# THE CINEMA OF THE BALKANS

First published in Great Britain in 2006 by
**Wallflower Press**
6a Middleton Place, Langham Street, London W1W 7TE
www.wallflowerpress.co.uk

A catalogue for this book is available from the British Library


ISBN 1-904764-80-0 (paperback)
ISBN 1-904764-81-9 (hardback)


Printed by Replika Press Pvt Ltd. India

# THE CINEMA OF
# THE BALKANS

EDITED BY

## DINA IORDANOVA

**WALLFLOWER PRESS** LONDON & NEW YORK

**24 FRAMES** is a major new series focusing on national and regional cinemas from around the world. Rather than offering a 'best of' selection, the feature films and documentaries selected in each volume serve to highlight the specific elements of that territory's cinema, elucidating the historical and industrial context of production, the key genres and modes of representation, and foregrounding the work of the most important directors and their exemplary films. In taking an explicitly text-centred approach, the titles in this list offer 24 diverse entry-points into each national and regional cinema, and thus contribute to the appreciation of the rich traditions of global cinema.

Series Editors: Yoram Allon & Ian Haydn Smith

OTHER TITLES IN THE **24 FRAMES** SERIES:

THE CINEMA OF LATIN AMERICA *edited by Alberto Elena and Marina Díaz López*

THE CINEMA OF THE LOW COUNTRIES *edited by Ernest Mathijs*

THE CINEMA OF ITALY *edited by Giorgio Bertellini*

THE CINEMA OF JAPAN & KOREA *edited by Justin Bowyer*

THE CINEMA OF CENTRAL EUROPE *edited by Peter Hames*

THE CINEMA OF SPAIN & PORTUGAL *edited by Alberto Mira*

THE CINEMA OF SCANDINAVIA *edited by Tytti Soila*

THE CINEMA OF BRITAIN & IRELAND *edited by Brian McFarlane*

THE CINEMA OF FRANCE *edited by Phil Powrie*

THE CINEMA OF CANADA *edited by Jerry White*

FORTHCOMING TITLES:

THE CINEMA OF AUSTRALIA & NEW ZEALAND *edited by Geoff Mayer and Keith Beattie*

THE CINEMA OF RUSSIA & THE FORMER SOVIET UNION *edited by Birgit Beumers*

THE CINEMA OF NORTH AFRICA & THE MIDDLE EAST *edited by Gönül Dönmez-Colin*

# CONTENTS

# INTERNATIONAL EDITORIAL BOARD

# NOTES ON CONTRIBUTORS

**ADINA BRADEANU** is a doctoral student at the University of Westminster, London, where she is completing a thesis on documentary film practices in socialist and post-socialist Romania. Prior to that she worked as a film journalist for the Bucharest-based monthly *Pro-Cinema* and conducted video-based research in the Visual Anthropology Department of the Museum of the Romanian Peasant, Bucharest.

**STRATOS E. CONSTANTINIDIS** is Professor of Theatre and Film at Ohio State University, USA. He is author of *Theatre under Deconstruction* (Garland, 1993) and *Modern Greek Theatre: A Quest for Hellenism* (McFarland, 2001). He has edited works on modern Greek culture and has published on Greek drama and film, and is the new editor of the *Journal of Modern Greek Studies*. His research papers have appeared in numerous refereed journals such as *Comparative Drama*, *New Theatre Quarterly*, *Journal of the Hellenic Diaspora*, *Journal of Modern Greek Studies*, *World Literature Today* and *Film Criticism*.

**NEVENA DAKOVIĆ** teaches Film Studies at the University of the Arts, Belgrade. She also teaches at different European universities and publishes widely on Yugoslav and Balkan cinema, including contributions to *Afterimage* and *Film Criticism*. She is the author of *Melodrama nije znar* (Prometej, 1994) and *Dictionary of Film Theorists* (CD-ROM, CSUB-FDU, 2002) and is the co-editor of *Gender and Media* (Mediation, 1996) and *Media(ted) Identities* (Bilgi University Press, 1999).

**DAN GEORGAKAS** is Adjunct Associate Professor at New York University. He is the editor of *Cineaste*, the co-editor of *The Cineaste Interviews 1 & 2*, *In Focus: A Guide To Using Films* and the Greek edition of *Film Criticism*. He has written on cinema for numerous publications and film anthologies, has organised film festivals and has engaged in film criticism on radio and television.

**ALEXANDER GROZEV** is Professor of Film History at NATFIZ-Sofia and YZU-Blagoevgrad in Bulgaria. One of the best-known Bulgarian film critics and historians, he is currently Executive Director of the National Film Centre Agency. He has authored several monographs, including

*The Beginning: Bulgarian Cinema History 1897–1956* (Nauka i Izkustvo, 1985). Having edited a number of books on the history and theory of cinema, he is also the author of studies on leading Soviet directors such as Vsevolod Pudovkin, Alexander Dovzhenko and Mikhail Romm. Has lectured widely internationally on issues of Bulgarian and Balkan cinema.

**MARINA GRŽINIĆ MAUHLER** works at the Institute of Philosophy at the Slovenian Academy of Science and Art and also teaches at the Academy of Fine Arts in Vienna. A freelance media theorist, art critic and curator, she has been involved in video art since 1982 an d has collaborated with Aina Smid on numerous video art projects, as well as on documentaries and shorts. Their work has been presented at international video festivals and has received important awards. She is also the author of theoretical texts and the editor of nine books.

**ANDREW JAMES HORTON** is the Editor-in-Chief of the online film journal *Kinoeye* (www.kinoeye.org), for which he also writes on Central and Southeast European film. He was previously Culture Editor of the internet weekly *Central Europe Review* and editor of *Slovo*, a peer-reviewed journal published by the School of Slavonic and East European Studies, University of London. He is also the editor of the e-book *The Celluloid Tinderbox: Yugoslav Screen Reflections of a Turbulent Decade* (Central Europe Review, 2000).

**DINA IORDANOVA** is Professor in Film Studies at the University of St Andrews, Scotland. She has published widely on Eastern European and Balkan cinema and is author of *Cinema of Flames: Balkan Film, Culture and the Media* (British Film Institute, 2001), *Emir Kusturica* (British Film Institute, 2002) and *Cinema of the Other Europe: The Industry and Artistry of East Central European Film* (Wallflower Press, 2003). She also co-edited the *BFI Companion to Eastern European and Russian Cinema* (British Film Institute, 2000) and *Framework*'s special issue on images of Romanies in international cinema. She is currently directing the AHRB-sponsored research project entitled *Balkan Cinema: Film and History*.

**ANNE JÄCKEL** is Visiting Research Fellow at the University of the West of England. She is the author of *The European Film Industries* (British Film Institute, 2003) and of numerous book chapters and journal articles published in *Cineaste*, *Media, Culture and Society*, *European Journal of Communication*, *National Identities* and *Historical Journal of Film, Radio and Television*.

**PAVLE LEVI** is Assistant Professor in the Department of Art and Art History at Stanford University. He has recently edited a selection of Annette Michelson's writings on modernist film and art. His book *Disintegration in Frames*, about aesthetics and ideology in the Yugoslav and post-Yugoslav cinema, is forthcoming with Stanford University Press.

**NIKOLA MIJOVIĆ** is an artist and filmmaker from Montenegro.

**JOHN PAPARGYRIS** is a doctoral student at the University of Birmingham, where he teaches Greek Film and is completing a thesis on the work of Theo Angelopoulos.

**MARGIT ROHRINGER** was a post-doctoral researcher on the AHRB-funded project *Balkan Cinema: Film and History* at the University of Leicester. She studied Sociology and Communication at the University of Vienna and wrote a thesis on Yugoslav cinema. Her monograph *Der jugoslawische Film nach Tito: Konstruktionen von kollektiven Identitäten* is forthcoming from Böhlau. She has published various articles, reviews and essays related to Balkan cinema and culture and has curated film programmes featuring the cinema of the region. Her current work is on the representations of memory and identity in Balkan documentary filmmaking.

**RADA ŠEŠIĆ** worked as a film critic and journalist for Radio-Television Sarajevo and for the film magazine *Sineast* in Bosnia and Herzegovina. Since 1993 she has lived in the Netherlands where she lectures on Indian cinema at the University of Amsterdam, and collaborates with the Rotterdam Film Festival and the International Documentary Film Festival in Amsterdam. She is also selector of documentary programmes for the Sarajevo Film Festival and for the Kerala Festival, India. Rada is also a filmmaker (*Room Without a View*, 1997, *Soske, In Whitest Solitude*, 2001) and a writer for *Skrien, Dox, Film Guide* and *Film Annual*.

**SVETLANA SLAPŠAK** is Professor of Anthropology of Ancient Worlds and Anthropology of Gender at Institutum Studiorum Humanitatis, Ljubljana Graduate School of Humanities, Slovenia. She has lectured widely in Europe and the US, and has published widely in cultural history and gender studies. Her book *Women's Icons of the Twentieth Century* (XX vek, 2001) deals in great part with images of Balkan women and international film. She also authored a booklet on *Anikina vremena* (*The Times of Anika*, 1954, directed by Vladimir Pogačič) published by Fifth Women's Pocket Festival Red Sunrises 2004, in English and Slovenian.

**VLASTIMIR SUDAR** is an artist and filmmaker of Serbian origin living in London. His work has been exhibited in London, and his short films have been screened both nationally and internationally. He is currently completing a doctoral thesis about the life and work of Aleksandar Petrović.

**LILLA TÖKE** is a doctoral student in Comparative Literature and Cultural Studies at Stony Brook University; her thesis is on Eastern European political film satire. She has completed an MPhil degree in Gender Studies at the Central European University, Budapest in cooperation with the Open University, UK. She has published book reviews on the subject of Eastern European and Balkan cinema and has presented her work at numerous conferences.

**VASSILIKI TSITSOPOULOU** holds a PhD from the Department of Cinema and Comparative Literature at the University of Iowa. She presently works at the Kaneb Center at the University of Notre Dame in Indiana. She has taught Greek cinema at the University of Iowa and published on the topic in the *Journal of Modern Greek Studies*. She has also given lectures on genre, politics and the Balkan dimensions of Greek cinema and cinema culture at the University of Florida and at Yale University. She is currently researching the cultural politics of the Greek reception of Emir Kusturica's films and the notion of postmodernity in Greek cinema.

# ACKNOWLEDGEMENTS

This project was made possible due to a large research grant from UK's Arts and Humanities Research Board (AHRB), enabling various activities intended to foster the study of Balkan cinema, a neglected yet aesthetically important area of European film historiography.

Even though not listed by name here, the main acknowledgment goes to the authors who contributed to this volume. This was a laborious project, which could not have come to successful completion without the authors' distinctive expertise, determination and endurance. Margit Rohringer was a post-doctoral fellow at the University of Leicester in 2004; she coordinated the administrative side of the project, communicating with authors, researching stills and efficiently taking care of the administrative and technical details. Dušan Makavejev, a key figure of Balkan cinema, persistently encouraged my work and kindly contributed the preface.

I would like to thank also Agorita Bakali, Dimitris Eleftheriotis, Daniel Goulding, Sergio Grmek Germani, Frank Hess, Andrew S. Horton, the late Kostas Kazazis, Violetta Petrova, Tassos Rigopoulos, Maria Stassinopulou and Marko Živković for sharing their knowledge and views on these cinemas; Dimos Avdeliodis, Victor Friedman, Julian Graffy, Rajko Grlić, Pavlina Jeleva, Irina Kanousheva, Krassimir Kroumov-Gretz, Bozhidar Manov, Goran Marković, Vesna Maslovarić, Eno Milkani, Dominique Nasta, Misha Nedeljković, Mitko Panov, Lydia Papadimitriou, Nick Potamitis, Petar Volnarovski, Vanja Valtrović, Miča Vučković, the late Bill van Wert, Želimir Žilnik, as well as DS Sound and Greek City Video in Toronto for helping with copies of the films, stills, bibliography, other materials and language queries; Dudley Andrew, Paul Coates, Natasa Ďurovičová, Herbert Eagle, Thomas Elsaesser, Fredric Jameson, David Norris, Cathy Portuges, Eric Rentschler, Robert Rosenstone, Milos Stehlik, Katie Trumpener for their persistent interest in Balkan cinema; Phillip Lindley, Guy Barefoot, Nicholas Watkins, Joanne Shattock and Bob Burgess at the University of Leicester and Brian Lang, Keith Brown and the members of our new Film Studies department at the University of St Andrews who made it possible for me to catch my breath, amidst all administration, and bring this volume to successful completion. Holly Charles for her work on the bibliography and filmography, Karen Drysdale for her help in the final stages, Yoram Allon at Wallflower Press for his unrelenting support throughout this project, and, last but not least, to Vessela Brakalova, Miloš Lazin, Nina Maleeva, Menelaos Panagiotakis, Sasho Rajkoff and Maria Viskaduraki for being such good friends. And to George for being such a perfect son.

# NOTES ON LANGUAGE AND STRUCTURE

No other area covered by the *24 Frames* series reflects a region of such linguistic diversity as this volume on the Balkans: here we deal with a cluster of languages that are mutually incomprehensible (various South Slavic languages, Greek, Albanian and Romanian) and use three different alphabets (Cyrillic, Greek and Latin). This linguistic tapestry is challenging to work with also because of on-going changes in the region that have put in circulation various highly politicised views on linguistic issues. Thus, I constantly had to take into consideration the intricate debates on language and cultural heritage.

As a film historian, however, I did not have particularly strong views on the linguistic debates nor did I want to take sides in disputes which were not of my competence. In most cases where decisions had to be made about transliteration and orthography, the rationale used was straightforward and simple: a) to ensure that the record about a film is correct in relation to the time of its original release and b) to use transliteration and spelling that would enable successful computerised searches at the most commonly used Internet sites (the Internet Movie Database [www.imdb.com] and other search engines) where the linguistic idiosyncrasies usually do not figure.

In cases where alphabets different than Latin were involved (Cyrillic is used in Bulgaria, Macedonia and Serbia and Greek in Greece) we have decided to transliterate to Latin.

On concrete issues regarding transliteration and orthography I consulted with Victor Friedman, the Andrew W. Mellon Professor in Balkan linguistics at the University of Chicago, who also happens to be the only person I know who is sufficiently familiar with all these languages and debates and whose pronouncements I deem competent.

The break-up of Yugoslavia and the proliferation of newly emancipated countries in the region created a range of dilemmas. As all films included in this volume were made before the country's break-up in the early 1990s, I thought that the correct approach is to list them all as Yugoslav as this was the producing country at the time of their release, even if some of them figure in the book in order to represent the cinema of the newly emancipated republics. Throughout the volume I have adopted some commonly accepted English spellings (for example Ustasha instead of Ustaša). I have also decided to avoid the special character for 'đ' (as in Đorđe or Srđan) and use the commonly used transliteration 'dj' instead (Djordje, Srdjan).

The transliteration of the Greek 'gamma' revealed a range of inconsistencies. According to Professor Friedman, Greek gamma should be transliterated with 'g', although 'y' is sometimes used before front vowels. So we have used Grigoris Grigoriou (rather than Yriyoris Yriyoriu) and Yiorgos (as in Yiorgos Arvanitis rather than Giorgos), which was also consistent with the IMDB referencing.

As a result of a recent language reform, the orthography of some words in Romanian has changed, but we have opted to retain the orthography that was in use at the time a film was made (for example, *Pădurea spînzuraţilor*).

All contributors were asked to follow the *Sight and Sound* style in structuring their essays: to open with a synopsis of the film followed by the review. This approach reflects my belief that keeping the account on the storyline and narrative structure somewhat separate from the analysis is suitable when introducing films that are little known.

Last but not least, some of the authors occasionally express strong opinions that I do not necessarily share. I decided not to interfere in such cases as it appeared appropriate to give readers a taste of the wide range of views that circulate in the studies of Balkan cinematic and cultural history.

**Dina Iordanova**
St Andrews University, Scotland
June 2006

# PREFACE

The end of the world

is coming close,

Let it come,

Nothing much to lose…

> – from a Gypsy song performed in *Biće skoro propast sveta* (*It Rains in My Village*, Aleksandar Petrović, 1968)

Writing about films for people who could not see them brought a recollection of Werner Herzog's documentary about a group of blind people gathered on a small airport and being shown an aeroplane.

They are encouraged to touch and feel the wings, the propeller and the wheels, the moving parts of the tail and some wires. They are clumsy and funny, curious, bumping into each other while climbing on the plane. Once they are in the passenger seats, we see the rest of the event on their faces: the plane taxies a little, takes off, and they fly. I cannot adequately convey this delicate sight, the minute movements of their heads, the shy smiles, and the moving quiet in the passenger cabin.

To label Herzog a magician would be wrong because no illusions were involved. He is a hands-on filmmaker, a mechanic who, using the camera, moves people's souls according to their needs. The needs they did not even know about. Over the course of only few minutes, the blind learn and experience what it feels like to be a bird.

The last time I saw Werner Herzog, born Stipetich, he was looking for a Croatian general of the same family name. He wanted to climb the steep, barren mountains above the Maslenica Bridge at the Adriatic coast, to reach the Serbian positions. He wanted to stop the war between the Croats and the Serbs.

The Balkan director dearest to me is Elia Kazan. He left Anatolia at the age of four. The image from his childhood that stuck with him was that of his father walking down a cobblestone street, keeping himself close to the walls of the houses. The middle of the street was kept for the Ottomans who, if they stumbled upon a Greek, would use the whip to teach him a lesson.

Telling me this story, Kazan himself walks by the wall imitating his father. It is in a Greek restaurant at Times Square, an older woman at the next table glances discreetly at Elia. At some point she catches his eye, leans towards him a little, and whispers: 'Can I touch you?' He blinks slowly, nods and slightly turns his head away. She lightly touches his upper arm, and moves her hand back.

Unspoken language has no written vocabulary and grammar – you learn it at an early age in the Balkans, by osmosis. Growing up in the multicultural world of the Balkans makes one understand world cinema better: reading details in one's behaviour, paying attention to the eyes, the hands and the short silences. Understanding the language of space. When a group enters a village, singing: 'Run for your life!'

Twenty-four films are presented here by multiple writers. These films were shot in about ten different languages, but they all speak a single, unique and unifying language of images in motion, a language of dreams.

After a few years of fresh air in the 1960s, communication between the Balkan countries went back to being erratic, nonexistent or very limited. Countries were separated by the barbed wire, minefields and bunkers bursting with machine guns. Not even a stray dog or a lost lamb could any longer innocently find itself on the neighbours' territory.

Each country cultivates its own history. Textbooks are incompatible.

After long isolation and new wars, ordinary people cannot perceive their closest neighbour as someone with whom they would want to have a cup of coffee.

The first retrospective ever of films from the Balkans was presented in April 2000 at the Biennale in Venice, under the directorship of Alberto Barbera. Eighty features were assembled by Sergio Grmek Germani. For more than a year Grmek was criss-crossing the Balkans, tracing rare prints in remote corners. The retrospective had an excellent catalogue.

The plan was to have the Venice retrospective play across Italy. Starting with the wonderful Yugoslav film *Ciganka* (*Gypsy Girl*, Voja Nanović, 1953), it was like the appearance of a lost island from under the sea. An Ali-Baba's Cave of film treasures opened its doors! In spite of different languages and a long absence of contact between national cultures, the films echoed each other, revealing similar vitality and humour, and eccentric storytelling. The diversity of directorial styles was remarkable.

The bad news is that the whole collection mysteriously disappeared. According to some semi-official information, immediately after the screenings some eager Venice administrator returned the painstakingly collected prints to their remote points of origin.

This collection is a new expedition searching for Ali-Baba's Cave.

Hollywood has been mining Balkan stories for ages, without knowing where the Balkans are exactly, who lives there and how. Hollywood's favorite bad dreams are about the blood-thirsty Transylvanian count and vampire, Vlad Tepes – Dracula. A website about this son-of-the-Balkans counts 307 films produced up to the present day – all about the gentleman and his fangs. A similar fantasy can be found in Jacques Tourneur's *Cat People*, a 1942 horror about historical Serbs who morphed into ferocious black panthers now living, for some unexplained reason, in the heart of Manhattan, in cages at the Central Park Zoo. Another Balkan connection is Agatha Christie's *Murder on the Orient Express*. This sleeping-car story is about a reality TV-style murder by eleven stabs from eleven relatives. The Pullman car was a smart choice of a crime site. When we look at the map, we see that by some uncanny coincidence, Lady Agatha's 'relatives-only perfect crime' happened in the same place where fifty-seven years later, in 1991, the Yugoslav Peoples' Army staged its brutal attack on the city of Vukovar, marking the break-up of Yugoslavia and triggering an endless chain of choreographed crimes committed by relatives only!

I held the map of Europe looking north-by-northwest. The biplane was flying low over the cornfields looking for me. Some connections ominously emerged when I drew a straight diagonal line from Belfast to Jerusalem. Passing past Flanders, and then through to Alsace/Lorraine and South Tyrol, it perfectly connected the recent killing fields in the Balkans all the way to the latest concrete monument to intolerance among the next of kin.

Jokers are still talking of the Balkans as unpredictable: the past is changing daily while the future resists appearing. As a basic guide into the uncertainties of Balkan life, I recommend *Who is Singing Over There?* (Slobodan Šijan, 1980), a Yugoslav film unfortunately missing from this book.

'Wonderful vitality!' I wrote as the concluding sentence.

The list of macabre-sounding titles unfolds on the computer screen. *When I am Dead and Pale, Forest of the Hanged, The Fall of Italy, Return of the Dead Army…*

OK! Cut out 'Vitality'!

**Dušan Makavejev**
Belgrade
April 2006

# INTRODUCTION

## *Connecting the disconnected space*

The claim that there is such a thing as a unified Balkan culture may sound unacceptable to some. They have been told repeatedly that people in the Balkans do not share a feeling of togetherness, that the culture of each Balkan country stands for itself, separated from the others by linguistic and religious barriers, and that there is more hostility than exchange among the groups in the region – Albanian, Bosnian, Bulgarian, Croat, Greek, Macedonian, Montenegrin, Romani, Romanian, Serb, Slovenian, Turk, Vlach and more.

A closer examination of Balkan cultural output, however, reveals an astonishing thematic and stylistic consistency. Cinema in particular testifies to a specific artistic sensibility, possibly coming from shared history and socio-cultural space. The issues, across borders, are the same: turbulent history and volatile politics; a semi-Orientalist positioning which some see as marginality, and others define as a crossroads or a bridge between East and West; a series of adverse encounters between Christianity and Islam; a legacy of patriarchy and economic and cultural dependency.

In collating this volume, I have faced numerous challenges. Many people I have consulted with often concluded with the line, 'I would not like to be in your shoes', because it is simply impossible to be politically correct in the Balkan context. The main reason is the question of Balkan mutuality. Regularly lumped together as Europe's South Eastern periphery, there appears to be little evidence that these countries add up to a plausible 'region'. After all, does 'Balkanised' not imply a mode of co-existence which is precisely the opposite of togetherness? A mode of being where people live next to one another yet think of themselves as completely different from their neighbours?

So was this project an artificial one by default? It involved grouping entities whose reluctance to turn to each other had become legendary and looking for shared identity patterns where such patterns had been vigorously rejected for decades. It was a project of 'connecting a disconnected space', as film director Dušan Makavejev has put it.

When seeking advice which films to include in this volume, everybody's reaction would normally be: 'Unfortunately, I only know the films from my own country; I don't recognise a single one of the other titles that you are asking my opinion on. Some names maybe, but not a single film.' People from former Yugoslavia knew next to nothing about Greek or Bulgarian cinema; most of the people I talked to had never seen an Albanian film; Romanians knew French cinema much better than any of the neighbouring Balkan traditions.

Had the Balkans ever functioned as a clearly defined cultural space? This problematic notion of the togetherness of a region was compounded by an array of difficult questions. First of all, no other part of Europe featured such a cluster of mutually incomprehensible languages (a range of South Slavic idioms were juxtaposed to Romanian, Greek, Albanian, Turkish, Romanes, Armenian, as well as many other smaller minority languages). Secondly, a range of religions had been present here side by side, sometimes fiercely clashing over centuries: variations of Orthodox Christianity, Islam, Catholicism, all existing in a general context of overall religious scepticism and lively pagan traditions. Third, countries in the region had belonged to opposite sides in Europe's political system during those decades of the twentieth century that were definitive for the development of their national cinematic cultures (1945–90). Following World War Two, Greece was placed in the Western sphere of influence while most other countries in the region were assigned to the Soviet sphere. But the divisions went even further: while Bulgaria was often described as the sixteenth Soviet republic for its unreserved loyalty to the Soviet regime, countries like Romania, Yugoslavia and Albania had the reputation of communist mavericks, each one inhabiting an idiosyncratic universe of its own and behaving stubbornly in asserting its strong-headed independence (from the paranoid Albania of Enver Hoxha through the peculiar goings-on of Ceauşescu's Romania to the bon-vivant spirit of Tito's non-aligned Yugoslavia). Fourth, political factors led to substantial differences in the industrial infrastructure. Some countries routinely co-produced with the Soviets (Bulgaria) while others opened the doors of their studios for co-productions with the West (Yugoslavia, Romania). Privately-financed Greek cinema blossomed up to the mid-1960s but was pushed into a crisis with the arrival of the junta's dictatorship in 1967, while the best works of Yugoslav cinema were made in the late 1960s; the war in former Yugoslavia in the 1990s resulted in a film production boom while, paradoxically, peaceful Albania, Romania and Bulgaria saw a serious overall decline during the same period.

With all this complexity, the question of the existence of Balkan cinema remains. Could it be that it is an imaginary entity, a newly consolidated concept that may appear convenient for the moment but cannot withstand the test of time?

The fact that I have committed to editing a book on Balkan cinema answers my feelings on this question: I believe it exists. It is true that a high level of editorial interference was required on my part, and it may have taken some work of imagination as well. While most of the people I talked to said that they can speak only of their own national cinemas, my simple act of watching films from all these countries asserted the realisation of similarities, shared themes and sensibilities. They were all there, but they needed to be seen to be acknowledged. For me, the act of construction of Balkan cinema came down to the act of watching it. I would expect that this would be everybody else's experience as well. As soon as one overcomes the lack of cross-cultural knowledge (which also implies the will to change one's watching pattern from a national to a transnational mode), a powerful discovery emerges and takes over: the cinema of the Balkans can be described as an entity of clearly discernible thematic and stylistic affinities. They are all there, just waiting to be seen and acknowledged. I hope this book will help such an acknowledgment.

The study of Balkan cinema still has some way to go – not because of shortages in cinematic traditions to be explored, but because of a shortage of scholarship that recognises the affinities within the region and draws it all together. My work on this book was an exercise in connecting the disconnected Balkan space.

## Making choices

Each one of the volumes in this series covers 24 films from a national or regional cinematic tradition. I looked with interest at the table of contents of some other volumes in the *24 Frames* series and counted how many of the films included there I had seen. It varied: in the case of Italy, France and Central Europe I had seen most of the films, while in the case of Japan and Korea or Latin America I had only seen about a third.

How many of the films in this book on Balkan cinema, I wondered, would have been seen by its potential readers? Very few, probably. But even if this is the case, I thought that for scholarship on Balkan cinema to flourish one needs to begin somewhere; better do little than nothing. And while this volume does not present a comprehensive picture, it will at least bring some great Balkan films out of obscurity and highlight some lesser known cinematic texts that are important for understanding the culture of the Balkans.

In the process of selection I had to make some tough choices. For each film to make it into the volume I had to drop several others that were equally worthwhile. In a context where

Balkan cinemas are so little known, I realised that the films included in this book were likely to come to be perceived as some sort of canon. Yet a word of caution is needed here: no 'canon' of Balkan cinema can possibly come about from this collection as the number of films included here is highly insufficient to be deemed as a representative selection for these rich cinematic traditions.

One of the most daring decisions I made was to include via exclusion: in order to open up space for films I considered important but which remain unknown, I opted to exclude the work of the best-known filmmakers from the Balkans in order to open up place for others. My rationale was that directors like Theo Angelopoulos and Emir Kusturica had been the subject of several monographs and there has been plenty of writing and festival panoramas on Dušan Makavejev and Lucian Pintilie, whereas many other Balkan directors have never been in the international spotlight and remain unknown outside their own country.

This decision was triggered in part by a comment made by one of these filmmakers: in a conversation a few years ago, Makavejev said he was hoping that one day film historiography in the West will find a way to honour the work of all those hugely important and yet unknown Balkan cineastes (he was talking specifically of the late Žika Pavlović). So I left out Makavejev's classic *WR – Misterije organizma* (*WR: Mysteries of the Organism*, 1971) for the sake of including work on Pavlović as well as Želimir Žilnik. Similarly, instead of including Kusturica's acclaimed *Time of the Gypsies* (1989), I opted for *Valter Brani Sarajevo* (*Walter Defends Sarajevo*, Hajrudin 'Šiba' Krvavac, 1972), one of Kusturica's favourite films, on the set of which the director was reportedly introduced to filmmaking. And so on.

I did not include here the work of directors who worked internationally (such as Costa-Gavras, Danis Tanović or Milcho Manchevski) nor of Westerners who were based in the Balkans (such as the American Jules Dassin who worked in Greece). A crucial omission for which I cannot really offer any plausible excuse is the non-inclusion of a single film made by a woman. If I have the chance to produce another volume on the cinema of the Balkans, I will make sure that the work of remarkable female directors such as Tonia Marketaki, Binka Zhelyazkova, Vesna Ljubić, Elisabeta Bostan and others is properly featured.

Various criteria occupied my mind at different points of the selection process. What to do about properly representing earlier times, for example? Cinema in the Balkans had begun, like elsewhere, at the very dawn of the twentieth century. The famous Manaki Brothers – Yanaki and Milton, Vlachs from Aegean Macedonia who had purchased the three-hundredth Bioscop in 1905 and had chronicled life in the region on film over the following decades – had lived and worked here. The most important historical events since the beginning of the twentieth century were registered on film. In the periods between the wars feature films were made by enterprising artists across the region. Yet I left out of consideration the whole period preceding World War Two. If I had more space I would make sure to commission chapters on films such as *Golfo* (Costas Bahatoris, 1915) or *Maria Pentagiotissa* (Ahilleas Madras, 1929), representative of the Greek *foustanella* genre, the Bulgarian satire *Balgaran e galant* (*The Bulgarian is Gallant*, Vassil Gendov, 1915) or the Lesbos-set *Dafnis kai Hloi* (*Daphnis and Chloe*, Orestis Laskos, 1931). Another possibility would be to feature essays on the first 'talkies', such as the Greek *O agapitikos tis voskopoulas* (*The Shepherdess' Lover*, Dimitris Tsakiris, 1932) or the Serbian *Nevinost bez zastite* (*Innocence Unprotected*, directed by stuntman Dragoljub Aleksić, 1942, parts of which are recycled in the famous 1968 avant-garde film of the same name by Makavejev).

I was tempted to open with a chapter on the Albanian epic *Skenderbeu* (*The Great Warrior Skanderbeg*, 1953), but dropped it as its national origin was dubious. Even if co-produced by Albania, it is still better known as a Soviet production directed by Sergei Yutkevich and with Georgian actors in the leads. I opted instead to begin in the mid-1950s with *Stella* (1955) an international breakthrough for Melina Mercouri and Michael Cacoyannis.

Does my selection not have too many films from the 1960s and the 1970s? Maybe, but I want to ensure that important films that remain unknown are highlighted here (whereas recent films are more likely to have played internationally). After all, with the peak of production of Finos Film in Greece in the mid-1960s and the new Greek cinema of the early 1970s, the New Yugoslav film of the 1960s, the Bulgarian 'poetic cinema' and the strong work of Romanian directors in the 1960s and 1970s this period appears to be the most important one in the cinematic history of the region.

Dividing the 24 chapters in this book between the countries was another area of tricky choices, as these had to represent about ten national cinematic traditions. In the case of Yugoslavia, where before we talked of one, albeit diverse, national cinema, now we had to honour the filmmaking of Croatia, Slovenia, Bosnia, Macedonia, Serbia and Montenegro, and were confronted with difficult decisions as to who and what belongs where. One cannot be politically correct in such an environment; the newly emancipated countries could only be included here with one representative film (made during the Yugoslav period). Turkey was not included in our selection (it features in the *24 Frames* volume on North Africa and the Middle East), but at moments I felt that Turkish cinema could also have been considered here as well.

My leading selection criterion, however, has been a thematic one: the shared history of the countries in the region highlights many of the common themes. I have therefore looked for films that are significant artistic achievements but that would also present important features of Balkan life and identity.

It is often the case that shared history – Ottoman presence, resistance to foreign occupiers and totalitarian governments, migration from villages to cities – has found similar treatment in cinema. Everybody in the Balkans has fought against everybody else and has practiced large-scale assimilation at some point; everybody has their version of the past and their idiosyncratic approaches to reconciling historical narratives. The negative representations are almost identical from whichever side one may look, and so are the depictions of farcical characters whose actions are marked by specific Balkan inferiority complexes. The mischievous humour was the same across all territories.

Each one of my selections is intended to represent a specific Balkan topic; for each one of these topics I could have chosen a different film from another country in the region. It was important to make sure that there was at least one film that represented key features and concerns: Historical super-productions on nation-building (*Mihai Viteazul* (*Michael the Brave*, 1970–1)), the Ottoman period (*Koziyat Rog* (*Goat's Horn*, 1972)), the struggle for national liberation (*Mera Spored Mera* (*Measure for Measure*, 1981)), the fratricide of World War One (*Kradetsat na praskovi* (*Peach Thief*, 1964), *Pădurea spînzuraților* (*Forest of the Hanged*, 1964)), various aspects of the struggle during World War Two (the partisan action-adventure genre in *Walter Defends Sarajevo*, the existential dimension of war traumas in *Tri* (*Three*, 1965), the difficult historical choices in taking sides in *Pad Italije* (*The Fall of Italy*, 1981) and the resistance by happenstance in *Ti ekanes ston polemo, Thanassi?* (*What Did You Do in the War, Thanassis?*, 1971)), the political violence and the twisted philosophy of power and dictatorship (*Petrina Hronia* (*Stone Years*, 1985), *Kthimi I Ushtrisë së Vdekur* (*Return of the Dead Army*, 1989)), the ubiquitous anti-intellectualism (*Rani radovi* (*Early Works*, 1969), *Splav Meduze* (*The Raft of Meduza*, 1980)). Issues of the specific idiosyncrasies of the Balkan 'national character' with its respective absurdist humour had to be well represented in films that took place in villages, Balkan cinema's most important setting (*Lachenite obuvki na neznainiya voin* (*The Patent Leather Shoes of the Unknown Soldier*, 1979), *I Earini Synaxis Ton Agrofylakon* (*The Four Seasons of the Law*, 1999), while other films stress aspects of village-to-town migration (*Nunta de piatră* (*Stone Wedding*, 1972), *Petrijin venac* (*Petrija's Wreath*, 1980)) and the resulting social disorientation as seen in the 'drifter' films (*Kad budem mrtav i beo* (*When I am Dead and Pale*,

1968), *Proba de microfon* (*Microphone Test*, 1980)). Issues of diaspora and displacement are addressed in *Crveniot Konj* (*The Red Horse*, 1981) while *Tirana Year Zero* (2001) features the post-1989 migratory obsession. Several chapters present films featuring predominantly female characters and address the quintessential questions of restricted opportunity and patriarchy (*Stella* and *Evdokia* (1971)).

Still, an important range of specifically Balkan themes remain unrepresented: the Gypsy films, none of which have been included. There are also no films that directly focus on Stalinism and other forms of communist totalitarianism (yet the genre that exposed communist-era absurdities was particularly prevalent in the Balkans). The representation of the 'urban' theme is somewhat neglected in favour of including films featuring village life. It is not possible to cover the important output of animators, documentary filmmaking or the avant-garde, even though the cinema of the region has contributed an array of important works in each one of these traditions. Popular cinema – comedy, musical, action-adventure – is also under-represented in this volume; it would take another entire volume to cover it properly.

In the (unlikely) event I am asked to present a list for another 24 Balkan films, what would I include? A tentative selection would be balanced along the same lines of division between national traditions. From Greece I would seek to include chapters on *O drakos* (*The Ogre of Athens*, Nikos Koundouros, 1956), *I thia apo to Chicago* (*The Aunt from Chicago*, Alekos Sakellarios, 1957), *Anaparastassi* (*Reconstruction*, Theo Angelopoulos, 1970), *To proxenio tis Annas* (*The Engagement of Anna*, Pantelis Voulgaris, 1972), *I timi tis agapis* (*The Price of Love*, Tonia Marketaki, 1984), *Kali patrida, syndrofe* (*Welcome home, Comrade*, Lefteris Xanthopoulos, 1986), and I would still be struggling to accommodate popular genres (like the films with Aliki Vougiouklaki) or the work of directors from the younger generation like Constantine Giannaris or Olga Malea. From Romania I would include *Reconstituierea* (*Reconstruction*, Lucian Pintilie, 1969), *Dincolo de nisipuri* (*Beyond the Sands*, Radu Gabrea, 1973), *Veronica se întoarce* (*Veronica Comes Back*, Elisabeta Bostan, 1973), *Morometii* (*The Moromete Family*, Stere Gulea, 1988), *Patul conjugal* (*Conjugal Bed*, Mircea Daneliuc, 1993) and *È pericoloso sporgersi* (*Don't Lean Out the Window*, Nae Karanfil, 1994). I would still have a chapter on some film directed by Sergiu Nicolaescu and seek to represent his work in popular genres by including either the action-adventure *Revansa* (*Revenge*, 1978) or the comedy *Nea Marin miliardar* (*Uncle Marin, the Billionaire*, 1979); I would consider including most recent work out of Romania, maybe the award-winning *Moratea domnului Lazarescu* (*The Death of Mr Lazarescu*, Cristi Puiu, 2005). The alternative selection from Bulgaria would include

*Privarzaniyat balon* (*The Attached Balloon*, Binka Zhelyazkova, 1967), *Avantazh* (*Advantage*, George Dyulgerov, 1977), *Matriarchat* (*Matriarchy*, Lyudmil Kirkov, 1977), *Vreme na nasilie* (*Time of Violence*, Lyudmil Staykov, 1988), and I would have a tough time deciding which one of Eduard Zahariev 1970s features to include, as all three of them are of definitive importance (*Prebroyavane na divite zajci* (*The Hare Census*, 1973), *Vilna zona* (*Villa Zone*, 1975), *Mazhki vremena* (*Manly Times,* 1977)). The alternative titles from Albania would be *Colonel Bunker* (Kujtim Çashku, 1998) and *Slogans* (Ghergy Xhuvani, 2001). From the countries of former Yugoslavia I would still look to include, first and foremost, the work of Živojin Pavlović such as *Budjenje pacova* (*The Rat's Awakening*, 1967) or *Zaseda* (*Ambush*, 1969). Other entries would include *Skupljači perja* (*I Even Met Happy Gypsies*, Aleksandar Petrović, 1967), *Jutro* (*Morning*, Mladomir 'Puriša' Djordjević, 1967), *Breza* (*Birch Tree*, Ante Babaja, 1967), *Nevinost bez zaštite* (*Innocence Unprotected*, Dušan Makavejev, 1968), *Bitka na Neretvi* (*Battle of Neretva*, Veljko Bulajic, 1969), *Tko pjeva zlo ne misli* (*He Who Sings Means No Harm*, Kresimir Golik, 1970), *Plastični Isus* (*Plastic Jesus*, Lazar Stojanović, 1971), *Crno seme* (*Black Seed*, Kirli Tsenevski, 1971), *Slike iz života udarnika* (*Scenes from the Life of Shockworkers*, Bato Čengić, 1972), *Simha* (Vesna Ljubić, 1975), *Čuvar plaže u zimskom periodu* (*Beach Guard in Winter*, Goran Paskaljević, 1976), *Miris poljskog cveča* (*Fragrance of Wild Flowers*, Srdjan Karanović, 1977), *Okupacija u 26 slika* (*Occupation in 26 Scenes*, Lordan Zafranović, 1978), *Ko to tamo peva* (*Who Is Singing Out There*, Slobodan Šijan, 1980), *Sječas li se, Dolly Bell* (*Do You Remember Dolly Bell?*, Emir Kusturica, 1981), *Rdeči boogie* (*Red Boogie*, Karpo Godina, 1982), *U raljama života* (*In the Jaws of Life*, Rajko Grlić, 1984), *Tajvanska canasta* (*Taiwan Canasta*, Goran Marković,1985), *Ovo malo duše* (*A Little Bit of Soul*, Ademir Kenović, 1986), *U ime naroda* (*In the Name of the People*, Živko Nikolić, 1987) and *Mi nismo andjeli* (*We Are No Angels*, Srdjan Dragojević, 1992). My book *Cinema of Flames* (2001) focused on the films that were made in the region as a reaction to Yugoslavia's break-up in the 1990s, so I have not included any of these here. If I was to make a selection of films that I consider most important from this period, however, I would probably go for *Tito po drugi put medju srbima* (*Tito Among the Serbs for the Second Time*, Želimir Žilnik, 1993) and *Kordon* (*The Cordon*, Goran Marković, 2002), both from Serbia, while simultaneously acknowledging that an important range of films reflecting on the break-up were made in Bosnia and Croatia. It should be noted that in recent times a number of exciting films are coming out from the younger generation of Slovenian directors, and that important films are being realised as international co-productions, like *Before the Rain* (Milcho Manchevski, 1994) or *No Man's Land* (Danis Tanovic, 2001).

*Mutuality in progress*

Throughout the twentieth century, the Balkan countries have been struggling to 'join' Europe, to catch up with its achievements and be admitted as equals. The history of each country in the region has been defined by this emancipatory drive toward Europe. Yet the endeavour has not been particularly successful, mostly on account of the Balkans' presumed incompatibility with the truly European, which can be traced back to the Ottoman legacy that is declared as inherently non-European and is identified as a major obstacle for the South East periphery to belong to the 'real' Europe. It is a framework in which the Balkans are rejected as a culturally irreconcilable civilisational chunk. Reacting to the dismissal each individual country in the region has been trying to negotiate a deal for itself, to shed off the alleged impure non-Europeanness by denouncing its affinity with the others from the area and highlighting aspects of its heritage that could affirm its fundamentally Western cultural lineage. But whereas the Balkan countries believe they are individually clearly distinguishable and expect to be treated as distinct from each other, the reality is that in the Western mind they are all lumped together via the vision of one big Oriental periphery of Europe.

No matter how hard one tries to assert a less rigid and more flexible vision of what Europe actually is, the Balkans are still looked down upon as a subaltern South-East corner that is somewhat insufficiently European and not fully compatible with the West. The Balkans continue to be marginalised, misrepresented and denigrated in their totality (and not as individual countries). This is why I argued in *Cinema of Flames* that the Balkans could gain powerful ground if they capitalise on the togetherness that is bestowed on them and try to turn the undistinguished qualification of 'being Balkan' from liability into an asset. A range of other writers have argued along similar lines as well. And, as of recently, this line of thinking has begun to take hold; if it is not possible to avoid this semi-Orientalist frame of reference, then one may as well embrace it. As soon as 'being Balkan' is no longer a troublesome position but is recognised instead as a tolerable agenda, the surreptitious reluctant togetherness and the acquiescent ignorance of one's own neighbours may come to an end. The main trope of national identity would then no longer be to deny one's own disadvantageous positioning (one has somehow just happened to be in the Balkans, a place where a nation does not really want to be and therefore does not properly belong), but acknowledge the location and assume it as an apposite frame of reference. The next step would be emerging mutuality, the key manifestation of which is the intensification of cultural exchanges and contacts, leading to an overt recognition of those stylistic and thematic affinities that lay the ground for conceptualising Balkan culture as one dynamic entity.

The involvement with pan-Balkan themes and cross-Balkan creative collaborations is not a new feature; it only takes a moment to unveil a range of such examples from past decades. Working in Germany in the 1970s émigré Yugoslav Želimir Žilnik, for example, made a short film entitled *Antrag* (*Appication*, 1974) tackling the complex relations of two guest workers, a Turk and a Greek. Greek star Irini Papas and composer Mikis Theodorakis were engaged in the Yugoslav partisan drama *Sutjeska* (Stipe Delić, 1973), Yugoslav star Rade Marković had a lead in the Bulgarian film *The Peach Thief*, Romanian director Lucian Pintilie made his *Paviljon VI* (*Ward Six*, 1973) in Yugoslavia, and Romanian Maia Morgenstern played all female roles in the Greek film *To vlemma tou Odyssea* (*Ulysses Gaze*, Theo Angelopoulos, 1995). One can easily provide more examples of such exchanges from the past. What is more important, however, is that these interactions are much more intense today, powerfully asserting the newly discovered interest of Balkan filmmakers in each other.

If we wanted to represent this new pan-Balkan consciousness of mutuality and the reawakened attention to each other, we could look at some relatively recent films that have tackled the theme from different angles. Maybe starting with Srdjan Karanović's *Za sada bez dobrog naslova* (*Film with No Name*, 1988) which sensibly pointed at the dangers of ethnic intolerance before the troubles in Yugoslavia had escalated, we would then feature films addressing pan-Balkan issues like *Lovtzi na sanishta* (*Dream Hunters*, Kostadin Bonev, 1991) from Bulgaria, the Romanian *Un été inoubliable* (*An Unforgettable Summer*, Lucian Pintilie, 1994), and Angelopoulos' *Ulysses Gaze*. Throughout the 1990s Balkan cinema put out many more films that sometimes took on the comical side of this pan-Balkan revitalisation (of which Sotiris Goritsas' *Valkanisateur* (*Balkanizateur*, 1998) a co-production of Greece, Bulgaria and Switzerland, is the best example) and at times offered a somewhat idyllic and nostalgic picture of multicultural ethnic harmony, and featured members of the main ethnic groups living peacefully side by side with Jews, Armenians, Turks and Gypsies in blissfully serene co-existence which is gradually disturbed and corrupted, leaving an aftertaste of wanted reconciliation: *Sled kraya na sveta* (*After the End of the World*, Ivan Nichev, 1998), *Train de vie* (*Train of Life*, Radu Mihaileanu, 1998), *Politiki kouzina* (*A Touch of Spice*, Tassos Boulmetis, 2003) and *Çamur* (*Mud*, Dervis Zaim, 2003). Including a text on Adela Peeva's seminal documentary *Chiya e tazi pesen?* (*Whose is This Song?*, 2003) would be a must for such a volume. In this film, the director travels across all countries of the region in an attempt to trace the origins of a well-known popular tune which all members of a party of Balkan filmmakers sitting in an Istanbul tavern claim to have originated in their own country. In every place she visits, she finds more and more versions of the song sometimes performed as a belligerent Islamic hymn and sometimes chanted by nationalist Orthodox Slavs. No matter what seemingly contradictory disguises and conflicting manifestations there may be for this melody, at the end of the day it is the realisation of commonly inhabited space that dominates, in resonance with the underlying motif of pan-Balkan mutuality.

There are many more aspects of this newly rediscovered Balkan togetherness, from the Balkan sidebars at the festivals in Thessaloniki, Istanbul, Sarajevo, Sofia and others, all showcasing the recent production of the region, through the South East European film network, to a variety of projects and publications. It is a new development which began taking shape in the 1990s and is still in development. Contrary to the widely shared belief that the Balkan countries are permanently at odds with each other, evidence from the annals of pan-European film funding bodies reveals that the Balkan nations collaborate more frequently today than even well-established older international partnerships. A large number of co-productions include participants from at least two Balkan countries – Bulgaria and Turkey, Cyprus and Greece, Cyprus and Bulgaria, and even the unlikely pair of Greece and Turkey – not bad for countries that are believed unable to leave behind a long history of political tensions.

The project of Balkan mutuality is being consciously cultivated with the intention of acknowledging the supra-national dimensions of the regional heritage and give a boost to an appreciation of a shared regional identity, thus offering a framework for a new, critical examination of sense of belonging and positive thinking about 'being Balkan'. The purpose is not to invalidate the individual national cultures but rather to transcend them, to highlight similar cultural patterns and spaces in a manner that would assert the background of a shared transnational identity, and show in the process that it is a matter of will and determination to turn a disconnected space into a connected one.

**Dina Iordanova**

# STELLA

## MICHAEL CACOYANNIS, GREECE, 1955

The Stella of the film's title is the lead singer at Paradise, a bouzouki club in the Plaka district of Athens. A sexual rebel at a time when there was no mass feminist movement, Stella (Melina Mercouri) views marriage as a prison that deprives women of their freedom. The film opens as Stella is ending an affair with Alekos, a man from a good family who has offended her by proposing marriage. She then begins a tempestuous relationship with Miltos, a local soccer star. When Miltos also insists on marriage, Stella, partly fearing a violent reaction if she refuses, ruefully accepts. On her wedding day, however, she finds the courage to literally leave Miltos standing at the altar. It also happens to be a national holiday, celebrated with numerous public events. Stella soon encounters Andonis, a youthful admirer from Paradise. They enjoy the parades and marching bands all day and then dance all night at nightclubs. When they part at dawn, Andonis begins to speak of a permanent union. Stella just walks away and heads home, even though she knows a crazed Miltos is surely awaiting her. When they meet, with knife in hand, he will demand that Stella choose between marriage or death.

*Stella* (Michael Cacoyannis, 1955) is set in Greece in 1953. While most of Europe was rebuilding itself in the post-World War Two years, Greece had experienced a brutal civil war that did not end until 1949. Tens of thousands of Greeks were forced into exile and thousands more were jailed on island prison camps.

Exactly what constituted genuine Greek culture remained very much at issue, and the first real film industry in Greece was a new element in that national discourse. Operating on the Hollywood studio model, national production would be prodigious, exceeding one hundred films a year by the turn of the decade. Most of these films were comedies, musicals, melodramas and other popular genres, but a handful of filmmakers working at the edges of the studio system managed to access its resources for more ambitious projects.

Among the most gifted of the new filmmakers was Cyprus-born Michael Cacoyannis, who had spent the war years in England working for the BBC. His first film, the light-hearted *Kyriakatiko xypnima* (*Windfall in Athens*, 1954) had been a domestic box-office success, the

Greek selection for Cannes, and the opening film at the 1954 Edinburgh Film Festival. Opting for a more serious theme for his second film, Cacoyannis teamed up with Iakovas Kamabanellis for a screen adaptation of the latter's hit play, *E Stella me ta kokkina gantia* (*Stella with the Red Gloves*). The resulting film, bearing the shortened title *Stella*, became the number one box-office film in Greece in 1955, was celebrated at the Cannes Film Festival, won the Golden Globe for Best Foreign Film in 1956 and would go on to enjoy success internationally.

Although *Stella* offers stark neo-realistic scenes of Greek tavernas, marketplaces and cityscapes, the film is better understood as a clever fusion of popular melodrama spiced with elements of classical Greek mythology. The theatrical references commence with the opening images. As a young Greek male walks along a stone walkway toward a taverna named Paradise, the film's credits are rendered as a series of wall posters of the kind that advertised taverna attractions at that time. The sombre lighting, soulful music and measured pace of the walker suggest all is not well. We will soon hear Maria (Sophia Vembo), the owner of Paradise, a woman who indeed mothers all in her realm, saying, 'Come inside and make your dreams come true.'

The bouzouki culture of Paradise, the social setting for *Stella*, was unique to the early 1950s and should not be confused with the taverna culture that evolved in the decades that followed. With its creative roots in the Near East, bouzouki music did not become well-known in Greece until the Greek-Turkish War of 1922 brought a million and half Asian Minor Greeks as refugees to the Greek mainland. The newcomers were not particularly well-treated in an extremely poor nation that had been engaged in a series of costly wars for more than a decade. Some of the refugees became petty criminals whose drug-centered social life evolved in small tavernas that featured bouzouki music. The plate-smashing that became so celebrated in later years began in these clubs as an expression of contempt for bourgeois propriety and the sanctity of property.

Bouzouki evolved into an urban Greek blues and was considered so subversive by pre-World War Two Greek governments that its performance was banned. Bouzouki joints began to reopen during the chaos of the war years, and by the onset of the 1950s, they had begun to attract intellectuals and affluent Athenians in a social dynamic not unlike the Harlem speakeasies of the 1920s or the New Orleans bawdy houses that featured jazz at the turn of the twentieth century. Cacoyannis wanted a musical score for his film that would explore the relationship of the new music to other Greek musical traditions. He wanted pianos, saxophones, guitars, bouzoukia and other instruments to serve as social and psychological markers. His choice to create such a score was Manos Hadjidakis. Although classically trained, Hadjidakis was a habituate of the bouzouki clubs and already had begun to incorporate bouzouki into his own work.

In one of the first sequences of the film, Stella attempts to update her act by dancing to a recording of music with a Latin American beat. Dressed in a tawdry outfit inspired by popular magazines, she wants to be spot-lit on a darkened stage in a manner she has seen in movies. Her effort initially works, but during the middle of a seductive dance, the record gets stuck, repeating one refrain over and over, destroying the mood. The waiter, sitting precariously on a stepladder in order to control the taverna's new spotlight, loses his balance and highlights Stella's knees rather than her face, leaving her to perform in the dark. An enraged Stella breaks the record across her knees and rushes into her dressing room. When we next see her on stage, she is singing with the house orchestra. Competent but not extraordinary and compelling because of her personality rather than her voice, she sounds best when she sits amidst the musicians, her voice joyously blending with the bouzoukia.

Although Stella flirts shamelessly with her mostly male audience, she is neither a whore nor a prostitute. She simply seeks lovers who will treat her as an equal. She states repeatedly that all she wants to do is dance and sing as a free woman. Stella denounces marriage as a condition that drowns a woman's liberty in the kitchen sink and breaks her dignity with a barrage of pots and pans. Her distress is not a conflict between career and domesticity; she is just not interested in domesticity and never takes up the issue of whether she ever wants to be a mother. In that sense, Stella is not a realistic character exploring a new sexual role for Greek women but a poetic embodiment of the irresolvable conflict between absolute independence and the commitments associated with a permanent relationship.

Stella is obsessed with her own image. She has photographs of herself prominently displayed in her apartment and has had a poster advertising her act put up across the street from her window, so she can look at herself whenever she wishes. She admits to one of her lovers that it pleases her to look at herself. Not coincidentally, her name in Greek means star, as in the heavens. We will learn nothing of her family or the source of her views. All we know is that she lives alone in an apartment outside the entrance to Paradise.

The other singers in Paradise, Maria and the younger Annetta (Voula Zoumboulaki), are a contrast to Stella. Annetta wants the kind of relationship Stella disdains and is always trying to win the affection of Stella's current beau. Her mother, who never passes up a chance to berate Stella, is constantly working on Maria to give her daughter better billing. Older than the others, Maria sings as well as them and constantly offers good advice as she strives to make her taverna as congenial an environment as possible. During a county outing that takes place midway through the film, Maria picks up a traditional guitar and sings an old village song. Stella, Annetta and the others at the gathering are touched by her performance, but they and the audience sense that Maria's music is rooted in a village culture whose time is rapidly passing, if not already gone.

The first of Stella's lovers we encounter is Alekos (Alekos Alexandrakis), a rather gentle, upper-middle-class dropout. He has pleased Stella by buying her a much-desired piano for her act, but not grasping her true nature, he proposes marriage. Stella is insulted and will shortly declare their affair is over. In fact, Alekos has inadvertently doomed their relationship with his gift. When an exhilarated Stella goes to an outdoor wedding to arrange for her favorite piano player to return to Paradise, she meets Miltos (Yiorgos Foundas), a local soccer hero. The contrast between the athletic, open-shirted Miltos and the effete, buttoned-down Alekos is absolute. Rather than using the polite language characteristic of Alekos, Miltos speaks brashly, revealing an ego as broad as his huge smile. He is clearly at home in a setting featuring traditional Greek music and dancing. Although intrigued by Miltos, Stella, unimpressed by his chauvinistic style, walks away. Miltos vows she will soon see him again.

That night a drunken Miltos appears outside Paradise. When he threatens to drive his truck through the front gates, Stella boldly bars the way with her body. Miltos guns his truck forward but brakes at the last moment. Thrilled by her daring, he persuades her to go for a ride. When he makes crudely possessive sexual moves, Stella rejects him and returns to Paradise. Much later that same night, Miltos returns. This time, he seeks to gain his will by threatening to blow up the taverna with the stick of dynamite that he holds in his hand. When he lights the fuse to show his determination, everyone but Stella flees. The two now play a kind of Russian roulette. At the last minute, Miltos pulls out the fuse and declares Stella to be the only woman he has ever met who could be considered his equal. He states that he takes women as they are and never seeks to change them. Stella accepts him at his word and for a time Miltos is surprisingly attentive and gentle.

The rejected Alekos becomes physically and emotionally ill. Although his family considers bouzouki music to be 'unbearable' and judges Stella to be a gold digger, they send Alekos's sister to see Stella. The sister reveals that Alekos has had a previous 'nervous breakdown'. The family, fearing a repetition, has decided to approve the marriage on the condition that Stella retires as a performer. An irate Stella responds that if she wanted to marry Alekos, she would not require their consent. The piano Alekos has bought for her guarantees that he will forever be in her heart, but she has no wish to be married. Shortly thereafter, a dazed Alekos posts himself outside Stella's apartment. He stares at the closed shutters and knows Miltos must be inside. Either accidentally or deliberately, he steps in front of a car and is killed.

Stella goes to the burial ceremony but is turned away by the family who holds her responsible for Alekos's death. Although she genuinely grieves for a man she once loved, Stella has no sense of guilt. From her perspective, his family has made him unstable with their rigid social thinking. Miltos now proves as ill-suited for Stella as Alekos had been. He seeks to comfort her by announcing that he has decided to marry her. A bewildered Stella cannot find the strength to refuse outright, but she is surely the most-unhappy of brides-to-be. Despite comforting words from Maria and even the envious Annetta, she truly believes that love cannot endure in the institution of marriage. When she refuses to pay a formal visit to her perspective mother-in-law (Christina Koloyerkiou) as tradition requires, Miltos trumps her defiance by bringing his mother to Stella's apartment. He waits outside as the two women talk.

Miltos' mother proves to be an engaging personality. Under different circumstances, she and Stella might very well have been friends. She says her son can be a stubborn ass who would rather kill or be killed than change, but he is also a frank man. She thinks Stella has a similar character. Thus Stella must understand that the marriage means she will leave Paradise, will move to a new suburban home her husband has already purchased, will become a mother as soon as possible, and will leave family affairs to her mother-in-law. After Miltos' mother has departed, Stella laments, 'The first one wanted to turn me into a lady, the second into a housewife. Oh brother! What am I to them that they want to change me, a phonograph record?'

On her wedding day, instead of proceeding to the church where Miltos is waiting, Stella walks to a central Athens festooned with Greek flags in a massive celebration of the day the Greek government said *oxi* (no) to Mussolini's request to pass fascist troops through Greece. That *oxi* had set off Greece's involvement in World War Two, first marked by a victory over the invading Italians and then by a brutal Nazi Occupation. As Stella listens to very Western-sounding military marching bands and observes various groups parading, she is sighted by Andonis (Kostas Kakavas), an acquaintance from Paradise. Earlier that day they had had a conversation in which she had learned he was not yet twenty years old. They meander among the street festivities all afternoon and then seek out Athenian nightclubs with American-style be-bop bands.

While Stella has been listening to parading military brass bands and dancing to American jazz beats, the rejected Miltos has gone to Paradise where he dances feverishly to the accompaniment of bouzoukia. He insists everything is fine. He says he is not embarrassed by what has happened. Images of Miltos dancing at the neighborhood taverna begin to alternate at an ever accelerating pace with images of Stella dancing at the midtown nightclubs. Images of rows of bouzouki players vie with that of a saxophone soloist. Close-ups of the face of an anguished Miltos alternate with the face of a doomed Stella.

If the melodramatic merging of Stella's *oxi* to Miltos with the Greek *oxi* to Mussolini is likely to be missed by most non-Greek audiences, for the national audience it smoothly blends the question of Greece's power relationship to Europe with that of the power relationship between the sexes. Andonis, much gentler than Miltos but more virile than Alekos, is thrilled to have the fabulous Stella in his arms, but any illusions Stella might have about his character being different than that of the others are dissipated when he begins to speculate about their future in the same possessive terms as her previous suitors.

The Fates now control Stella's destiny as surely as any character in Greek tragedy. When she parts with Andonis at the break of a new day in the street outside Paradise, she tells him not to look back. He asks why and she replies, 'Bad luck.' 'Tomorrow,' he confidently whispers. She echoes his whisper as if affirming his hope, but she has already spied Miltos, waiting for her with knife in hand, as he once stood with a stick of dynamite. Miltos also has become a figure of Greek tragedy, compelled by tradition to slay the only woman he has ever loved. He shouts that if she will agree to go through with the marriage, he will throw away the knife. She keeps walking forward; perhaps hoping he will again pull the fuse. He pleads for her to flee until, in a cumbersome fusion of cheap melodrama and classic drama, he stabs her. Stella's last wish is that Miltos keep kissing her as she dies.

The people of Plaka pour into the streets as an immobilised Miltos holds the dead Stella in his arms. Annetta shouts that he must flee before the police arrive. A dazed Miltos, lost in the same despair Alekos must have experienced, cannot respond. A crowd surrounds him and the camera pulls back for a last wide-angle, crane's-eye view of a world that ultimately had no place for a woman like Stella.

Even the sympathetic Maria, while admiring Stella's style and bravery, had never fathomed her views. Stella's men – the gentlemen caller, the proletarian athlete, the boy/man – are just different faces of the same Greek patriarchy. A number of changes made from the play emphasise these themes. The Stella of the play had some conformist views and was sometimes awed by European and American fashion. In the film, she has neither of these qualities. Even if her tastes are often vulgar, she is genuinely intrigued by new things she hears about on radio, reads about in magazines or sees in motion pictures. Adroitly played by Mercouri, who is taller and fairer than most Greeks, she is not a drop-dead beauty but a handsome, working-class woman full of curiosity. By changing Miltos from a truck driver to a soccer player, the film gives him a star status equal to that of Stella; and like Stella's constellation of admirers, his admirers are also working-class men. Alekos, in contrast, is made weaker. Rather than having the honorable profession of surgeon as in the play, he is reduced to being an idler. These alterations render Alekos as an ineffectual representative of the old money elite while the dynamic Miltos represents a working class not always able to distinguish between its emotional needs and its emotional fears.

Although contemporary Greek audiences flocked to the film, some Greek critics considered the film's feminism to be vulgar and even offensive. Leftists, in particular, believed Stella's vague sense of free love was a distraction from class-based feminism that most certainly included marriage. They judged Miltos to be more a dangerous sub-proletarian than a worker, and they thought the Oxi Day sequence did not make it clear that the military had appropriated a genuine patriotic event for its own ends. Ideology aside, other critics were upset that the film glamorised a music associated with petty criminals. Over the decades these views about bouzouki would change considerably. Mikis Theodorakis, the nation's premiere musician, would incorporate bouzouki into what came to be called people's music. With *Pote tin Kyriaki* (*Never on Sunday*, Jules Dassin, 1960) and *Zorba the Greek* (Michael Cacoyannis, 1964), bouzouki would be recognised as one of the signature sounds of Greek culture.

All the principal actors involved in *Stella* would remain central to Greek cultural life for decades. Although Yiorgos Foundas never gained an international following, he would reign as one of Greece's major leading men, first in film and later in television. Foundas also appeared in two more international hits, as the chauvinistic village bully in *To Koritisi me ta mavara* (*A Girl in Black*, Michael Cacoyannis, 1956) and as the neighborhood nice guy whom Ilyia finally marries in *Never on Sunday*.

Mercouri would become the first Greek woman to achieve international stardom since Katina Paxinou's Academy Award role in *For Whom the Bell Tolls* (Sam Wood, 1943). Mercouri became an international celebrity with *Never on Sunday* and took on her most challenging screen role one year later as the lead in *Phaedra* (1962), also directed by her husband Jules Dassin. As a major opponent of the military junta (1967–74), Mercouri came to personify the best in Greek culture. In a later political career, she served as Minister of Culture in Greece's first socialist government. Using that office, she would transform the somewhat seedy Plaka area seen in *Stella* into a major tourist centre, would be a tireless supporter of state aid to Greek filmmakers, and would champion the return of the Parthenon marbles to Greece.

Cacoyannis' third film, *A Girl in Black* is arguably his best, but his biggest box-office hit was *Zorba the Greek*. Later, Cacoyannis proved to be more passionate about Greek tragedies than about contemporary Greece. Using his own translations, he often directed tragedies for the London stage and brought three to the screen: *Ilektra* (*Electra*, 1962), *The Trojan Women* (1971) and *Ifiyenia* (*Iphigenia*, 1977). Noted as a superb director of women, in addition to his success with Mercouri, he frequently directed Irene Papas in the roles that made her an international star and he worked repeatedly with Eli Lambetti, Greece's foremost stage actor. Always intrigued by the challenges of bringing theatre classics to the screen, at the age of 79, he wrote and directed an English-language adaptation of Chekhov's *The Cherry Orchard* (1999).

With his score for *Stella*, Manos Hadjidakis opened the door for what became a major presence of Greek composers in international film. He personally continued to compose for films of varied genres. Among his work are the scores for *The 300 Spartans* (Rudolph Maté, 1962), *Topkapi* (Jules Dassin, 1964), *America, America* (Elia Kazan, 1964), *The Invincible Six* (Jean Negulesco, 1970) and *Sweet Movie* (Dušan Makavejev, 1974). But he is best known internationally for writing the lyrics and music for 'The Boys of Pireaus', the lead song of Dassin's *Never on Sunday*.

Films about strong-willed women were also made in other countries of the region, typically by male directors (for example, Makavejev's *Čovek nije tica* (*Man Is Not a Bird*, 1965; Hristo Hristov's *Edna zhena na trideset i tri* (*A Woman at Thirty-Three*, 1982); Ademir Kenović's *Kuduz* (1989); Lucian Pintilie's *Balanta* (*The Oak*, 1992)) and sometimes, as in the case of Mercouri, launched the careers of important actresses (such as Yugoslav Milena Dravić or Romanian Maia Morgenstern). This type of strong woman is a more typical personage for Balkan cinema than the victimised wife seen, for example, in the recent *Maria* (Calin Peter Netzer, 2003).

*Stella* is of historic importance as the first Greek film to successfully bring Greek music, Greek images and Greek issues to the attention of international audiences. Having been shot mostly on location, *Stella* also offers a compelling portrait of post-war Athens. Especially noteworthy are the numerous bouzouki sequences that preserve the rebellious musical spirit of a time and place irrevocably gone. In addition, *Stella* is an example of how a commercial film industry aimed at a general audience can produce truly remarkable films. Finally, *Stella*'s feminist theme, however heavy-handed its execution, remains as relevant to Greek and international audiences as when the film was made, if not more so.

**Dan Georgakas**

## VULO RADEV, BULGARIA, 1964

Veliko Turnovo, 1917. World War One is drawing to an end, and ragged prisoners-of-war loiter in the streets. Memorial services are held every day for the Bulgarian soldiers killed on the front. The city's commandant, a pedantic middle-aged Colonel, keeps his wife Liza behind the thick walls of their period mansion, which is surrounded by a peach-tree orchard. One day Liza discovers Ivo Obrenović, a Serbian prisoner of war, picking peaches in the backyard. Having managed to slip out of the nearby camp for prisoners of war, the young man's relationship with Liza blossoms from compassion and an opportunity to find companionship amidst loneliness, to love. In the camp, Ivo strikes up a friendship with a French fellow-inmate, De Greville, whilst looking forward to his encounters with Liza. The lovers are aware that their love is doomed, but this only draws them closer together. The infatuation with Ivo brings about a change in Liza, giving her a different outlook on the world, a transformation not missed by the Colonel. After riots break out in the city, the Colonel orders the camp to be moved to another town. His orderly, under orders to shoot on sight anyone who approaches his home, catches Ivo as he breaks from rank to say farewell from Liza, and fatally shoots him.

The diversion from the aesthetic dogmas of Stalinism during the second half of the 1950s constitutes an interesting period in Bulgarian cinema, be it a short one. During these years, Bulgarian cinema managed not only to overcome its isolation, but also to succeed in modernising its cinematic language. Several works offered new avenues for cinematic expression, including Rangel Vulchanov's *Na malkiya ostrov* (*On the Small Island*, 1958), Khristo Piskov's *Bednata ulitza* (*The Poor Street*, 1960), Binka Zhelyazkova's *A byakhme mladi...* (*We Were Young*, 1961) and Ducho Mundrov's *Pleneno yato* (*Captive Flock*, 1962). These works allowed Bulgarian cinema to overcome its inherent provincial inferiority complex. It took part in the experiments and 'new waves' that characterise most Eastern European film industries of the early 1960s. Having come about as a result of weakened ideological pressure, this process of integration expressed the desire of filmmakers from the Eastern Bloc to participate more actively in the dialogue of world cinema, while protecting the unique character of their national film traditions.

Unfortunately, this drive was quickly suppressed, once again returning to the ideological dogmas of 'socialist realism'. For a time, artists with more 'liberal' views lost out to those whose films would commit to socialist ideology and propaganda.

In these times of stagnation, the arrival of Vulo Radev's *Kradetsat na praskovi* (*The Peach Thief*, 1964) was a remarkable event, in particular because the film was free from ideological bias. It revolutionised the Bulgarian film industry in its own unique and creative way, by introducing the theme of love, a topic that had lacked adequate appreciation in the Bulgarian cinematic tradition.

*The Peach Thief* brought to the fore a valuable debate on the problems of artistic merit. The film leaves a lasting impression not because of its plotline or the truthfulness of its details, but rather with the outstanding honesty with which it depicts the richness of human feelings, and with its skilful recreation of the characters' intimate world. It was the first time in the history of Bulgarian cinema that a film spoke of love so freely, unrestricted by ideological demands or paradigmatic representational requirements. The film became a real challenge to the stringent defenders of aesthetic orthodoxy, who saw the value of a work of art only in direct relation to its ideological message.

Radev's film is based on the novella of the same name of the important Bulgarian writer Emilian Stanev. The film differs significantly from its literary source, in shifting certain emphases and details, whilst remaining truthful to the spirit of the Stanev's work.

The novella is centred on a conventional love triangle. A prisoner of war falls in love with the wife of the army officer in charge of the town where the prison camp is located. After a series of memorable encounters, the love affair is brutally cut short and the feelings of love slowly fade. The writer recreates the rich emotional states of the characters and tactfully reveals the complexity of their relationship with sympathy for the pure beauty of their secret love. For the screen adaptation, Radev went even further in telling Liza and Ivo's story. The director was in search of the bigger projections of love on the personalities of his film's characters. He situates the romance against the background of World War One, which underpins the human fates within a serious social and historical context.

Other noticeable changes were made to Stanev's story. In the film, the Colonel is shown as a noble and world-weary person, tired and disillusioned with warfare. Additional camp scenes were included, as well as a subplot featuring the French prisoner-of-war, De Greville. The narrative structure became more linear and was presented more objectively. Reportedly, this new treatment triggered a degree of disapproval from the writer, who initially reacted angrily

toward the film. The controversy eventually calmed down, due in part to the enormous popularity of the screen adaptation. Even though writer and director approached the treatment of the protagonists and their relationship differently, their disagreement never grew into a bitter public showdown, as they realised that the differences were neither aesthetic or ideological, but concerned secondary elements. In this sense, Radev provided a novel reading of Stanev's text, placing it in a different cultural context, which resounded better with the concerns circulating at the time the film was made.

*The Peach Thief* was the directorial debut of Radev, previously known as one of the most skilled and sought-after Bulgarian cinematographers, whose work included Vladimir Petrov's Soviet co-production *Nakanune* (*V navecherieto/On The Eve*, 1959), an adaptation of Ivan Turgenev's novel, and Nikola Korabov's adaptation of Dimitar Dimov's classic novel *Tyutyun* (*Tobacco*, 1962). The release of Vulo Radev's first film as director marked the arrival of a new filmmaker of original creativity whose approach would challenge and revolutionise the artistic practices of Bulgarian cinema.

Interestingly enough, this film was also the first step toward mastering the principles of popular cinema, something to which Bulgarian filmmakers had been aspiring for many years. It also succeeded in balancing critical acclaim with public popularity. Sensitive toward the emotional modality of a wider audience, Radev consciously looked for those artistic devices that would bring the film closer to a mass audience without compromising his artistic vision. He was not afraid to play to mainstream tastes at a time when the dogma of *auteur* cinema dominated the creative and intellectual filmmaking arena.

After a series of high profile anti-fascist films populated by tired ideological clichés, *The Peach Thief* was a refreshing film about intimacy and human warmth. Instead of images of revolutionaries and underground party functionaries fighting for their ideals, Radev's film offered audiences people made of flesh and blood, characters that could yield to their emotions, suffer, make mistakes, experience love and affection and sacrifice themselves in the name of love. His decisions concerning the film's style allowed him to construct an involving story based on the motivations and psychology of his characters. His film engaged the audience on an emotional level, relying on sympathy and identification.

*The Peach Thief* takes place against the backdrop of a period marked by tragedy and loss within the Bulgarian nation. Although the bloody fighting of World War One was fading into the recesses of the country's collective memory, there were still thousands of survivors who had witnessed the bloody conflict, as well as the two equally devastating regional wars (The Balkan

War, 1912–13; The Serbian-Bulgarian War, 1913–14) that had preceded it. Those still serving in the army had long since lost any dignity, ordinary people had lost hope, and the failure of reunification had left deep scars in the everyday life of common Bulgarians. The adverse impact of the wars rules out a happy outcome for the lovers in *The Peach Thief*, as they belong to opposing sides: in this particular socio-historic context Serbian Ivo stands in for the 'enemy' by default.

The film features desperation and disillusionment at the end of a string of wars; such feelings defined the mood not only in Bulgaria but across the region where these wars brought national catastrophes, as shown also in the Romanian film *Pădurea spînzuraţilor* (*Forest of the Hanged*, 1964) and Bulgarian film *Lachenite obuvki na neznainiya voin* (*The Patent Leather Shoes of the Unknown Soldier*, 1979), both discussed in this volume. Triggered by irredentist ambitions (that customarily come as a reaction to the perceived inequitable territorial allot-ments established by the Great Powers at the disbanding of the Ottoman Empire), by the end of the period all Balkan nations become conscious that even after years of fighting they effectively have no say over their own fate. Realising that decisions over the future of their countries are not taken by their sovereign governments but are made by Western bigwigs leads to a situation where fighting each other has increasingly come to be seen as warfare against 'brothers' who are equally deprived and deceived and therefore not a real adversary. In the later historical film-making of the Balkans these wars are commonly represented as 'fratricidal.'

Life is monotonous and boring in a small provincial town like Veliko Turnovo; the atmos-phere is permeated by nostalgia for a time that has long passed into history. The melancholy of a war drawing to an unsatisfactory end dominates the Colonel's household; the invader breaks this spell. What begins as compassion for the shabbily-dressed captive, soon turns to passion and grips Liza and Ivo with a sweeping power. They know that their sudden, uncontrollable affection is doomed, but this feeling inspires them even more. Their love is stronger than the neighbours' narrow-mindedness and the prejudices of provincial society. Liza and Ivo fully succumb to their feelings, neglecting the reality of war-time relations, the dehumanising regime of the camp, and the stringent regulatory framework of mores that keep the young woman split between her love and the duties she would be expected to obey as a wife.

At first glance, *The Peach Thief* appears to offer little more than the staple elements of a love-torn melodrama, evolving within an even more trivial love triangle. However, Radev breathes life into the simple plot, by building rich and interesting characters with fates that mirror the historical context and drama of an entire nation. The story takes place in the aftermath of the Balkan wars that immediately preceded World War One. In this context of military confrontation, the love affair between a Bulgarian military wife and a Serbian war captive is no longer a simple emotional escapade, but acquires added historical significance. It is a situation that subtly challenges the concept of the 'enemy' in a context where affection is given the status of opposing the war, protesting against the divides of national, ethnic and racial belonging.

The love story can be seen as a pretext for a probing exploration of the deeper existential problems of human life and fate; conveying a message about the power and beauty of pure love, which cannot be burdened with prejudice and false moral norms. It clearly reveals the author's opinion that war emasculates people's natural feelings, by erecting unnecessary walls between them, and by destroying all beauty in life. *The Peach Thief* is a verdict against a world full of injustice, which would not disappear with the last bullets of war; it is an indictment of narrow-mindedness and bigotry.

A beguilingly confident debut, *The Peach Thief* recreates the real drama of those human conflicts without a trace of naïve sentimentalism or ostentatious rhetoric. And while the main narrative remains focused on the intimacy of the protagonists, the director uses the grim everyday life to provide a framework for the drama: the scenes showing the bleak existence in the prisoner-of-war camp mirror the gloomy daily goings-on of ordinary people in the town. The scenes of the struggle for survival in the camp amount to more than a simple background to Ivo and Liza's tragic love story; the point is to show that the suffering and denigration that people suffer as a result of war are the same on either side of the barbed wire.

In his quest for psychological truthfulness and the emotional integrity of the characters, Radev touches with delicate respect upon the theme of eternal human drama. The director carefully recreates the lyrical depth of Liza and Ivo's romance. Idealistically presented, this leit-motif represents the protagonists' yearning for the primeval beauty of feelings; it embodies the celebration of life over death.

The purity of this mutual infatuation is balanced by Liza's husband, a mature and considered man twice her age. The withdrawn Colonel plays an important role, playing a character far removed from the usual cliché of a cuckolded husband. The Colonel is, above all, a spiritually elevated intellectual who represents the wisdom and scepticism that come with a life experience acquired in testing times. Weary and wise, he clearly realises that his personal life is a failure and that his young wife is lonely and restless. This knowledge is overshadowed by a stronger awareness of the collapse of all other ideals for which he fought so ferociously. His world literally crumbles and he is incapable of preventing its destruction; all his ideas and dreams have transformed into illusions and unrealised hopes. The melancholic stoicism that the Colonel deploys to meet the challenges of fate is an expression of a life philosophy that elevates honesty and fanatic devotion to truth and principles above everything else.

Several of the secondary characters in the film also need to be considered carefully as their presence is of key importance for supplying the background of candour and existential quest. These secondary characters are introduced only in broad strokes and without much detail, but remain excellently psychologically observed and thus leave an impression that is memorable and profound. For instance, the image of intellectual sceptic Pierre de Greville, a French prisoner-of-war who has befriended Ivo, provides a much needed further dimension to Ivo's character, achieved by contrasting Ivo's romantic drive with the sophistication and the cynicism of Pierre's mature outlook. This character echoes the sarcasm of the war-weary protagonists in Jean Renoir's masterpiece *La Grande illusion* (*The Grand Illusion*, 1937). The voiceless orderly of the Colonel is also an important presence. Sorrow is hidden in his obedience; he moves as a shadow between the main characters only to yell out his pain at the very end of the film.

The constant alternation between extreme states of mind and moods imparts a rich emotional texture to the film. It allows the director to jump between episodes possessing different degrees of emotional intensity while keeping a distance from the outbursts of sensuality or sentimental energy. Each of the characters in *The Peach Thief* is an expression of pairs of categories: love/death, good/evil, war/peace, duty/passion, all seamlessly integrated into the way the story unravels. There is also an important emblematic image – the small wooden doll that Ivo has made. It represents a soldier suspended from a string stretched between two sticks; even the slightest squeezing of the sticks sends the soldier into a series of somersaults. The protagonists are frequently seen flicking the doll; these recurring scenes symbolising the restrictions faced by the protagonists in the whirlwind of history's whims.

In addition to serving the narrative well, the camerawork excels in its painterly use of black and white, and expressive yet unobtrusive camera angles. The compositions follow the overall style of intimate insight into the inner world of unspoken feelings and strong passions, of melancholy and sorrow. Landscape and cityscape (of the ancient Bulgarian capital Veliko Turnovo) are ascribed a special place here, as a counterpoint to the action. In Radev's poetics, Nature is interpreted as an equal participant in the ensuing confrontations: it either reveals its bounty in front of the film's heroes, or becomes a dull addition to their pain; it either shares the characters' sacred hopes and secrets, or mourns their lost illusions. The poetic attitude toward Nature and its role is part of the overall original stylistic concept of the film.

One of the main musical motives of *The Peach Thief* is the nostalgic war melody 'Tamo daleko' ('There, Far Away'), a classical song of exile and displacement, which was created in the winter of 1915 when surviving soldiers of the Serbian army had found temporary shelter on the island of Corfu near Albania and Greece. 'Tamo daleko' is still popular today, and some modern versions are in circulation (the best-known one is by diasporic Yugoslav Goran Bregović).

The powerful impact of *The Peach Thief* would be unthinkable without the strong performances: the actors not only responded to the director's vision of each character but were also set to become true co-authors in the directorial concept. In his memoirs, Radev reports that at the early stages of his work on the film there had been serious disagreements between him and the members of the cinematic establishment: reportedly, the bureaucrats attempted to wrest control of the casting by choosing an actress for the lead role. The director, however, remained adamant in his insistence in casting Nevena Kokanova, a young actress who, as Liza, delivered one of the top performances of her prominent artistic career. Later on, Kokanova was to become a major star of Bulgarian cinema, remembered for a range of leading roles in films by directors like Lyubomir Sharlandzhiev, Lyudmil Kirkov, Lyudmil Staikov and others.

Kokanova had already appeared in several films and had established herself as a popular actress. Being cast by Radev for the role of Liza at a relatively early stage of her career, she had been fortunate to meet a talented and insightful director who did not simply exploit her stunning beauty, but endeavoured to bring out the dramatic qualities in her performance, thus uncovering the full range of her expressive possibilities. Kokanova's Liza is a heroine of iconic importance, a memorably sensitive woman, ready to sacrifice herself for love but also harbouring the power to counteract prejudice, able to resist judgemental public opinion and to stand for her own feelings.

Nevena Kokanova's partners in the film are the celebrated Serbian actor Rade Marković in the role of Ivo and Mikhail Mikhailov in the role of Liza's husband. Marković came to this film having already established a reputation as a leading Yugoslav actor. His Ivo is a shy, lyrical character who lives with his romantic feelings for Liza, suffers honestly and is spontaneously sincere. In this he profoundly differs from the affable cynicism of the other character from the prisoner-of-war camp – the Frenchman de Greville, played by Naum Shopov. Mikhailov, in the role of the Colonel, commands respect with his controlled screen performance and use of restrained gestures and posture that suggests inner nobility and delicacy. The actor skilfully

portrays weariness and *ennui* while simultaneously recreating the protagonist's sharp feeling for justice and respect to others. Very different from Ivo, the image of the army officer is far from the trivial clichés of popular cinema.

Bringing together the artistic trio of Nevena Kokanova, Rade Marković and Mikhail Mikhailov was a significant achievement for Vulo Radev. By allowing actors of different sensibilities and various professional experience and backgrounds to work together on *The Peach Thief*, the director confidently constructed the framework of this tragic love story. Together with the remarkable supporting performances, the actors endow their characters with astonishing sincerity and human warmth, bringing forth the humanistic message of the film. The ability to balance the individual performances of each one of the actors and yet achieve the feeling of true acting ensemble is a rare quality for a directorial debut. In *The Peach Thief,* this feeling of togetherness and organic integrity of the acting performances is an inseparable part of the aesthetics of the film. Homogenous in all its aspects, *The Peach Thief* stands out as one of the most significant achievements in Bulgarian cinema.

**Alexander Grozev**

# PĂDUREA SPÎNZURAŢILOR FOREST OF THE HANGED

## LIVIU CIULEI, ROMANIA, 1964

*Pădurea spînzuraţilor* (*Forest of the Hanged*, Liviu Ciulei, 1964) tells the difficult story of an ethnic Romanian drafted in the Austro-Hungarian army who refuses to fight against his kinsmen and as a result faces the death penalty.

It is 1916 and Transylvania, a region of mixed population where Romanians are a majority, is still part of the Austro-Hungarian Empire. The independent state of Romania declares war on Austria-Hungary, a confrontation that will end with Transylvania's takeover by Romania in 1918. The entrance of Romania into the war poses a series of moral dilemmas for Apostol Bologa (Victor Rebengiuc), a young lieutenant of Romanian ethnicity who has been with the Austro-Hungarian army for some time, but is now transferred to fight in a region populated mostly by people of the same ethnicity. Bologa's moral torments begin with his appointment to a court martial that condemns a Czech deserter; he has to supervise the execution, a profoundly upsetting experience.

Later on, Bologa faces additional ethical predicaments. Sent to the Romanian front, he becomes entangled in a complex hierarchy of ethnicities that characterised the Austro-Hungarian army. He befriends Czech captain Klapka (played by director Ciulei); his fellow officers are a Polish priest and a Ruthenian, while his commander, General von Karg, is Austrian. He is influenced by pacifist Johann-Maria Müller, an Austrian private, argues with his Romanian orderlies Petre and his son, and has to interrogate Romanian war prisoners and Hungarian peasants thought to be traitors. His friendship with Varga, a Hungarian officer, and his eventual falling in love and engagement to Ilona, a Hungarian peasant girl, introduces further complex dimensions, provided that a certain degree of animosity between Romanians and Hungarians has been a feature of Transylvanian life for quite a long time. As these subplots reveal, however, coexistence in such ethnically diverse communities is mostly unperturbed at the level of individual relationships and interactions.

Bologa's initiative of crossing the front line with a handful of men in order to destroy an enemy searchlight pleases everybody and is considered an act of bravery. Bologa hopes that his newly acquired heroic aura will grant him the desired move to another front where he would not have to deal with Romanian 'enemies'. General von Karg, however, is displeased with Bologa's demand for a transfer and rejects the request, to realise only later that his brave lieutenant is an ethnic Romanian and thus forced to fight against his compatriots. Distraught by the rejection, Bologa tries to desert the front line but is wounded and hospitalised. He is then given leave of absence and travels to his hometown where he finds his fiancée, Maria, busy with joyful wedding preparations. Tormented by disquieting thoughts, Bologa breaks the engagement and returns hastily to the army barracks.

Spring seems to bring a moment of bliss: he falls in love with the peasant girl, Ilona, daughter of his Hungarian village landlord. But his happiness is short-lived; soon war brings him face to face with an even more personal drama: once again he is appointed to serve on a court martial, the purpose of which is to condemn twelve Romanian and Hungarian peasants who disobeyed orders and tried to plough near the frontline. Bologa does not want to be involved and tries to desert. He is soon apprehended, tried and sentenced to death. He refuses the suggestion to plea insanity as he believes that man should be responsible for his own deeds. Bologa awaits execution in a state of acceptance and serenity.

In 1965, director Liviu Ciulei received the award for Best Director at the Cannes Film Festival for his screen adaptation of Liviu Rebreanu's novel *Pădurea spînzuraților* (*Forest of the Hanged*, 1922), while cameraman Ovidiu Gologan was awarded at the festival in Milan. This took place as France seemed to resume its old links with Romania by engaging in a number of co-productions; Cannes was just one of the places where Romanians could distinguish themselves (in particular, Mircea Mureșan's award for *Răscoala* (*The Uprising*, 1965), an adaptation of a novel by Liviu Rebreanu).

Romania had to wait for many years before its cinema would receive further endorsements at major festivals: it was not until 1986, when director Dan Pița received a Silver Bear at Berlin for *Pas în doi* (*Paso Doble*), that such recognition was given. Only after the 1989 revolution did international success become more frequent again: in 1992 Pița was awarded a Silver Lion at Venice for *Hotel de lux* (*Luxury Hotel*), followed by Lucian Pintilie with another award at Venice for his *Terminus paradis* (*Next Stop Paradise*, 1998).

*Forest of the Hanged* represents both a moment of continuity and a landmark of innovation. It occupies a distinguished place in a long line of Romanian screen adaptations, traceable back to Jean Mihail's drama *Păcat (Sin,* 1924), an adaptation of Ion Luca Caragiale's story. Its main influence was the tradition established by directors Jean Georgescu (1901–94) and

Paul Călinescu (1902–2000), who had achieved a degree of international recognition prior to 1940 and who continued to make films during communist rule. Georgescu made several screen adaptations, most importantly of Caragiale's *O noapte furtunoasă* (*Stormy Night*, 1943) and of Tudor Mușatescu's play *Visul unei nopți de iarnă* (*A Winter Night's Dream*, 1946). Călinescu had received two prizes for documentaries at Venice before World War Two began. He then successfully took up fiction films with *Porto Franco* (1961), adapted from the novel by Jean Bart, and *Titanic vals* (*Titanic Waltz*, 1964), adapted from a Mușatescu play. Victor Iliu also reinforced the tradition with *În sat la noi* (*In Our Village*, 1951), and eventually with Ioan Slavici's adaptation *La moara cu noroc* (*The Mill of Good Luck,* 1956).

Liviu Rebreanu (1885–1944), the titan of Romanian literature, was heavily involved in theatre. On one occasion he even saw his work turned into a film: German director Martin Berger adapted his 1930 novel *Ciuleandra* almost immediately after its publication in a Romanian-German co-production known as *Verklungene Träume* (*Echo of a Dream*, 1930). At the time of this first adaptation (*Ciuleandra* was adapted once again in 1985, by Sergiu Nicolaescu) the critics thought the film was not faithful to the original and therefore a failure; Rebreanu even had to explain publicly that he had little to do with the script and attributed the film's faults to an inadequate budget. This adaptation, however, remains of importance as it is the first Romanian sound film.

As a work of literature, Rebreanu's acclaimed *Forest of the Hanged* is considered to be more than fiction, as it is inspired by the tragic death of the author's brother who was hung after being caught trying to cross the frontline. Both Rebreanu and Bologa, the novel's protagonist, come from intellectual families committed to defending the civil liberties of Romanians in Transylvania. Even the character's first name, Apostol, is eloquent: it is the Romanian form of 'apostle', here a messenger of Romanians' hopes. Most of all, however, the novel is seen as a deep analysis of the tragic fate of Romanians living in Austro-Hungarian Transylvania before the 1918 reunification. Rebreanu confessed that he intended to write a book 'not only about the war, but also about the human soul', so he wrote about an officer who has to face a tragic choice between military duty and national belonging.

In adapting this classic text for the screen, Liviu Ciulei changed the story in a way that remained faithful to the literary source and simultaneously reemerged as a modern treatment of the contentious issues of war and loyalty. By focusing on the protagonist's mental torments Ciulei avoided turning the film into a patriotic-nationalistic drama. Together with scriptwriter Titus Popovici, Ciulei decided to replace Rebreanu's character, Gross, with Müller, by adding to

the latter some of the features of another literary protagonist, Iţic Ştrul, taken from Rebreanu's original story. As the novel dealt with characters of different nationalities (Czech, Hungarian, Slovak, Romanian and Austrian), the authors had to decide on the languages to be spoken in the film. If the film was to be a truthful depiction of the multilingual reality of Austria-Hungary, it should have featured the range of idioms that were actually used at the time: Romanian, Ruthenian, Czech, Hungarian, Slovak, German, and maybe more, and the protagonists should have been shown switching back and forth between languages; in addition, the set of languages they would use would clearly delineate their social standing. If faithful to reality, Bologa should have spoken German with the officers, Hungarian with Ilona and Romanian with the soldiers, peasants and prisoners. But even though some of the actors were Romanian Hungarians (for example, Anna Széles and György Kovács) and many actors were fluent in German, the director decided in favour of one language, Romanian, thus avoiding any linguistic complexity during production and for audiences. But even though the linguistic diversity is not retained in the film, one should stress that the multi-language tapestry of life in the region is indeed one of its most important features. Istvan Szabo's Hungarian masterpiece Colonel Redl (1985), also set around the end of the Austro-Hungarian Empire, clearly reveals it by showing the multiple layers and subtle hierarchies of linguistic affiliations. Ciulei opted instead to make use of his background as an architect and set designer and to concentrate on rendering the atmosphere of the empire and its army through the verisimilitude of costumes and sets. Shooting mostly took place in Transylvania, including the use of a baroque eighteenth-century castle.

Ciulei and screenwriter Popovici dropped those aspects of the novel that dealt with the hero's background. They also changed Bologa's motivation for breaking off his engagement: in the novel Bologa gets a glimpse of his fiancée laughing and chattering in Hungarian; he is dismayed and ends the engagement, as she now appears as a stranger to him. Ciulei takes a more cinematographic approach by briefly showing Bologa standing silent and ignored by his fiancée while she cheerfully displays the trousseau. He does not say anything, but his sudden return to the front is more than telling.

It is with this type of change – diminishing the specifically Romanian dimensions and focusing on universal moral concerns, yet remaining faithful to Rebreanu's spirit with cinematographic means – that Ciulei's film displays its real achievement. The director confessed that he intended to make 'a film about the collapse of certainty, of everyday conformism and basic notions of life'. Thus, even though this novel dates back from the time before World War Two, international critics considered Ciulei's film to be an eloquent denouncement of war from a

more contemporary standpoint. The film was released at a time when society was overwhelmed by fears of a possible nuclear conflict in the aftermath of the Cuban missile crisis (1962) and Ciulei's film clearly addressed some of these concerns.

By telling the difficult story of an ethnic Romanian drafted in the Austro-Hungarian army who refuses to fight against his kinsmen and comes to face the death penalty, *Forest of the Hanged* links directly with Vulo Radev's *Kradetsat na praskovi* (*The Peach Thief*, 1964), the film discussed in the preceding chapter. The films may have been made in different languages and countries yet they tackle essentially the same theme (how war damages individual humans), contain the same message (the fratricidal essence of World War One) and are very similar in style (exquisite black and white photography and remarkable artistic performances).

*Forest of the Hanged* opens with images of a long march of troops moving away in disorder. The camera turns back and slowly approaches a hill overgrown by barren trees, then stops on a gallows under which two soldiers dig a grave. The soldiers are supervised by an old corporal who aimlessly paces back and forth across the muddy terrain; he then tries to clean his boots with his bayonet. The inadequate use of the bayonet and the manner in which he addresses the privates reveal he is more of a peasant rather than a trained soldier. Upon Bologa's arrival at the execution site the corporal realises that they forgot to bring a chair for the hanging; in addition, the hangman is missing. In his turn, General von Karg now warns them that it is against the regulations for a uniformed soldier to act as an executioner. Thus, every possible aspect – the weather, the nature, the people – is shown as ill-suited for the war.

During the execution scene, the camera slowly reveals the torment of those involved in the hanging. It moves alongside the convoy, then closes in at the distraught gesture of the corporal wiping the chair, showing the condemned man nervously gripping one of his buttons before moving on to the priest, the peasants, then back again to the terrified corporal who has meanwhile been appointed executioner. At the very moment of the hanging, the camera moves away, as if trying to escape.

Bologa will soon realise the whole absurdity of war. Tormented with guilt over his gutless compliance in the execution, after the hanging he tries to explain to Austrian soldier Müller that 'the state is above man and his interests'. The soldier, who in civilian life is a trinket dealer and philosophising pacifist, replies that 'nothing is above man' and 'only a monstrous state can send a Romanian to fight his own folk'.

Müller's fate will be at the core of a twisted subplot of misapprehensions resulting in the tragic loss of Bologa's orderly Petre, a Romanian peasant. In Bologa's absence, Petre accepts the assignment to quietly eliminate Müller, whose conscientious objector stance is believed to undermine the unit's morale. In exchange Petre is promised a short leave to go home in order to take care of his farm. However, Petre does not kill Müller but tells him to escape across the frontline. When Bologa hears of Petre's actions, he dismisses the orderly and sends him to certain death on the battlefield. It is only later that Bologa will learn from Petre's son that Müller survived; the revelation comes too late, however, as Bologa himself is in confinement at the time. Realising that he is indirectly responsible for the despondency of Petre's family, Bologa has yet another Romanian death on his conscience.

In a key sequence Bologa and Klapka are kept awake by the enemy's searchlight, talking with each other while their faces change appearance in the shifting light. The alternating light and darkness reveals and enhances their anguish; the conversation looks like an exigent interrogation. In the course of the conversation, Bologa tries to justify his behaviour at the hanging as well as to present his very enlisting as an act of courage. It does not take long for Klapka to persuade him that defying orders and keeping away from the trenches would have required more courage. Later on, at a moment of disorientation and insecurity, Klapka confesses that he was also planning to desert along with the executed officer but cowardly changed his mind.

Bologa remains apparently indifferent to this confession. Although he still looks naïve and innocent, his purity is becoming tarnished. He starts drinking, spends a night with the 'loose' Rosa Janosi and acts unkindly towards the Romanian prisoners. Beleaguered, Bologa now hopes that destroying the enemy's searchlight would get him the desired transfer to another front.

Even though the clashes between protagonists resemble an ancient tragedy, the film clearly reveals that the actions of most protagonists are completely logical nonetheless. This is the director's way to assert, once again, the absurdity of war. Apostol Bologa, for example, is often mistaken and comes across as flawed by war yet his comrades Klapka and Varga, as well as the audience, care about him as he remains ultimately more human, innocent and pure. Pacifists Müller and Klapka's repeated assertions that nothing is above man and that somebody who is responsible for raising a family should make sure to live at any cost (Klapka's excuse for abandoning his plan to desert) are fully justified and logical. Petre and the local peasants are right to worry about their crops in the context of their prevailing concerns of survival; the moves of General von Karg are also logical in the context of his military role.

Ilona, albeit a peasant girl, emanates a certain wisdom and moral superiority. She is the one who explains to Bologa how serious the locals' concern is that if they do not plough they will starve. She silently receives Bologa's marriage proposal and thanks him 'for the good thought'. With feminine instinct, she also guesses that he is thinking of deserting and offers to lead him over the mountains. As a former philosophy student and an officer, Bologa not only has an ethnic difference with Ilona but also a class one; it is this disparity of class and ethnicity that suggests their possible marriage would probably never take place; nonetheless she proves to be the most faithful presence in his life.

Ciulei's telling of the story is further enhanced by subtle irony. During their night of discussions Klapka wins Bologa's admiration and establishes a reputation for high moral standards. But this reputation is subverted almost immediately. Soon after breakfast Klapka is asked to go and see General von Karg, who receives him at the table and invites him to breakfast. Rather than admitting he ate already, Klapka accepts and eats breakfast one more time. His gorging on the food is a metaphor for the way he 'swallows' von Karg's opinions without question or hesitation. It is now clear that Klapka is little more than a coward. The general's rich breakfast, including cream and rolls from Vienna, represents a clear a contrast with the dilapidated castle where he lives (a metaphor of Austro-Hungarian decay). The contrast with the trenches full of water inhabited by raggedy soldiers who look like a bunch of vagabonds rather than a regular army is even more stark.

The employment of irony increases as the film progresses. When Bologa is apprehended trying to desert, the duty officer complains about having his sleep disrupted over such a trivial matter. Yet he is scrupulous enough to ask that the detainee is searched for maps and other documents. In another act of irony it is Bologa's friend, Varga, who has to carry out the search: as Bologa is seized in his sector, Varga must disregard their camaraderie and act as an officer, thus having to perform actions he does not believe in.

A subtle feature of Ciulei's remarkably austere approach is his ability to declutter the narrative and thus enhance the effect of the specifically cinematic means he uses (image, light, sound). At certain points in the film events accelerate and Ciulei uses just a few frames to cover the whole period of Bologa's injury, subsequent hospitalisation and trip back home: a couple of months have elapsed and the action has taken place in a range of locations, yet Ciulei tells this part of the story in just a few minutes of screen time.

The director skillfully draws on Theodor Grigoriu's minimalist musical score. Sometimes the music is shrill and merges with the sounds of nature, while in other scenes it completely withdraws in order to make us hear whispered dialogue or the pounding of cannons. An example of Ciulei's masterly approach to sound is evident in the scene at the end of the film, showing Bologa eating his last supper before the hanging. Ilona, his fiancée, has brought food to the cell; she is already dressed in black even though Bologa is still alive, and stares at him with unblinking eyes. Only the sound of rattling plates can be heard. Indeed, what could the protagonists – a simple peasant girl and an officer condemned to death – say to each other? Whatever they utter would reduce the scene to shallow melodrama.

Ciulei's approach included masterly handled dialogues and natural sets of an awe-inspiring impact. Little of the war is directly shown – more puddles than combat action. Instead of ploughs, cannons turn the land over, but war will bring forth just mud and gallows, not trees and crops. Even nature is discoloured during this rainy winter without snow. When taken into confinement, Bologa passes by the gallows and stares at the dead bodies of peasants that hang there as the absurd fruits of the war. This is the 'forest of the hanged', the allegory that provides the harsh image of the title.

Light in all its forms is also a decisive feature of this superbly crafted black and white film. While in the novel the searchlight episode is a minor one, it has a haunting presence in several short but effective scenes in the film. Blinding luminosity faced by the camera is also the leading cinematic element of the exquisite closing scene, showing the embrace of Bologa and Ilona where their silhouettes fade away graciously in the sunlight.

Ciulei's team consisted of regular collaborators (composer Theodor Grigoriu, Mihai Mereuța, who played the corporal at the hanging, and Stefan Ciubotârașu as the orderly Petre) and veteran film professionals (cameraman Ovidiu Gologan). He also introduced new faces on the screen (Emerich Schäffer as Müller, Mariana Mihut as Bologa's first Romanian fiancée, Marta, Ana Széles as Ilona, Bologa's second Hungarian fiancée) and offered the principal part to Victor Rebengiuc who later became one of the leading Romanian actors and distinguished himself in films by Dan Pița and Lucian Pintilie.

Before *Forest of the Hanged*, Ciulei had made two other films that presented praiseworthy, yet trivial, stories. *Eruptia* (*The Eruption*, 1957) was a film about the heroism of everyday life, the kind of theme that was customarily glorified in the early years of communism, but in the hands of a talented filmmaker such as Ciulei it presented the work of drillers in romantic light. His second film, *Valurile Dunarii* (*The Danube Waves*, 1959) was a World War Two story of two men and a woman on a barge moving down the mined Danube. It was compared to Jean Vigo's *L'Atalante* (1934) and received an award at the Karlovy Vary Film Festival in 1960.

Yet in spite of the international acclaim for *Forest of the Hanged*, Ciulei never directed another film. Ironically, the success at Cannes, a symbolic beginning for Romanian cinema, was also the end of the director's career. Ciulei went on working mostly in theatre. In the 1960s he acted as vice-president of the Romanian Association of Filmmakers and was manager of a theatre company in Bucharest. Around 1966 he contemplated adapting Mihail Sadoveanu's novel *Baltagul* (*The Hatchet*); the novel was finally adapted by Mircea Mureşan in 1969, in an Italian co-production. Around 1967–68 he planed to direct *Bacantele* (*Bacchantes*) using Euripides' literary source, as his personal answer to Fellini's *Satyricon*, but this was probably too bold a project for its time. During the 1970s he acted in seven films and a television series, and worked as production designer for several other films.

It is not clear why Ciulei never directed again. Although he did not speak publicly about this, he seems to have tired of working in cinema and chose to dedicate himself to theatre which allowed him to put on stage plays he liked and to work at home and internationally. When asked about this he tried to avoid a direct answer but sometimes he referred to 'getting tired' (of censorship) and made allusions to professional envy. Between 1980 and 2004 he lived and worked often abroad, where he worked mostly as a stage director, especially in Germany and the USA. Since 2004 he has been living in Bucharest and Germany and is rarely seen in public.

*Forest of the Hanged* not only brought international acknowledgement for Romanian cinema, but was also successful at addressing the difficult issues of Austro-Hungary's dissolution at the end of World War One and in exploring its intricate Transylvanian dimension, while staying away from propagandistic patriotic leanings. Ciulei's stylish adaptation of Rebreanu's novel is a memorable historical fresco that addresses complex Balkan confrontations and reinforces the importance of this early analysis of Balkan history.

**Marian Ţuţui**

PĂDUREA SPÎNZURAŢILOR

# TRI THREE

## ALEKSANDAR PETROVIĆ, YUGOSLAVIA, 1965

*Tri* (*Three*, Aleksandar Petrović, 1965) is structured in three chapters, featuring protagonist Miloš Bojanić (Velimir 'Bata' Živojnović), all taking place at different stages of World War Two. In the first, Miloš witnesses the arbitrary slaughter of an innocent man amidst wartime panic and insecurity. In the second, Miloš, who has joined the underground resistance, comes face to face with the brutal demise of a fellow-partisan. In the third part, he is a seasoned partisan commander who succumbs to a short-lived infatuation with a woman, before returning to his more solitary, hard-edged loner personality.

*One.* Spring 1941; Yugoslavia is invaded by Nazi Germany. In a village near Belgrade a group of civilians have gathered at the railway station. They are running away from the advancing Germans and hope to get on whatever train arrives, but the police are holding them back from getting on the platform. Miloš Bojanić, seen here as a handsome and well-groomed young man, approaches the group and is immediately shouted at by the police. At this time he is still a student in Belgrade, and is visibly dismayed by the harsh treatment he has just witnessed. As a train passes by, the crowd grows more desperate and impatient; they venture to ransack a wagon-load of food and fuel supplies but an army patrol shows up firing in the air. Announcing that the front line is now very near and that martial law is introduced, the soldiers begin a random ID check. The crowd panics.

A stranger approaches the station. He comes across as particularly suspicious as he cannot produce an ID on request and claims to be escaping from Belgrade and speaks with a slightly odd accent. Although he insists that his wife and little boy are here with him, the family is nowhere to be seen. The soldiers questioning him do not believe his story and the crowd starts to jeer, believing a spy has been caught. Only Miloš, raises his voice against rushed judgement, but is warned not to get involved. The soldiers take the man to a nearby tree, shoot him, and then leave. The crowd, in a state of shock and disbelief, appear to regret their original excited state. A woman with a child approaches and enquires about her husband who should be at the station. The crowd remains silent; people avoid looking her in the eyes while boarding the train that has arrived.

*Two*. Somewhere in Yugoslavia, the war is in full swing, as is the resistance fight against the German occupiers. Miloš Bojanić, unshaved and in rugged clothes, is running through woods, chased and shot at by a group of German soldiers. He tries to escape by jumping into a river but the Germans do not give up. At a graveyard, Miloš meets another partisan who tells him that he has been in hiding for ten days after the Germans killed the rest of his unit. The only ammunition of the pair consists of two hand grenades and an empty handgun. A German patrol discovers them. Miloš convinces the partisan to escape while staying behind, throwing the grenades against the patrol and then running away.

Arriving at the shore of a large marsh, the men believe they can get to safety if they manage to cross to the liberated territory on the other side. As they advance through the shallow water, the partisan tells Miloš of the fear he experienced while on his own. As they tread through the tall grass they realise they are now surrounded by Germans and followed by a reconnaissance plane. They decide to split, hoping that at least one of them will make it; the partisan tells Miloš that he is not afraid anymore. Miloš hides in the marsh, but the partisan is captured and taken to a derelict shepherd's hut which is set on fire and the partisan burned alive. Miloš, who witnesses it all from his hiding place, screams in horror and desperation.

*Three*. The war is coming to an end; the partisans come out of hiding. Mature Miloš Bojanić, clean-shaven and in an officer's uniform, sits in front of the typewriter on the upper floor of a village house. As he is trying to write a report on his unit, a group of captured soldiers and alleged civilian collaborators are brought into the yard below. Among them is a beautiful young woman. Miloš watches her, their eyes meet.

An intelligence officer tells Miloš that it will be easy to prove that all detainees collaborated with the Nazis and will be shot. A peasant woman cautiously tries to plead for the young woman's life, insisting that forgiveness is needed if hostilities are to come to an end. Miloš dismisses her reasoning, asserting that those responsible ought to be punished.

The officer soon confirms that everyone deserves the death penalty. The young woman is revealed as a Gestapo officer's companion throughout the war. Miloš's eyes remain fixed on the woman's across the yard, but as he hears the news, he turns away. The young woman, evidently taking this gesture as a verdict, tries to flee. She does not get very far before partisan soldiers apprehend her and drag her off to her death. Anxiously, Miloš dashes into the yard. But his attention is diverted by a loud wedding party on the other side of the street. The last shot of the film is a close-up of his weary and tired face.

\*\*\*

*Three* is a study in dehumanisation caused by war, depicted via the complex and shocking experiences the main protagonist lives through. Focusing on the adverse effects of war on the protagonist's psyche, director Aleksandar Petrović portrays one man's lonely struggle to survive and remain sane. Andrew Horton describes *Three* as a 'general existential study of men and women under pressure', a film that presents a deep and tender but simultaneously pitiless observation of what was most commonly depicted as a romantically heroic and victoriously defiant struggle of Yugoslav people against the occupying fascist forces.

For its masterful study of anxiety and psychological conflict, *Three* is often seen as the finest war (or partisan) film to come out of the former Yugoslavia. It set Petrović on a path to success, along which he was considered the greatest Yugoslav director, and was certainly the filmmaker most bestowed with accolades. The film ended up on the shortlist for an Academy Award for Best Foreign Language Film in 1966. (Petrović's next film, the acclaimed *Skupljači perja* (*I Even Met Happy Gypsies*), was also nominated in 1968.)

Petrović's interest in the psychology of those affected by war is rooted in personal experiences, some of which are described in his autobiography, *Sve moje ljubavi* (*All My Loves*, 1994). Born in 1929, World War Two coincided with his coming of age. The director and his family spent most of the war evacuated to a village near Belgrade. With the increasing triumph of the Soviet Red Army and Yugoslav Partisans, in 1944 Petrović, although just a teenager, joined the Yugoslav Communist Youth Organization (SKOJ) and the Partisans. He did not get the chance to participate in fighting but witnessed episodes of cruel treatment of prisoners of war and, worst of all, the cruel settling of political scores between the rival resistance groups (leftist Partisans, monarchist Chetniks). One of the most traumatic experiences for the director was his witnessing the execution of four hundred members of a large unit of Montenegrin Chetniks, who awere shot over a few hours, in groups of five. Attempting to seek protection from the Anglo-American forces at the border, the Chetniks (monarchy loyalists) were intercepted by Petrović's partisan group and hastily disposed of. When a few tried to run away, Petrović's 16-year-old comrade hit one of them with the handle of his unlocked rifle and shot himself in the stomach. Petrović rushed his wounded friend to hospital but he died on the way. It is this bizarre and disturbing incident that Petrović would later identify as his strongest memory of war; an afterimage of relentless brutality and senseless carnage.

Soon after the end of the war Petrović left the Communist Party, but remained convinced that the struggle against the Nazis was justified and necessary. The knowledge and understanding of human nature he acquired during the war convinced him that warfare is a corrupting and

dehumanising experience; he could never accept war's unforgiving ruthlessness and disrespect for human life.

Petrović was determined to express his familiarity with war through film as soon as he could. He began making documentary films in collaboration with another filmmaker and war veteran, Vicko Raspor. After several successful shorts, they were given the chance to direct their first feature, based on an incident from World War Two. Although they collaborated well on the documentaries, their differences became an insurmountable problem when working on fiction and they parted company after completing just one feature together, *Jedini izlaz* (*The Only Exit*), in 1958. On his own, Petrović became interested in the cinema of the emerging French Nouvelle Vague and was influenced by the writings of André Bazin and the *Cahiers du cinéma* group. Over the next four years Petrović directed two features that focused on contemporary urban life and dilemmas (*Dvoje* (*Two*, 1961) and *Dani* (*Days*, 1963)), which were strongly influenced by the work of his French peers. By the time he came to make *Three*, he had become an outspoken advocate of *auteur* cinema.

In the 1960s, the Belgrade-based production studio Avala Film invited Petrović to work on a project based on the prose of Antonije Isaković, a pre-war communist and partisan with whom the director had already collaborated on *Jedini izlaz*. Isaković's writing, which also served as the basis for other significant film projects (for example, Živojin Pavlović's *Zaseda* (*Ambush*, 1969) and for several films by Stole Janković), was very popular; his work was seen as radically new and modern in form. Isaković's stories usually follow the psychological meanderings of protagonists caught in difficult and morally compromising wartime situations. The resistance fighters' struggle was the predominant point of focus, with the various perils of combat, fear, hunger, adverse weather conditions and isolation painting a finely detailed, naturalist image of warfare. Although classified as realist, Isaković's approach was both fresh and original, and most importantly for Petrović, pervaded by feelings quite similar to those he experienced.

Petrović and Isaković wrote the script together, turning four stories into three. They created a new character by combining existing and new features, calling him Miloš Bojanić; he was to become the protagonist of the film in which he would live through encounters with death in three distinct episodes. Every time he would witnesses an execution, his empathy with the victim would be obvious, and he would ask himself what he could have done to prevent the fatal demise. In the final story, he would be the one effectively authorising the death and would live through a tragic infatuation with the captive. The film was shot in black and white and completed in 1965.

According to a widely held view, all the former Eastern Bloc countries, including Yugoslavia, were producing only one kind of war film: those glorifying the heroic struggle of permanently righteous and faultless communist resistance fighters opposed to the cowardly occupiers and traitors. Indeed, Veljko Bulajić's epic *Bitka na Neretvi* (*Battle of Neretva*, 1969) and Stipe Delić's *Sutjeska* (*Battle of Sutjeska*, 1973), with their cast of international stars like Richard Burton, Orson Welles and Yul Brynner, are now seen as classic examples of the high-budget Yugoslav Partisan film genre. These projects were endorsed and promoted by the authorities as they were seen to cater for specific social needs, even though the influential society of Partisan war veterans (SUBNOR) sometimes objected to their one-dimensional portrayal of the war. (These objections culminated following the release of Hajrudin Krvavac's *Partizanska Eskadrila* (*The Partisans' Squadron*) in 1979, which, according to the veterans, had oversimplified the war effort to the point of ridiculousness.) These examples seem to confirm the commonly shared belief that an honest and complex portrayal of the war was impossible, and the only concern of filmmakers was to satisfy the so-called 'party line'.

In reality, however, all East European countries produced numerous works that featured psychologically complex characters and dealt with the war and its consequences in the courageous and honest way of which *Three* is a fine example. A number of other films made across communist Europe around the same period – at a time when war memories were still fresh and so were the traumas afflicted on the rest of the population – portrayed the war in a psychologically truthful and dignified manner. The best-known example is probably Mikhail Kalatozov's acclaimed Cannes-winner *Letyat zhuravli* (*The Cranes Are Flying*, 1957), which de-glamorised all superhuman representations by focusing on the intimate experiences of a couple of lovers tragically separated by the war. Andrei Tarkovski's feature debut, *Ivanovo detstvo* (*My Name is Ivan*, 1962) was another example of war experienced by a vulnerable, sensitive and traumatised boy. Other finely crafted psychological war films included works from Poland (Andrzej Wajda's war trilogy: *Pokolenie* (*A Generation*, 1955); *Kanał* (*Canal*, 1965); and *Popiół i diament* (*Ashes and Diamonds*, 1958); or Andrzej Munk's *Eroica* (1957)), Hungary (András Kovács' *Hideg napok* (*Cold Days*, 1966)) or from the GDR (Konrad Wolf's *Ich war 19* (*I Was Nineteen*, 1967)). The interest in making 'serious' films on the war did not wane with time: Elem Klimov's *Idi i smotri* (*Come and See*, 1985), which offered a terrifying portrayal of life and death in Byelorussia under Nazi occupation, remains, with its almost unbearable cacophony of fear and violence, one of the most powerful cinematic indictments of any war. Even though film scholars traditionally identify the 'partisan genre' as specific to Yugoslavia it is important to stress that resistance films were also made in the other countries of the region. Some Bulgarian art-house films that belong to this category, for example, include the German co-production *Sterne* (*Zvezdi/ Stars*, Konrad Wolf, 1959), *A byahme mladi...* (*We Were Young*, Binka Zhelyazkova, 1961) or *Chernite angeli* (*The Black Angels*, Vulo Radev, 1970).

Along these lines, *Three* was an existential work of art, substantially different from what was considered to be the ideologically correct way to portray the glorious partisan fighters. Its focus on the inner life of the protagonist was probably the main reason for the film's great success. Its innovative narrative structure, fragmented into three seemingly unrelated stories has, as Petar Volk has stated, 'expressed the story visually rather than describing it in literary terms', and confirmed Petrović as an upcoming modern(ist) *auteur*. The film has a fable-like, almost abstract quality; its strong anti-war message is not inferred through strict didacticism but comes as an implication of the strong emotions.

The opening sequence is comprised of black and white still photographs taken by the German army during their occupation of Yugoslavia in 1941. Most of the footage shows the manifestation of might and the advancement of German forces; there are several images of hanged patriots who opposed the occupation. The titles are superimposed on top of these images and are accompanied by an abrasive, minimal soundtrack consisting of a drum pattern. Reference to the opening sequence will re-appear throughout the film, accompanied by a loud siren sound reminiscent of an air raid alarm. The drum pattern resumes in each of the three stories, evidently intended to underline moments of heightened anxiety experienced by the protagonist and to reinforce the tensely rhythmic but well-paced editing.

Petrović's focus on a group of civilians trying to escape the invading German army in the first part of the film is an interesting portrait of a state that is about to collapse and will soon be no more, at least not in that form. Although this first part of the film runs for just under 25 minutes, thus almost functioning like a short film in itself, it represents a strikingly wide spectrum of society, showing peasants, pensioners, journalists, students, civil servants, police, army and new recruits, and revealing the people's distrust in their own army. Here the director even includes a group of Gypsies playing their famous folk song *Djelem, djelem* (a song that will figure prominently in Petrović's next and celebrated feature film, *I Even Met Happy Gypsies*). The three soldiers from the army patrol are apparently restless and suspicious, their weakness is revealed in the forceful demand to carry out random identification checks and thus maintain the illusion of order and control. One soldier warns the crowd that a civilian has been shot for fiddling with the telephone wires; it is precisely at that inopportune moment that the stranger approaches the station. His alleged foreign accent, possession of a photographic camera and lack of identification are deemed to make sufficient ground for his execution. The aggressiveness of the soldiers, however, is nothing else but a manifestation of their own insecurity.

The only person raising his voice in defence of the accused is the Belgrade student, Miloš Bojanić, pointing out that such rushed conclusions cannot justify taking someone's life. But the soldiers are already taken in by the war's whirlpool of paranoid misjudgements and brutality. It only takes minutes for the awful truth to come to light, clearly suggesting that the coming struggle will not only be against the occupiers but against inner demons as well, against one's own injustice and ineffectiveness.

In the second part of the film, the Germans who chase Miloš are better equipped and more determined to destroy him; he has to run for his life. Unaware of the connection between the reconnaissance plane and the German units on the ground, the partisans fall into a trap; Miloš' partner is brutally executed. By the final shots of this part, the protagonist is mentally wrecked after witnessing the terrifying end of his comrade. Someone he has just shared his fears with (while partisans had to be fearless by default), and has just established a tender and understanding rapport with, has been cruelly slaughtered in another act of war's relentless lunacy. Miloš's cry to life in the last shot of this part reveals his profound doubt in the value of human endeavour.

The longest section of the film is probably the most successful and memorable of the three, not least due to Tomislav Pinter's stunning photography. Pinter was to become one of the most celebrated cinematographers in former Yugoslavia, filming a large number of projects, including some of the high-budget partisan films already mentioned. A Croat by origin, Pinter is one of the most prolific and influential cinematographers from the Balkans, with a career that spans more than fifty years and with more than a hundred films to his credit. Besides the cinematography of *Petrijin Venac* (*Petrija's Wreath*, 1980; discussed in this volume), Pinter shot many other famous Yugoslav films (including Petrović's *I Even Met Happy Gypsies*; Ante Babaja's *Breza* (*The Birch Tree*, 1967); Dušan Makavejev's *Montenegro* (1981); Rajko Grlić's *Samo jednom se ljubi* (*You Love Only Once*, 1981) and *U raljama zivota* (*In the Jaws of Life*, 1984)). He also worked internationally, most notably with Hungarian master Miklós Jancsó in the 1970s.

In *Three* the choice to shoot primarily in exteriors, in order to underline the protagonist's solitude during his ordeal, works best in the second part. Pinter carefully uses filters to increase the contrast of clouds against the sky, the sky against the gently waving marsh grass, or the soldiers' uniforms against the washed-out stones. He makes the most of aerial shots taken from the perspective of the German reconnaissance plane that follows Miloš's escape trajectory. These shots reveal spectacular vistas of southern Herzegovina and Dalmatia where the Neretva flows into the Adriatic Sea and where, during the war, Yugoslav partisans were out of reach for German troops. This part of the film also gave Bata Živojinović (playing Miloš) the chance to establish a lasting reputation, which later on made him the prominent choice for this type of role in other films. *Three* will specifically be remembered as a film that revealed the best of his wide-ranging skills and allowed him to create a psychologically complex character.

In the third encounter, Miloš has suppressed his anxieties and fears as the liberation fight is about to come to an end and a new order of fairness and justice is about to be established. Is it that simple, however, to defeat brutality and leave cruelty behind? Petrović and Isaković put the protagonist to a final test which lets them deliver a subtle warning to the new system, as the struggle for a humane and just society is a never ending one.

Here, Miloš is seen as commanding officer of a unit that just captured German soldiers and local collaborators. His intelligence officer hastily concludes the captives should all be shot; the plan is to have it all dealt with by the evening. Miloš is obviously dismayed by this answer but he does not intervene. Neither does he react to the peasant woman's plea for forgiveness, even though he is noticeably attracted to the young woman. Miloš seems troubled by his new position of power, which puts him in charge of people's lives. In the first wartime episode he had tried to stand up against a cruel and pointless execution; by the end of the war he is the one sanctioning executions. He apparently does not have the strength to overcome this brutal morass; war has triumphed over him, to a corrupting effect; viewers are left to question if the new country, forged in a vicious circle of violence, will be able to do any better.

With its unequivocal portrayal of war's 'side effects' on an individual's mind, *Three* is newly resonant in view of the recent violence in former Yugoslavia. Even though a representative work of the 1960s art-house cinema, seeing *Three* today reverberates strikingly and sadly within the disturbed region. With the world increasingly 'Balkanised', it seems that the bitter lessons of the past are too often repeated, especially where they have never been learned.

**Vlastimir Sudar**

Horton, A. (1987–88) 'The Rise and Fall of the Yugoslav Partisan Film: Cinematic Perceptions of a National Identity', *Film Criticism*, 12, 2, 22.

Volk, P. (1986) *Istorija jugoslovenskog filma.* Belgrade: Institut za Film, Partizanska Knjiga.

**04**

TRI

# KAD BUDEM MRTAV I BEO  WHEN I AM DEAD AND PALE

## ŽIVOJIN PAVLOVIĆ, YUGOSLAVIA, 1968

*Kad budem mrtav i beo* (*When I am Dead and Pale*, Živojin Pavlović, 1968) tells the story of Janko Bugarski, nicknamed Džimi Barka (Jimmy the Boat), a youth in his twenties who, having no permanent employment or regular living habits, aimlessly wanders around the Serbian province in the late 1960s. He is first seen with his girlfriend Lilica, leaving an agricultural cooperative on which they have spent some time as seasonal workers. The manager, Milutin, shows no sympathy for Jimmy's complaint that they have nowhere else to go, so the two reluctantly join the crowd of other seasoners on a departing tractor.

Paying a visit to his mother, a launderer in an impoverished worker's settlement, Jimmy finds out that she has remarried and has had another child. Although genuinely affectionate to Jimmy, she is unable to help him financially. Jimmy then applies for a temporary job on a building site. No sooner does the manager hire him (and show him to the workers' dormitory, where Jimmy is given 'half a bed'), than he is stabbed with a knife (off-screen). Jimmy immediately makes use of the chaotic situation that ensues, and steals his fellow-workers' wallets. Fleeing the site, he meets up with Lilica in the vicinity.

The bus on which the two drifters continue their journey is stopped by the police. Running away from them Jimmy loses Lilica, but he meets Duška, a sexually-predatory bar singer. Jimmy becomes Duška's lover and, with her help, he also begins to sing. His voice is horrible, but this is no obstacle for performing in roadhouses and at provincial fairs. However, he soon tires of spending time in the company of drunken musicians and promiscuous singers, so he leaves Duška without even bothering to collect his bag.

Jimmy is next seen illegally riding in the mail-wagon of a train, where he is discovered by Mica, the post-woman. Lonely and ageing, Mica immediately makes use of Jimmy for her sexual gratification. Afterwards, she takes him to her home in the town of Užice, where she bathes him and cooks for him. Mica's brother is an army officer who hires Jimmy to sing to soldiers and workers, in military garrisons and industrial settlements. In one of these settlements, Jimmy meets a bored dentist's assistant, who naively believes him to be her ticket to a more fulfilling, middle-class life. The two of them decide to go to Belgrade, where Jimmy will take part in a youth singing competition. But in the city, his lack of talent and his obvious rooting in the roadhouse culture, provoke sneer among the audiences whose 'urban' views hardly conceal their own provincialist background. Jimmy is ruthlessly booed during the audition and, for the first time, visibly undergoes a crisis of identity.

On a small ship sailing away from Belgrade, the failed singer and the (by now) disenchanted girlfriend have an argument, which culminates with Jimmy hitting her. Leaving the girl, he discovers Lilica on the same ship, simulating pregnancy and pick-pocketing. Together again, the two return to the cooperative from which they initially departed, and start blackmailing Milutin, claiming that Lilica is bearing his child. However, Milutin soon discovers their deception and tries to force Lilica to have sex with him. When she resists, he beats her. Jimmy, who has been playing soccer on a nearby field, hears Lilica's screams and runs to her rescue. He humiliates Milutin by forcing him, at gunpoint, to crawl in front of his workers. Jimmy then goes to a field-toilet, while the infuriated manager orders him to come out and publicly apologise. From inside the toilet, Jimmy responds with a curse. As the soccer game continues without Jimmy, two gunshots are heard. Other players keep calling upon him to hurry up. In the end, one of them opens the door and finds Jimmy sitting on the toilet … dead, shot in the head.

'A clear diagnosis about the absurd senselessness of reality is by itself an undisputedly positive reactant. Even if it does not cure, it gives rise to an irresistible need to be cured.'

– Miroslav Krleža, quoted by Živojin Pavlović

*When I am Dead and Pale*, the fourth feature directed by Živojin Pavlović, is a piece of rough cinematic naturalism, a portrayal of the 'uglier side of reality', of life on the margins of socio-economic existence. With *Budjenje pacova* (*The Rats' Awakening*, 1967) and *Zaseda* (*Ambush*, 1969), it forms an informal 'trilogy' of socially engaged films, grounded in Pavlović's obsession with 'the poetics of viciousness' and 'the aesthetics of the disgusting', which marked the peak of the first half of the director's prolific career. Between 1963, when his debut feature, *Povratak* (*Return*), was shot (held back for release until 1966, for painting 'too dark' a picture of the Belgrade crime-world), and 1998, when his death interrupted the completion of the project entitled *Država mrtvih* (*The State of the Dead*), Pavlović made fourteen films. He is considered a foremost *auteur* of the New Yugoslav Film (*novi jugoslovenski film*, also known as the 'Black Wave'), a current of thematically and stylistically diversified, ideologically often provocative works that flourished in the cinema of the Socialist Federative Republic of Yugoslavia (1945–

1991) from the mid-1960s until the early 1970s, when a campaign mounted by the political and cultural watchdogs of the socialist apparatus brought about the movement's end.

The film was a product of the 'liberal era' of Yugoslav state socialism, characterised by impulses towards decentralisation of the governmental and communist party control, and an increase in democratisation of the social and cultural spheres. It was Pavlović's second project (*The Rats' Awakening* was the first) produced by the Centre of Film Workers' Cooperatives, an independent production house formed in Serbia as an alternative to the highly bureaucratised, government overseen Avala Film Studio (under the auspices of which Pavlović worked earlier). Having an administratively, as well as ideologically, less burdened producer provided the director with favorable, relaxed working conditions. Pavlović liked to point out the following: 'This was the moment of complete freedom. I had no artistic directors, no councils, no one above me … *The Rats' Awakening*, *When I am Dead and Pale* and *Ambush* were made … without anybody's blessing … That was highly inspiring.' The shoot lasted twenty-four days, and locations – on the periphery of Belgrade, and the nearby town of Pančevo – were chosen to convey the sense of an environment in which Pavlović typically situates his protagonists: economically impoverished, dilapidated mud-filled settlements, collective farms and provincial fairs; in short, locations evocative of harsh living conditions, and characterised by an 'anti-aesthetic' visual appearance (that is, ugliness).

The film marked Pavlović's second collaboration with both the cinematographer Milorad Jakšić-Fandjo, and the screenwriting duo Gordan Mihić and Ljubiša Kozomara (again, in both cases, *The Rats' Awakening* was the first collaboration). The original screenplay had the title *Jimmy Barka*, but Pavlović decided to change it; inspiration for the new title came from some verse by the German poet Wolfgang Borchert. Significantly, Pavlović also radically changed the ending of the screenplay. Originally, it concluded with Jimmy and Lilica simply returning to the collective farm from which they initially departed. The director, however, strongly felt that Jimmy's nomadic, in no small measure absurd, life could only have an equally absurd, yet by no means tragic, ending. Thus was the final, memorable scene of Jimmy's sudden death on the toilet invented (Arthur Penn is said to have paraphrased this scene in *The Missouri Breaks*, 1975).

Centered around Jimmy's 'journey through life', *When I am Dead and Pale* has a loose, episodic narrative structure, akin to that of a 'road movie'. Jimmy (Dragan Nikolić) is an aimless, ambitionless and disoriented character – in the director's own words, 'a man without a compass'. As such, he is not really representative of the protagonists commonly found in Pavlović's films and literature (besides being a director, Pavlović was also an established writer of short stories and novels, an essayist and, during the early period of his career, a film critic and theorist). Typically, these characters tend to be ideologically disillusioned individuals – often disappointed communists (as is the case in *Ambush* and *Crveno klasje* (*The Red Wheat*, 1970)) – who embody the gap between ideological idealism and practice/reality, the discrepancy between 'how we would like things to be' and 'how they in fact are'. Knowing 'neither what he wants, nor what he does not want', Jimmy is, on the other hand, envisioned as somewhat representative of what, according to Pavlović, was a state of mind widespread among the Yugoslav youth in the period preceding the student uprisings of 1968: an intellectual and moral apathy, an attitude of resignation towards issues of ideology, provoked by an all-out exhaustion of the grand narratives of human emancipation, be they traditional (religion) or modern (Marxism).

Yet even if he is disoriented, Jimmy does not lack energy or vitality: the force of life pulsates in him. As film scholar Nebojša Pajkić and others have suggested, he is not simply a character without a clear identity, but a character with an identity that falls 'outside ideology': a social outcast whose life is a trajectory without a past or a future, a series of intense moments belonging only to the permanent present. In the film, Pavlović emphasises this aspect of the character by presenting the viewer with a succession of scenes typically deprived, in the process of editing, of proper dramatic exposition and resolution – a technique inspired by Jean-Luc Godard's elliptical approach to narrative in films such as *À bout de souffle* (1959). Thus, Jimmy may also be understood as a local, Yugoslav version of Godard's Michel Poiccard (Jean-Paul Belmondo), or as something of an equivalent of such literary anti-heroes as Saul Bellow's Augie March (*The Adventures of Augie March*) or Jack Kerouack's Dean Moriarty (*On the Road*).

Each 'stop' on Jimmy's journey is defined by a relationship with a different woman: first Lilica, then Duška, Mica, the unnamed dentist's assistant and, once again, Lilica. All of these characters are portrayed as more decisive than Jimmy, and superior to him in their ability to economically sustain themselves. But their identities and aspirations remain clearly formulated from within the patriarchal framework: despite, or perhaps because of, Jimmy's complete lack of commitment, the women in the film function as agents of his (potential) social integration. The partnership with Lilica (ever ready to fake pregnancies) is the best way to sustain the lifestyle of a social parasite; Duška begins to build Jimmy's career as a singer; Mica provides him with a temporary home (she is the clearest maternal surrogate in the film), and gives a further boost to his career by helping 'institutionalise' him as a singer in the military garrisons; the dentist's assistant expects Jimmy to stop wandering, marry her and lead a socio-economically stable life. Yet as some recent analyses of the film have pointed out (such as those of Branko Dimitrijević and Goran Gocić), while the behaviour of the female characters seems to reinforce the standard patriarchal myth about the 'taming' of the unbound male Eros, at the same time it is Jimmy – not them – who is regularly sexually objectified and fetishised. Thus, for example, he temporarily occupies the place of the 'young male game' in Duška's busy sexual life, and satisfies ageing Mica's fantasy about still being sexually desirable. Finally, as a follow-up to his debacle at the singing competition, Jimmy hits the dentist's assistant in response to her complaint that his aimlessness is 'ruining her life'. With this aggressive manifestation of Jimmy's frustration over a feeling of impotence ('Do you think I wouldn't want things to be better?' he asks, standing in front of a prominently displayed Yugoslav flag), his wandering is also revealed as grounded in a crisis of patriarchal masculinity. His persistent refusal to accept society's rules of the game has, partially at least, been a refusal to assume those roles and 'duties' which the pronouncedly patriarchal order he inhabits has been expecting him to assume.

The film's defining stylistic feature is its use of the sequence-shot, proceeding from Pavlović's shooting technique which tends to avoid scene fragmentation. Dialogues, actors' movements, even background activity dictate the flow and rhythm of individual scenes, while the long-take camera movements strive to preserve and reproduce with minimal intrusions the integrity and unity of the depicted events as they evolve in space and time. ('In both literary fragments and cinematic shots, I strive to create an atmosphere that will by no means seem arranged, but rather as a consequence of incidental occurrences,' Pavlović has stated.) The result is an overall naturalistic, even veristic, cinematic form, often evocative (in its apparent absence of directorial intervention) of documentaristic factography.

An acclaimed example of Pavlović's directorial style is the long panning shot depicting Jimmy and an army officer walking by a group of chatting peasants, then crossing paths with some protesting workers (who criticise the building of 'political factories'), while in the far background a platoon of singing soldiers is on the move, followed by a group of playful children. Another example frequently praised by critics is the scene of the singing audition in Belgrade, in which the emerging urban youth culture is compared and contrasted with the thus far depicted culture of the Serbian province. Featuring Black Pearls (one of the first Yugoslav rock bands), this scene is entirely filmed in the *cinéma verité* style. In its lengthy opening shot, the camera patiently focuses on the drummer awaiting his cue; only when he energetically begins to play does the camera embark on a sideways track, in order to reveal the location and introduce other musicians.

Pavlović's propensity for integral narration, for *mise-en-scène*-driven organisation and control of space, developed as a consequence of his abandonment of the montage-based types of storytelling with which he initially preoccupied himself in his early days as an amateur-film-maker associated with the Belgrade Kino Club. (This cine-club was one of the major centres of a fervent network of amateur filmmaking in the country during the late 1950s and early 1960s; a number of the foremost Serbian representatives of New Yugoslav Film – Dušan Makavejev, Kokan Rakonjac, Marko Babac and others – made their first shorts in it.) Among the key influences upon the emergence of Pavlović's style were such Italian directors as Luchino Visconti (his 1942 *Ossessione*, in particular), Antonio Pietrangeli, Mario Monicelli, but also Jean Renoir, Carl Theodor Dreyer and Robert Bresson. Naturalism, however, is not each filmmaker's primary goal, but rather the expressive means they prefer to use. It is in the film's numerous raw images – workers gathered around their slain manager; Lilica urinating behind Jimmy as he counts the money he stole; an attempted conversation between a politician and an army officer, while the latter is going through the agony of his teeth being fixed; Milutin's attempted rape and beating of Lilica; and, of course, the final shot of dead Jimmy sitting on the toilet, while the camera slowly dollies in to reveal his bloody face – it is in images such as these, coupled with an abundant use of debased language and topped with Jimmy's horrendous singing, that the central function of Pavlović's veristic aesthetic is revealed. A powerful, visceral, at times shocking impact on the viewer is what he seeks to provoke: his aim is to nurture the impulsive, irrational, destructive manifestations of human existence ('the poetics of viciousness'), while maintaining respect for the laws of realism. This ambition – described by the filmmaker as 'naturalism in the service of the drastic image's unpleasant associativity' – developed, first and foremost, under the sign of Luis Buñuel and Sergei Eisenstein's masterful use of drastic images, and their pronounced directorial intensification of the filmically constituted reality. Among Buñuel's works, Pavlović was particularly fond of those 'unburdened by surrealist caprice and artificiality', such as *Las Hurdes* (1932), *Los Olvidados* (1950) and *El* (1952). As far as Eisenstein is concerned, Pavlović adored *Bronenosets Potyomkin* (*Battleship Potemkin*, 1925) and the great Soviet director's theory of 'montage of attractions'. Significantly, in his own film practice – and *When I am Dead and Pale* is exemplary in this respect – Pavlović would always maintain an interest in producing raw visual 'attractions', while increasingly moving away from editing as a means towards accomplishing this goal.

The film's socially critical dimension resides in what may be summed up as its demythologising portrayal of the Yugoslav socialist everyday, an authorial vision in sharp contrast with

the official stories of socio-economic prosperity taking place under the sign of an enthusiastic commitment to communist goals. Specifically, considered against the contextual background of a large-scale economic reform introduced in 1965, the film takes the viewer on a tour of what may unambiguously be read as symptoms of this reform's failure. In this unapologetic exposure of Yugoslav reality, as well as in its exploration of the relationship between individual freedom (Jimmy's) and collectively defined interests and norms (one of the key themes of Pavlović's oeuvre, also masterfully pursued in his later film *Do vidjenja u sledećem ratu* (*See You in Another War*, 1980), *When I am Dead and Pale* pronouncedly bespeaks some of the central concerns of the 1960s New Film tendency (Petrović, Makavejev, Krsto Papić, Bato Cengić, Želimir Žilnik and others). As Daniel Goulding has concisely put it, New Film 'claimed for itself the right to serve as a critic of all existing conditions ... to be a conscience – often an unavoidably sombre one – of the land, the nation, the society and the individuals that comprise it'. What generated this, sometimes more and sometimes less piercing, socially critical attitude was a desire to, first and foremost, assert the autonomy of subjective truth, and of the independent authorial vision; 'to replace', as Dušan Stojanović, a preeminent Yugoslav film theorist, put it at the time, 'one collective mythology with endless individual mythologies'.

The bleak outlook on social reality typical for the films of the Yugoslav 'black wave' has its correlative in a range of works made in the other East Central European socialist countries of the region during the same period: Evald Schorm's *Kazdy den odvahu* (*Courage for Every Day*, 1964), Irina Aktasheva and Hristo Piskov's *Ponedelnik sutrin* (*Monday Morning*, 1965 – banned until 1988), Lucian Pintilie's *Reconstituirea* (*Reconstruction*, 1968) or Lyudmil Kirkov's *Shvedskite krale* (*Swedish Kings*, 1968).

New Yugoslav Film, and Pavlović's contribution to it, needs to be situated within a wider framework of progressive intellectual activity in the country during the 1960s, a major aspect of which was the school of Marxist humanist thought known as *Praxis* (a group including Milan Kangrga, Gajo Petrović, Rudi Supek, Mihajlo Marković, Ljuba Tadić and others). Particularly influenced by Marx's early manuscripts, in dialogue with other contemporary forms of progressive social theory (Marcuse, Bloch, Habermas and so on), these revisionist thinkers declared themselves against all forms of authoritarianism, in favour of an open, democratic socialist society. Making individual freedom a necessary precondition for collective, societal freedom, *Praxis* advocated a 'merciless critique of everything existing', and argued that socio-political ideals are neither absolute, nor can they be fully accounted for in advance. Correspondingly, the socialist revolution became thinkable for them only as a never-ending process.

In his own reflections on the relationship between film and revolution, Živojin Pavlović similarly asserted that the essence of the latter is 'not the change in the name of something, but the change for change's sake, as the meaning of lasting existence. That is why I do not think I would be able to say in the name of what I am engaged, but I do know that I must be engaged.' But while the *Praxis* intellectuals worked primarily within the framework of Marxist-humanist theory, and invested in the idea of constructive socialism, Pavlović tended to consider the problem of freedom from a historically less specified and politically less optimistic perspective, which made humanist ideals as such an object of critique. The central problem, as Pavlović saw it (in rather Nietzschean terms), is that of human nature stretched between its two, ultimately irreconcilable, poles. On one side, there is life as a biological phenomenon: as a pulsating irrational force, a series of drives for food and sex, but also violence and destruction. On the other is what he calls a 'carcinoma of nature' which distinguishes humans from all other living beings: consciousness. Seeking to make human existence pleasurable, or at least tolerable, consciousness, in the end, always either 'degenerates life itself or its efforts result in failure'.

The function which Pavlović, operating with this understanding of the human condition, assigns to art is that of socially destructive criticism: of expressing the 'paroxysms of existence', of tapping into an 'unhealthy ground' upon which affective, impulsive forces and senseless acts manifest themselves in situations of suspended or, at least, loosened consciousness. In *When I am Dead and Pale* one finds elements of this type of critique applied to the Yugoslav socialist system itself, and emanating from the basic fact that, from any socially constructive point of view, Jimmy's character is entirely useless, 'pure waste'. Not only is he usually out of work, but he prefers not to have to work at all (at one point he even boasts that he is 'too lazy to work'). Pavlović uses this 'inassimilable' dimension of Jimmy's personality as a point of reference: in relation to it, he presents the Yugoslav system of 'workers' self-management' (which envisioned workers as decision-makers, as direct participants in the management of production) as a system concerned primarily with managing the *appearances* of productivity and social prosperity. As Saša Radojević has put it: 'All that is expected of the many characters in the film … who constantly talk about work, but actually do not work, is socialisation. They are not desperate because there is no production but because there is no socialisation. Proletarians and soldiers are not supposed to enthusiastically fulfill their duties at work, but to endorse a spirit of friendship and leisure, a castration of revolt that might bring down the glass-tower in which the foundational myths of the socialist society are piled up.'

At the most prestigious film festival in former Yugoslavia, held annually in the Croatian coastal town of Pula, *When I am Dead and Pale* won awards for Best Film and Best Director in 1968. It also received a number of notable international prizes, including the top award at the Karlovy Vary Film Festival, and had a good share of screenings in the West, including in France and the United States. (John Schlesinger, who saw the film in New York, claimed that it inspired his *Midnight Cowboy*, 1969.) However, at the time of its release, critics were divided in their assessments of the film. Some, such as Bogdan Kalafatović, praised it for its advanced use of realism, and a 'life-like' narrative. Others, who situated the film primarily in relation to Pavlović's earlier works, found it to be dramaturgically and visually inferior to its predecessor, *The Rats' Awakening*. Film critic Slobodan Novaković even argued that Pavlović's 'ominous documentarist ambitions' clearly signified a decline of the filmmaker's creativity.

By the early 1970s, as the politicised offensive against the New Film gained momentum, Pavlović's 'ominous', unscrupulously destructive authorial vision also proved a fertile ground for frequent attacks on him as a paradigm of the supposedly harmful social nihilism that had contaminated Yugoslav cinema. This critique culminated in 1973, when Pavlović was declared morally, politically and pedagogically 'inappropriate', and removed from his teaching post at the Belgrade Academy of Dramatic Arts (to which he returned eight years later). To be true, during these attacks on the director, *When I am Dead and Pale* was less frequently singled out than his *Neprijatelj* (*The Enemy*, 1965), *The Rats' Awakening*, *Ambush* (which, although never officially banned, was kept out of distribution until the early 1990s) or *The Red Wheat*. Without any doubt, however, the film did have its place in the mosaic of works – built by Pavlović, Žilnik (*Rani radovi* (*Early Works*, 1969)) and other 'Black Wave' filmmakers – which, according to some unfavourable opinions at the time, presented an image of 'the entire country as one big toilet'.

Time proved to be on the film's side. By the early 1980s, the younger generation of critics (such as Nenad Polimac, Nebojša Pajkić and Dinko Tucaković) praised *When I am Dead and Pale* as, among other things, a work which thematically and narratively anticipated some of the counter-culturally influenced developments in the cinema of New Hollywood. In 1997, the Belgrade Film Institute published a volume of six new essays, entirely devoted to the fresh critical re-evaluation of Pavlović's landmark film.

**Pavle Levi**

REFERENCES

Dimitrijević, B., V. Džogović, G. Gocić, S. Markuš, S. Radojević, S. Vučinić (1997) *Kad budem mrtav i beo: film Živojina Pavlovića*. Belgrade: Institut za film.

Goulding, D. (1985) *Liberated Cinema: The Yugoslav Experience*. Bloomington: Indiana University Press.

Kalafatović, B. (1985) *Znaci sa ekrana*. Belgrade: Institut za film.

Novaković, S. (1970) *Vreme otvaranja*. Novi Sad: Kulturni centar.

Pajkić, N. (2001) *Jahač na lokomotivi: Razgovori sa Živojinom Pavlovićem*. Belgrade: Studentski Kulturni Centar.

Pavlović, Ž. (1996) *Djavolji film*. Novi Sad: Promete/Belgrade: Jugoslovenska kinoteka.

_____ (1990) *Jezgro napetosti*. Belgrade: BIGZ, Srpska književna zadruga, Narodna knjiga.

Stojanović, D. (1998) *Velika avantura filma*. Novi Sad: Prometej/Belgrade: Institut za film.

# RANI RADOVI EARLY WORKS

## ŽELIMIR ŽILNIK, YUGOSLAVIA, 1969

*Rani radovi* (*Early Works*, Želimir Žilnik, 1969) takes place in the territory of former Yugoslavia, during the student riots of 1968. Three young men and a beautiful young woman, Yugoslava, leave home and move across the country in search of a true revolutionary spirit and a society that believes in truth. Yugoslava also wants to find out if it is possible to improve the position of women in society; she is appalled by the disastrous patriarchal structures that rule over her own family and by the pressures that her drunken and despotic father imposes on everyone around him.

In order to grasp and perpetuate the revolutionary ideas of socialism, the four protagonists first try to express their solidarity with the members of the working class; so they engage in all sorts of manual work. Their acts are accompanied by communist revolutionary slogans recited throughout the film, like 'Down with the red bourgeoisie!' But the workers do not appreciate the four quasi-revolutionaries, whom they see as hollow impostors. The three male members of the gang are therefore turned over to the police. The policemen punish them by giving them a radical haircut, thus engaging in a bizarre combination of fun and 'torture'.

Rejected by the workers and frustrated in mind and body, the four decide to abandon the factories and engage instead in a series of actions to bring radical ideas to the peasants, the other component of the working class. The four move to the countryside with the intention of raising the peasants' revolutionary consciousness. The peasants, however, prove to be equally disinterested in their preaching and beat them up. The four end up squatting near the wall of a collective farm, amidst squalor and dirt, surrounded by ugly and primitive people who engage in vulgar dialogue. Together, they smear dung, mud and dirt over their bodies and faces.

Now rejected both by workers and peasants, the four find themselves back at square one, immersed in the same rebellious emptiness that they experienced at the beginning of the film. But what can be done? All they can do is chant old socialist hymns and slogans, such as 'Communist Party – Precious Treasure!'

Yugoslava, the female member of the gang, decides to return home, leaving her friends behind. But the others are not willing to let her go and soon arrive to find her. What follows is a clash powered by the male chauvinism that is still deeply rooted amongst the comrades; their deep-seated bigotry cannot coexist peacefully with the hippie-style communal forms of sexuality. At first they simply chat with Yugoslava but then the mischievous fooling around turns into sexual aggression. The woman shouts: 'Who'll be the first? You always horsed around and you never finished anything!'

After rehearsing with shooting guns and setting off gasoline bombs for fun, the men shoot Yugoslava, drench her with gasoline and set her body on fire. The macabre and cowardly 'revolutionary act' takes place under the accompaniment of one of the numerous popular communist songs from the beginning of the century, invoking fraternity and communal bondage.

Director Želimir Žilnik grew up in what was known for decades as the Socialist Federative Republic of Yugoslavia. It was here he studied and worked until the 1990s, when the country fell apart. Pressured by forces such as ethnic belonging (Serbian) and other personal and professional considerations, Žilnik had to choose which one of the new territories he was to belong to. Today, Žilnik is one of the most important film directors in Serbia and Montenegro.

Yugoslavia's break-up was, figuratively speaking, announced about a decade before the formal disintegration took place: in that mythical year of 1980, when Josip Broz-Tito, who had appointed himself president of the country for life, died. However, Žilnik's films had foretold the future collapse of the country at an even earlier point.

His film career is defined as much by the leading film trends and concerns of the 1960s as it is defined by key situations of historical and existential collapse. He focuses on radical content, on the desire to challenge entrenched social norms by confronting the audience, and on radically subverting his own position. Few other directors have remained as committed to the idea of socially provocative and politically engaged filmmaking as persistently as Želimir Žilnik.

Žilnik is an extraordinary figure in cinema, not only because his work represents a remarkable synthesis of different avant-garde traditions but also because his films present an elliptically vertiginous path of obsessions within the socio-historical and political contexts of past (former Yugoslavia) and present (Serbia). The process of Žilnik's personal formation and his filmmaking career can be seen through the prism of post-World War Two Yugoslav history: the promise of socialism (as it was imagined by the once thriving Marxist left in the West); the bloody communist dictatorship (as it appeared from behind the iron curtain); the non-aligned 'third way' movement (as it looked from the point of view of the Third World's aspirations, a movement that was swallowed and then spat out as the refuse of capitalism at the end of the 1970s); the dimension of 'bastard capitalism' (the one that 'brought freedom' on the other, totalitarian side of the 'iron curtain' that used to be called Eastern Europe until the fall of the Berlin Wall in 1989); and lastly, Žilnik's films supply an adequate framework for understanding the courtroom performance of the former Yugoslav president, Slobodan Milošević, at The Hague.

Žilnik was born in 1942 in Niš, Serbia. He completed his studies at the Law Faculty in Novi Sad before he began his career in film, editing a special youth programme featuring cultural criticism and political discussions. Later on he acted as the editor of *Polja*, a prestigious journal covering artistic, cultural and social issues, published out of Novi Sad. His involvement with amateur film production dates back to the 1960s when he got drawn into the amateur filmmaking circles, acted as a film critic and worked as an assistant director for Dušan Makavejev.

Žilnik's early series of shorts: *Žurnal o omladini na selu zimi* (*Newsreel on Village Youth in Winter*, 1967), *Nezaposleni ljudi* (*The Unemployed*, 1968), *Lipanjska gibanja* (*June Turmoil*, 1969) and *Crni film* (*Black Film*, 1969), are comparable, in terms of singularity of vision and of the way issues of identity, violence and sexuality are explored, as well as in their visual elements and editing, to Russ Meyer's films, such as *Lorna* (1964) or *Faster, Pussycat! Kill! Kill!* (1966). The 'early works' of Žilnik mark a trajectory comparable to the esoteric cult cinema of Japanese director Koji Wakamatsu and, in particular, to his *Tenshi no kokotsu* (*The Angelic Orgasm*, 1972). For both, the juxtaposition of images of self-destruction is paired with a radical questioning of basic social concepts such as democracy, truth and lies, all concerns that become a quintessential motif in their film work. Wakamatsu's films, however, are mostly preoccupied with issues of extreme terrorism and sexual anarchy, while Žilnik's interest lies more in investigating the communist pathology and the specific Yugoslav 'third way' into socialism (known as self-management) and in the cinematic recreation of the hellish conditions of life and freedom. The venture here is not to gamble with the simple crossing of established limits; it does not matter if we are invited to think about the limits of capitalism (Wakamatsu) or socialism (Žilnik), or to subvert other not yet known areas of social practice. It is much more about highlighting the connection between safeguarding the limits and the disintegration of social, political and moral domains.

*Early Works* is structured around a series of juxtapositions: it mixes fast cars, lovely women, bread, alcohol, sports and the Communist Manifesto, as well as no less than seven acts of promiscuous fornication within one night. The film is full of black humour and overt sexuality, all meant to point at the (im)possibility of changing a world that is ruled by inner conservatism and patriarchal attitudes. Between tears and smiles, Marx and Lenin are contextualised with various ways of cooking cabbage. For this film, Žilnik hijacked the basic framework of the 1968 student riots and filled it with scopophilia, rape and murder, developing a remarkable series of surrealist, grotesque and stylised images of decomposition and decay that later on became basic features of his radically innovative and subversive approach to film.

The film's title is borrowed from the general heading under which Karl Marx and Friedrich Engels' early writings on political philosophy and their political economy interpretations of the capitalist system was published. In addition, a literary and political leitmotif in the film is the usage of quotes from letters written by the young Marx to Arnold Ruge in 1843, usually applied to scenes of perverse tenderness interspersed with meta-textual intervals within the film's narration. The inventive narrative structure and subversive effect of Žilnik's *Early Works* can be appreciated even better if one establishes another parallel, to John Waters' *Pink Flamingos* (1972). In order to prove that Divine and his entourage are the 'filthiest people alive', Waters made the overweight drag queen eat dog faeces on screen; Žilnik, instead, simply incorporated in the film references to the 'socialist' shit that jammed the reality around him to achieve an even more seditious and bleak effect. A radical disruption and reformulation of the official film form and content rules prescribed by the state socialist aesthetic codex is carried out within the processes of re-inscription, inversion and displacement of Žilnik's constantly nihilistic themes of lawlessness, rebellion and sexual deviancy; his engagement with these themes made his influences go far beyond cinema into the more general spheres of aesthetics and politics. It is no surprise that the *punk-geist* groups of the Yugoslav underground scene of the 1980s were influenced by Žilnik's 1960s films in their political and rock'n'roll video experiments.

From today's point of view the film's political resonance – of a story foretold – is particularly significant. Yugoslava, the female protagonist, comes across as an allegory of the brotherhood and unity of ex-Yugoslavia, where, according to the official ideology, working people had dropped all antagonisms and bad thoughts. By showing Yugoslava brutally attacked and killed, Žilnik exposed this imaginary fairytale long before the horrifying 1990s, when the federation imploded and was torn apart.

When *Early Works* opened in Yugoslavia in 1969, it was an immediate success because the film captured so precisely many of the most pertinent political and social issues of the time. Nevertheless the film's subtle plea for political and sexual liberation was so disturbing for the authorities that it was temporarily banned. The ban, which was imposed two months after the film's release, reflected Josip Broz-Tito's reaction to the film. Reportedly, after watching the first 15 minutes, Tito had angrily stopped the screening and demanded it be withdrawn from public circulation. Trained as a lawyer, Žilnik decided to challenge the ban. The court ruled in his favour, although he was forced to remove some politically sensitive footage referring to social unrest. Žilnik was subsequently expelled from the Communist Party. He then began to experience difficulties in making films. Around the same time, however, the film was awarded the Golden Bear at the Berlin International Film Festival. Berlinale historian, Wolfgang Jacobsen wrote: 'Žilnik's film portrays society using a farce as its means; it is critical of the orthodoxy of the older generation, self-critical of the verbal radicalism of the younger and of the left, to which Žilnik himself belonged.' The award gave *Early Works* the aura of a powerful underground testament and turned it into an icon of the European left. In the aftermath of the Berlin triumph, *Early Works* was invited for a showing at the Museum of Modern Art in New York, followed by the opening night premiere at the Chicago Film Festival in 1970.

The adverse reaction to *Early Works* in Yugoslavia led to Žilnik's emigration to Germany where he worked for several years in the 1970s. Closely connected with the Oberhausen festival, here he continued making shorts of the same radically critical type focusing on awkward issues. One of his key themes was the investigation into the lives of socially marginalised guest-workers; his short *Antrag* (*Application*, 1974) centred on a fierce clash between Greek and Turkish guest-workers who quarrel over the Turkish incursion into Cyprus that developed at the time. A favourite of Oberhausen, Žilnik worked closely with people like Rainer Werner Fasbinder and Hanna Schygulla who were set to star in a feature project that was never to materialise. Žilnik soon realised that in Germany he was subjected to similar levels of censorship and scrutiny as at home, so he returned to Yugoslavia and has since worked in Novi Sad, mostly on guerrilla-style independent productions and in theatre. His later work has remained equally critical and socially committed; he has been a relentless commentator on awkward political issues such as the violent break-up of Yugoslavia (*Tito po drugi put medju srbima* (*Tito Among the Serbs for a Second Time*, 1993) and *Dupe od mramora* (*Marble Ass*, 1995)), on migrations (*Trdnjava Evrope* (*Fortress Europe*, 2001)) and on Romani discrimination (*Kenedi se vraca kuci* (*Kenedi Goes Back Home*, 2003)). During the period Žilnik spent working in Germany, another important filmmaker from the Balkans, the Romanian Radu Gabrea, also worked in the film circles gravitating around Fassbinder; Gabrea later directed the Fassbinder biopic *Ein Mann wie EVA* (*A Man like Eva*, 1984).

*Early Works* can be described as a socialist *Easy Rider* (Dennis Hopper, 1969) in that it focuses on general discontent, social disturbance, erotic violence and exploitation. The film explored the radical protests of the young generation against the daunting reduction of elevated socialist values into a rigid system of absolute command. This was a protest against those Communist Party members who, a decade earlier, had been revolutionaries and who, by the 1960s, had become members of the new nomenclature and now enjoyed unlimited powers. Some of the slogans that the protagonists of *Early Works* shout in the film ('Down with the red bourgeoisie!') were intended to challenge precisely this fallacy of socialist ideology. It had proclaimed that power belonged solely and entirely to the people, to the workers and to the peasants, while in fact the power was now totally concentrated in the hands of the political elites at the top of the Yugoslav Communist Party; they also possessed all material benefits (money and luxury goods).

Žilnik's cinema was part of the so-called Black Wave, which made its direct task to fuse political and aesthetic rebellion with the radical dismantling of social and sexual taboos. Besides Žilnik's films, the cinema of the Black Wave included the work of masters such as Živojin Pavlović, Alexander Petrović and Dušan Makavejev. With its austerity, the cinema of the Black Wave was a drastic shift from the aesthetic requirements of the socialist realist doctrine. It radically subverted the simplistic Manichean representation of the post-war reality. The new Yugoslavia had been born from the debris of the war; the Black Wave healed the war wounds by developing an absolute critical stance in the form of a new, rebellious and almost hyperrealistic approach to film. The attention here was on the everyday existence of the working class, on their poverty, and on the betrayal of the socialist ideals by the red bourgeoisie, often challenged through references to radical thinkers such as Wilhelm Reich (whose initials, WR, formed part of the title of Makavejev's 1971 seditious *WR – Misterije organizma* (*WR: Mysteries of the Organism*). The past was also closely scrutinised, thus revealing the multiplicity of recurring traumatic narratives of history, nation and patriarchy.

*Early Works* was made as a reaction to the 1968 student demonstrations in Belgrade and remains one of the few Yugoslav feature films dedicated to these riots. Yugoslavia's reaction to the unrest differed from the other countries of state socialism. Contrary to the practice in other Stalinist Eastern European countries, the army was not sent in to disperse the protestors and there was no intervention by the secret police. More importantly, as a result of the turbulence, the bureaucratic structure came under genuine pressure. The concurrent occupation of Czechoslovakia by the Warsaw Pact, however, led to a widespread paranoia in Yugoslavia. It

was feared that the country's relatively higher degree of liberalism could be used as an excuse by the Soviets who would happily make it the next target to invade. At the beginning of the 1970s these fears led to an increased dogmatisation of Yugoslav social life, a process that had drastic repercussions on film production as well.

It was in this context that, in March 1971, Želimir Žilnik co-signed a special Manifesto entitled *This Festival is a Cemetery*, which he read aloud at the 18th Yugoslav Documentary and Short Film Festival in Belgrade. In this Manifesto, Žilnik resolutely expressed his deep disapproval of the way recent political developments were affecting filmmaking:

> The suggestion that there is something like a young Yugoslav film can be considered yet another manipulation of the situation in our cinema. There is no such thing. Those who declare themselves young are in fact middle-aged, but what is worse is their total collaboration with the existing conditions of production and their consenting identification with the environment they originate from. None of the film authors present at this festival would be willing to accept risks and responsibilities beyond what is permitted. Compared to the young international film our so-called 'young cinema' is absolutely reactionary; it simply reproduces the traditional circumstances of Yugoslavia's non-autonomous cinematography, only too familiar to us because of their intrinsic evil.

In addition, Žilnik argued that 'If we do not want to wallow in the mire of our own decomposition, which already begins to smell dangerously, the next festival will have to be guided by completely different principles.' He demanded that screenings be organised for ordinary people beyond the festival auditorium. In addition to those films produced with state subsidies (and thus by default not particularly interested in transgressing boundaries), Žilnik demanded the inclusion of more independent and personal productions, shot in the 16mm and Super-8 formats. In conclusion, not even sparing his own work, Žilnik stated: 'This festival is a cemetery: everything in this festival is a grave; everything is here laying grave to grave, including – obviously – those signing this declaration.'

*Early Works* is fully consistent in questioning the unresolved boundary between the elements of fiction and fact. Using a specific cinematic strategy – inserting quasi-documentary shots into the fictional story – Žilnik powerfully exposed the utopia of the Socialist Revolution and brought into cinema the Freudian concept of the return of the suppressed. Žilnik searched not only to develop a new visual narration. Most of all, he tried to develop new stylistic dimensions of mixing life experience with artificial film structure. Žilnik's new approach to correlating documentary and fiction significantly advanced the expressive nature of the film medium as it allowed for a head-on attack on the complex power structure of social institutions.

*Early Works'* new expressive realism strongly reflected the cultural shift in cinema. Many scenes in the film were not a direct reflection of reality but rather of presupposed documentary and ideological views about that reality. It is a well-known fact that Žilnik's passion for documentary and his appreciation of the genre remain as much alive today as they were back in the 1960s. The verité quality of 'Black Wave' cinema has been extensively commented on by various observers. In Žilnik's case it is important to stress that his dedication to socially analytical documentary is a lifetime passion: his feature films are more appropriately described as docudramas rather than as fiction filmmaking. Although *Early Works* does not attempt to blur fact and fiction or try to fool audiences into believing that the film is a documentary record of real events, it nevertheless engages with a specific vision of the interaction between actuality and interpretation and thus fundamentally erodes the authoritarian model of governance. In *Early Works* fiction is derived from non-fiction, resulting in a wonderfully weird version of realism. It is a fiction film yet it looks and feels like *cinéma verité,* leaving the audience with the strange illusion of fictional legitimacy. In this way the film radically differs from the socialist realistic paradigm preoccupied with creating a fictional and clearly regulated conceptual universe for the spectator.

Želimir Žilnik is a unique personality in European cinema, a provocative filmmaker dealing with new forms of film narration, relentlessly exposing important political and social ills and using film as a powerful tool of reflection. Marx's *Early Works* laid the foundations of the anarchic and rebellious subtext of the future communist ideology; Žilnik's *Early Works* critically engaged in performing revolutionary acts that cut through conventionally approved barriers. *Early Works* had a profound effect on the way in which Yugoslav intelligentsia perceived all social, political and aesthetic processes from then on. The film is still a powerful and ingenious tool for critical minds.

**Marina Gržinić**

REFERENCE

Jacobsen, W. (2000) *50 Years Berlinale.* Berlin: Nicolai.

# MIHAI VITEAZUL MICHAEL THE BRAVE

## SERGIU NICOLAESCU, ROMANIA, 1970−71

A two-part epic, *Mihai Viteazul* (*Michael the Brave*, 1970–71) loosely follows events between 1595 and 1601, telling the story of Prince Mihai, the ruler of Wallachia who waged a war against Turkish domination and, as traditional accounts of Romanian history would have it, briefly succeeded in uniting Wallachia with Romanian-speaking Moldovia and Transylvania under one crown. The film focuses on one of the most important episodes in the formation of the Romanian nation and puts the emphasis on the Romanian resistance to the invading Ottomans, thus endorsing the government-sponsored vision of the nation's history.

The opening scene shows the Turkish army in the marshes of Călugăreni in August 1595. Their 'victory' claim is immediately contradicted by flashback sequences showing Mihai (Amza Pellea) as a fugitive riding across the country, and the ruler of Wallachia, Prince Alexandru, enjoying a gruesome dinner with the Ottoman Empire representative Selim Bei (played by the film's director Sergiu Nicolaescu), whilst watching his people die on spears and making promises of chariots of gold in exchange for Mihai's head. Mihai's wife, Stanca, wants nothing to do with the fugitive; neither his family nor his friends understand Mihai's stubborn quest for the Wallachian throne, which pushes him to strange friendships with people like Selim. Mihai ends up in Istanbul, trying to raise money to buy back Wallachia from the Turks. There he meets Countess Ventini. By standing up to the sultan Murad, Mihai proves himself worthy of the crown, while his rival Alexandru is speedily executed.

A few months later, as Selim Bei comes to collect dues for the Ottoman Empire, he witnesses the first of the extreme measures taken by the new prince: the killing of his creditors, who are burnt to death. This not only makes Mihai look callous in the eyes of the Western Alliance led by the Prince of Transylvania, Szigmond Báthory (Ion Besoiu), who was planning to oppose the Turks, but also incites the Turks against him. Mihai seems to have his own agenda: fighting back the Turks while trying to forge an alliance with the Vatican. He conquers fortress after fortress, freeing the Southern Romanian territory all the way to the sea, and soon is on his way to attack Istanbul. Unhappy at the West's decision to delay sending him troops for five months, he progresses with his plans, forging an alliance with Szigmond in exchange for military assistance. However, when the decisive battle between Mihai and Pasha Sinan takes place in the Neajlov marshes at Călugăreni, Szigmond withdraws his promise of support, and Mihai must confront the powerful Turkish army alone. After a spectacular battle scene Mihai emerges from the bloodbath claiming victory.

After the Western crusaders lose the battle against the Turks at Kerestes in 1596 (also known as the battle of Mezőkeresztes), Szigmond's Báthory cousin, Andrei, takes over the throne, allowing Mihai's most daring move, to change sides in an attempt to claim Transylvania and Moldavia in the battle of Şelimbăr. Mihai's intention to unify all Romanian-speaking principalities is now facilitated by the Moldavians refusing to fight their Wallachian brothers. While soldiers celebrate on the battlefield, Mihai is offered the traditional bread and salt as well as Moldavia's flag and crown. He enters Alba-Julia in 1600 and is crowned king of Wallachia, Transylvania and Moldavia, thus fulfilling his dream of unification.

But his reign does not last long. Szigmond Báthory attempts to reclaim Transylvania. General Basta, surprisingly, joins Mihai against Szigmond, only to betray him in the middle of a decisive battle. Mihai not only loses the battle, but also the crown and his son, Nicolae. A fugitive again, he wanders through his beloved country, finding only distress and poverty as a result of endless wars. At one point he is forced to part with his last possessions to pay for a room.

Having lost the territories he has just conquered, Mihai turns to the Austrian Emperor for support, but it is only when Szigmond betrays Emperor Rudolf and pledges alliance with the Turks that the Emperor receives Mihai and accepts to finance his campaign against Szigmond. Impressed by Mihai's dignity, the Emperor finds him 'too big for his small country'. Szigmond, chased down in a sea of mud, loses the battle. Yet Mihai's future is far from secure. Weakened by his travels, his only comfort is the ghostly apparition of his mother. On his way to be crowned, Mihai is joined by two of Basta's men for an outdoor dinner – a visual evocation of the Last Supper – where he is shot in the back and killed.


In the 1970s, the historical figure of Michael the Brave inspired not only Sergiu Nicolaescu but also film directors like Mircea Drăgan (*Ştefan cel Mare – Vaslui 1475 (Stephen the Great – Vaslui 1475,* 1975)) and Constantin Vaeni (*Buzduganul cu trei peceţi (The Mace with Three Seals,* 1978)). In contrast to Vaeni's film, where Mihai is faced with a cobweb of diplomatic intrigues, Nicolaescu's prince-soldier remains resolute and brave, however strong the opposition of his relatives and friends or terrible the wounds of war are. All three films use Romanian history as a backdrop for large-scale battle scenes but the most memorable ones are those from *Michael the Brave*. It may be because director Nicolaescu not only had the services of the national army at his disposal but was also able to work with a cast of fifty for the key parts and with another two hundred actors for the episodes. *Michael the Brave* contains seven breathtaking battle scenes, one of which featured 30,000 extras and 150 cannons. Today, Nicolaescu claims his battle scenes inspired Steven Spielberg and still talks of how, on the set of the international super-production *Lupta pentru Roma I* (*The Struggle for Rome I*, 1968), he taught Robert Siodmak how to create instant chaos on a shoot involving over a thousand extras (a third of whom were provided by the Romanian army). Nicolaescu's name is attached to a string of lavishly financed historical super-productions spanning over four decades, including *Dacii* (*The Dacians*, 1966), *Nemuritorii* (*The Immortals*, 1974), *Pentru Patrie* (*For Motherland*, 1977) and, more recently, *Mircea* (*Proud Heritage*, 1989) and *Triunghiul Morții* (*The Death Triangle*, 1999). However impressive this list may be, it also reflects the megalomania of a director who did not hesitate to adjust his strategies to accommodate contemporary political agendas.

*The Dacians* and *Michael the Brave* can be regarded as Nicolaescu's first contributions to the nationalist trend of the times. *The Dacians*, his first feature film, is an impressive fresco set in the year 87AD when Dacia was faced with the first invasion of Imperial Rome. Showing the Dacians struggling for survival alongside the strategically superior Romans led by emperor Trajan, the film offers a mythic reinterpretation of Romanian history as a blending of the Roman and Dacian peoples.

Along with other state-sanctioned Romanian epics of the time, the film fully endorses the popular theory of Daco-Romanian continuity, first propounded by Prince Dimitrie Cantemir (1673–1723) and popularised by Bishop Ioan Micu in the eighteenth century. According to this theory, the Romanian peoples are descendents of indigenous Dacians and Roman settlers. Claiming racial and cultural continuity, nationalists have made ample use of this theory that allowed Romanians to assert rightful ownership of Transylvania and dismiss their Magyar rivals as usurpers. In *Michael the Brave*, the hero champions the cause of national unification and freedom. Before each battle, Michael the Brave is seen expressing his nationalist ideals in a passionate address to his men.

Theories describing the origins of the respective nation as a cross-breed between tenacious tribes and more sophisticated peoples characterised the national discourse of countries like Bulgaria (nomadic Bulgars and sedentary Slavs) and Romania (Dacii and Romans), as well as Hungary. In each case the arrival of superior civilising influence was seen as a key element in the nation-building process. Nicolaescu's *The Dacians* is one of the important super-productions illustrating these theories. Its Bulgarian equivalent was Lyudmil Staykov's *Khan Asparukh* (1981), made for the 1,300th anniversary of the founding of the Bulgarian nation (the film is better known in its abbreviated version *Velichieto na hana* (*681 AD: The Glory of Khan* (1984)).

Like other Romanian productions meant to boost national consciousness, Nicolaescu's epics are often sparse with historical facts. Mihai may have been briefly welcomed by the Vlachs in Transylvania, but he was most certainly not the liberator portrayed in the film. Even though poverty is seen as the disastrous result of wars, the exploitation of the lower classes was not strictly explored (something that comes across as surprising, given the class-conscious context of the time the film was made; yet, as Andy Medhurst has observed, class hierarchies were not really challenged in any of the other heritage epics across Europe). When asked about his view on the relationship between history and fiction at the time he was shooting *The Dacians*, Nicolaescu asserted that when artistic interpretation is concerned, 'the truth or untruth of a fact – if it is not a very important one – must not be judged by the criteria of the veracity of a chronicle but by the spirit of history'. To him, as well as to other Romanian directors of similar ideologically conformist ilk endorsing the nationalist agenda, the highlights of Romanian history are best represented in films depicting the efforts to prevent the Ottomans from spreading into Europe as Romania's major historical achievement.

Beginning in the late 1950s, the historical Romanian epic really flourished throughout the 1960s and the 1970s. Lavish heritage super-productions fulfilled the needs of romanticised representations of national history and, as such, were encouraged and supported by various cultural and educational institutions determined to foster national consciousness. Lucian Bratu's *Tudor* (1963), depicting the exploits of the leader of the 1821 popular uprising against the Turks, is usually credited for having paved the way for the patriotic film epics that Nicolaescu, Mircea Drăgan, Constantin Vaeni and Gheorge Vitanidis were to go on to make. Nicolaescu's *The Dacians* was the first of what Romanian film historians have called 'The Dacians Trilogy'. It was followed by Mircea Drăgan's *Columna* (*The Column*, 1968), an ambitious film about the founding of Romania by Roman emperor Trajan and *Burebista* (*The Iron and the Gold*, Gheorghe Vitanidis, 1980) which was meant to mark the 2,050th anniversary of the first step toward the formation of the Romanian nation.

The trend of depincting Romania's great national heroes peaked in the 1970s. Supported by a government eager to draw on historical figures to foster and consolidate a particular brand of Romanian national identity, a number of directors contributed to the nationalist epic genre. Vitanidis's *Ciprian Porumbescu* (1972), for example, was a historical drama depicting the tragic life of the Romanian composer (1853–83) who dreamt of Romania's freedom and unity through the recovery of Bucovina and Transylvania (under Habsburg rule at the time), while his *Muşchetarul Român* (*A Man From the East*, 1978) was a swashbuckling period piece recounting the adventures of Prince Dimitrie Cantemir. Doru Năstase's *Vlad Ţepeş* (*Vlad the Impaler*, 1979) was yet another epic. The heroes of these films often earned their fame through their tireless political and military exploits against the Ottoman Empire. The epic treatment of the subject matter relied on narratives depicting the resistance of ordinary Romanians to the rule of foreign masters, in particular Turks and Hungarians. Thus, these films contributed to the growth of nationalist sentiment that reinforced the arguments put forward by Romanian historians on Romanian ethnic origins and the respective territorial claims that came along; they were, unsurprisingly, highly popular with Romanian audiences at the time.

Why were such super-productions made in Romania before and during the Ceauşescu era? The 1950s was a period of key developments for the Romanian film industry; as well as the foundation of the I. L. Caragiale Institute of Theatre and Film (IATC) and the Alexandru Sahia documentary and short film studio in 1950, the decade saw the construction of the Buftea studios (1950–57), a 150-acre complex built on the outskirts of Bucharest. With superb technical facilities at their disposal, Romanian filmmakers were encouraged by the Romanian authorities to make ambitious films that complied with the nationalist policy of the times. By the mid-1950s, the increasing refusal of Gheorghiu-Dej – Ceauşescu's predecessor – to follow the Moscow line was a great success domestically, tapping into a vein of popular nationalism that was exploited even more systematically by Ceauşescu, who came to power in 1965. The cultural reliance on the Soviet Union was replaced by a compelling nationalist discourse and a desire to consolidate the works of Romanian artists. Films could not be made without government approval, so it was no coincidence therefore that many filmmakers embarked on a spate of films glorifying the past. The history of Romania became a source for spectacular historical dramas, and the epic a new 'sub-genre' in the rising wave of Romanian nationalism. Writing at the time Ceauşescu was still in power, ideologically conformist film historian Manuela Cernat contended that Romanian filmmakers had 'a duty' to produce films exalting the past. Referring to 'the cinematic portraits and effigies of the great personalities doomed to the martyrdom of carrying on their shoulders the burden of history', Cernat asserted that only 'history as a tragic parable could lend Romanian films the universal dimension required for their penetration into the consciousness of audiences – particularly foreign ones'. However, the fact that schoolchildren and workers were actually taken to see these films in organised cohorts seriously challenges Cernat's officially approved cinematic version of Romanian film history.

Under Ceauşescu, the production of national epics was also part and parcel of the 'independent foreign policy' that earned Romania the reputation of being 'the maverick' state of the Eastern bloc; a substantial number of these patriotic epics were planned and/or made in collaboration with foreign partners. Official co-production agreements with France, Italy and Germany included advantageous deals for more 'spectacular' films; distribution was left to the national agencies of the countries involved. *The Dacians* was a Romanian-French co-production, *Michael the Brave* was planned in cooperation with Columbia (USA), and Mircea Drăgan's *The Column* was co-produced with the Federal Republic of Germany. In the late 1950s, Buftea studios boasted some of the finest technical talent in the East and provided foreign filmmakers with cheap labour and modern facilities. After Romania's political regime established cultural links with France and other Romance-language nations of Europe and South America, they attracted reputed foreign – particularly French – filmmakers. Literary adaptations became fashionable and French Communist directors like Marc Maurette and Louis Daquin were invited to film in Romania. In the 1960s, it was the turn of Henri Colpi and René Clair to come to Romania's large production complex. However, the hey-day of multinational collaboration was in the late 1960s and 1970s, when the studios offered their services to a substantial number of foreign film and television companies. In 1968, Robert Siodmak shot *The Struggle for Rome* there, with Laurence Harvey and Orson Welles. The series was co-produced with Germany and Italy, and co-directed by Sergiu Nicolaescu. That same year, Nicolaescu also adapted works by Mark Twain and James Fennimore Cooper in a series of films co-produced by the Paris-based company Franco London Film. It was also in 1968 that Terence Young made *Mayerling* (1968) with Omar Shariff and Catherine Deneuve, while Jean-Paul Rappeneau came to shoot *Les mariés de l'an II* (*The Newly-Weds of the Year II*, 1970) with Jean-Paul Belmondo, and Michael Anderson made *Pope Joan* (1972) starring Maximilian Schell and Liv Ullmann. More importantly for Romanian cinema, it was in this 'Cinecittà of the Balkans' that a new generation of Romanian directors, cinematographers, scriptwriters, actors and technicians were soon to prove their talents. Likely to have been influenced by various Cinecittá-based projects of the late 1950s and early 1960s, super-productions of similar scale were made also in other countries of the Soviet bloc. Multinational ones were patented by Soviet director Sergei Bondarchuk (*Waterloo*, 1970) while in Poland the tradition was mostly linked to the names of directors like Aleksander Ford (*Knights of the Teutonic Order*, 1960) and Jerzy Hoffman (*Pan Wolodyjowski* (1969); *Potop* (*Deluge*, 1974)). Around the same time Yugoslavia made several large-scale partisan epics which are reminiscent of Nicolaescu's super-productions not so much in historical theme but in production recipe. *Bitka na Neretvi* (*The Battle of Neretva*, Veljko Bulajić, 1969) featured a range of international actors, such as Sergei Bondarchuk, Yul Brynner, Franco Nero, Curd Jürgens, Orson Welles and Sylvia Koscina. Romania and Yugoslavia developed the reputation of 'mavericks' of the so-called Second World, which is probably the reason for their less rigid and ultimately more diverse international cultural contacts, resulting in a range of co-productions that attracted a genuinely international scope of participants.

Nicolaescu and scriptwriter Titus Popovici were among the most prolific film person-alities of the period. They collaborated on seven films including *The Dacians* and *Michael the Brave*. Popovici, who worked on the script with Nicolaescu, also worked on the adaptation of *Pădurea spînzuraţilor* (*Forest of the Hanged*, 1964; discussed in this volume). One of the most influential Romanian screenwriters, he is responsible for the script of other historical epics, such *The Dacians* and Mircea Dragan's *Columna* (*Trajan's Column*, 1968), as well as for nearly thirty other scripts. A 1953 graduate of Bucharest University, he also adapted his own novels for the screen. *Setea* (*Thirst*, 1960) and *The Column* were filmed by Mircea Drăgan and *Atunci i-am condamnat pe toti la moarte* (*Ipu's Death*, 1971) by Nicolaescu. By contrast, Nicolaescu had left school at the age of 16. He started his film career as a mechanical engineer at the Sahia Studio for documentary and short films. A jack-of-all-trades, he served in almost every capacity in film production including cameraman, scriptwriter and director of shorts. The green light for a director's career was given to him after his short films *Primavara obisnuita* (*Ordinary Spring*, 1960), *Memoria trandafirului* (*Memory of the Rose*, 1962) and *Lectie în infinit* (*A Lesson in the Infinite*, 1963) won several national and international prizes. Between *The Dacians* and *Michael the Brave*, Nicolaescu directed six films – all of them co-productions with Western partners. By 1971, he had become the most popular Romanian filmmaker both at home and abroad. Film critic Mircea Alexandrescu talked of him as director who did not behave like 'an artist addressing just a handful of people', but as one whose creed was 'to address broad audi-ences'. To date, Nicolaescu has directed 48 films (including adventure series for West German and French TV studios), switching from historical epics to fast-paced thrillers like *Un comisar acuză* (*A Police Inspector Calls*, 1973), *Revanşa* (*Revenge*, 1978) and *Duelul* (*The Duel*, 1981), melodramas like *Osânda* (*The Doom*, 1976) and *Ultima noapte de dragoste* (*The Last Night of*

*Love*, 1979), comedies like *Nea Mărin Miliardar* (*The Elusive Billionaire*, 1979), aesthetic experiments like *Ipu's Death* and contemporary dramas like *Punctul Zero* (*Point Zero*, 1996). *The Dacians* marked both his acting and directing debut in features. (In the film, he plays the small part of a Roman soldier who is beheaded.) Having built his acting career on his good looks, Nicolaescu proved to be a charismatic star as comfortable in military roles (*Noi, cei din linia întâi* (*The Last Assault*, 1986); *Triunghiul morții* (*The Death Triangle*, 1999)) as well as playing the lead in the popular action-adventure franchise about the indestructible police inspector Moldovan (*Un comisar acuză, Revanşa, Duelul*).

*The Dacians* and *Michael the Brave* reflect Nicolaescu's skill, talent, versatility and enormous ambition as well as his undeniable flair for popular appeal and political malleability. A consummate opportunist, he quickly realised that the awards bestowed on his early shorts gave him instant credibility and, as long as he followed the ideologically conformist line, he could aim for more significant assignments. For his first national epics, Nicolaescu was able to enlist a multinational cast which secured wide international distribution for the film. Co-produced by a Paris-based company, *The Dacians* claimed a prestigious cast led by Romanian actors Amza Pellea and Ilarion Ciobanu, and including Italians Antonella Lualdi and Amedeo Nazzari, and the French Marie-José Nat, George Marchal and Pierre Brice. Following his successful collaboration with American actors in Siodmak's 1968 film, Nicolaescu's intention was to have a cast of even higher international profile for *Michael the Brave*. Charlton Heston was to be cast in the lead role and Richard Burton as Szigmond Báthory, the other roles were to go to Elizabeth Taylor, Orson Welles, Laurence Harvey and Edward G. Robinson. However, the Minister of Culture and reportedly Ceauşescu himself objected to such a heavy American involvement in a production aimed at glorifying the history of Romanian people. As a result, Nicolaescu and Popovici had to recruit Romanian actors and renounce the American partnership.

Three years in the making, *Michael the Brave* was shot in Romania, Turkey and Austria. First developed as a co-production with Columbia, the film was ultimately financed by the Romanian government. The American connection was not totally lost: picked up for distribution by Columbia, the film boasts the largest international distribution for a Romanian film (130 million viewers worldwide); it was Romania's official entry for the Academy Awards in the Best Foreign Language Film category.

Romanian actor Amza Pellea plays Mihai, a casting decision that was reached after extensive discussions. Titus Popovici had insisted that Nicolaescu himself should play the main character. Along with the director, several other actors were tested for Mihai's role and the scouts

were sent to Hollywood for the American producers to choose which actor would be most suitable. Again, Nicolaescu was their preferred choice. After shooting started, however, Nicolaescu realised he did not want the lead role; he went to the Ministry of Culture and declared he was not going to direct the film unless he could have Pellea in the lead. And he got his way. Pellea was to become Nicolaescu's favourite actor. Like many other Romanian actors, he had a remarkable stage career; it was for his roles in historical epics, however, that he became an institution in Romania.

Both Pellea and Nicolaescu went on to play national heroes in *The Immortals*, a film written and directed by Nicolaescu. A sequel to *Michael the Brave* and set in the year 1611, *The Immortals* depicts the adventures of a group of soldiers who fought under Michael the Brave. After long wanderings across Europe, they return home to hoist once more the flag of the Union briefly achieved by their prince, only to be welcomed by bullets, as the new prince does not share their ideal. In 1977, Nicolaescu directed and acted in *For Motherland*, a film dedicated to the anniversary of the 1877 Independence War. In a 1986 leaflet Romania Film, the national production and distribution company, hailed *For Motherland* as a film 'pervaded by enthusiastic, deep-seated patriotic feelings [that] shows the heroism and self-denial of Romanian soldiers and officers'. In *Mircea*, a film he also directed, Nicolaescu played the role of Prince Mircea, another historical figure who gained his badge of national hero in fierce battles to stop the expansion of the Ottoman Empire at the end of the fourteenth century. Preventing the Ottoman invasion from spreading into the western parts of Europe is the basis for one of the most important ideological tropes of the Balkan discourse on history and national identity: by putting on heroic resistance to the Ottomans (often resulting in defeat), these nations have made it possible for the West European nations to continue their Christian development uninterrupted by the Muslim Ottomans. Many epic films from the Balkans explore aspects of this resistance, be it in battles (as seen in Zdravko Sotra's *Boj na Kosovu* (*Battle of Kosovo*, 1989)) or in resistance to forced religious conversion (as seen in the Bulgarian film *Vreme na nasilie* (*Time of Violence*, Lyudmil Staykov, 1988) or the Albanian film *Balada e Kurbinit* (*Ballad of Kurbini*, Kujtim Çashku, 1990)).

Today, Nicolaescu claims that, as someone who comes from a wealthy family, his life was not made easy under the regime of Ceauşescu, as the 'Conducator' bestowed privileges to people of more humble origins. Yet he does not seem to have suffered any of the ills inflicted on the Romanian people over several decades. Somehow, he managed to always remain in power, no matter what political changes there were. He does acknowledge that, under Ceauşescu, he could do everything he wanted, but he also insists that he never compromised, neither in his professional capacity (he did not go to Hollywood) nor in his personal views. Such statements by a filmmaker who, somehow, always managed to stay on top, are taken to task today by film historians who point out that not challenging the official line was already enough of a compromise. Indeed, under the Ceaușescu regime, a number of other filmmakers were silenced and/or were driven into exile.

Even though today he is one of the most controversial Romanian filmmakers; he has managed to keep himself abreast of change and has proven to be the ultimate survivor and pragmatist. Since the fall of Ceaușescu in 1989, he became involved in politics by first joining the CFSN (the Democratic Front of National Salvation, renamed the Party of Social Democracy in Romania in 1993) and becoming a member of the CPU (the Provisory Council of National Union). He then served as a member of the Romanian parliament (PDSR).

But he also continued working in film. After 1990, following the example set by other Romanian filmmakers of a less conformist persuasion, Nicolaescu undertook the running of the creative unit Star Film 22. He also acted as President of the Filmmakers Union of Romania (UARF), and throughout the 1990s directed several films. Set during World War One and starring Nicolaescu himself as General Averescu, *Triunghiul morții* (1999) is the director's most ambitious project and another tribute to the heroes who fought and died for Romanian unification. Nicolaescu claims that the film's completion was hampered by a lack of production money, a deficient distribution system and run-down exhibition outlets.

An ultimate survivor-type who has resurfaced in high-profile public roles all over again no matter what volatile developments may come about, director Sergio Nicolaescu is an extremely strong person who also appears to be universally disliked. Nicolaescu's work, however, is important as it represents the popular strand that is usually neglected in the study of Eastern and South European cinemas. This prolific director has worked in virtually all popular genres (action-adventure, crime, comedy, historical epics, and so on) and has displayed a remarkable inclination toward self-promotion, a feature which would normally be suppressed in the context of state socialism. The result is a larger-than-life figure who certainly should be studied more closely.

In *Michael the Brave*, Nicolaescu presented the achievements of his hero as a triumph of nationalism. Imbued with the political agenda at work in the nation-building process under the Ceaușescu regime, Nicolaescu's historical super-production reflects more than any other Romanian epic the megalomania and the opportunistic ambitions of its director. The film has become one of the Romanian national epics broadcast on occasions like 1 December, Romania's national day.

**Anne Jäckel**

REFERENCES

Alexandrescu, M. (1986) 'Sergiu Nicolaescu: A portrait', *Romania Film* leaflet.

Cernat, M. (1982) *A Concise History of the Romanian Film*, trans. A. Bantas. Bucharest: Editura Siinţifică şi Enciclopedică.

Medhurst, A. (2001) 'Sexuality and Heritage', in G. Vincendeau (ed.) *Film/Literature/Heritage*. London: British Film Institute, 11–14.

# TI EKANES STON POLEMO, THANASSI? WHAT DID YOU DO IN THE WAR, THANASSIS?

## DINOS KATSURIDIS, GREECE, 1971

Froso lives with her brother, Thanassis Karathanasis (Thanassis Vengos), a 44-year-old bachelor who works in a factory run by Greeks under the supervision of the German and Italian military during the occupation and famine in Athens in 1942. Their neighbour, Mrs Cleopatra, sues Mr Vasilis, the local tavern owner, for cooking her pet cat and serving it to his customers. When Froso, a member of the Greek Resistance, learns about the lawsuit, she tells Thanassis that he must testify as a defense witness because they are indebted to Mr Vasilis for the food he has been giving them, and, after all, he served the cat to three Greeks who were German collaborators.

In court, the judge sentences Mr Vasilis to three months in prison for stealing the cat and deceiving his customers, while Thanassis gets twenty days of imprisonment for perjury. Thanassis is sent to jail but due to an error he is transferred to the prison reserved for Greek resistance fighters. Among his cellmates is Ivan, one of the respected and resourceful leaders of the Greek Resistance. All of his cellmates follow Ivan when he escapes – except for Thanassis who does not realise the gravity of his situation and thinks that the Italians will release him when his twenty-days sentence is over. A Gestapo officer and his men arrive at the prison to interrogate Ivan and find only Thanassis. So they torture Thanassis for information and he realises that he must escape. He does so disguised as a prostitute with the help of Danai, a member of the Greek Resistance and one of the prostitutes locked up in the next cell.

Thanassis returns to his apartment and, while he is taking a bath, Apostolos, his nephew – a medical student and a member of the Resistance – arrives with a radio hidden in a bag of groceries, and asks Froso to hide it. Furthermore, Froso uses Thanassis as a courier without his knowledge to get copies of a subversive flyer, O Eleftherotis (*The Liberator*), inside the factory where he works, by hiding them in his lunch pail. An insider removes the flyers from the lunch pail and distributes them to all of the factory workers. One of the flyers falls into the hands of the Gestapo officer, and an investigation begins.

The following morning at the factory, the German soldiers frisk Thanassis and the other workers before they are allowed to work. Froso, Apostolos and Danai learn about the search and realise that they must warn Thanassis to get rid of the new copies of the flyer that Froso has, once again, hidden in his lunch pail earlier in the morning. Danai arrives at the factory where the workers are lining up for their lunch ration. She succeeds in catching Thanassis's attention and signals him to open his lunch pail. When Thanassis sees the copies of *The Liberator*, he panics and leaves the line. Hans, the German military cook, sees him and orders him to carry a barrel of sardines over to the lunch line. The copies of *The Liberator* fall out; Hans – who does not read any Greek – picks them up and uses them to wrap up each worker's ration of sardines as he hands them out. The Gestapo officer sees how the copies of *The Liberator* are being distributed to the workers, and orders his men to arrest Hans and Thanassis. Thanassis manages to flee the factory and returns to his apartment unaware that the Gestapo officer and his men are already there, awaiting his return. He is arrested and is thrown in prison with Hans.

In the Italian-controlled prison, Thanassis (who is mistaken for 'Ivan'), is forced to watch the Germans torturing Hans. When Hans passes out, both of them are taken back to the cell. Thanassis slips out from the cell but Hans is too weak to follow. The Gestapo officer returns, and, as Hans does not answer his question about how 'Ivan' escaped, is killed by the officer. Disguised in a German uniform and helmet, Thanassis exits the building with the other soldiers. He gets on a motorcycle to escape, but two German soldiers get on the motorcycle with him and he has to follow the convoy. He realises that the soldiers have orders to raid his apartment when they stop at his home. Thanassis races up the stairs before anyone else to warn his sister. He enters his apartment and tries to bar the door. Nonetheless, the Germans manage to push their way into the apartment. Thanassis sees Danai standing next to his sister holding her belly, looking very pregnant. Surprised by her sudden pregnancy, Thanassis makes her raise her arms. Her 'baby' drops on the floor. It is the radio, so Thanassis immediately picks it up, wraps it up in a blanket like an infant, and runs down the stairs. He misses a step and tumbles down. The radio accidentally comes on and broadcasts a speech against fascism. Thanassis runs out in the street with the radio as the speech ends and the Greek national anthem begins to play: '…Freedom, born from the sacred bones of the Greeks, I salute you, I salute you for taking a brave stand like in old times.'

Dinos Katsuridis was awarded the Golden Alexander Prize at the Greek Film Festival in Thessaloniki in 2000 for his contribution to every aspect of Greek cinema, in a career that spanned over half a century. He was born in Nicosia, Cyprus, in 1926. In the mid-1940s he went

to Greece to study medicine at the University of Athens, but changed his major to economics, which he failed to complete as he had decided to become a filmmaker. He began his long career in film in November 1950, as an assistant director on *Pikro Psomi* (*Bitter Bread,* 1951), directed by Grigoris Grigoriou. He continued his apprenticeship in other films as a set photographer, assistant cameraman, assistant editor, and then cameraman, editor and director of photography throughout the 1950s. He made his debut as film director in 1960 with two films – *Ime athoos* (*I am Innocent*, 1960) and *Englima sta paraskinia* (*Crime in the Wings,* 1960) – which broke new ground in making elements of *film noir* palatable to Greek audiences.

Katsuridis made his debut as a film producer in 1970 with *Ti ekanes ston polemo, Thanassi?* (*What Did You Do in the War, Thanassis?*, 1971). He co-authored the screenplay with Asimakis Gialamas, and called it an 'anti-war satire' ('antipolemiki satira') because, during the heyday of the Papadopoulos military dictatorship (1967–74), he would not have been permitted to call it an anti-fascist or anti-dictatorial satire. The screenplay was the Greek response to Hollywood's *What Did You Do in the War, Daddy?* (Blake Edwards, 1966). The subject matter of war has been approached humorously in other Balkan films as well, most notably in the Yugoslav classic *Who is Singing Out There?* (Slobodan Šijan, 1980); the 'Thanassis-style' mischievous resistance by necessity is probably most closely replicated in Emir Kusturica's *Underground* (1995).

Katsuridis and Gialamas tailored their screenplay to fit the acting style of Thanassis Vengos, a rising star in Greek cinema in the 1960s. Vengos had made his debut as an actor in *Magiki polis* (*Magic City*, 1952) directed by Nikos Koundouros. He met Koundouros on Makronisos (Long Island) where both of them had been exiled by the Greek government because of their communist beliefs and affiliations. Born in New Faliro (near Piraeus) in 1926, Vengos was in his mid-twenties when his acting career was launched. In the late 1960s, he was ascending the Greek star system. Playing the leading role in *What Did You Do in the War, Thanassis?*, his name appeared in the title of the film in the manner of a tradition that had been established during the era of the Karaghiozis Shadow Puppet Theatre shows in Greece.

The comic persona of Karaghiozis depended largely on the improvisational routines of the Karaghiozis shadow puppet players who responded to the demands of each new story. Likewise, the comic persona of Thanassis Vengos depended largely on the improvisational routines of this comedian, adapting his performance to the demands of each new screenplay. He enjoyed a name recognition and popularity in Athens in the late 1960s comparable to that of Karaghiozis in the 1920s. Katsuridis had seen the persona of Thanassis Vengos and the public's responses to it in films such as *Psila ta heria, Hitler!* (*Hands Up, Hitler!,* 1962),

*Enas trelos, trelos, trelos Vengos* (*A Mad, Mad, Mad Vengos*, 1965), *Voithia! O Vengos faneros praktor 000* (*Help! Vengos is Obvious Agent 000,* 1967) and *Pios Thanassis* (*Which Thanassis?,* 1969).

Katsuridis was familiar with the range of Vengos's acting style and improvisational routines because he had worked as the director of photography for two films directed by Vengos – *Doctor Zivengos* (1967) and *Thu-Vu falakros praktor epihirisis yis Madiam* (*Bald Agent Thu-Vu: Operation Havoc,* 1969). More importantly, Katsuridis had the opportunity to direct Vengos in two other films – *Enas Vengos gia oles tis dulies* (*A Vengos for All Jobs,* 1970) and *O Thanassis, i Iulieta, ke ta lukanika* (*Thanassis, Juliet, and the Hotdogs,* 1970). Banking on this experience, Katsuridis went ahead and directed *What Did You Do in the War, Thanasis?* himself. In this film, the collaboration between Katsuridis and Vengos reached its peak.

*What Did You Do in the War, Thanassis?* was a sensation at the Greek Film Festival in Thessaloniki in 1971. Both the public and the festival jury liked the film, which won awards in three separate categories: Best Picture, Best Screenplay and Best Actor. It also became an instant blockbuster throughout Greece much to the annoyance of the military dictators and their collaborators. It sold 640,471 tickets in the first-run movie theatres of Athens and Piraeus alone. It climbed to first place on the charts for ticket sales during 1971–72, as three million Greeks went to see it during the first year of its release. *S'agapo* (*I Love You,* 1971), starring Aliki Vougiouklaki, took second place with 393,137 tickets in the first-run movie theatres of Athens and Pireaus. Reportedly, the Greek Ministry of Press attributed the success of Katsuridis's film to an 'outlawed machination of the Communist Party of Greece'.

Through the story of cowardly Thanassis and his brave sister, the makers of this film publicly and courageously aired a political message calling for resistance against dictators – whether domestic or foreign – and against totalitarian cultures of the nationalist or imperialist kind – both in their past forms and present legacies. In the film, the lives of Froso and Thanassis have become difficult and dangerous due to Hitler's 'Blitzkrieg', which, in 1941, annexed Greece to the occupied territories of the Third Reich. Inflation increased dramatically and the buying power of the drachma was reduced to nothing when the Germans covered their campaign and occupation expenses in Greece from the coffers of the Greek government. Famine spread following the requisition and shipment of food supplies and raw materials from Greece to Germany, worsening with the blockade of Greece by the allied powers. Work at the factory would earn Thanassis his daily ration of food which he could bring home and share with his sister.

Thanassis's behavior is driven by the fear of being slaughtered in reprisals that weakened the will of some Greeks to resist the Axis powers, and the fear of succumbing to the famine that killed tens of thousands of Greeks during the occupation. The themes of famine and slaughter combine when Thanassis, on the way home from the factory, first picks up the scent of a meat-with-onion stew and traces it to Mr Vasilis's neighborhood tavern; and then, on his way out of the tavern, he sees a speeding motorcycle with two German soldiers – one driving and the other firing his submachine gun – that is racing towards him. Thanassis runs for his life. What must be the longest and most famous chase in Greek cinema begins because Thanassis, who dashes through a backyard into the next street, is unaware of the fact that the German soldiers are not chasing after him, but are in hot pursuit of a young Greek man who is also running for his life.

During the chase, the tragic figure of the brave young Greek man and the comic figure of cowardly Thanassis criss-cross, in this 'tragic comedy' (Katsuridis's term), before they are hunted down. The motorcycle catches up with both of them on the street where Thanassis lives. Thanassis who is running at full speed, passes an old man and two starving boys before he knocks himself unconscious when he fails to notice that the garden gate to his apartment is closed. Instead of helping him up, the boys devour the food ration in his lunch pail, scrape up the crumbs that were spilled on the sidewalk and run off. The young Greek man, in a last effort to dodge the motorcycle at his heels, climbs up a wall to jump down in a fenced courtyard and, for a very brief hanging moment, is no longer a moving target. It is at this moment that the German soldier shoots him dead. Unmoved by this incident, the old man picks up Thanassis's lunch pail and wanders off.

This suspenseful manhunt in the streets of Athens turned an unarmed young Greek man into 'dead meat,' but also presented a dinner opportunity for two hungry boys. The well-known Greek expression, 'I will cook you with onions' ('Tha se kano me ta kremidakia') is repeated in various forms throughout the film. More importantly, however, it becomes a visual metaphor that affects plot development and connects several emotionally-charged scenes – especially those in which the powerful imperialist military machine renders its victims helpless and then takes away their humanity and dignity. The point, however, that this film ingeniously drives home is that dehumanisation is a two-way street, affecting the degradation of both victims and victimisers – whether they are Italian guards, German cooks, Gestapo officers, Greek collaborators, two famished boys, an old man or Thanassis. Because of this, it is not surprising that Thanassis does not show any interest in making inquiries about the slaughter of the young

Greek man in his neighborhood, and is more interested in returning to the tavern where the Greeks, who are German collaborators, have finished eating. He finds evidence that they were served meat. Thanassis picks up the evidence in one hand and a knife in the other, and threatens the tavern owner. 'I'll slaughter you,' Thanassis says, 'and I'll cook you with onions' ('Tha se sfakso ke tha se kano me ta kremidakia'). Mr Vasilis admits that he cooked meat for the German collaborators, but he lies when he says that the meat was a hare, not Mrs Cleopatra's pet cat. Thanassis rushes over to their table and devours the leftovers in a few seconds. Next, he runs into the kitchen and, with a piece of bread, wipes off the bottom of the empty pot.

The thin line between dignity and degradation is crossed again in court by Thanassis, the judge and Mr Vassilis's defense attorney. The defense attorney claims that, anatomically, one cannot tell the difference between a skinned cat and a skinned hare. Thanassis, in turn, thoughtlessly testifies that the hare was a Persian. And the judge, who tries to supplement his caloric intake by nibbling on raisins, takes Thanassis to the side and asks him if cooked cats taste as good as cooked hares.

Degradation prevails in the prison when the Italian guards find out that, except for Thanassis, the rest of the Greek resistance fighters had escaped. They beat up Thanassis by mercilessly banging his head against the wall. However, when the Italian guards begin hitting each other and one of them bangs his head against a large ceramic jar, Thanassis instinctively places his hat between the head and the hard clay to protect him from concussion. This act of kindness does not prevent the Gestapo and the Italians from taking Thanassis to the torture chamber where he is tortured to the tunes of Mozart's *Le nozze di Figaro*, a German opera with an Italian libretto. At long last, a speck of dignity is temporarily restored when a group of Greek prostitutes, who were locked up because they had refused to keep the German and Italian soldiers company, help Thanassis escape disguised as a 'dumb broad'.

Thanassis would never have agreed to possessing, reading or disseminating subversive literature against German and Italian occupiers – let alone consenting to become a courier of copies of *The Liberator*. He even tells his sister how insane and hopelessly dangerous it is for people to join the Resistance. She replies that he is not any saner for not joining the Resistance. Annoyed by her indifference to his point of view, Thanassis asks her to turn off the radio. In the middle of his sentence, he realises that his sister is a member of the Greek Resistance, and more importantly, that she is endangering him by hiding a radio in his apartment and by listening to a BBC broadcast in Greek about the war developments. Froso refuses to turn the radio off. 'Have you gone insane?' Thanassis protests. Scared out of his wits, he tells her that he will not tolerate underground activities in his home. 'Very well,' Froso replies, 'I will collect my things and leave tomorrow. The entire world has awakened and only you are still fast asleep.' Thanassis's response reveals his motive and fear. 'You want me to wake up?' he asks, 'If I wake up, they'll stand me up against an execution wall, and they will put me to sleep once and for all.' He takes a copy of *The Liberator* to the kitchen with his and destroys it in the flames of the burner.

Freedom's premium for Thanassis has increased dramatically since he last tasted the left-over bones of the Persian cat. He is imprisoned for a second time because he ran away with Hans when the cook was seen handing out sardines wrapped in copies of *The Liberator*. When Hans is tortured and killed, Thanassis escapes from prison disguised as a German soldier and follows the convoy, which has orders to search his apartment. On the way to his apartment, Thanassis sees a puppy trying to cross the street, and stops his motorcycle, forcing the entire convoy to stop behind him. He dismounts, picks up the puppy and carries it to the sidewalk. He returns to his motorcycle and the convoy resumes its course.

The struggle for freedom is presented by director Katsuridis as a daily affair in a series of 'little' acts of defiance (as in the case of Froso) and 'great' acts of endurance (as in the case of Thanassis). What elevates this 'tragic comedy' is the arresting simplicity of its direction that does not historicise the experience of totalitarianism in Greece – both imperialism and nation-alism in their fascist, Nazi and praetorian variations – from 1941 to the 1971, and does not limit the presence of totalitarianism and its agents in Greece to the past. *What Did You Do in the War, Thanassis?* emphasises that the war against totalitarianism is not over and that freedom fighters must be saluted for taking a brave stand at all times. The film ends with the Greek national anthem, praising the Greeks as glorious freedom fighters over centuries.

Admittedly, Thanassis Vengos did not construct Greek masculine bravery (*levendia*) in the manner that was constructed by other actors around the same period of time, like Manos Katrakis. The comic persona of Thanassis is closer to that of Karaghiozis whose frequent self-referential praise 'What a brave guy!' ('E re levendia!') made people laugh at or with the irony and the paradox of his situation. This type of irony was missing from the bulk of films in the third quarter of the twentieth century because they stuck to the melodramatic construction of Greek bravery by featuring incredible heroic deeds that exploited the actual anxiety and waning self-confidence of the viewers. Thanassis Vengos's screen persona was closer to the hard-working Greek everyman – honest, naïve, cowardly and kind – who, in order to survive, has to keep up with a rapidly changing world.

Between 1969 and 1982, Katsuridis directed nine films with Thanassis Vengos in the leading role. Following *What Did You Do in the War, Thanassis?*, Katsuridis and Vengos made *Thanassi, pare t'oplo su* (*Thanassis Get Your Gun*, 1972), their second 'comic tragedy'; *O Thanassis sti hora tis sfaliaras* (*Thanassis in the Land of Slaps*, 1976), which became their second blockbuster; *O palavos kosmos tu Thanassi* (*The Crazy World of Thanassis*, 1979); *O falakros mathitis* (*The Bald Student*, 1979); *Vengos, o trelos Kamikazi* (*Vengos, the Mad Kamikaze*, 1980); and *O Thanassis ke to katarameno fidi* (*Thanassis and the Damned Snake*, 1982). During their long collaboration, Katsuridis's directorial style and Vengos's acting style each developed, inspiring a fruitful mutual influence.

**Stratos E. Constantinidis**

# EVDOKIA

ALEXIS DAMIANOS, GREECE, 1971

*Evdokia* (Alexis Damianos, 1971) recounts an episode from the life of a beautiful young prostitute who makes a desperate effort to escape her destiny. The film follows the titular Evdokia's affair and subsequent marriage to Yiorgos, a sergeant of the Greek army. Mainly due to Evdokia's trade, their relationship immediately faces the mockery of Yiorgos's fellow soldiers and the hostility of Evdokia's entourage; their marriage cannot withstand the social pressure it is subjected to and comes to a dramatic end with serious consequences for both protagonists.

The opening shots of the film present a view of the Attican landscape – dry, barren and rather inhospitable – as Maria, an aging friend and supposedly a former prostitute, is on her way to pay a visit to Evdokia. During that visit, Maria, in a highly symbolic fashion, predicts a troubled future for Evdokia. That same night, Evdokia and Yiorgos, accompanied by a fellow soldier, meet for the first time in a rundown tavern. Evdokia, a frequent visitor, is with her pimp and his friends, a particularly aggressive group. As Yiorgos dances and openly courts Evdokia, a fight breaks out between him and Evdokia's pimp. The two soldiers escape unharmed and return to the barracks. As they are leaving the tavern, a delighted Evdokia, noticeably flattered by the fight, warns them that the landlord has made a phone call to the military police. On their way back to the station, Dimitris, Yiorgos's friend, informs him of Evdokia's trade.

The next morning, Evdokia visits the barracks as Yiorgos leads his men through a series of exercises. She stands outside the fence, watching the drill. The soldiers notice her and start making jokes to the disdain of Yiorgos, who asks Dimitris to tell him how he knows Evdokia. Again, he will not be satisfied with Dimitris' portentous reply. 'I know her,' he says, implying that his 'knowledge' comes from personal experience. Later that night Yiorgos visits Evdokia at her house. When he arrives, he finds the pimp threatening Evdokia with a knife; Yiorgos chases the pimp away. Evdokia and Yiorgos spend the night and all of the next day together, a period presented as the most idyllic and pleasant time of their relationship. They go out in the hills where Yiorgos proposes to her. After a momentary pause of disbelief, she accepts.

On the day of the wedding, Evdokia has summoned her family and the whole group is waiting for the groom. But Yiorgos fails to show up. Evdokia is extremely distraught. She remains in her room and refuses to talk to anyone for days. Her only companion is her older friend, Maria. Yiorgos is soon back to express his regret and apologise, which she accepts. However, marriage fails to improve their situation. People, especially Yiorgos's fellow soldiers, cannot take the marriage seriously and treat it with disrespect. The difficulties continue, putting pressure on their relationship.

Having nearly completed his military service, Yiorgos is about to leave the army. One morning, however, after they have slept together, he disappears. Evdokia, bitterly disappointed, returns to prostitution. A few days later, Yiorgos turns up. Their feelings are apparent, but they are both too discouraged and disillusioned to hold a proper conversation and Yiorgos leaves again. Three days later, Maria unexpectedly tells Evdokia that she saw Yiorgos in the same tavern they once met. Evdokia hurries to the tavern, where they have a fight, as Yiorgos is drunk and flirts with another woman in precisely the same fashion as he once did with Evdokia.

Evdokia tries to kill herself by swallowing the pieces of a broken mirror she pulls out of her purse, but he stops her. They leave the tavern together; Yiorgos, despite his apparent drunkenness, tries to reassure Evdokia that everything will be fine from now on. All of a sudden, Evdokia's pimp arrives at the scene with his gang and they attack Yiorgos. In a fight that lasts several minutes they eventually run him over with their truck and then severely beat him. As they hear the police arriving, they disappear leaving Yiorgos to die but taking Evdokia with them. In the closing sequence of the film they drive around Athens with no apparent destination.

*Evdokia* is the second film of Alexis Damianos, a director who made few films but who nonetheless enjoys a position of high esteem in Greek cinema. He was born in Athens in 1921 and studied at the Drama School of the National Theatre and at the Department of Philosophy at the University of Athens. He then worked as an actor for both cinema and theatre, wrote a number of plays and directed three films. His first contact with cinema was as an actor, starring in *O Kleftis* (*The Thief*, 1965) by Pantelis Voulgaris and in *O fovos* (*Fear*, 1966) by Kostas Manoussakis, before going on to direct his first film, *Mehri to plio* (*Until the Ship Sails*) in 1966.

*Until the Ship Sails* tells the story of a Greek emigrant as he leaves Greece and of his successive encounters with three women. Artfully directed, it won the prize for Best Foreign Film at the 1967 Hyeres festival in France and was awarded the Golden Apollo by the Greek

Union of Film Critics in 1968. *Evdokia* was his second and most successful film. In 1995, he returned to cinema to direct *Iniohos* (*The Charioteer*), a three-hour film, mostly remembered for the difficulties it faced throughout its long production. Telling the life story of a partisan and spanning over fifty years of Greek history it was a deeply political film, which was awarded the annual Ministry of Culture prize. Damianos has also published three theatrical plays and acted for television.

Originally entitled *The Prostitute and the Soldier*, *Evdokia* was at first censored for its provocative content, although the ban was eventually lifted. It was an exceptionally successful endeavour, especially if one takes into consideration the bleak conditions in Greece at the time. It sold an impressive 70,852 tickets in the year of its release, and won the French prize, *Cineclubs*. Maria Vassiliou (Evdokia) won the prize for Best Actress at the prestigious film festival in Thessaloniki in 1971. In 1985, *Evdokia* was voted among the ten best Greek films of all time by the Pan-Hellenic Union of Film Critics. In 1993, it was included in the list of fifty most representative Greek films and shown as part of the Greek cinema retrospective in New York. In 1995 it was selected and screened as one of the hundred most representative Greek films by the Centre Georges Pompidou in Paris.

*Evdokia* occupies a special position in the history of Greek cinema, not only because of its artistic properties, but also because of the politically sensitive time it was made. Commercial Greek cinema had been booming in the early 1960s, with the period 1966–67 reaching record levels of production (117 features) and attendance (137 million cinema visits). With the coup of 1967, Greece came under the rule of a military junta that immediately imposed strict censorship rules. The repercussions of the policies of the dictatorship were felt across the country, as well as in each and every aspect of cultural and cinematic production. Along with the introduction of television, which in many ways destroyed the existing popular film industry, the commercial output of Greece's film production companies suffered a great blow and the production shrunk dramatically (down to 47 films in the period 1974–75 and further down to 16 in the period 1976–77). Greek cinema soon turned into a wasteland, lacking in terms of production, reception and, above all, in a clear sense of national identity and direction.

However, at the time *Evdokia* was filmed in 1970, significant new developments were already taking place. In 1971 several younger directors satisfied the need for a new, innovative national cinema, in the tradition of the French Nouvelle Vague and other European cinematic movements. The New Greek Cinema, as it came to be called later, made its appearance around 1971, with the release of films such as Theo Angelopoulos's *Anaparastassi* (*Reconstruction*,

1970) and *Meres Tou 36* (*Days of '36*, 1972), Voulgaris's *To Proxenio tis Annas* (*The Engagement of Anna*, 1972) and Damianos's *Evdokia* which constituted the foundations of the movement. New Greek Cinema has since been regularly characterised by its intention to emphasise the artistic aspects, its political involvement, its innovative drive and, up to a point, its devotion to the fate of the nation, often explicitly revealing concerns that may have resided in the Greek psyche for decades without ever finding expression. By attempting to contain expression and subdue artistic creation, the dictatorial regime became in many ways the catalyst that freed or even generated the political aspects of Greek filmmaking and had, subsequently, a reverse effect from the one desired. Thus, the significance of the emergence of New Greek Cinema lies not only in its artistic achievements but also in its revisionist approach to historiography and politics. Yet, despite the critical acclaim, New Greek Cinema has never been truly popular among wider audiences. This has resulted in a particular lack of continuity and coherence, mainly due to the absence of suitable conditions, as far as funding and production is concerned.

*Evdokia*'s place in the canon of New Greek Cinema is non-negotiable, due to the film's quality and the crucial timing of its production. Damianos's gritty, at times even crude, cinematography, however, also emerges as an exception to a cinematic movement largely characterised by its emphasis on style. *Evdokia* may not display the stylistic flawlessness of Angelopoulos's films; it manages, however, to generate an unequivocal balance between content and aesthetics. Damianos has been able to keep proximity to the spirit of everyday life with its mundane preoccupations and characters and at the same time to keep his work away from the trap of excessive dramatisation. His simple and innovative approach to filmmaking established his reputation as a leading Greek *auteur* and has rendered him irreplaceable in the canon of New Greek Cinema.

In terms of filming techniques, *Evdokia* is influenced by Italian neorealism. The Italian movement had a great impact on Greek cinematography, not only due to the geographical proximity of the two countries, but also due to the influence that neorealism exerted on world cinema. Earlier attempts towards the establishment of a Greek neorealism had included films such as *Pikro Psomi* (*Bitter Bread*, Grigoris Grigoriou, 1951), *To Xypolito Tagma* (*The Barefoot Battalion*, Gregg C. Tallas, 1954) and *Synoikia to Oneiro* (Alekos Alexandrakis, 1961). In accordance with neorealism's main objective to present issues of concern to the working class these films draw their thematic concerns from the contemporaneous Greek reality (German occupation, poverty, unemployment).

The casting choice of non-professionals in *Evdokia* (both Maria Vassiliou and Yiorgos Koutouzis were not professional actors), the script theme and the simplicity of the plot, the location shooting in peripheral urban areas (in Lavrio, Attica), suggest that this film, characterised by intense and even cruel frankness, was also conceived and executed in the tradition of Neorealism. Indeed, *Evdokia* bears direct parallels with Federico Fellini's *Le notti di Cabiria* (*Nights of Cabiria*, 1957), not only in regard to the main motif of both films, that of the disheartened prostitute, but also in relation to the isolation of the setting and the barrenness of the landscape. Interesting parallels can also be drawn between *Evdokia* and other Italian films of the early 1960s, like Pier Paolo Pasolini's *Accattone* (1961) or Bernardo Bertolucci's *La Commare secca* (*The Grim Reaper*, 1962), again with reference to representations of prostitution and the barren landscape at the city's periphery.

*Evdokia* takes place at the margins of the capital, in Lavrio, a small working-class port in the outskirts of Athens. The location immediately becomes a focal point with regard to the symbolic aspects of the film. The marginalisation of both characters and location is central to the narrative. It is because of the total and unconditional exclusion imposed on the whole of the filmic representation that the attempt of the young couple to stay together appears so improbable, and this is skilfully reflected in the inhospitable landscape.

As critic Vasiles Raphaelides suggests, *Evdokia* constitutes a conscious attempt towards a critique of urban ethics. Yiorgos's proposal to Evdokia marks the turning point in the fortunes of the two protagonists. Their common aspiration to adopt middle-class practices (marriage) will not be successfully realised within their working-class, even lumpen, environment, which defines and limits their actions and prospects. Their failure will be dramatic. Evdokia will return to her previous life of prostitution and exploitation. We never learn how her relationship to Yiorgos will affect her in the long run, as we only witness this very specific episode of her life. It would not be unfounded, nevertheless, to propose that by returning back to her old lifestyle nothing much has changed except for her realisation that this state of affairs cannot be escaped. In this sense and as far as the role of fate is concerned, *Evdokia* is reminiscent of a classical Greek tragedy where fate determines the tragic moves of the protagonists and the futility of their actions. Yiorgos, on the other hand, will be severely punished for his 'hubris' and excessively daring arrogance. Yet fate here is much more a manifestation of the inexorable social determinism that remains the main defining force of the protagonists' fortunes and a reminder of the characters' fundamental powerlessness to be in command of their lives.

The passionate attraction of the couple collapses under the weight of social convention, and the instinctive nature of their conduct leads them into conflict with well-established, institutionalised boundaries, against which they stand no chance. However pessimistic and bleak the conclusion of the film may be, Damianos does not search for scapegoats. The process of the rejection of the young couple is a systemic one and no single character appears to bear any individual responsibility. It is the urban value system that, according to Raphaelides, Damianos seeks to denounce with *Evdokia*.

Maria, Evdokia's only friend and mentor, plays an important role in the film. When alone, Maria reminisces her past in black and white flashbacks, suggesting that she was abandoned by her sailor husband and never recovered; it appears she was also engaged in prostitution at one time; she still longs for love but she can no longer sell her body as her flesh is sagging and her face is wrinkled. Her evident suffering over aging and bitter nostalgia over the past present a fast-forward glimpse into Evdokia's only possible future. The other secondary personage in the film, Evdokia's pimp whose name is also Yiorgos, is, despite the severity of his actions, presented in a sympathetic manner. It would not be an exaggeration to argue that he is seen as a victim of the circumstances in the same way that Evdokia or Yiorgos are.

Some of the most important scenes in *Evdokia* take place in the local tavern, a quintessential setting for Greek cinema, as seen in a range of films, from *Stella* (Michael Cacoyannis, 1955; see Dan Georgakas's chapter in this volume) and *Pote tin Kyriaki* (*Never on Sunday*, Jules Dassin, 1960) through *Parangelia* (Pavlos Tassios, 1980) to *Ola ine dromos* (*It's a Long Road*, Pantelis Voulgaris, 1998). The tavern traditionally provides the atmospheric backdrop for passionate male dancing and plate-breaking, it is an enclosed arena preserved mostly for sweaty macho outbursts (and only occasionally for emancipatory assertions by females).

The 'Greekness' that the film demonstrates is another issue widely discussed in relation to *Evdokia* and in particular within the context of New Greek Cinema. Many of the concerns expressed in the film are characteristic of the troubled social reality of Greece at the time. Yiorgos comes from a village and, albeit reluctantly, would have to go back. He considers leaving for Germany in order to find a job there. Emigration was indeed an option adopted by many Greeks with no opportunities in a country with high unemployment and no realistic prospects of improvement. Excessive internal migration towards the cities and especially towards Athens is another key issue in the demographic history of Greece; the theme of migration thus occupied a rather prominent position in the cinema of the 1960s and 1970s.

Another important symbolic aspect of Yiorgos's character is his involvement with the army. The choreographed stylish scenes showing Yiorgos engaged in military drills with his unit are directly reminiscent to the later but wider-seen *Beau travail* (Claire Denis, 1999). Yiorgos is doing his obligatory military service; his life abruptly ends at a time when he is nearly done and would have to make some critical decisions for the future. It is in this context that the scene of Yiorgos's emblematic death at the end of the film stands out: not only because of its exceptional cinematic quality, extensively discussed in the critical literature about the film, but also because of the particular symbolic weight that it carries.

As film historian Yiannis Soldatos points out, the sequence where the pimp and his gang are fighting with the soldier, with Evdokia screaming helplessly in desperation, is one of the most moving scenes in Greek cinema. This is essentially the last scene (not of the film, but definitely of the narrative); it provides the ideal example of Damianos's approach to filmmaking – even though the events that evolve on the screen are extremely harsh, the camera keeps a critical distance, not getting involved at any point, thus creating and maintaining a certain degree of detachment between the events and the spectator. Thus, the emotional involvement of the 'gaze' is severely hampered by the persistent preference to use long shots and the insistent rejection of point-of-view shots. The only point-of-view shot used by Damianos in this scene is a momentary one, on the part of Yiorgos, as he suddenly sees the lights of the truck coming onto him. This subjective shot is used to express the raw crudity and the coarseness of the moment.

A very particular generation and an exceptionally sensitive period of Greek history have found their expression in *Evdokia*. At the time of the film's making Greece was in the middle of the military dictatorship, which had started in 1967 and was to last until 1974. The film reveals the intrusive nature of the army in the period of the junta as it sets Yiorgos against a questionable set of values imposed on him against his will. His absurd death at the moment of his discharge from the army represents Damianos's scepticism of a future free Greece.

Last but not least, the most powerful of all symbolic identifications in the film is that between Evdokia and Greece. The representation of Greece as a prostitute, unable to take her fate in her own hands, constantly trapped and exploited by powers beyond her control, has been a popular trope of Greek writing from various periods; this comparison is also made by Soldatos. The self-destructiveness, which often characterises Evdokia's behaviour, is a manifestation of the despondency that governs her life. Again, Evdokia's failure to escape her destiny is a clear indication of Damianos's pessimistic outlook to the prospect of a really independent

Greece. In this, the director clearly has encapsulated the visions, hopes and anxieties experienced by many Greeks during the dictatorship era.

The use of music in *Evdokia* is particularly significant. The score is by Manos Loizos, a popular composer who has encapsulated the atmosphere and the mood of the film in superb melodies characterised by strength and intensity. The composer has made skilful use of the rhythms that are believed to embody the working-class musical preferences, like Zembekiko. The soundtrack was a commercial success and is considered a classic even today. The exterior settings of the film are large open spaces, often characterised by a distinctive, even haunting, brightness. When Yiorgos and Evdokia go out, they do not head towards the city centre but go to the mountain and the beach instead. Apart from their desire to be alone, these choices speak of the impetuous and impulsive nature of their relationship and its incompatibility with the urban patterns of courtship. The narrative is largely driven by the clash between the protagonists' instinctive drives (sexuality, violence) and their respective institutionalised forms (prostitution, the military). The interior settings are sparsely furnished and rather open, not strictly defined. The bed appears to be the centre of all life events in both Maria's and Evdokia's rooms. Although the filming is done in colour for the most part, black and white is used for the flashbacks that are referencing Maria's past memories. The film also turns to black and white for the final scene, probably to suggest the bleak state of affairs, when the group of those who just beat Yiorgos to death roams the streets of Athens.

*Evdokia* is remembered as an authentic and insightful portrayal of life in Greece during the junta period; it is a film that is representative of Damianos's ability to encapsulate the harshness of the period whilst at the same time allowing the dramatic intensity of its tragic plot to develop fully within the same cinematic entity. As a filmic creation on the other hand, *Evdokia* does not reach the full artistic consistency of New Greek Cinema, but Damianos's passionate and convincing approach to direction makes up for the possible technical shortcomings. *Evdokia* is a film which is extraordinarily original and frank; it is an exceptionally straightforward film in that it displays obvious tendencies towards cinematic realism without actually demonstrating a coherent compliance with the axioms of this approach.

In conclusion, we should once again stress the multifaceted character of the film and make sure to indicate that it occupies a special position within the canon of Greek cinema. *Evdokia* is not only a highly artistic work of cinema but also one that has reached out to wider audiences and has been extremely popular with them. This is of great significance, especially if one takes into consideration the fact that many of the masterpieces of New Greek Cinema,

while celebrated within the festival circuit, have not managed to reach the hearts and minds of ordinary Greeks. *Evdokia*'s appeal goes significantly beyond the art-house cinemas and, seen in this context, the film acquires an even greater importance. It is a pity that a director like Alexis Damianos, who is one of the few to find the balance between the highly artistic and the popular, has been largely absent from the Greek film production scene. The result is that films like *Evdokia* have remained rare and singular occurrences.

**John Papargyris**

REFERENCES

Raphaelides, V. (1995) *Ellinikos Kinematografos: Kritike (1965–1995)*. Athens: Aigokeros.
Soldatos, Y. (1993) *Alexis Damianos*. Athens: Aigokeros.

# VALTER BRANI SARAJEVO WALTER DEFENDS SARAJEVO

10

## HAJRUDIN 'ŠIBA' KRVAVAC, YUGOSLAVIA, 1972

It is late 1944. In occupied Yugoslavia, Sarajevo has become an important refuelling post for the German army, which is withdrawing from the Balkans and passing through the mountains of Bosnia. The German command plans a complex operation to secure its army supplies; the intelligence service is doing everything to ensure secrecy and safety.

The opening sequence shows a confidential meeting of top German officers discussing details of the operation. A mysterious, unbeatable Bosnian, a charismatic undercover resistance leader known by the code-name Walter, is identified as the biggest threat to the German operation. Famous all over the country, Walter appears to be the only one who could jeopardise the plan, so even the Nazi generals fear him. The German commander of Sarajevo admits that he has been searching for Walter since his arrival in Bosnia a year ago yet has not been able to learn much about him: 'No one knows who he is. I have come to believe that Walter is a ghost. That he actually doesn't exist.'

The resistance movement in Sarajevo operates across the entire city. Citizens of all classes and ethnicities – Muslims, Serbs, Croats and Jews – take part in the underground activities: hiding communists, organising various sabotage operations and disobeying most of the German orders. When several members of the resistance are in danger of being identified, they are transferred to the territories liberated by Tito's Partisans.

Infiltrated by a traitor, one of the underground resistance groups is seriously shaken. Betrayal after betrayal follows: nobody knows where intelligence is leaking and who is working for whom. Everybody is under suspicion.

Rumour has it that Walter is a courageous, daring and smart man, inventive and witty, yet hardly anybody knows what he looks like. That is why a Gestapo agent, Condor, finds it easy to infiltrate the Sarajevo resistance team under the false pretence he is the famous Walter. Condor hints that a young photographer, Zis (Ljubiša Samardžić), could be the traitor. Yet Zis, who has already gained the sympathy of the audience by teasing German soldiers, does his best to prove that he is, in fact, a trustworthy patriot. Towards the end of the film, Zis will become one of the closest collaborators of the real Walter.

A newcomer from Mostar, who will later be revealed as the real Walter (Velimir 'Bata' Živojinović), joins the group. Smart and uncompromising, he finds out that a young woman, Mirna, has betrayed the group and has been recruited as a spy following her capture and torture in prison. Even though she confesses and tries to correct her mistake, Mirna is soon killed by the treacherous Condor (who still pretends to be Walter).

At the same time, another drama takes place in the city. Azra, the only child of a lonely old Muslim watchmaker, is also involved in the underground resistance. One night she is killed in action. The next morning her body is dumped in the city square along with the corpses of other dead resistance fighters. The families are supposed to claim the dead, but the German soldiers are ordered to shoot anyone approaching. When the devastated father comes forward to take Azra's body home, he is surrounded and protected by the crowd. Faced with such a degree of solidarity among local people, the German soldiers give up their orders. The agrieved father, who also works for the resistance, will also lose his life soon. But he will manage to rescue the real Walter after confronting the traitor in the yard of a picturesque mosque in Sarajevo.

While Condor continues sabotaging the resistance movement, the real Walter not only has to uncover the traitor but also to disrupt German fuel distribution. The fuel transport is disguised as an ordinary wounded soldiers transfer, but the heavy security raises Walter's suspicion and he soon realises that the train, which will use the narrow gauge railway from Sarajevo to the nearby town of Višegrad, carries something more dangerous. Walter soon manages to penetrate the convoy, which indeed turns out to be the fuel cargo. One of the top German generals is in charge of this secret manoeuvre. Walter and his closest war companion, Suri, board the train and are joined by the charming and daring Zis. The three Sarajevan heroes attack the German soldiers and a fierce battle ensues, which the three heroes survive through their bravery and military skill, in outflanking their enemy.

Following the success of the partisans' sabotage on the fuel line, the German general is forced into retirement. He is shown standing on a hill overlooking Sarajevo and commenting to his successor: 'From the moment I arrived in Bosnia, I was trying to trace Walter; now I am leaving and I think I know who he is.' The new officer is flabbergasted: 'You do?' 'Yes, I do. Have a good look at this city! ... This is Walter.'

The end credits roll, accompanied by glorious music, over a marvellous panoramic shot of Sarajevo and its surrounding mountains.

\*\*\*

The fourth film by Bosnian director Hajrudin 'Šiba' Krvavac, *Valter Brani Sarajevo* (*Walter Defends Sarajevo*, 1972), along with two other films, *Diverzanti* (*The Demolition Squad*, 1967) and *Most* (*The Bridge*, 1969), forms a loose trilogy of romanticised war dramas inspired by true events concerning the Sarajevo underground resistance during World War Two that made the director famous not only at home but abroad as well. All these films are bound by a similar approach. They were not so much the grand epic war spectacles commonly made at the time in former Yugoslavia but rather enthralling populist stories of mythical bravery displayed by ordinary humans against the background of adverse historical events.

*Walter Defends Sarajevo* was made at a time when Yugoslavia was undergoing important liberal reforms: it was a period of national 'awakening', which also included attempts at political decentralisation and cultural emancipation. The most pronounced political and cultural movement, usually referred to as the Croatian Spring, had taken place in Croatia in the late 1960s and had profoundly impacted the whole country. The central political establishment in Belgrade reacted to these emancipation tendencies in the republics by interfering in the work of filmmakers. Many films were censored; prominent politicians were dismissed. About that time, big changes occurred in Bosnia and Hercegovina as well. The Muslim population of Yugoslavia was officially recognised as a constitutive ethnic group (until then Muslims could define themselves only either as Serbs or Croats, or as 'undecided'). A dozen nationalities lived in Bosnia and Hercegovina; the largest ethnic groups were Muslims and Serbs (almost equally represented) with Croats close behind. Many of these people declared themselves simply as Yugoslavs, denying any national attribution. The idea of 'brotherhood and unity' was cherished and promoted in Bosnia mostly because of this intricate ethnic mixture.

Treating contemporary themes in film became quite a sensitive issue in the context of such turbulent politics. Filmmakers resorted to the 'safer' subject of glorifying the National Liberation War in Yugoslavia and the values it was based upon, themes that they were treating during the 1950s. As the only producer, the Yugoslav state had specific ideological requirements. As Croatian scholar Hrvoje Turković suggests, cinema was expected to present the advent of the socialist system as a 'historically necessary' and superior development, a requirement that implied the need to reassess past and present historical events. Partisan films – a sub-genre of war films in which the Liberation Movement of freedom fighters during World War Two was presented in a rather superlative manner – were particularly favoured. The place and the time of the specific war events would vary but the excessive idealisation and demagogic simplification would be a permanent feature. The clash between good (Partisans) and bad (Nazis and their collaborators) became imperative for every war film. Partisans were portrayed as people of extraordinary human qualities who sacrificed everything for higher goals while domestic traitors were pictured in the darkest tones available.

According to Turković's lucid observation, the poetics of the classical Western style at the time was compatible with the requirements of socialist realism. Yugoslavia was a country where the doctrine of socialist realism was never implemented as rigidly as in the countries of the Eastern Bloc; American and European films were shown in cinemas and filmmakers could use an assortment of narrative patterns without obviously defying the socialist realist doctrine. A dramatic storyline and individualised characters placed in the framework of the partisan struggle, done with the skill of a capable director like Krvavac, were just what was required from a partisan film.

Serbian scholar Nevena Daković describes the partisan films as 'red westerns'. She emphasises that if the American western is the most explicit example of mythologising American history, then the 'red western' plays the same function in the mythology surrounding the birth of socialist society. Both types of films, Daković suggests, are loaded with action scenes depicting the elevated dedication of tough freedom fighters and glorifying heroic myths even with some adjusting of historical facts.

The best examples for the conventional partisan genre are the films of Veljko Bulajić, the busiest director of partisan films. One of his first films, the popular *Kozara* (1962), takes place on the Kozara mountain in Bosnia, the site of one of World War Two's biggest battles. The drama shows how 35,000 partisans and 80,000 women and children, surrounded by the Germans in the spring of 1942, heroically manage to break out of the blockade. Bulajić's biggest hit, however, was the expensive blockbuster war spectacle *Bitka na Neretvi* (*The Battle of Neretva*, 1969), also based on a real event. The plot focuses on a partisan operation that involved destroying the bridge across the Neretva River, thus preventing the Germans from moving ahead and rescuing 4,500 typhus-infected soldiers to safe territory in Hercegovina (by carrying them over an improvised bridge that was built overnight).

Bulajić's movies were often realised in collaboration with several Yugoslav filmmaking centres, with the participation of actors and crewmembers from Zagreb, Belgrade, Sarajevo and, almost as a rule, from abroad. In order to gain international attention for the communist-glorifying war sagas, Bulajić would persuade the powers-that-be to entrust him with sizable budgets that would allow the casting of well-known foreign actors. *The Battle of Neretva*, for example, featured Yul Brynner, Orson Welles, Sergei Bondarchuk, Franco Nero, Sylva Koscina and others. The inflated budgets were balanced by the fact that most partisan films used the complimentary services of the Yugoslav Army, which readily supplied extras and resources. But even though Bulajić's war spectacles were given numerous awards, most of his films were perceived as straightforward and not particularly persuasive propaganda; they were praised only by the critical establishment close to the regime. The main audience for these films consisted of school children, who were taken to the cinemas in organised visits.

A year after *Walter Defends Sarajevo* was made, Stipe Delić, another Yugoslav director specialising in the partisan genre, released one of the biggest epic spectacles ever, *Sutjeska* (1973). This war saga revived the story of Marshall Tito's great combat leadership and focused on the famous partisan battle on the Bosnian River Sutjeska in which Tito was wounded. The production also used celebrated and costly foreign stars: Tito was played by Richard Burton while Orson Welles impersonated Sir Winston Churchill. Greek composer Mikis Theodorakis wrote a memorable score, and Greek actress Irene Papas gave an impressive performance. Nonetheless, *Sutjeska* never became popular with Yugoslav audiences.

In spite of the requirement to structure war films as glorious epics, Yugoslav cinema saw the release of many masterpieces on the war theme that did not comply with the official ideological recipe of glorious partisan representation. It is interesting that almost all of these films dealt with the revolution and the war from the perspective of intimate emotional experiences. The Croatian production *Ne okreći se sine* (*Don't Turn Back, My Son*, 1956) by Branko Bauer, for example, was a masterful psychological study on the uneasy relationship between father and son in times of parting along fault lines brought about by the war. The Serbian film *Tri* (*Three*, 1965) by Aleksandar Petrović was a moving triptych on wartime fear, uncertainty and determination, once again explored through the story of an individual (see Vlastimir Sudar's chapter on the film in this volume). *Jutro* (*Morning*, 1967), made by another Serbian director Puriša Djordjević, treated a story of love and betrayal during wartime through the destiny of a young girl.

The resistance action-adventure films, to which we should add the popular television series *Otpisani* (*The Written Off*, 1974) and *Povratak otpisanih* (*Written Off Return*, 1976) directed by Aleksandar Djordjević, were typical not only for Yugoslavia. Even without casting major international stars, countries like Romania and Bulgaria also produced similar films, sometimes for the big screen but more often as television series. Best-known examples of the genre include Sergiu Nicolaescu's *Ultimul cartuș* (*The Last Bullet*, 1973), *Un comisar acuza* (*A Police Inspector Calls*, 1973), *Revansa* (*Revenge*, 1978) and *Duelul* (*The Duel*, 1981), all starring

Nicolasescu himself as the invincible Commissar Modlovan. The popular Bulgarian television series *Na vseki kilometar* (*At Each Kilometer*, 1969–71), directed by Nedelcho Chernev and Lyubomir Sharlandzhiev and starring Stefan Danailov, was another key output of the resistance genre (along with other films by directors Zako Heskia and Nedelcho Chernev). The prototypes of these films were probably the hugely popular Polish television series *Czterej pancerni i pies* (*Four Tank Soldiers and a Dog*, 1966) and *Stawka wieksza niz zycie* (*More Than Life at Stake*, 1968).

*Walter Defends Sarajevo*'s success is due, to a large extent, to the director's skill in creating a formulaic dramaturgy which mimics American westerns while remaining faithful to many socialist creeds. Fearless partisan fighters, brave resistance members and courageous saboteurs are all portrayed as cartoon characters. They are young, dressed in well-ironed uniforms, morally pure and impeccably handsome (like the charming and witty Zis and his smart, proud and likable boss Walter). They are not blinded by fanaticism, they are neither communist fanatics nor nationalists; they are simply people standing on the side of the ultimate Good.

Krvavac's romanticised invincible heroes were very much comic book characters: not particularly realistic yet providing comfort by fighting for the weak, the poor and the unjustly endangered. In this sense, Walter is comparable to the invincible James Bond. His multiple abilities are emphasised in the last sequence of the film where he not only drives a car and a truck, but also takes over a train, then shoots skilfully using various weapons, speaks fluent German and engages in witty dialogue in the most dangerous situations. His heroic aura is created through the use of dramatic close-ups, edited together in an exquisite rhythm that would provide tense action while making references to the disturbing dilemmas and traumas of the hero's inner life.

A specific characteristic of Krvavac's approach to the partisan film was to leave the plot driven more by the personal dilemmas of the protagonists and not so much by the war. In his first feature work, a contribution to the omnibus film *Vrtlog* (*Vortex*, 1964), Krvavac co-directed (with Gojko Šipovac) the first part called *Otac* (*Father*). The plot evolved around the dramatic confrontation between a father and his two sons who happen to be on opposite sides in the war. The plot of his short film *Bridge* evolved around the moral dilemma faced by an architect who has to decide whether to help the Partisans by destroying his own masterpiece, a stunning bridge, or to refuse but thus assist the progress of the German Army into Yugoslav territory. Being the only person who knows the weak spots of the heavily guarded bridge, the architect (brilliantly played by Serbian actor Slobodan 'Cico' Perović) is at a moral crossroads, clearly knowing that whatever decision he takes, it will be a painful one for him. In *Demolition Squad*, Krvavac focused on the heroic accomplishment of eight young patriots who decide to risk their lives in order to destroy the closely observed facilities of the German air forces based at the Sarajevo airfield. The task seems almost impossible but this is the only way in which the besieged partisan troops can be set free.

As with these other war films, in *Walter Defends Sarajevo* camera angles, editing style and music were resourcefully used to emphasise the dramatic content of a particular scene, whether it is glorious, disturbing or funny. As in almost all other war films by Krvavac, the invincible duo played by popular stars Velimir 'Bata' Živojinović and Ljubisa Samardžić miraculously succeeds in outwitting and outsmarting German officers as well as in eliminating all obstacles coming from the SS-troops or local traitors. The pairing of Živojinović and Samardžić worked perfectly well with Yugoslav audiences: one of them tough, smart and serious and the other one charming, funny and handsome. Strengthened by the presence of a third fellow partisan – Suri, played by Slobodan Dimitrijević –Walter and Zis single-handedly changed the outcome of the war. No wonder that all of their other associates were, by default, witty, sympathetic, often clumsy ordinary men with whom the audience could identify (especially Zis, the character played by Samardžić).

Krvavac used dramatic exaggeration creatively, making even the most implausible scenes look not only acceptable but enjoyable. The more striking, humorous, brave and resourceful the Good Guys were shown, the uglier, machine-like, heartless or distressed the Bad Guys came across. In this way *Walter Defends Sarajevo* was no different to other partisan films. Good always beat evil at the end, no matter how impossible the odds at the beginning of the film may have appeared. Those fighting for the good cause would somehow be lucky at the very end, culminating into a situation where only three lucky and resourceful partisans would fight dozens of well-equipped German soldiers. The partisans, of course, would succeed in killing most of the soldiers easily, before destroying the target of the operation.

The film fell in line with the ideals of 'brotherhood and unity', as is clearly seen in the important scene where the crowd unanimously steps forward to confront the Germans and claim the bodies of the fallen resistance heroes, thus showing that the private loss has grown into a public one. This scene symbolised the solidarity of all nationalities in Sarajevo who stood together in the anti-fascist struggle. The importance of their unity was further emphasised by the triumphant score by Slovenian composer Bojan Adamič (who worked with Krvavac on all his war films). In another episode of solidarity, Walter and two of his associates are being chased by Germans; bystanders throw rubble in the path of the Germans and the metalworkers in the old Sarajevo shops (Baš-čaršija) spontaneously clatter with their hammers, thus securing the successful escape of the heroes.

As many other pioneers of cinema in former Yugoslavia, Hajrudin Krvavac came to film-making under the guidance received from influential communists. He did not possess film education and had to master his trade along the way. He started in 1948 with documentary reports on the rebuilding of the country. These reportages would be edited into the newsreel series *Mjesečnik* (*Monthly*), usually screened in theatres before the feature presentation. It was in this context that Krvavac made some very interesting documentaries. *Skidanje zara i feredže* (*Taking off the Veil*, 1949), for example, focused on the emancipation of Muslim women in Bosnia; the reconstruction of the railroads was tackled in *Uspomene s pruge* (*Memories from the Railway*, 1952). Although the genre did not invite an auteurist approach, even in these works Krvavac showed a talent for incorporating the small personal story into the bigger historical context, as well as a talent for superb editing rhythm. An adventurous and curious person, Krvavac even tried his hand at making puppet films, thus pioneering animation art in Bosnia and Hercegovina. Even today, his 13-minute puppet film *Miss Zelengrada* (*Miss of the Green City*, 1962), is a thrill to watch. Other Bosnian directors picked up animation in his footsteps, while Krvavac returned to his favoured subjects of the heroic war struggle during World War Two. He wrote most of his scripts himself or in collaboration with professional scriptwriters, mostly frequently Djordje Lebović. The stories were mainly spy plots about special partisan troops, or the exciting adventures of underground resistance heroes.

It is peculiar that Krvavac, who entered the resistance at the age of 17, never joined the Communist Party formally. He was a real communist at heart, an anti-fascist and, as he used to point out, an anarchist. For the specific style he developed, Krvavac was nicknamed the 'romantic' of the war film. Only once did he make a blockbuster-type war spectacle, *Partizanska eskadrila* (*The Partisans' Squadron*, 1979), which focused on the combat of the air forces in World War Two. Although he received a Silver Arena for this film at the National Film Festival in Pula, it is considered his weakest work.

*Walter Defends Sarajevo*, on the contrary, was extremely well-liked. It is one of the most popular Yugoslav films; enjoyed and celebrated by peers, critics and audiences alike.

Walter was set to become a cult figure for the younger generations, ridiculed but liked. Younger generations would find the comic-book psychological characterisation of the heroes amusing and exciting. Lines of the film would be quoted, mocked, paraphrased and thus kept alive in Sarajevo. During the 1980s, a well-known rock band Zabranjeno pušenje (No Smoking) devoted a song to Walter. Besides, most of the cast were best-loved actors from Serbia, Bosnia and Kosovo. Young Emir Kusturica, set to become a famous director in his own right, was involved as an extra in the film.

Apart from the good reception at home, *Walter Defends Sarajevo* was sold to sixty countries and seen (according to the statistics of Yugoslavia Film) by hundreds of millions of people across the world. Today, three decades after Krvavac's films were made, they are still fanatically adored in China, and are so popular that, reportedly, children were named after their characters, songs from the films were sung by common folk and in the city of Szechuan, some streets were named after actors from Krvavac's movies. Together with *Bridge*, it is one of the most popular films of all time. Its protagonist even became a role model for many youngsters in communist China. A popular brand of Chinese beer is named Walter and carries the picture of the main actor on the label. Velimir 'Bata' Živojinović, who, according to some Chinese newspapers, was the second most popular person in the country after Mao Zedong, played the main role in both of the films. Currently there is an initiative to build a statue to actor Bruce Lee in the Bosnian city of Mostar and, in parallel, a statue of Walter in China.

Hajrudin 'Šiba' Krvavac died during the war in Bosnia and Hercegovina (1992–95). In spite of a weak heart he had refused to leave the besieged city of Sarajevo and, once again, chose to stay with his fellow Sarajevans in times of starvation, water and electricity shortages and heavy shelling. In this misery, he was thrilled to see, as he pointed out in one of his last interviews, that in the first days of Sarajevo's tragedy people protested on the streets shouting the slogan 'We are all Walter!'

**Rada Šešić**

REFERENCES

Daković, N. (2000) 'Rat u kuci ogledala', *Profemina*, 23–4, 211–21.

Turković, H. (1998) 'Against the Odds', *Catalogue of the Croatian Film Week in Lantaren/Venster*. Rotterdam, 3–4.

# KOZIYAT ROG GOAT'S HORN

## METHODI ANDONOV, BULGARIA, 1972

The Rhodopi mountains, eighteenth century. Bulgarian people are suffering under the violent rule of Ottoman occupiers. A group of Turks rape KaraIvan's wife while he herds his sheep in the mountains. His daughter, little Maria, witnesses her mother's attack and subsequent death.

This act of extreme violence defines the fate of the shepherd and his daughter. As he sets his house on fire, KaraIvan solemnly vows to avenge his wife's death and lost honour. He takes little Maria into the forest and raises her like a man, so that she can avenge her mother's murderers. Becoming a threatening weapon in her father's hands, young Maria receives her life education in situations that require typical male behaviour. She gradually begins to feel comfortable and confident in the new role that KaraIvan has allotted her – to be strong and merciless toward the objects of vengeance.

Years later, wearing a male sheepskin outfit and with her hair cut short, Maria stalks and kills the rapists one by one, with a sharpened goat's horn. At the same time, Maria transforms into a woman, something her father has denied her and a change that erodes her dedication to her acts of violence. One day she meets a young shepherd and falls in love; the feminine in her prevails and she is no longer capable of carrying out her mission. The encounter with the shepherd puts an end to KaraIvan's power over Maria; she has now unreservedly succumbed to her feelings. Hoping to bring back his daughter, KaraIvan kills the shepherd. After discovering her lover's dead body, Maria sets the barn she finds him in on fire and, pushed to utter despair, throws herself onto the flames. KaraIvan attempts to save her but to no avail. Confronted with the raw might of Nature on the one hand and his tragic helplessness to overcome evil on the other, KaraIvan climbs the highest hill, clutching Maria's lifeless body in his hands. In his fury, at the top on the mountain, KaraIvan throws stone after stone into the abyss, remaining impassive in his tragic solitude.

Published in the early 1960s, Nikolay Haytov's modest collection of short fiction, called *Wild Stories*, was acclaimed by critics and has become a cultural milestone. A little-known provincial writer at that time, Haytov (1919–2002) not only dominated the Bulgarian literary scene, but he also earned a reputation as one of Bulgaria's most respected screenwriters, credited with scripts for films such as Khristo Khristov's *Darvo bez koren* (*Tree Without Roots*, 1974), Eduard Zakhariev's *Mazhki vremena* (*Manly Times*, 1977) and the popular television series *Kapitan Petko Voyvoda* (*Captain Petko Voivode*, 1981).

*Wild Stories* appealed to audiences because of its laconic, almost ascetic style; its memorable morality tales turning it into a bestseller. Haytov's proud and free-spirited protagonists inhabit the beautiful Rhodopi mountains and live in a world of raw and primitive feelings and audacious impulses, which define their behaviour and values. They act with little hesitation and are unafraid to stand by their decisions. Their outward impudence hides nobility and generosity of spirit. To a certain extent, these characters compensate for the lack of icons in real life and for the dearth of heroes who would take responsibility for their actions, defending the values that constitute the meaning of their existence.

Towards the end of the 1960s, Bulgarian cinema faced the challenge of emancipating itself from the stylistic deadlock into which it had drifted, and fresh artistic approaches were needed to overcome ideological narrow-mindedness. In this context, Haytov's short stories became the literary material for a range of exciting cinematic projects that influenced the exploration of new artistic territories. It attracted filmmakers who were drawn to the vitality of Haytov's characters; their nonconforming attitudes, emphatic humanism and the narrative thrust of each tale.

Famous Bulgarian stage director, Methodi Andonov, whose film debut *Byalata staya* (*The White Room*, 1968) had been recognised as one of the most successful attempts to overcome the crisis in cinema, was among the first to adapt Haytov's work (other adaptations, from 1971, include Milen Nikolov's *Krayat na pesenta* (*The Song's End*) and *Gola savest* (*Naked Conscience*) and Georgi Dyulgreov's *Izpit* (*Test*)). The gripping events of *Koziyat Rog* (*Goat's Horn*, 1972) and the tragic destinies of the protagonists are rich in conflicting emotions and choices, and the narrative structure plays well to cinematic conventions. *Goat's Horn* is a classically simple moral fable, which effectively bridges traditional morality and modern sensitivity.

Set in the Rodopi Mountains, the film depicts the rough sensuality of mountain people who lead a monosyllabic primitive life. Similarly primitive and weird are the protagonists of other 'mountain' films where the landscape determines the characters and the plot (like in many of the works of Albanian cinema, in the films of Živko Nikolić which are regularly set in some remote village in the middle of the Montenegrin mountains or Bato Čengić's *Gluvi barut* (*Silent Gunpowder*, 1990) and Srdjan Karanović's *Virdžina* (1991), both set in the mountains of Bosnia). According to the 1920s theories of influential Yugoslav geographer Jovan Cvijić the mountains in the area are inhabited by a special kind of wild and primitive people, very different from those living in the valleys. Cvijić's contentions are enhanced by the way the violent yet tender protagonists from the mountains are depicted. It is a cinematic set up reminiscent to some works of Italian cinema where mountainous remote locations (as seen in Paolo and Vittorio Taviani's Sardinia-set *Padre padrone* (*Father and Master*, 1977) are shown as producing extreme manifestations of patriarchal oppression.

At the very basis of the story lies the tragic fate of one Bulgarian family during the prolonged era of Ottoman yoke over Bulgarian lands (1396–1878). The extreme violence of the opening rape scene in *Goat's Horn* more or less summarises the place that Ottoman Turks occupy in the Balkan imaginary: they are traditionally seen as the archetypal enemy and presented as arbitrarily cruel, treacherous and vindictive. And KaraIvan knows no better way to fight violence than with violence. Blinded by the brutality of his wife's rapists, KaraIvan craves vengeance: a primeval reaction triggered by the physical and spiritual slaughter of the person closest to him. His view on justice is not particularly sophisticated; the primordial principle of an-eye-for-an-eye automatically takes precedence over his actions, justifying his basic need for gratification. Responding to atavistic impulses, however, brings about a certain kind of fanaticism that overpowers KaraIvan, and takes him further away from his initial goal of revenge; he becomes a victim of his deadly passions.

Yet behind the chain of simple physical actions pulsates the tragedy of a human fate determined by concrete historical reality. KaraIvan is a true product of his time; his actions express a certain form of protest and individual self-defence. The clash of opposite ethical and religious systems begets an outburst of barely containable atavistic feelings and passions. He undertakes it to impose justice but in the end he falls victim to his fanatic fervour to take life. The archetypal simplicity of the story strengthens the epic capacity of the tragic plot.

Even though the story is situated within the specific historical context of the Ottoman Empire, the authors of the film overcome problems of historicity by searching for links with the contemporaneous social and cultural reality. The filmmaker portrays the tragic complexity of KaraIvan's character on a level that exceeds the purely regional dimensions. This illiterate shepherd's drama from the eighteenth century remains topical even at the dawn of the twenty-first century. Besides the peculiar inner conflict, the hero's tragic guilt and doomed cause, there is celebration of an audacious human being who dares to challenge Fate. Torn between his basic grasp of justice, honour and dignity on one hand, and the strength of his character and his will to act according to his own notions of morality on the other, he exists outside time and space; he belongs to eternity. KaraIvan's character synthesises an archetypal tragic conflict, hence the message of the film is a universal and existential one, geared toward modern sensibilities.

KaraIvan's tragic story and his struggle for justice can be interpreted on several levels, which the director skilfully incorporates into the film's structure. The literary source is restructured in pursuit of a vivid and memorable cinematic expression which enriches the austere plot. Delicately and compellingly, director Andonov delves into the deeper dramatic dimensions of this human, historical and moral conflict.

A representative feature of Andonov's directorial style which significantly enhances the narrative is the repetition of the same motif in different cinematic contexts throughout the film. Some of the more memorable motifs include the image of fire. At the opening of the film, the house in which the Turkish oppressors plunder, rape and kill KaraIvan's wife, is set on fire. It is mirrored at the end of the film by the fire that Maria sets to the barn where she has tasted happiness with her lover. Another motif is the recurring climb of the mountain hill that KaraIvan makes carrying Maria in his arms – the first time after his wife's death, and for a second time after Maria kills herself when, holding her lifeless body, KaraIvan walks his own Golgotha of suffering and redemption. A third motif is the shot of a bleeding hand: in one instance KaraIvan discovers Maria's wounded hand and in another Maria sees her father's hand bleeding.

There is also the leitmotif of the musical theme, which often counters the action in its dramatic, lyrical or tragic context, thus sculpting the necessary inner meaning for each scene of the film. Written and performed by Maria Neykova, the song enjoyed something of a cult following in Bulgaria throughout the 1970s.

Andonov consciously sought to contrast individual sequences, a device used to facilitate further dramatisation of the emotional charge of the story. Furthermore, instead of taking advantage of trite and established ways of contrasting atmosphere, mood and meaning, he looked for the indirect and often subtly-observed clash within the same dramatic scene. For instance, when Maria, ready to avenge her mother's death and desecrated honour, crawls secretly into the house of one of the murderers and hides behind a wall. There she becomes an unwitting witness of the tranquil and serene life in the garden of her intended victim; she watches him gently caressing his young lover and cheerfully playing with his dog. A different, unknown reality unfolds in front of Maria's eyes; for the first time she encounters a world where worries and ubiquitous death are not everywhere present. Encountering such a beautiful and unattainable existence, doubts over her mission crawl into Maria's mind.

The director displays particular attention to representing the contrasting states of Nature. Cameraman Dimo Kolarov, one of the most visually stimulating and accomplished Bulgarian cinematographers, created a lively imagery that adhered to the overall ascetic style of the film. However, even limited within the black and white tonal range, his work powerfully under-scored the depth of the storyline. The mountain hills, the soft outlines of the knolls, the rocky protrusions, the forests, the rivers and the fresh meadows replicate the characters' sensibilities, their uncomplicated lifestyles, and their simple world perceptions, inseparable from the mighty power of Mother Nature. Nature literally overflows in harmonious beauty in the short moments of Maria's happiness. The mythical presence of Nature is also felt during the crucial moments of KaraIvan's ordeal, whose vitality and stamina are held up to the standards of Nature's raw beauty.

*Goat's Horn* also explored the intimate dialectics of the masculine and feminine in Nature. The masculine is represented by aggression, violence and the relentless urge for change; it is seen as the active element in life, and begets all that disrupts the status quo and the dynamic balance in reality. The feminine, on the contrary, is lithe, subdued, conservative and stands for family, equanimity and peaceful tranquillity.

KaraIvan typifies the male element. His actions yield a sense of prowess and confidence; standing for and defending his principles seems to be in his nature. He achieves personal fulfilment only when engaged in decisive, uncompromising and ultimately destructive action. Spiritually, he is a typical action hero, which explains his extreme reaction to the desecration of his world – house and family. KaraIvan's antagonists, on the contrary, personify the negative side, the destructive outbreak of male brutal force. Family and honour do not mean much to them; human dignity is easily sacrificed for the sake of uncontrollable sex drive.

Sexuality plays a special part in the semantics of the film. The act of sexual intercourse (be it coercive or consensual) not only defines the characters but also reveals the experien-tial complexity of the conflicts. Phallic symbols are present throughout the film, both on a literal and on a symbolic level. The rape scene, however, also directs the viewer's attention to specific historical events – the 500-year-long era of Turkish oppression and occupation of the Bulgarian lands – and represents the cruel fate that the Bulgarian nation had to endure during those dramatic times. In the love scene between Maria and the young shepherd, the sexual act symbolises quite the opposite: it signifies the triumph of the forces of Nature and celebrates life. The repetitive change of clothes that Maria performs in the course of the film (male to female before going to the lover; female to male when returning to the father) is also important for the film's reading, as it alludes to the ambivalence of existence, and to the relativity of the opposition of male and female. Subtle hints to incest made in the scenes where KaraIvan gazes at his daughter's womanly figure also yield interesting lines for interpretation.

The feminine force, though less articulate in the semantics of the narrative, becomes a natural counterpoint to the merciless and hostile masculine world. While only delicately hinted at in places where it is just a soft image of a certain state of mind, the feminine surfaces clearly as the centre of attention in the love scenes between Maria and her shepherd lover.

In his casting choices, Andonov sought performers who could also represent certain ethnic types. In his pursuit for appropriate features, the director made the radical decision to give the main parts of the film to actors whose faces were relatively unknown to Bulgarian audiences: Anton Gorchev as KaraIvan and Katya Paskaleva as Maria. Make-up and costumes augment the sense of male force of Gorchev's character. His physique, however, is quite different from the trivial image of what a rough mountaneer would be expected to look like. Rather than displaying brawn and muscles, Gorchev concentrates on presenting a tough and unyielding character. The director is primarily concerned in showing the conflicting emotions that this otherwise primal and ascetic character struggles with.

Andonov's considerations in casting Katya Paskaleva were different. She was to play a double part: Maria the daughter and Maria the mother. The director relied on the actress's ability to transform from one state of mind to another. She succeeded in combining decisiveness and fanatic determination with tenderness, warmth and sorrow. The actress revealed the feminine in her heroine without resorting to a simplistic reliance on her erotic aura. Her physical appearance was austere, yet the actress demonstrated her attractiveness and emotional depth through her talent as a performer.

Even though they are meant to represent two opposite and contradicting extremes, Maria and KaraIvan's characters are not mutually exclusive but rather function as complementing parts of something higher and revered. Their inner contradictions echo the historical tragedy of Bulgaria. Maria and her father, like her mother, are victimised by Ottoman villains, their position serving as an allegory for the historical fate of the nation. All this defined specific cinematographic choices, embedded on different semantic levels in the film and augmented with references that actively encouraged Bulgarians to examine themselves. In this sense, *Goat's Horn* was a major breakthrough in the evolution of Bulgarian cinema, marking the beginning of its creative emancipation and maturity. Andonov's stylistically unique film successfully surmounted the simplistic understanding of the limitations of the past, an attitude that has often led to provincial isolationism.

Of course, the film can (and should, at least on a narrative level) be interpreted as the reconstruction of specific historical realities. But the authors were not satisfied with only this dimension. They made references to a range of cosmogonic and theosophic beliefs, radically rejecting any narrow-minded clerical dogmatism. The film opened up a discussion of this tragic guilt which is examined not only in the everyday interpersonal relations of the characters but also as a daring challenge to superior divine forces. In pursuing his own kind of justice, KaraIvan attempts to measure up to transcendental forces. In the scene where KaraIvan and Maria climb up the mountain hill ready to punish the first assailiant, their figures gradually fill up the frame, in sharp contrast to the disappearing sky. Wearing picturesque costumes made of sheepskin and reminiscent of Bulgarian pagan mythology, they appear ready to perform a ceremonial ritual. Their actions, the choreography of their movements and the composition of the shot are heavy with symbolic connotations: positioned between Earth and Heaven, their intimate human drama now assumes the significance of a universally-shared tragedy. Freed from the trivial details of an everyday existence, the protagonists do not simply avenge the evil but rather perform an act of absolute justice, a deed that in traditional mythology is solely Fate's prerogative.

In his rejection of quiet obedience, KaraIvan infringes upon the norms of Christian ethics. Audaciously challenging Fate and taking over God's license to justice, KaraIvan must stoically endure his punishment. The price is high, and KaraIvan has to make a dear sacrifice: he will lose the daughter that he has brought up and has trained to avenge without a trace of hesitation. The film ends with a commanding metaphor, which effectively summarises the filmmaker's philosophical viewpoint and the message of his film: from the high mountain hill, as if a hero from the ancient Greek tragedies, KaraIvan hurls the stones of his ire to Mother Earth. Mighty and lonely in his infinite suffering, KaraIvan proudly stands up to counter the challenges of Fate.

*Goat's Horn* is perhaps the most serious artistic achievement of post-war Bulgarian cinema, confirmed by its critical acclaim and continued success amongst audiences. Its accomplishments were also fundamental in fostering the enthusiasm of several generations of filmmakers who had until then been curtailed by ideological restrictions and archaic artistic norms, and who were then free to explore the existential problems of human nature.

Further, *Goat's Horn* prompted the search for a truly modern film aesthetics and transcended the traditional paradigms of Bulgarian cinema. Included were scenes where graphic violence – physical and sexual – dictated the characters' behaviour. The opening scene of the film, showing the cruel rape and murder of KaraIvan's wife, sets a precedent for Bulgarian cinema. Hiding behind a self-confessed hypocritical aesthetic puritanism, this cinema had consistently avoided the treatment of explicit violence. The way shots were assembled in this scene – deliberately odious and aggressive – was meant to shock the viewer's senses. However, Andonov did not compromise good taste nor yield to aimless naturalism in the enactment of these violent sequences. A gifted director, he was able to integrate all elements and make them work toward an artistic representation of the story. Thus, the film affects the viewer as a whole instead of breaking apart with every scene, each requiring a different level of interpretation.

The screen adaptation of *Goat's Horn* was a key cultural phenomenon of the early 1970s. Time has done little to hinder the power of the film's artistic and philosophical underpinnings, but it has given birth to new ways of filmic interpretation. More than twenty year later, young director Nikolay Volev, chose to remake the film. *Goat's Horn 2*, released in 1994, constituted a specific challenge to the poetics and aesthetic premises of the original film. Relying on the same literary source yet having writer Nikolay Haytov collaborate on an updated screenplay for the new version, Volev's film stressed different dimensions of the narrative. The original 1972 film tackles issues of suppressed sexuality and sensuality yet the dominant themes here remain patriarchy and rejected revenge. The 1994 remake of the film (by director Nikolai Volev) refocuses and pays more explicit attention to the incestuous motives that drive the action. What had been delicately suggested by Andonov now grew to become crucial elements of the story's plotline. It invited a more decisive psychoanalytical interpretation; sexual instincts define the behaviour of all protagonists, and Maria's actions in particular. The incest theme is foregrounded, no longer a moral problem but now the manifestation of atavistic behaviour resulting from the fact that Maria has been raised in isolation from society and is thus oblivious to its norms and taboos. That is why she has no remorse when succumbing to her awakening desires.

In the remake, KaraIvan's character (Alexandar Morfov) is also approached differently, the stress being more on vengeance rather than on his daring and ultimately blasphemous search for justice. Maria (Elena Petrova) is also changed, her feelings now more important than her actions. The most curious development, however, is that the shepherd is made a Muslim (Petar Popyordanov); an alteration that brings the problem of religious and ethnic (in)tolerance to the forefront, thus introducing additional issues into Maria's relationship. In Andonov's original film, the figure of the shepherd-lover was only briefly outlined; his character remained peripheral and sketchy, functioning only as a trigger for the development of the tragic conflict. In *Goat's Horn 2*, Maria's involvement with the Muslim shepherd becomes an indispensable feature of the film whose tragic ending seems to not only re-emphasise the doomed love but also the religious conflict. In an outburst of jealousy, KaraIvan kills Maria's lover; soon thereafter father and daughter lay down, shot by a horde of avenging Muslims. In interview, Volev referred to the love between Christian Maria and the Muslim shepherd as a Balkan version of Romeo and Juliet.

Given the various inter-ethnic tensions of the 1980s and the conflict in Yugoslavia throughout the 1990s the theme of peaceful co-existence between Christianity and Islam in the Balkans gained new importance. A number of films ventured into testing the boundaries of mutual prejudice (for example, the Romeo-and-Juliet story in Srdjan Karanović's *Za sada bez dobrog naslova* (*Film With No Name*, 1988) featuring the tragically constrained love between a Muslim woman and a Christian man). While in the original story and film version of *Goat's Horn* Maria's lover was a Christian (who at one point even takes her to an Orthodox shrine), for the 1994 remake he was turned into a devout Muslim (who at one point even utters: 'It seems that God is one, but we all call him by different names'), thus bringing to the film a whole new range of issues related to inter-faith tolerance.

One story, two interpretations. Two similar yet singular films, each rethinking in its own way Haytov's short story. Methodi Andonov's *Goat's Horn* occupies an important position in the canon of Bulgarian cinema. It is a film that triumphs over the limitations of a work of art of regional meaning and importance. Critics have rightly voted this film as the best Bulgarian film of the twentieth century.

**Alexander Grozev**

# NUNTA DE PIATRĂ STONE WEDDING

## MIRCEA VEROIU & DAN PIȚA, ROMANIA, 1972

*Nunta de piatră* (*Stone Wedding*, 1972) comprises of two short films based on the writings of classic Romanian writer Ion Agârbiceanu. The first part, *Fefeleaga*, directed by Mircea Veroiu, is set around the turn of the century. It presents us with Maria Fefeleaga, a widow living in the Carpathian Mountains, who has lost her husband and all her children except for one daughter. This last daughter is also fatally ill and Maria takes care of her while simultaneously working at the gold mine nearby. Maria struggles hard to save money for a wedding dress, her daughter's only desire. But in spite of all her efforts, she does not manage to buy the dress before the young girl dies. In order to fulfil the dead daughter's wish, Maria goes to the town and sells her white horse, her sole companion and help at the mine. With the money she buys the white dress and buries the young 'bride' near her house, alongside the rest of her family.

The second part, entitled *La o nuntă* (*At a Wedding*) and directed by Dan Pița, is set in a small semi-rural town on the cusp of modernisation, at the beginning of the twentieth century. It opens with a scene showing soldiers searching for a deserter. A musician, while on his way to play at a wedding, meets the deserter and they decide to go on together. At the wedding party, it turns out that the marriage was an arranged one. The bride is visibly unhappy and keeps looking at the musician while the groom is busy eating and drinking. The musician and the young bride exchange long looks and, under the accompaniment of the ubiquitous wedding music, gradually grow attracted to each other. The groom becomes suspicious but remains passive and does not intervene. Later, the bride and the musician run off while the soldier keeps playing dance music for the guests. When the groom and the family finally realise what has happened, they beat the soldier to death. The lovers escape; the final scene shows them running hand in hand along a lake.

*Stone Wedding* was released at a turning point in Romania's history when a relatively liberal stance on censorship that had come about in the 1960s lapsed into a more restrictive one.

As part of Nicolae Ceaușescu's general policy to project an image of ideological and economic openness in Romania, artists and intellectuals had witnessed a certain cultural liberalisation, which created hope for breaking away from strict communist dogmas in the late 1960s. The decentralised production system (five autonomous film companies were established instead of a central directorate) and the move away from Soviet ideology and aesthetics had resulted in increased production (from 15 to 25 feature films per year), and in improved social sensitivity and artistic quality (experimentation with genres and cinematic language).

However, in the context of growing international tensions after the Warsaw Pact's invasion of Czechoslovakia in 1968, at a party activist meeting in 1971 Nicolae Ceauşescu delivered a speech that was severely critical of the intelligentsia, claiming that they did not show enough support in building the ideal communist state. Soon thereafter, political scrutiny of artistic content became much tighter. Yet this was accompanied by a certain relaxation of control in the area of artistic forms of expression, maybe precisely because the attention was so strictly fixated on content.

Directors Mircea Veroiu and Dan Piţa emerged in this historical moment when intellectuals were trying to find artistic liberty 'within the strictly delimited field of "allowed" subjects'. Veroiu and Piţa were the most important members of the '1970 generation' of Romanian filmmakers. This generation, which included personalities such as Alexandru Tatos, Constantin Vaeni, Radu Gabrea and Stere Gulea, emerged at a time when the freedom of artistic expression seemed to have come to an end. Despite strong political censorship, their films brought hope that Romanian cinema could still produce texts of high quality and originality. The manifesto of the group was an impressive, collectively-directed documentary, *Apa ca un bivol negru* (*Water Like a Black Buffalo*, 1970), which presented the dramatic struggle of villagers affected by a devastating flood.

It is not by accident that literary adaptations were common in post-war Romanian cinema. The imposed socialist realist framework had set severe limits to artistic expression. Adapting classical Romanian literature for the screen was one of the ways to avoid the oppressive regulation of cinema. Many literary masterpieces had been turned into films such as Ioan Slavici's *La Moara cu noroc* (*The Mill of Good Luck*, Victor Iliu, 1955) or Liviu Rebreanu's *Pădurea spînzuraţilor* (*Forest of the Hanged*, Liviu Ciulei, 1964; see the chapter by Marian Ţuţui in this volume). Ion Luca Caragiale's comedies were especially popular because their comic form allowed for pointed, even indirect, social criticism. Thus, adapting acknowledged literary works for the screen was considered by filmmakers to provide a 'safe space' mostly because these literary classics enjoyed something of a canonised position.

Ion Agârbiceanu's short stories provided perfect material for Veroiu's and Piţa's interest in formal experimentation. One the one hand, working with acclaimed literary texts that established a historical distance and dealt with the 'safe theme' of peasantry ensured getting around political censorship. On the other, Agârbiceanu's naturalism and basic mythical narrative provided a rich soil for aesthetic experimentation. The qualities of *Stone Wedding* lay in searching for fresh means of cinematic expression; in the visible passion to create drama strictly through the language of film.

*Stone Wedding* is a prime example of the preoccupation of the new generation filmmakers with creating a sophisticated cinematographic language that established film as an authentic and true form of artistic expression. It opened the road of innovation by being the first instalment of the specific tradition of 'silent' style in the new Romanian cinema, where dialogue is reduced to a minimum and the cinematic signification is almost exclusively visual. This film is also one of the few works from Romania to break into the international arena; it was successful at several international festivals including Cannes, and received various awards for direction and cinematography, as well as for the performance of Leopoldina Bălănuţa (Maria Fefeleaga).

Each of the two parts of the film follow different narratives and display distinct directorial approaches. However, both parts reveal a tense sense of tragic, strong visuals and rely on a narrative tone that is close to folk ballads. The same director of photography, Iosif Demian, shot both parts of the film. In order to recreate the gloomy space of these archetypal dramas one needs to know, as Grid Modorcea asserts in the volume by Călin Căliman, 'how to tell a story through images, an action almost entirely without words. One needs to tell not real facts, with people remembering real people, with psychological activities and progressive development, but atemporal conflicts, the eternal problem of death, given once and forever, fixed within the "laws of the universe".

Maria Fefeleaga, the protagonist of Mircea Veroiu's piece, is a tragic character resembling the protagonists of ancient Greek dramas, where Fate stands above all human actions. She lives in a remote place in the Western Carpathian Mountains with her only daughter who is fatally ill. Maria is a victim of her own fate and just like the heroes of ancient dramas, she accepts it without resentment. She silently follows the predetermined path, as if being fully aware that one cannot fight destiny. She does not show particular attachment or affection even to her own daughter. Her life seems to be a series of mechanically performed duties. Both Maria and her daughter bear their tragic fate submissively; the daughter faces death while the mother faces the loss of the daughter and that of her horse, all this being played out with complete resignation. In a fundamentally tragic mode of existence there is no space for strong feelings.

Maria is trapped in her monotonous life. The long takes in the goldmine disclose cyclical movements and routines, repeated over and over again. She digs the dirt, then she fills the baskets on the back of the horse, then she walks slowly leading the horse to the water mill. The sound of the mill's non-stop spinning and the non-diegetic music determined by the rhythm of the drumbeat magnify the monotonous nature of Maria's life. It is a world where emotions as well as relationships are fully restrained. Maria is alone working or running chores in town; her daughter is also alone waiting in the house while walking her dolls. In this environment verbal communication is restricted to the minimum; all communication is carried out through the visuals and the music. At the moment of her death the daughter will be alone and silent.

The idea of unavoidable Fate known from ancient tragedies is replayed both on narrative and visual levels. Besides the archetypal characters and relationships (mother/daughter, human/animal) the tragic end forecasts itself in visual symbolism. The film is structured around basic archetypal oppositions. Shot in black and white, it relies on the metaphorically charged relationship between these two colours. Maria's black clothes are in contrast with her faithful companion, the white horse as well as with the white wedding dress. The white stony landscape of the mine is punctuated by the tiny black dots of the people working there. The black frames of doors and windows disrupt the clean, continuous surfaces of the white walls in Maria's house, and so do the framed photographs and a mirror. The repeated contrast between black and white symbolises the hidden omnipresence of death and life.

The square frames that reoccur everywhere around Maria are further visual signs of the tight framing of her world. Forces beyond her own will determine her trajectories within this universe. Many of the images are static, as if frozen in their frames, creating the feeling that one is watching photographs. The frames are composed in another set of binary oppositions, namely of horizontal and vertical lines. The almost surreal, but certainly inorganic flat landscape, which appears in both films, is regularly disrupted by vertical lines such as a tall water-tower and the bar-irons of a swing. The juxtaposition of the horizontal and the vertical is paired with another opposition, which lays in the paradox of the richness that the goldmine symbolises and the unbearable poverty that Maria has to cope with day by day. While in the immediate presence of gold she cannot afford to buy a white dress for her daughter.

In Romanian folk tradition, those who die prematurely before being married are buried in a symbolic wedding ritual. The special ceremony has a specific function described by anthropologist Gail Kligman as a resolution with a calamitous event that is 'out of phase with the "time" for death in the life cycle'. In this context, the daughter's wish for a white wedding dress becomes a sign of her own awareness of the inevitable tragic end. The fact that Maria cannot afford to fulfil this last wish further heightens the sense of tragedy. The whiteness of the horse and that of the young dead 'bride' enhances the feeling of a fatalistic surrender of all that is pure and innocent to dark forces such as death and poverty.

The oppositions, however, reveal inherent connections as well. As Kligman claims, 'the relationship between marriage and death is paradoxical, characterised by opposition and identity, difference and likeness – all the stuff of metaphor'. Death is to life just as black is to white and poverty is to affluence. Conflicting entities such as black and white, rich and poor, horizontal and vertical, urban and rural cannot exist separately from each other, they define and require their counterparts, and one cannot be perceived without the other. Veroiu's film visually describes Maria's perception of a world that is heavily reliant on these eternal and universal binaries. Maria's whole existence depends on accepting these oppositions, on living within a fundamentally metaphorical universe based on polarised coordinates. She can only understand what is happening around her and carry on living this seemingly meaningless life if she subordinates herself to the paradoxical controversies that her world is built on.

Fefeleaga's fatalist outlook is very similar to the fatalism of Petrija in *Petrijin venac* (*Petrija's Wreath*, 1980; see the chapter by Nevena Daković in this volume), both women inhabiting very similar smalltown settings that have retained some features of idyllic rural life while simultaneously taking on devastation coming from the industrialisation that takes over the bigger urban centres nearby and leads to depopulation and moral decline. The rural-on-the-verge-of-destruction setting of *Stone Wedding*'s first part bears direct parallels with the settings of other films made in the region at about the same time, such as Alexis Damianos' *Mehri to plio* (*Until the Ship Sails*, 1966), Theo Angelopoulos' early feature *Anaparastassi* (*Reconstruction*, 1970) and the Bulgarian films *Posledno lyato* (*Last Summer*, Hristo Hristov, 1974) and *Spomen za bliznachkata* (*Memoir of the Twin Sister*, Lyubomir Sharlandzhiev, 1976).

One other significant feature of *Fefeleaga* is reminiscent of Greek tragedies: from time to time a singing voice outside the narrative comments on the events. Embedded in the music with folkloric elements this lyrical voice serves a function similar to that of the chorus in ancient Greek dramas. It asks questions, explains what is unknown to the spectator, presents the conflict and analyses what is shown. The choir can be understood as a kind of close link between the spectator and the film text. Faithful to the overall metaphorical world of the film and to folklore, the chorus speaks in a highly symbolic and poetic language to the spectators.

The chorus appears in Piţa's film too, with very similar functions. *At a Wedding* comments on the tragedy unfolding around the arranged marriage. Although the directorial techniques of the two filmmakers are clearly distinct, there is an evident effort to connect the films by sharing important structural, thematic and symbolic elements. Like *Fefeleaga*, *At a Wedding* also displays a fatalism reminiscent of ancient tragedies. Starting from the very first scene, when we see some soldiers in the search for a deserter, a sense of doom lingers over each subsequent deed. The music, dominated by drumbeat, is virtually the same throughout the two movies, even though in the second part the drum intensifies the tension besides creating a monotonous rhythm. Thus, music becomes an important narrative element. The two musicians play polka and folk music at the wedding as entertainment for the participants. Their music hypnotises the guests so powerfully that no one notices the escape of the bride and the violinist. Towards the end of the film, a classical-type tragic chorus is also incorporated into the film text.

The two films share some of the landscape and characters. For instance, the same shop-keeper appears in both films, even if only seen from a distance selling different items. On their way to the wedding, the two men walk across the same plane and surreal field with the water tower and the swing where the ill daughter used to walk her dolls. The white horse also appears unexpectedly on the road. These elements, however, never come to play a signifying role in the second film but remain more as decorations, self-explanatory and therefore slightly forced indications of a link between the two films. There is a more functional similarity in the archetypal figures that both films use. Piţa's piece pushes the symbolism of his characters to an extreme in depriving them from having names. The bride, the groom, the drummer-soldier and the violinist symbolise quintessential protagonists of ancient tragedies. Through them the drama is elevated to a mythological level. Fate is replaced by universal tragedy, by sacrifice of the innocent, by revenge and by contradictions between the individual's desires (love) and society's demands (marriage) taking ritualistic forms (such as wedding or burial).

Piţa's film follows the Greek dramatic formula also because it prepares the viewer for the unavoidable rupture from early on. The tension is increased through music and different forms of narrative suspension such as the long and slow sequences showing guests dancing and eating. The viewer is denied access to the characters' inner life: there is an evident lack of close-ups at the beginning, and only with time does the camera get closer and closer to the faces and reveals, for example, the bride's unhappiness. However, the more we know about the characters' state of mind, the closer we come to realising that tragedy is predestined. The gloomy end lingers above all actions, the question is only when, how and who will die. Yet *At a Wedding* also departs from ancient drama because Fate does not seem to overpower all human actions. The bride and her lover challenge it and get away successfully; the soldier has to be sacrificed, however, so that the broken order is reinstalled.

Similarly to *Fefeleaga*, *At a Wedding* is structured around significant binary symbolism. The most obvious is the repeated coupling of the theme of death and wedding. Life and death, wedding and bereavement are inseparably connected. The young lovers – the bride and the musician – may escape happily, yet this happens in parallel with the innocent soldier's demise. The contrasts between the bride's white dress and the groom's black suit, between the white house where the wedding takes place and the dark forest where the dead body lies in the end function as visual metaphors for the same binary between life and death. The polarity between poverty and prosperity also plays an important role in the film. The girl has to marry the much older groom because her family is poor and he is rich. The guests at the wedding are completely taken over by eating and drinking, endlessly stuffing themselves as if it is their last ever chance to eat. The fiesta is out of all proportions, which only underlines the poverty of everyday life from which these people try to escape.

Both films are set at the turn of the twentieth century, the historical period of acceler-ated industrialisation and modernisation. In *Fefeleaga* these developments bring about tension between the urban and rural environment, between innovation and tradition. The shopkeeper cannot understand why Maria does not want to remarry, while Maria gets irritated when she is asked this question. Town life is noisy, busy and often immoral, while the mountain hamlet is associated with solitude, tranquillity and strict moral laws. There is no communication between town and village, they seem to be worlds apart, with distinct and irreconcilable values. The signs of modernisation in *At a Wedding* are seen in the appearance of a phonograph to replace the traditional live folk music by pre-recorded Western orchestral melodies. The opposition here seems to emerge between the 'civilised' new world of technology and rationality and such eternal human drives as love, jealousy and revenge. The visual and narrative binaries in the second film signify an inconsolable opposition between the idea of social and historical devel-opment and the power of universal human desires.

The wedding is one of the key tropes of Balkan cinema. It is a trademark image for directors as diverse as Theo Angelopoulos and Emir Kusturica who usually stage at least one wedding in most of their films. *Lachenite obuvki na neznainiya voin* (*The Patent Leather Shoes of the Unknown Soldier*, 1979; see the chapter by Alexander Grozev in this volume) also evolves around the central wedding sequence. It is noteworthy that films that feature a wedding regularly counterbalance it with the representation of a funeral procession.

*Stone Wedding* was the first in the two directors' continuous collaboration, an unprecedented partnership that remains unique in Romanian cinema. Their *Duhul aurului* (*Lust for Gold*, 1974) was something of a sequel to *Stone Wedding* both in reworking two other stories by Agârbiceanu and in the intense experimentation with cinematic style. Although after *Lust for Gold* the two directors went on to make films on their own, later on they repeatedly consolidated their careers. For example, they introduced the genre of the western to Romanian cinema. Pița made the first western in 1978, *Profetul, aurul și ardelenii* (*The Prophet, the Gold and the Transylvanians*, 1978), and another one in 1981, *Pruncul, petrolul și ardelenii* (*The Baby, the Oil and the Transylvanians*), while Veroiu continued the series with the parody *Artista, dolarii și ardelenii* (*The Actress, the Dollars and the Transylvanians*, 1979).

In his later career, Mircea Veroiu worked mostly with cinematographer Călin Ghibu, making six films together over the next seven years. The first was an 'artistic-detective story', *Șapte zile* (*Seven Days*, 1973). In 1976 Veroiu made *Dincolo de pod* (*Beyond the Bridge*), a highly personal adaptation of an important Romanian novel, Ion Slavici's *Mara*. Critics described the film as 'a beautiful gallery of living pictures', and a 'great victory of the image'. In *Între oglinzi paralele* (*Between Parallel Mirrors*, 1978) Veroiu continued relying on literary inspirations, adapting two novels by Camil Petrescu. Films he made in the 1980s, such as *Sfîrsitul nopții* (*The End of the Night*, 1982), *Să mori din dragoste de viață* (*To Die from Love of Life*, 1983) and *Adela* (1985) reveal thematic and stylistic consistency by keeping in line with Veroiu's continuous preoccupation with aesthetic experimentation. The director went into self-exile in Paris before the official screening of *Umbrele soarelui* (*Shadows of the Sun*, 1986), the last film he made in communist Romania, only to return in 1990. His first film of the post-communist period, *Somnul insulei* (*The Slumber of the Island*), a poetic piece about life in exile, was released in 1994. This movie launched a series of intimate films that Veroiu, diagnosed with a terminal illness, made as his artistic testament: *Craii de curte veche* (*The Debauchees of the Old Court*, 1995), the made-for-TV *Scrisorile prietenului* (*The Friend's Letters*, 1997) and his last work, *Femeia în roșu* (*Woman in Red*, 1997). The director died in 1997.

After *Stone Wedding* Dan Pița next made *Filip cel Bun* (*Good Philip*, 1975), a historical film that, according to Irina Coroiu, combined 'at present tense the refusal of a cohabitation of mediocrity'. After dedicating a couple of years to making unique Romanian westerns, he directed films such as *Bietul Ioanide* (*Poor Ioanide*, 1980), *Concurs* (*Contest*, 1982) and the highly symbolic *Faleze de nisip* (*Sand Hills*, 1983), all of which were set in the present and dealt with contemporary themes. In *Dreptate in lanţuri* (*Justice in Chains*, 1984) his attention turned towards the past again, using a legend to scrutinise 'the condition of a rebellious individual towards an order arbitrarily established', according to Coroiu. Piţa directed three more films before 1989: *Pas în doi* (*Paso Doble*, 1985), *Noiembrie, ultimul bal* (*November: The Last Ball*, 1989) and *Rochia albă de dantela* (*The White Lace Dress*, 1989), thus showing a continuous concern with emblematic, mythological characters and eternal human metaphors. His first film in the 1990s, *Hotel de lux* (1991), which received the Silver Lion at the Venice Film Festival, used an allegorical form of expression with a tendency, again in the words of Coroiu, 'to disclose reality through the imaginary'. In his latest films, *Eu sunt Adam* (*I Am Adam*, 1996) and *Omul zilei* (*The Man of the Day*, 1997) the director has showed persistent interest in Mircea Eliade's existentialist-mystical theories, an interest that can be traced back to *Stone Wedding*. According to Eliade, human life is organised around a set of fundamental primordial archetypes, forming temporal and spatial configurations that are displayed in various festive practices and initiation rituals. Human beings have to constantly pass through initiations in order to overcome their fundamentally tragic existence in time.

*Stone Wedding* remains a pioneering work in Romanian cinema with its aspiration to overcome restrictive socialist political agendas and achieve emancipation from aesthetic dogmas. It combines minimalist narrative with strong visual symbolism, formal experimentation with pure cinematic language; it positions the human drama within a framework of universal binaries such as life and death, individual desires and communal laws, tradition and modernity. Mircea Veroiu's and Dan Piţa's masterpiece fully deserves the canonical position that it occupies in the history of Romanian cinema.

**Lilla Tőke**

REFERENCES

Coroiu, I. (2002) 'Dan Piţa: Famous Author, Well-Known Model', *MovEast*, 8, 49–53.

Căliman, C. (2000) *Istoria filmului românesc 1897–2000*. Bucharest: Editura Fundaţiei Culturale Române.

Kligman, G. (1988) *The Wedding of the Dead: Ritual, Poetics and Popular Structure in Transylvania*. Berkeley: University of California Press.

# LACHENITE OBUVKI NA NEZNAINIYA VOIN THE PATENT LEATHER SHOES OF THE UNKNOWN SOLDIER

## RANGEL VULCHANOV, BULGARIA, 1979

The plotline of *Lachenite obuvki na neznainiya voin* (*The Patent Leather Shoes of the Unknown Soldier*, Rangel Vulchanov, 1979) follows the associative imaginary travels of the film director in the distant world of his own childhood. There, trailing the whimsical and unexplainable logic of haunting memories, he finds himself amidst the whirlwind and the noisy chaos of a traditional Bulgarian village wedding.

At the opening of the film, filmmaker Vulchanov is seen recording the guard change ceremony at Buckingham Palace. An abrupt jump in space and time, enhanced by the super-imposition of musical score where a drawling Balkan song interferes with the stately British march, relocates the hero from present-day London into the reality of an ordinary Bulgarian village of the early 1930s, a time when the country is still recovering from the wounds of World War One. (The film is shot in Krivina, near Sofia, the director's native village.) The past rushes suddenly and aggressively into the story, and colours it with the unknown aroma and beauty of patriarchal mores and customs of everyday life. This sudden shift is accompanied by the director's voice-over commentary, which makes it clear that the grown-up protagonist, Simeon, is now transformed into the little Mone, his childhood's *alter ego*. While Mone's presence will dominate the screen from now on, the voice-over commentary will be delivered by the director's mature voice, thus establishing an uninterrupted intimate link between the various dimensions of the protagonist: child, adolescent and adult. The retrospective narrative is provoked by the encounter with the majestic display of Empire's rituals: majestic yet eccentric, the guard-change ceremony incites the protagonist to delve into his unconscious and examine the roots of his own identity.

The central part shows the prolonged ritual of a noisy and populous village nuptial celebration. A 'White Aunt' is married to a 'Black Uncle'. To the child these are two mutually exclusive entities, which become symbols for Beautiful and Ugly and are juxtaposed in the spiritual heritage of the nation as sublime and deformed, refined and primitive. These are presented along with a kaleidoscopic picture of harvest and war, floods and hot summer days, child-births and deaths. Mone's memories extend into various subplots: daily life is punctuated by wars, weddings and funerals. Fire devastates the whole household and all one hundred relatives die with Mone and the Grandfather as the only survivors. White Aunty also burns to death but then returns reincarnated as a while bird. The Grandfather mourns his lost relatives and decides it is his time to leave this world; he lies down in his coffin and begins growing smaller and smaller. In a symbolic gesture of coming of age, Mone travels to Sofia where he marvels at the outsized urban architecture and the elegant yellowish street pavement; he freezes in awe in front of the wondrously immense Alexander Nevski Cathedral. At a boulevard corner he listens to a street musician singing praise to the 'unknown soldier', and he finally acquires the pair of patent leather shoes he has been dreaming for. But he is also intimidated and overtaken by agoraphobic insecurity: the bittersweet memory of the lost patriarchal home lives deep inside him. He is unsure as to whether modernity is what he desires.

Rangel Vulchanov inhabits a special space in the history of Bulgarian cinema. Today, he rightfully carries the authority of a timeless filmmaker whose films are an inseparable part of Bulgaria's national culture. Having undergone an uneven professional development, driven by experimentation and remarkable persistence of vision, the director continues to be the object of discussions and wide-ranging interest among film researchers. His films enjoy an astounding longevity, and are constantly rediscovered by new generations of spectators. Without searching for the elements of a popular style and without compromising his aesthetic vision, Vulchanov has mastered an approach that makes his work communicative and understandable, despite the complexity of his imagery and his multi-layered narratives.

*The Patent Leather Shoes of the Unknown Soldier* is a deeply personal film in which the director goes back to his own childhood in order to reveal a bizarre world at the intersection of real-life images and a child's fantasies. The film is an introspective philosophical speculation which presents Bulgarian traditions and social concerns in various images and quasi-magical visions and reflects on the peculiarities of the national character shaped by adverse historical events. The film is not only the most sacred, personal and homogenous work of the director but is undoubtedly one of the most original Bulgarian films: it has no analogy, it refuses to gravitate around an established thematic orientation, and it does not fit into the traditional genre registry. Nor does it have predecessors to be compared to. A singular artistic phenomenon, this film lays out the beginning of an interesting and productive tradition.

The story is told in a bizarre way that defies genre conventions; various subplots balance each other into a delicate equilibrium between external occurrences and private verve. War is represented as a histrionic squabble between peasant neighbours forced to drop their daily chores and chase the whims of obsessive leaders. Disasters strike out of the blue and function as acts of nature that resolve all tensions in the extended household, helping to restore law and order. The imposing urban image subverts the village idyll but it is ultimately the latter that has a more powerful role in Mone's formation. And even though the film constructs a dreamlike image of innocent village life as painted by the child's imagination, its narrative is infused with the distanced and ironical stance of the matured grown-up who casts a reflective look on his reminiscences. *Patent Leather Shoes* addresses the perennial Balkan theme of the previously harmonious relationship between rural and town cultures, now disturbed by urban modernisation. Here it is explored within the framework of a coming of age narrative, an identity quest that plays out both on personal and national levels.

It opens with a sequence showing the director filming the Changing of the Guards at Buckingham Palace in London; from there on the storyline abruptly cuts to the rest of the narrative which takes place in a Bulgarian village. With such an opening, the frame of reference is established as 'European', turned to the West. Such narrative framing that sets up (and simultaneously problematises) the relationship with Europe and particularly the peripheral, marginal positioning of the Balkans in relation to the West figures as a key element in many of the Balkan films that tackle issues of national identity.

The film is a magic philosophical parable rendered in quasi-*verité* terms: the cast includes no professional actors. Rangel Vulchanov chose to play himself quite intentionally, a fact that further underlines the film's confessional character. However, if one decides to scrutinize *Patent Leather Shoes* in terms of its plotline and eventful narrative, one would discover that the film does not overcome the traditional structure of a tested dramatic construction within a familiar framework. According to its internal logic, the filmmaker (who is also the protagonist of the film) delves into his childhood memories looking to discover general moral principles that would provide the framework to his present-day existence, and to rediscover the meaning of forgotten values. In building his film's narrative, however, Vulchanov does not rely solely on tested narrative techniques. While such techniques may form the foundation of the plotline's first turn, they are soon overpowered by the far more powerful influx of multi-faceted memories. Mone (the director as a child and his *alter ego*) keeps coming up with seemingly naïve questions, an approach which allows him to encounter the secrets of life, to catch the echo of human experience and discover the wisdom of suffered knowledge. The return to childhood is a *sui generis* homecoming toward the source of the artist's personality, a trip toward oneself. The initial drive is the escape into the delicate material of childhood memories, augmented by the urge for scrutinising the surrounding world in its complexity and of the way ancestral memory defines the creativity of the filmmaker.

Little Mone faces the eternal questions of human existence and attempts to find explanations within his naïve system of beliefs. The little boy tries to figure out why people are different, what governs their actions, and why they do not always share the same notions of good and bad. The drive and the ability to analyse abstract concepts like 'dignity', 'duty' and 'patriotism', though limited within the framework of a child's mind, are deeply ingrained in the narrative. Again and again, Mone reflects upon complex ideas where life and death, holidays and workdays, war and peace co-exist in an astounding unity. At times, the child does not comprehend his surroundings; the inability to fully grasp the causes behind events is the driving force of his spontaneous reactions toward occurrences. The director presents his reactions by blending in peculiar humour and open irony and enriches them with a personal commentary from an adult point of view. Though sometimes paradoxical, the child's reflections are profoundly philosophical thoughts that express the author's attitude toward central human concerns: those of war, death or happiness. Misleadingly naïve, this attitude nevertheless charms with its shrewd ambiguity as it reveals the same set of problems that contemporary cinema has been dealing with in a non-traditional and engaging fashion.

For instance, World War One is shown as a vanity fair; a pageant of lavishly festooned people proudly displaying their shiny medals. Compounded by a range of shabby flags and pyrotechnic fireworks, conspicuously meaningless and alienating, the grotesque rituals of all the participants in this hysteria are brought to absurd extremes. This explains the single-handed determination of Mone's peasant grandmother who treats the self-indulgent generals by scolding them like disobedient boys. All that it takes to put an end to the fighting is a decisive granny. With her unceremonious behaviour, this coarse and strong woman personifies the simplistic ideas of Bulgarians about world order and justice. In their scale of values, war and destruction come last as they mean an end to the eternal circle of life.

Similarly, death is represented as a truce negotiated between the irreconcilable opposites of reality; after a big fire sweeps through the house where his extended family lives, Mone's grandfather lays down in a wooden coffin and gets ready to depart from this world. For this dignified old man life has lost meaning as of the moment the sweet hubbub and the delightfully noisy stampede of family routines no longer surrounded him. He feels lonely, and accepts his way out of life with poise and decorum. Death is nothing else but another event in the continuity of life – like his going to war, his harvesting, and his holiday celebrations. Thus, the grandfather begins his voyage towards his end in the same way that he has approached every other activity in his life – with calmness and with the conviction that it is the necessary thing to do.

Little Mone also carries the wisdom of his predecessors. He resists the obvious violation of harmony in Nature with childish stubbornness. Black Uncle and White Aunt's marriage is a true infringement upon Mone's notions of beauty and perfection. The overall joy from the wedding ritual – its noise, colourfulness, and laughter – and all the happiness of the multitude of guests cannot compensate for the conspicuous disparity of the couple, evident even to the child. The age-old ritual of publicly displaying the blood-stained underskirt of a virginal bride obliterates human dignity, and Mone's inquisitive mind cannot help realising how demeaning it is. Drunken Black Uncle looks even uglier next to the pallid White Aunt after this first night. It is beyond Mone's comprehension to understand why the beauty of the village has to marry such a hideous man. The child is not familiar yet with the adult world where the hierarchy of values is different.

Soon thereafter all of Mone's relatives find their death in the big fire which devastates the house. Only White Aunt survives or, at least, this is what Mone believes: she is now rein-carnated into a mysterious white dove that comes to the little boy as messenger from another world, not governed by concerns over money and property. This symbol, taken from Bulgarian folklore, is an expression of the naïve vision of a child for an ideal human society where natural harmony and beauty reign.

Vulchanov's film builds up a world of its own, populated with picturesque characters and memorable customs and traditions. The past's significant presence throughout the film perme-ates the elegiac landscape compositions, the ethnographic details of various folk traditions, the drawling songs, and the pastel colours of the film images, as if directly imported from the colourful folk dresses. Tightly placed in a system of cyclically repetitive events (birth, harvest, traditional holidays, death), village life excites the viewer's imagination with its sincerity and simplicity. The raw surface cannot hide the inner intensity of the peasant mentality, however. Primitive forms of expression conceal a rich spiritual life, captured in specific patterns of behaviour. The protagonists express their attitude toward the surrounding reality not in words, but in songs. One can sense good-natured humour and sentimentality in these drawling melodies which soften the burden of existence and poeticise life in an extraordinary fashion. Simultaneously, raw prosaic life is powerfully ubiquitous in *Patent Leather Shoes*: the viewer can easily sense it in the coarse fingers of the protagonists and in the pain and sorrow in their eyes.

The feeling of carnival emanates from every shot in the film. Led by certain outer similarities, some critics have tried to describe *Patent Leather Shoes* as a magic realist film. Indeed, the fascinating symbolism of a world so foreign and unfamiliar to modern civilisation is widely present here, a world with a distinct system of beliefs, vows, curses and mythological rituals, all making up an organic part of human existence. Furthermore, the peasants' hardship-ridden daily life is revealed through the imagination and inspirations of an artist enticed by the beauty of this world, so archaic and close to Nature. The inner organic closeness of the filmmaker's style, however, carries the codes of expression of authentic Bulgarian folklore: in such a context the parallels with the poetics of Latin American magic realism remain somewhat superficial and reliant on accidental similarities.

Still, the direct citations of Bulgarian traditional folk culture in *Patent Leather Shoes* are not many. Instead, the author's style displays creative mastery of Bulgarian heritage through the reworking of typical plot juxtapositions (wedding/funeral; birth/death), as well as through the usage of typical folklore themes, used to develop characters that otherwise lack in psychological and dramatic complexity. These characters are present on the screen as certain types, as signposts that express part of the spirituality of one entire nation. Vulchanov takes advantage of the impact of this technique of contrasts and anti-theses, as seen in the example of Black Uncle and White Aunt, and in the persistent contrast between city and village life. This stylistic approach brings to mind pagan beliefs about the dualist symmetry of the world. The director relies on the instinctive collective experience, which unceasingly seeks inner harmony in everyday existence.

The peasants in Vulchanov's film live in an extraordinary world of spiritual composure that balances the extremities that surround them. The peasants take the misfortunes that befall them with an almost ritualistic stoicism. Their contained sorrow naturally flows into the poetic lyrics of their songs. At the same time, they possess an ability to meet the difficulties with a remarkable sense of humour that speaks of optimism. Like his relatives, little Mone experiences war as a carnival fair of pyrotechnical celebration and operatic generals. In the child's naïve perception, life is one big game with its own rules, however incomprehensible and illogical.

The simplest way of conquering the power of this polarised existence is to convert its diversity into a simplified binary system that employs the principle of contrast. And this is quite characteristic of Bulgarian folk tradition. That is why the main characters and the central themes in the film are represented as 'coupled' notions: the quarrelling grandma and the silent grandpa, the hideous uncle and the beautiful aunt, the female and the male, the enduring dichotomy of Nature/civilization, the white and the black as a continuous movement in Nature, and even the gaudy folk dresses and the kitsch city clothes.

But Vulchanov's abundant imagination does not merely link the separate elements of the plotline into an astounding filmic spectacle. The director's staging of village life impresses with its inner energy: it is a spectacle whose rhythm follows the crescendo of emotional Bulgarian folk songs. The filmmaker has mastered to perfection the art of transforming the spectators into true co-authors and making them active participants in the carnival of life that he has filmed. He openly enjoys himself by throwing word puzzles at the viewers and by playing with multiple meanings in the recreation of his childhood memories. He looks with amazement into the lives of his predecessors seeking to explain the stamina that secures their perpetual survival.

In the context of these thoughts, as though jokingly, Vulchanov challenges the audience with opinions and arguments that allude to the fundamental issue of dialogue between civilisations. The film intentionally opens with documentary footage showing the director filming the change of guard at Buckingham palace, thus presenting a well-known ritual that symbolises the long-standing traditions of the imperial West. Yet in the middle of this footage, the narrative is relocated to the contrasting realities of the Balkan patriarchal village community. In foregrounding these distinct ways of social organisation, however, Vulchanov is not unnecessarily judgemental and does not come across as excessively opinionated in favour of one or the other.

The binary juxtaposition of city and village is of particular importance for the director; it reflects his views on the historical maturing of the nation. Village and city are two distinct dimensions of existence in which the protagonist's fantasy continuously dwells. They supply the framework for the complex trail of emancipation from a patriarchal lifestyle toward more modern forms of social organisation. The director nostalgically summons up the idyllic paradise of his old village but he does it without denying its backwardness, its rude customs and its cruel intolerance. He foregrounds the poetics and beauty of village labour, the allure of traditions and of sincere and simple relationship. He then juxtaposes village life with all its shortcomings and the forces that will soon come to destroy it: the modernising supremacy of the big city that comes to dominate with new mores and rites. The patent leather shoes that Mone dreams of throughout all this work as a specific metaphor of the inevitable modernisation; like his slick but tight patent leather shoes, a new world unavoidably comes and takes over, one that is glamorous and attractive but not particularly cosy to inhabit. And as soon as he has brought the awareness of inexorable modernisation to its extreme, Vulchanov drops it all; having alerted his viewers that all progress comes at a cost, he leaves it up to them to choose and decide.

Vulchanov is concerned with recreating a world that he knows in depth; his mission is to appeal for a tolerant acceptance of various cultural practices that can co-exist and preserve the diverse traditions and peculiarities of an idiosyncratic national development. To the film-maker the ascent to modernity gradually obliterates long-lasting customs and erodes many of the moral values that various societies have harboured for ages. Hence the nostalgic feeling of his outlook on the world of bygone childhood: it is nostalgia that also contains a healthy dose of wise scepticism.

*Patent Leather Shoes* can be seen as a natural culmination of other rewarding creative processes in Bulgarian cinema of the 1970s. During this decade, many filmmakers became interested in studying the inner world of the Bulgarian. Some of them went deeper into the problems of national self-consciousness delineating the mentality and the specific social character. But it is Vulchanov who offered the most comprehensive artistic expression of this interest by combining modern day cinematic language with what Ronald Holloway describes as the traditions of Bulgaria's 'poetic cinema'.

The film is of true significance for Bulgarian cinema. It is a film that completes the integration of the relatively inexperienced local cinematic tradition with the processes of modern cinema. Vulchanov daringly rejects the tested techniques of theatrical forms, and instead populates his film with real peasants, not actors. The amateur performers not only add authenticity to the film; they also eloquently express the director's own belief that the creative power of the spontaneous is ultimately more productive than a perfectly controlled acting routine. The screen presence of Vulchanov's non-professional actors is vivid and sincere; their enthusiasm is genuine. The director's contribution lies as much in the astounding discovery of these performers as in his skilful organic integration of their presence with the other artistic and stylistic components of the feature.

The seemingly eclectic style supplies original and powerful stylistic means for the unique dramaturgy and confessional tone. The director's imagination is unleashed into discovering new worlds and in populating them with characters that come straight out of fantasy fairy-tales. Ironic and sentimentally drawn toward the magic reality of his childhood memories, Vulchanov thoroughly examines the signs of his contemporary world looking for a trace of the irretrievably lost vitality of gestures and rituals.

Another significant detail from the film's biography deserves a mention. The screenplay of *Patent Leather Shoes* was written in the early 1960s and published in 1966. It was received as an avant-garde work that was far ahead of its time; the filming was held back for more than a decade for various ideological and aesthetic reasons. The then powers-that-be could hardly accept an approach that so boldly and daringly diverged from the postulates of socialist realist doctrine. All this free play of the imagination and the film's whimsical associations appeared to be out of tune with the ideological canons of the period; they countered the existing artistic dogmas and became factors that built a barrier for the realisation of Vulchanov's screenplay.

The decade that separated the screenplay's conception from the film's realisation, however, was not a lost time for the director. These were the years during which Vulchanov matured as a filmmaker capable of undertaking a project of such personal and complex character. During the decade that separated the publication of the script from the film's realisation, Vulchanov not only built up his filmography by making one film after another but, more importantly, he steadily perfected his style. The director also had the opportunity to exercise his talent in the context of the Czechoslovak film industry. Around the Prague Spring period, he shot three co-productions there – *Ezop* (*Aesop*), *Tvár pod maskou* (*Face behind a Mask*) and *Šance* (*Chance*), all released in 1970 – each experimenting with avant-garde narrative structures.

If one takes into consideration the overall growth in quality of Bulgarian cinema from the 1970s together with the filmmaker's Czechoslovak experience, one can accept that the advent of *Patent Leather Shoes* is an organic emanation of the artistic growth of an individual filmmaker as well as of a national cinema.

In the years after *Patent Leather Shoes*, Vulchanov continued developing these well-tested stylistic methods. In his next film, *Posledni zhelaniya* (*Last Wishes*, 1983), he unequivocally succumbed to idiosyncratic visions, an approach that facilitated his demystification of the ugly face of war. From a strictly Balkan point of view, World War One here was represented as a carnival panopticum, its main players a motley crew of grotesque characters, and its main events a series of absurd situations. Caricature, exaggeration and hyperbole, all stylistic means that had first been tested in *Patent Leather Shoes*, were widely employed.

In his oeuvre, Vulchanov endeavoured to balance the carnivalesque and dramatic elements in cinema. His example inspired many followers: a host of Bulgarian filmmakers embraced his stylistic approach and further developed Vulchanov's artistic efforts. These included Lyudmil Staykov (*Ilyuziya* (*Illusion*, 1980)), Ivan Andonov (*Byala magiya* (*White Magic*, 1982)) and Nikola Korabov (*Poverie za beliya vyatar* (*A Tale of the White Wind*,

1990)), as well as some younger directors such as Alexandar Morfov (*Hulmat na borovinkite* (*Blueberry Hill*, 2001) and Petar Popzlatev (*Poseteni ot gospoda* (*Visited By God*, 2003), who all made films influenced by Vulchanov's style while diversifying the approach into various other thematic contexts of identity exploration. Vulchanov's influences, however, should not be reduced to a simplistic imitation; it is more about a certain cultural intimacy, a merger between individual viewpoints and existing national tradition which he continued developing in such highly personal films like *Za kade patuvate?* (*Where Are You Going?*, 1986) and *A sega nakade?* (*And Where Do We Go from Here?*, 1988). It is essential to underline how fruitful these processes – of reaching an insight into the characters' intimate world and thus getting an insight into the specifics of national character and identity quest – have been for the enrichment of Bulgarian cinema.

The film's director of photography, Radoslav Spassov, is the most important Bulgarian cinematographer. Besides being responsible for the remarkable camera work of all Rangel Vulchanov's films since *Patent Leather Shoes*, he also shot all the films of director Georgi Dyulgerov (including *Mera Spored Mera* (*Measure for Measure*, 1981; see the chapter featured in this volume). Before turning to directing in the 1990s, Spassov also worked on a range of important films by directors Eduard Zakhariev, Ivan Andonov, Kiran Kolarov and, most notably, on the national epic *Vreme na nasilie* (*Time of Violence*, Lyudmil Staykov, 1988).

*The Patent Leather Shoes of the Unknown Soldier* is a work of cinematic art that allows for multi-dimensional reading. The most popular critical interpretations are those that focus on the 'architectural' uniqueness of the film form and on the skilled use of stylistic archetypes. Indeed, these particularities stand out during a first viewing. In addition to them, however, the film reveals a further philosophical standpoint where the filmmaker traces and reconstructs his own path in art. Even though the film is focused on the past, it bids farewell to the patriarchal world of childhood and turns to the world of tomorrow. The director looks back to yesterday's idyllic existence with open nostalgia as he clearly realises that today the remembrance of the past can only be used as a means for a self-directed search of values for the future. That is why the author's viewpoint of present-day reality is full of vitality and a wisdom born of experience. It is the reality of today that allows him to accept the contradictions of invading modernity and progress with a tongue-in-cheek irony and yet preserve faith in the strength of the individual capable of resisting historical cataclysms.

**Alexander Grozev**

REFERENCE

Holloway, R. (1986) *The Bulgarian Cinema*. Rutherford, NJ: Fairleigh Dickinson University Press/London: Associated Presses.

**13**

LACHENITE OBUVKI NA NEZNAINIYA VOIN

# SPLAV MEDUZE THE RAFT OF MEDUSA

## 14

## KARPO GODINA, YUGOSLAVIA, 1980

In its opening credits, *Splav Meduze* (*The Raft of Medusa*, Karpo Godina, 1980) is defined as a 'tear-jerking comedy'. In Yugoslavia, during the 1920s, a postcard reproduction of Théodore Géricault's painting *The Raft of 'Medusa'* is part of the portable memorabilia/art collection carried by a small group of Yugoslav metropolitan artists (poets, painters, authors of manifestos, photographers from Belgrade) heading out to the world and its avant-garde centres in Russia and in Western Europe.

A photographer uses provocative photos of his sister, Ljiljana, a school teacher, to lure rich bourgeois men into visiting the village where she works, in order to blackmail them. Ljiljana shares her teacher's position and lodging space in a remote village on the Banat plane, near the Romanian border, with a more serious Slovenian girl, Kristina, an aspiring poet. The girls are visited by the brother and his avant-gardist friends Aleksa Ristić, Mišić and Borivoje Lazarević, who arrive together in the car. Kristina discovers mutual sympathy with Aleksa, a tuberculosis sufferer, poet and painter, who pins Lenin's portrait under *The Raft of 'Medusa'* postcard on the wall. Most of the dialogue between the protagonists are quotations from Yugoslav avant-garde texts of the 1920s.

After a couple of days of feasting and artistic debates, made possible due to the school's director having a stroke, they all decide to launch a road show, joining their programme with a travelling strongman, 'Giant' Žnidaršič (a retired Slovenian miner), and his female partner and financer Nadežda. In addition to his performance they dance, read poetry and, to the amazement of an ambivalent and penny-pinching provincial audience, unfold banners with communist slogans and symbols. Among other provocations, Lazarević shoots Aleksa in the chest; Aleksa protects himself with a copy of Petar Petrović Njegoš's *The Mountain Wreath*, a model work of Yugoslavist romantic epic national poetry, so the bullet makes a hole in the Montenegrin poet's book.

Workers in Belgrade are not impressed by the revolutionary show and Žnidaršič, concerned about his dwindling takings, seeks a way out; a smart capitalist persuades Lazarević to leave the group and begin publicity work for him. German writer Hannah Kluge arrives in an airplane to deliver a revolutionary letter from Mayakovsky to Mišić, but it transpires that the Soviet poet sent a love letter by mistake. After several scenes of jealousy, Žnidaršič decides to go on with Ljiljana. Nadežda commits suicide by taking poison in front of the group. The group reaches the Yugoslav-Italian border where the Yugoslav frontier guards mistake them for Comintern agents and Aleksa is shot. The group disperses.

The epilogue reveals Kristina's ill fate. She is shown residing in a morbid Catholic school for the blind in Slovenia, under a tyrannical director. This position is supposed to be punishment for her former behaviour. Kristina receives a letter from her friend, Ljiljana, who has married a rich Dutchman and is now writing from a boat headed for a colonial destination in South East Asia. Following the instructions to burn the letter, Kristina causes a fire in the school. While saving her blind pupils, Kristina get caught in the fire and is left blind and disfigured. We are told of her death some twenty years later, on a day when a film crew arrives to make a documentary about the blind children in the school; in the commotion around the filming her dead body is put in the cellar among sacks of potatoes and donated American canned food, to be buried later.

There are two possible readings of *The Raft of Medusa*. One would be within the context of the contemporary situation at the time of the film's making in 1980, a period of short and promising thaw that soon degenerated into the nationalism in the decade following Tito's death that year. Yet another reading is possible in the aftermath of Yugoslavia's dissolution. This second reading is further legitimised by the specific events and atmosphere leading to the country's disintegration, in which cultural and intellectual production played the key role of inventing, furnishing and disseminating new discourses and narratives which were then, through the state-controlled media, recycled for use by the various political, clerical and military circles.

Film, as an art form of the highest influence, of representative clout (and of state-dependency when it comes to financing), held a very special place in the Yugoslav political and sociocultural system. We should not forget that even in socialist Yugoslavia where popular movies were making money, the financial success of a film was not the real issue, since all the films, except a few rare independent specimens, had to be approved for financing from the state agencies. The rapid degradation of the administrative system in the 1980s did not allow for a prosperous film production that would have significant influence in the formation of new discourses and narratives; this work was primarily done by television, radio and the printed media. Thus, *The Raft of Medusa* remains an exclusive example and an important source of ideas and images, a monument of cinematographic historic poetics, and a turning point in a culture that, at the time, felt an urgent need to look at its recent cultural and intellectual past.

The Raft of Medusa is a rare, if not a unique, Yugoslav feature film in that it deals with the intelligentsia. Artists and intellectuals generally figured in film plots as metaphors, or as typical characters, usually hinting at a certain degree of disengagement with reality, and especially with current politics. There is no big difference between this kind of social and cultural representation and the rather similar construction of artists and intellectuals in Western European countries, in the cinematic discourse of which this group remained equally neglected (except for the intriguing love life and genre stereotypes of a mad artist/scientist). A film dealing with a certain artistic movement and its poetics is such a rarity that none of the overall interpretative templates can apply here. It brings to light a number of challenging problems and questions pertaining to the history of ideas. One of the most demanding is the social invention of artists and intellectuals in the film, chronicling the constant tension between the group's vulnerability, social liminality and lack of political power on the one hand and, on the other, the attention of the authorities who prove eager to manipulate, seduce or repress the group's obvious capability to subvert established ideological narratives and conveniently re-adjust and enhance new ones for the profit of the powers-that-be. With all this, The Raft of Medusa emerges as a high point in a significant period in the cultural history of former Yugoslavia, the so-called 'lead years' after 1968, a period of cultural confrontation, usually associated with the last period of Tito's life (1971–80) in which an informal dissidency tried and succeeded to turn the theme of freedom of expression into the main subject of public debate (often repressed along with its participants) and position the creative and thinking parts of society against the sturdy, wooden language-burdened office-holders of the nomenclature. During this period, Tito's personality cult became so obvious that, after his visit to North Korea, it was even appropriated in some of that country's features. Repression against intellectuals and artists, especially those active in the 1968 events, became very heavy; some of the academics belonging to the so-called Belgrade Group were fired from the University, periodicals banned (Student, Praxis, Vidici, among others), and trials against freedom of expression became commonplace.

Karpo Godina (sometimes listed as Karpo Aćimović-Godina), the director of The Raft of Medusa, was born in Skopje, Macedonia, in 1943 and began his career as a cameraman. His first shorts were awarded prizes at domestic and international film festivals (Piknik v nedeljo (A Picnic on Sunday, 1968), which received awards at festivals in Belgrade and Krakow, and Sonce, vsesplošno sonce (Sun, Sovereign Sun, 1968), awarded at the Belgrade short feature and documentary film festival). Working almost always as both director and cameraman, he continued with a short feature film *Gratinirani mozak Pupilije Ferkeverk* (*Brains au gratin by Pupilija Ferkeverk*, 1970), featuring a famous Slovenian avant-garde performing group, and a documentary, *Zdravi ljudi za razonodu* (*Healthy People for Fun*, 1971), about a multiethnic community in Vojvodina. He made several films on artists and art, and also distinguished himself, both artistically and politically (with his opposition to dull nomenclatural directives), by working as a photographer on controversial films such as Želimir Žilnik's *Rani radovi* (*Early Works*, 1969; see the chapter by Marina Gržnić in this volume), Bato Čengić's *Uloga moje porodice u svetskoj revoluciji* (*The Role of My Family in the World Revolution*, 1971) and Lordan Zafranović's *Okupacija u 26 slika* (*Occupation in 26 Frames*, 1978). All these films came under direct attack from conservative and hardline critics operating with entrenched and rigid ideological and aesthetic concepts, and by the nomenclature itself.

The Raft of Medusa was Godina's first full-length feature film. The author of the script, Branko Vučičević had been active as a film critic since the late 1950s; he was also known as an English translator and a connoisseur of avant-garde cinematography and the artistic movements of the 1920s. Along with Dušan Kovačević, Gordan Mihić, Mirko Kovač and Ljubiša Kozomara, Vučičević is one of the 'auteur' screenwriters responsible for the definitive image of Yugoslav cinema. Vučičević cooperated with Dušan Makavejev on his two feature films, *Ljubavni slučaj ili tragedija službenice PTT* (*Love Affair, or the Case of the Missing Switchboard Operator*, 1967) and *Nevinost bez zaštite* (*Innocence Unprotected*, 1968) as well as working with Bato Čengić and Želimir Žilnik. Besides sharing key creative personnel with *Early Works*, *The Raft of Medusa* also compares to Žilnik's film in its scepticism with regard to the chances of successful revolutionary propaganda and in featuring the dismal failure of communication between the 'masses' and their alleged radical leaders. In both cases we have a traveling group of intellectuals trying to enlighten the proletariat without success. Ultimately, it is this same premise of communication breakdown between the group of actors and their provincial audiences that is the core of the stylistically very different film by Theo Angelopoulos, *O Thiassos* (*The Travelling Players*, 1975). Bulgarian cinema also addressed these issues in well-known films from the same period (*Zvezdi v kosite, salzi v ochite* (*Stars in Her Hair, Tears in Her Eyes*, Ivan Nichev, 1977); *Dom za nezhni dushi* (*A Home for Gentle Souls*, Evgeni Mikhailov, 1981)). The theme of communication deficiency between intellectuals and the peasant/worker classes has been addressed in many other Balkan films as well, often using a plot evolving around an intellectual protagonist who is shown leading an isolated life within a community dominated by anti-intellectual leanings (be it a village setting or a provincial town). Yet another aspect of this same theme is tackled in films revealing the impossibility to be a true intellectual even in big cities in the region as life in the Balkan metropolis is dominated by peasant or petit-bourgeois values (as seen in Yugoslav films like Rajko Grlić's *U raljama zivota* (*In the Jaws of Life*, 1984) or Goran Marković's *Tajvanska kanasta* (*Taiwan Canasta*, 1985)).

In 1982, Godina directed *Crveni Bugi* (*The Red Boogie*), a feature film on the influence of jazz on Yugoslav culture shortly after World War Two, with Branko Schömen as a scriptwriter. Vučičević's and Godina's cooperation peaked later in their film *Umetni raj* (*Artificial Paradise*, 1990), which can be seen as the last Yugoslav film, formally and conceptually. It built on recently discovered research materials concerning the short yet intensive stay of director Fritz Lang in Slovenia during World War One and tackled the problems of film history and poetics, as well as of the relation between talent and power. This fruitful cooperation between director and scriptwriter, both interested in art, historical poetics and in the way the relations with authority affects artists and intellectuals, was shaped, to a large extent, by the unique visual culture and knowledge of the matter possessed by Godina and Vučičević. This thematic sphere can be recognised as one of the leading schools in the context of 1970s and 1980s Yugoslav filmmaking.

The two other schools were represented by the 'Prague Group' and by the group represented by Živojin Pavlović, who often adapted his own writing for the screen, or Mića Popović, who followed the same stylistic orientation in his painting and filmmaking: an orientation that connected the literary group of hyper-realistic authors and the authors of the so-called 'Black Wave' films. While the directors of the Prague Group perpetuated the sensibility of their Czech teachers (such as Miloš Forman), and displayed certain reservations in committing to a clear-cut political view (by hiding their political utterances under layers of irony and thus completely blurring the political message), the Black Wave authors insisted on raw images and raw characters, branding patriarchal violence and pointing, sometimes quite explicitly, to the (communist) ideology which, in their view, 'corrupted' people, especially the rural population. The works of the Black Wave directors alarmed the bureaucrats while those of the Prague Group did not disturb the system as profoundly. The film that initially alerted the authorities was a student feature by Lazar Stojanović, *Plastični Isus* (*Plastic Jesus*, 1971), which linked a clear anti-ideological and anti-nomenclatural political message with surrealist metaphors (using the folklore of the student movement). Using Eisensteinian parallel montage, *Plastic Jesus* established clear associations between the fascist and nationalist movements from World War Two with the present-day communist regime (some unseen archive footage was used for this), bringing these philosophies together under the common denominator of totalitarianism. The author was put on trial and sentenced to five years; his mentor, the film director and professor at the Belgrade Academy of Performing Arts Aleksandar Petrović, best-known for his film *Skupljači perja* (*I Even Met Happy Gypsies*, 1967) was also in trouble with the authorities and distanced himself from Stojanović, even though he had been recognised as his most talented student.

The film school represented by Karpo Godina and his *The Raft of Medusa* was more subversive than the two other groups. The history of recent (pre-war) artistic movements, which became an attractive topic for research in academic circles in the 1980s, was still not acceptable for the communist nomenclature, but was silently tolerated. The anachronistic twist enabled those who wrote about the pre-war and thus pre-communist times, to criticise totalitarian practices in history, before they had become part of Yugoslavia's post-war reality, yet this clever 'transfer' of meaning was rather transparent to the educated Yugoslav public, which was accustomed to coming across metaphors and figures of so-called 'Aesopian language'; they were often attacked by the regime's watchdogs. Godina's attitude was to use a rationalist approach, to take the stance of an educated, enlightened individualist who questions everything, even his own pleasure in culture. When faced today with the international success of the 'colonial wisdom' of Emir Kusturica, who cannibalised Yugoslav film tradition by presenting glossy pseudo-folkloric images and loose narratives of the central Balkans, funded generously by Slobodan Milošević, one cannot but despair at the Western and European lack of serious film culture and taste – but also knowledge – when it comes to small cinema traditions.

*The Raft of Medusa* is structured around multiple layers. The central narrative is of a group of avant-garde artists who want to escape the banality of everyday life and are cruelly punished for this; it is a basic plotline, which is most transparent in the somewhat overdone finale with the ill-fated Kristina. The *épater le bourgeois* layer includes mimicking of the movies, the contrasts between artists and villagers, as well as the almost total rejection of artistic provocation. The connection of art and popular culture is explored through images of technology (dancing to radio tunes, messages brought by a woman pilot, a 'revolutionary' watch), and in dangerous manipulation suggesting how easily art can be sucked up into publicity (the case of the artist who sells himself to a capitalist); the artists join a strongman in an attempt to include the unconscious and the kitsch into avant-garde poetics; Kristina's misery and death in an atmosphere in which the electricity is switched off underlines the linkage of art and technology.

The idea of a travelling show that makes equal use of circus and intellectual attractions, of the use of popular culture as a smokescreen for more demanding reflections, is imbedded in the ideology of many avant-garde movements from the beginning of the twentieth century. The nomadic-picaresque layer of the plot is represented by a car from which the group displays changing banners and slogans (mostly in red). It plays ironically with a romanticised representation of Romanies (walking by the car, for instance), an image that had become part of the Yugoslav cinematic folklore by the 1980s. But there is also a hint of the Yugoslav cultural situation, before World War Two and after, as a gateway culture which cannot live in isolation. Mobility against provincialism as a more general slogan also has its subversive meaning hinting at the ideological staleness and isolation perpetuated by the Yugoslav communist nomenclature: the fear of the 'foreigner' was and still is – more than ever – one of the basic discursive components of the totalitarian/nationalist narrative in the region. The characters in the film have different ethnic backgrounds; their mobility within Yugoslav space also means mobility of political messages; the restriction of their mobility serves as a warning of imminent developments in Yugoslav society. No doubt Godina and Vučičević were right in this respect.

The love interest in the plot is problematised through a 'private is political' point of view: sexual liberty and promiscuity blend well with revolutionary movements and avant-garde projects. The sexual emancipation of the two schoolteachers, however, is already in place by the time the male members of the group arrive in the village. Therefore, only the backlash into the formatted, banal passion (Žnidaršič/Nadežda/Ljiljana triangle) can drag the love ideology back to the popular narrative. Otherwise, there is not much sexual interaction between the male and the female counterparts of the nomadic artistic group. The gender problematisation was not really high on the agenda of Yugoslav film artists at that time, so Godina's use of women in the film is quite a rarity. Independent, clever, capricious, seductive women were certainly not often seen in these years; rather, women were just too often raped on screen, or represented in a restricted range of characters (a crying mother, a treacherous whore/wife, a victimised virgin/sister).

Almost all the dialogue in the film comes from quotations of various avant-garde poems, manifestos and revolutionary slogans. Appealing to the masses, making high art accepted and acceptable by the proletariate was a widely appropriated strategy of the intellectual ideologues of Communism. The fact that the group is neither accepted nor acclaimed, and that Žnidaršič does not approve of mixing subversive political ideas with his straightforwardly commercial act 'injects' additional irony and allows for the interpretation that art is by definition elitist, and it should not seek mass approval. An esoteric reference to Marcel Carné's *Les Enfants du paradis* (*Children of Paradise*, 1945) can be found in this.

The characters in the film *perform* their communication; the 'natural' language is erased from the film, except for a few direct examples of repression. Lovers also exchange quotations, and this engagement with the arbitrary nature of the sign represents one of the basic propositions of the film, as well as of avant-garde poetics. A sudden change of tone occurs in the finale: the neutral female voice narrating Kristina's miserable fate can be understood as the voice of history, exemplifying the 'generic' fate of artists, universalising the situation of the clash between creative individuality and collective patterns of behaviour.

The historic layer of the plot features, through quotations, a number of avant-garde artists and movements from the 1920s, a particularly vivid period of culture in the new state of Yugoslavia. A number of 'isms' lived together, in continuous polemics and mutual denial: Zenithism, Expressionism, Hypnism, Sumatraism, Surrealism, Tank movement, Futurism, and so on. Many of these movements had special relations with Communism, and certainly all of them copied one or more features of revolutionary folklore which in the 1920s seemed to be thriving, especially among European intellectuals. The favourite genre of the period was the manifesto, a form that derives directly from the contemporary political programmes of the Left, all modelled on Karl Marx's 1845 *Thesis on Feuerbach*, even though the various American and French revolutionary pronouncements from the end of the eighteenth century should not be forgotten either. Zenithism is most often quoted in the film. This movement's inventor and leader, Ljubomir Micić (Mišić in the film), was forgotten for decades; his work (mostly published in his periodical *Zenith*) was re-discovered in the 1980s. Even though its followers were based in different countries, one of its main ideas was the almost mystical belief in the force of 'the Balkan', a certain Balkan 'barbarogenius'. The film itself 'quotes' the technique of *collage*, so popular with the avant-garde movements. Many international avant-garde names are referenced in the film, such as Tristan Tzara, Kurt Schwitters, Vladimir Mayakovsky, F. T. Marinetti and Bertolt Brecht.

*The Raft of Medusa* proposes the idea of a travelling exhibition, for which art is necessarily adjusted to small transportable forms, although some large-sized paintings also travel with the artists. The postcard with the reproduction of Géricault's painting functions as a *mise-en-abŷme* for the film, a condensed semiotic framework in which all meanings merge and form new meanings: it is a sign of poetics, not a symbol bearing a message. Therefore, the 'message' of the film is certainly not 'survival of the strongest'; rather it focuses on travel, death and art as subversions of 'beauty'. The complicated poetics of the film are combined with a 'horror of the story' inherited from the European cinema, especially the French Nouvelle Vague from the late 1950s. The non-narrative, or the arbitrary can also be interpreted as a reference to the film poetics proposed by Angelopoulos in *The Travelling Players*; instead of the nervous, mobile off-hand cinematography of the Nouvelle Vague, the camera here is more or less static as in the early days of cinema, and people enter and exit the restricted, stage-like space that is framed by the lens, often posing still as if for a photograph. Taking photographs is a leitmotif in the film: the brother takes lurid photos of his sister; the group poses for a photo before taking off.

Black and white cinematography is used in the documentary-styled ending featuring shots of blind youngsters who explore relief maps of Yugoslavia and the globe, powerfully suggestive of the post-war backlash of socialist realism. The final shot freezes on a letter written in Braille. Compared with the archaic-looking 'masks' used in other episodes in the film, as if extracted from old movies, this reference to a much more recent documentary style suggests that the previous avant-garde irony has been completely forgotten – just like the oblivion that surrounds the paintings and the poetry by Aleksa, Kristina and Mišić. The lack of historic continuity or memory forces an awkward quasi-naïve approach, evocative of the old maxim that, if forgotten, tragic history repeats itself as a farce.

Many scenes in the film are organised as tableaux, as if they were staged; the effect is strengthened by the quotations *performed* by the actors. This is meant to stress the episodic character of events and to enhance the feeling of lacking plot development and absent hierarchies, including the director's and scriptwriter's authority. But this 'invisibility' of the author is just a trick: the absence of a progressing plot can also be seen as an expression of the author's ultimate will. The theme of *The Raft of Medusa* is historic and pedagogic at the same time (revealing hidden aspects in the cultural past); Godina's approach can be interpreted as a reaction to the undemanding understanding of the past in official history as straightforward progress. In most of his films, Angelopoulos also tried to denounce the inanity of official history; he did that by dedicating a lot of 'slow time' to tell the history of oppressed individuals. Godina's and Vučičević's concept is different: they 'translate' avant-garde poetics into the official record and are not so concerned with the fate of an individual in history. There is a point – at the end of the film – where the plot coincides with an individual historic fate; it is here where the story overlaps with the postulates of avant-garde poetics and becomes over-verbalised. Kristina's downfall into realism is simultaneously a symbolic blindness to the forward-looking poetics of the avant-garde, so her life comes to an end.

One of the main elements of the avant-garde poetics used in structuring of *The Raft of Medusa* is time. The main timeframe, which moves from one desperate provincial school at the start to one in a worse condition at the end, is intersected by other timeframes: the utopian European avant-garde, represented by a woman pilot in her airplane, bringing the message from an avant-garde friend; the local avant-garde, presented by a rather slow car, especially in the scene where the car has to be transported over a river on a barge; the contrast between the perpetual routine lifestyle of the general populace and the 'happening', event-based lifestyle of the artists. The *mise-en-abŷme* of Géricault's painting concerns timeframes, too; because it represents the movement (end of a long and catastrophic voyage, final hope). Finally, *The Raft of Medusa* questions the self-sufficiency of the socialist Yugoslav regime, which erased from memory some of the avant-garde movements and personalities (Zenithism) while favouring those that acted more loyally toward the new communist ideology (Surrealism). Thus, reconstructing the cultural memory in *The Raft of Medusa* is a warning against the disrespectful ideology which establishes the new value system. However, it is also a warning to artists in view of their possible irresponsible collaboration in inventing (and selling out) utopian projects. In this respect, *The Raft of Medusa* was a prophetic film which bears qualities that any avant-garde movement of the twentieth century would claim for itself. Thus the two proposed interpretations mentioned at the start of this chapter are justified in the film's own manifold poetics.

**Svetlana Slapšak**

# PETRIJIN VENAC PETRIJA'S WREATH

## SRDJAN KARANOVIĆ, YUGOSLAVIA, 1980

The story of *Petrijin Venac* (*Petrija's Wreath,* Srdjan Karanović, 1980) takes place in a small mining town in Serbia called Okno ('Shaft'). The events span over three decades – before, during and after World War Two – from 1937 to 1967. The tragic life of the illiterate peasant woman Petrija (Mirjana Karanović) is structured as a triptych, with every part marked by a new man she loves.

The story begins with Petrija's marriage to Dobrivoje, an unhappy union ruined by the brutality of the husband and the hostility of the mother-in-law, Vela Bugarka. Routinely abused and neglected, Petrija's first pregnancy ends with the death of her son at birth. Later, she gives birth to a girl, Milana, who survives only a few years before succumbing to meningitis, near the end of World War Two. The marriage falls apart and Petrija is compelled to leave the family home.

Ljubiša, a *kafana* owner, gives Petrija a job waiting tables, rescuing her from her despair and thus prompting her gradual emancipation. But soon the *kafana* is nationalised and Ljubiša leaves town; Petrija accepts the marriage proposal of Misa, a local miner. She begins a new life under socialism but her happiness does not last long. Misa's drinking becomes excessive; he survives a mining accident but is now handicapped and suffers severe psychological pain. He dies a few years later and Petrija is once again left alone.

In the 1960s, the mine is shut and the railroad closes down the train service to the town. Yet Petrija's lonely life goes on. She finds comfort in the visits of the ghosts of her loved ones, Milana and Misa. She knows that one day Misa will call her to join him, but she is in no hurry as she feels life is still worth living.

Srdjan Karanović, the film's director, belongs to the so-called (Yugoslav) Prague Group. The term refers to a group of ex-Yugoslav directors (including Goran Marković, Goran Paskaljević, Lordan Zafranović, Rajko Grlić) and cameramen (Živko Zalar, Predrag Popović) who graduated from the famous Prague Film School (FAMU) in the late 1960s. This was the first generation of formally educated and cine-literate directors in Yugoslavia to come out of the same film school. The members of the Prague Group deny its existence, arguing that it is an artificial moniker invented by film historians and critics as a matter of convenience. Goran Marković, for example, has claimed that these filmmakers are connected mostly by friendship, by the memories of their youth and studies, while the extensively discussed influences of the 'Czech New Wave' are, in fact, sporadic and barely recognisable. According to Karanović, the work of each member of the Prague Group should be analysed as a separate entity: 'For a long time now we do not belong to the same "compartment" … we all deserve separate ones.'

And indeed, the work of the Prague Group directors is marked by diversity and richness rather than by shared stylistic or thematic features or generic preferences. There are significant stylistic differences in the auteurist-type filmmaking of its members. Throughout his oeuvre, Goran Marković explores various genres, from the teen social drama (*Specijalno vaspitanje* (*Special Education*, 1977)) to fantastic adventure (*Sabirni centar* (*Meeting Point*, 1988)). Goran Paskaljević, probably the director with the best commercial instinct, plays upon melodrama and knows how to develop images of helpless marginals in order to earn the audience's sympathy and emotional response, as seen in his *Pas koji je voleo vozove* (*The Dog Who Loved Trains*, 1977), of children or old people, as seen in *Tango Argentino* (1992) and *Tudja Amerika* (*Someone Else's America*, 1995). Lordan Zafranović has used cinema to re-articulate Yugoslavia's World War Two history, most notably in his excellent epic *Okupacija u 26 slika* (*Occupation in 26 Scenes*, 1978). Rajko Grlić passes a whole range of sophisticated love stories intertwined with urban, generational or class conflicts with poise and elegance; he is best known for *Samo jednom se ljubi* (*That Melody Haunts My Reverie*, 1981), *U raljama života* (*In the Jaws of Life*, 1984) and *Za sreću je potrebno troje* (*Three for Happiness*, 1986). Despite the stylistic differences, however, the grouping of these directors (facilitated by the fact that they have often collaborated) has proved to be a useful analytical tool that facilitates analysis of their work.

Karanović, the director of *Petrija's Wreath*, has explained that within his work one can distinguish three tendencies. The first one is 'experimental'. These are films that offer space to amateur actors to allow them to gain a reputation, films where improvisation allows different versions of popular culture to become the prevalent element of fiction (*Drustvena igra* (*Society Game*, 1972); *Pogledaj me, nevernice* (*Faithless Woman Look at Me*, 1974); and *Miris poljskog cveća* (*The Scent of Wild Flowers*, 1977)). The second tendency is represented by films preoccupied with characters from the director's generation, where the plot is located in a middle-class environment (*Nešto izmedju* (*Something In-between*, 1983); a section of *Za sada bez dobrog naslova* (*Film With No Name*, 1988)). Here, the middle-class setting usually determines both the psychology of the characters as well as their morality: it imposes values and lifestyles, and determines relationships. The third tendency involves films that are, foremost, of 'ethnological interest'. These are based on myths and stories of the past, which include sufficient material to fuel the telling of a story, as in films like *Petrija's Wreath* and *Virdžina* (*Virgina*, 1991). In these films, 'it is popular tradition, manners and customs that determine the framework, and it is their dynamics that create the necessary conflicts in the plot'.

In the 1990s, finding it painful to cope with the break up of ex-Yugoslavia, most of the FAMU graduates moved abroad. But their lives continued to follow the same generational pattern. Marković stayed as professor at FDU (the faculty of Drama Arts in Belgrade); Grlić and Karanović taught at American universities; Zafranović returned to Prague. Paskaljević continued his career with feature fiction films in France, while others turned to documentaries, making compelling testimonies about politics and art. After spending a period abroad, in 1998 Karanović resumed his Belgrade University career. Since 1999, Grlić has divided his time between Ohio and Zagreb, Paskaljević has commuted between Paris and Belgrade, while Zafranović returned for a large retrospective organised in 2002 by the Belgrade Film Archive, and stayed on to work on new projects. After more than a ten-year break, Marković and Karanović made feature films – *Kordon* (*Cordon*, 2002) and *Sjaj u očima* (*Loving Glances*, 2003) – ensuring not only the continuity of their careers but also the continuity of the Prague Group.

*Petrija's Wreath* was adapted from the novel of Dragoslav Mihajlović, a Yugoslav writer of cult standing. Survivor of Goli Otok, the Stalinist working camp for political prisoners set up after Tito's break with Stalin in 1948, Mihajlović had been one of the first writers to reveal the hard truth about communist-era repressions. A 1969 theatrical adaptation of his novel *When the Pumpkins Blossomed* (1968), directed by Boro Drašković, had been banned soon after the opening night after Tito alluded to it in critical terms in one of his speeches. A member of SANU (the Serbian Academy of Science and Art), Mihajlović enjoyed the aura of politically engaged and quasi-dissident author.

Literary historian Jovan Deretić considers Mihajlović among the 'novostiliste' ('new stylists') whose work is characterised by the rejection of all things artificial or construed. For these writers it is not enough to simply offer a realistic reflection of modern life and its rough aspects; rather they seek to recreate it in vivid speech, which sounds emphatically different from the normative literary language. The critic, Novica Petković has commented that 'the themes and language of everyday life are put together, so that narration in the first person can be equally done in jargon or in a dialect'. Mihajlović used both options to build symbolic and lyrical meanings as well as to 'transform the low and the vulgar' into moving poetic symbols. Published in

1975, the novel *Petrija's Wreath* received the newly established Andrić Prize (named after the Nobel Prize winner Ivo Andrić). As well as being adapted for the screen, it was later made into a four-part television mini-series, and adapted for the theatre. The film was awarded the Golden Arena and screened as part of the Special Retrospective of the best films of Pula's Festival for its fiftieth anniversary in 2003.

Chronologically, *Petrija's Wreath* occupies the mid-position in Karanović's oeuvre and is pivotal in both connecting and opposing the rest of the Prague Group's generational oeuvre. Karanović transfers the urban periphery heroes from the films of Grlić or Marković to the Serbian rural landscape. Whereas Marković uses popular beliefs about life after death and structures the plot of his *Meeting Point* (based on Dušan Kovačević's play) around the fact that the living are not allowed to know that they will go on living after they have actually died, Karanović's simple protagonists are immune to intellectual scepticism; their firm belief in life after death determines most of their actions.

In the context of the predominantly macho Yugoslav cinema, Karanović stands out as a director adept at representing women – be they ordinary or heroic – on the screen. In the wedding scenes, in the *kafana*, in the hospital or at the railway station Karanović continues to use 'naturschiks'. This allows him to concentrate on the exploration of Balkan borderline identities, tracing rural-urban migration. He would return to this with *Something In-between*, which would explore the relations between Balkanism and Europeanism, or via the way in which *Film With No Name* would deal with the multiethnic society, or *Virgina* would question gender identity. Most obviously *Petrija's Wreath* is of the same 'blood type' as *Virgina*, as it explores the same theoretical (ethnological and anthropological) and generic (melodrama, women's film) foundations.

The ethnographic background here is provided by the *vlaško* surrounding. The Vlasi are an ethnic minority who inhabit the northeastern parts of Serbia and speak a Romance language that is believed to be close to Latin. They live near the Bulgarian and Romanian borders and are known for magical talents that take on a certain primitive and atavistic sensibility, as well as for a supernatural heritage that finds expression in various superstitious beliefs, healing practices and fortune-telling rituals. As with Emir Kusturica's *Dom za vešanje* (*Time of the Gypsies*, 1989), the old women of this group are respected and simultaneously feared as they are seen as shamans or soothsayers. One of these women, Vlajna Ana (Olivera Marković), a secondary figure who is nonetheless present in all key moments of the film, provides help or comfort to Petrija. She recommends stoic endurance: 'You just be ready … you just wait and hope.' The second uncanny character is Vela Bugarka. Swathed in black, she silently tiptoes around and lurks behind windows. She is like a black cat or an evil witch, casting her spells over the dowerless bride (and causing the death of her newborn baby boy). In this animal-like life, which is simultaneously full of mysticism and rituals, a woman's existence is two-dimensional – there is the domineering witch and there is the mother giving life. The world's order is matriarchate; thus the film's genre can be described as matriarchal melodrama. Petrija's greatest tragedy, accordingly, is in her inability to bear or keep a child.

In the second part, Petrija embarks upon a trajectory of emancipation. She confirms her definitive break with the obedient existence of silent patriarchal wife by changing her appearance. She dresses in a quasi-urban way and, more importantly, she drops the scarf and uncovers her hair, then cuts it short and puts a wig on. It is this change in appearance (and, effectively, iconography) that marks her 'liberation'; the changed hairstyle represents an awakening of a new sexuality, which is played out in the relationship with Ljubiša. As the story develops, it is easy to mistake Petrija's habitual stoicism for regained passivity. She is again married and again obeying a husband, yet she is now able to talk back and persevere even if she gets slapped in the face. But it does not mean that she accepts it thoughtlessly: she can never be truly submissive again; she expects to be rewarded for her suffering.

The multiple framing and the flexible positioning of the gaze neatly structure the sociological reading of the patriarch-matriarch binary. In the beginning, Petrija is framed as a woman in waiting, often shown as standing behind or beside the window. She does not dare to look through the window or to explore openly her reflection in the mirror; she turns back the photos and pulls down the curtains and remains a passive object in the camera's gaze. Later on, after she has grown into an active heroine, she is transformed into a brave subject that leads the camera. She looks in the mirror to check out her new look; she follows Ljubiša's advice and no longer avoids eye contact with men; at the end of the film she will even directly address the camera, thus triumphing by daringly returning the gaze.

The changing gender dominance is also underlined by the narration. The narrator is a woman who tells the story through voice-over or direct to camera. Quite systematically that voice-over is provided by a real 'Petrija', amateur Darinka Živković who also appears on screen several times – most notably bookending the film. (The actual woman who served as prototype for the novel was called Milica Stevanović; she died at the the age of eighty.) With her wise and calm voice, she ensures the transition between the present and the narrated flashbacks remain smooth.

The young Petrija was played by Mirjana Karanović, in her screen debut. At the time she was only in the second year of her studies, yet for the role of Petrija she received the two highest national cinematic awards (at film festivals in Pula and Niš). Petrija's role, a woman with a weather-beaten face and a strong east Serbian accent, revealed Karanović's talent in full scope and established the image of the common-sensical, long-suffering wife and mother that the actress would develop later in two of Kusturica's films – *Otac na službenom putu* (*When Father was Away on Business*, 1985) and *Underground* (1995). Even today, after a rich cinematic and theatrical career that took her all over ex-Yugoslavia, Mirjana Karanović considers Živojin Pavlović, Emir Kusturica and Srdjan Karanović as the directors she most enjoyed to work with. Along with other stars (like Milena Dravić, Olivera Marković and Mira Furlan), Karanović is one of the most important film actresses in former Yugoslavia. Various aspects of her career make her compatible to leading female stars from the region who belong to different generations, such as Hungarian Mari Törőcsik, Bulgarian Nevena Kokanova, Pole Krystyna Janda or Romanian Maia Morgenstern.

Unlike the films of Grlić or Zafranović, history and social circumstances remain of secondary importance in the context of this film. Although Karanović draws continuous parallels between the ups and downs in Petrija's life and the corresponding social and political developments, the latter are little more than a vivid backdrop for Petrija's story. In the 1940s, there are momentary glimpses of German patrols, partisans and youth brigades, as well as scenes of preparations for a Labour Day Parade. Railway tracks or smoking train chimneys, similar to those in classical westerns, gradually punctuate the idyllic village landscapes, signalling industrialisation and urbanisation. The closure of the railroad line is marked by the removal of the tracks, symbolically cutting-off the life-line to the village, after which the village is left behind, abandoned for the city that has attracted the rural population who have rejected the traditional lifestyle. Society has neglected the old villages and mining towns, which are now left without their vital lifeline. By 1967, Okno is a half-deserted ghost town, similar to the Welsh mining village seen in John Ford's *How Green Was My Valley* (1941), although Petrija's story does not contain the same level of sentimental and nostalgic overtones, relying instead on a more hard-hitting, murky realism. The time of the historical background is linear, progressively changing as witnessed by the people who are not sure if the manifestations of Destiny are truthful clues or only deceptive appearances. The time in the foreground, focusing on Petrija and her suffering, is the mythical circular time of a Fate foretold. It is something that is felt, believed in and accepted yet remains invisible. The turning points in life occur when the 'spear' of reality time pierces the mythical circle of this invisible other dimension. Petrija accepts everything as repetitive tragedies and evil, 'as something not only inevitable but also normal, accepting the world as the stage' according to Bogdan Kalafatović. She is a typical Karanović character, besieged by Destiny and split between a melodramatic and a tragic world.

One of the more frequent themes in Karanović's films is usually made up of a meta-cinematic essay containing dedications to film history, as seen in *Something In-between*; reflections upon the relationship between reality and illusion, as seen in *The Scent of Wild Flowers* or upon issues of media manipulation as seen in *Film With No Name*. In *Petrija's Wreath*, the reflective mode is inscribed through formal design and the densely interwoven ethnographical and anthropological elements of the narrative. The film's opening and end as well as its 'chapter headings' are marked by the insertion of still photographs of the main characters. The credits roll over a sequence that shows these same photographs being manipulated in various ways – coloured, rearranged and put together in a collage – opening with a photograph of Petrija and in closing with an image of all the protagonists. Each chapter opens with the photo of the man who will become the main presence in Petrija's life and closes with Petrija leaving with his photo. When her first husband, Dragiša, chases her away, she takes their wedding photograph with her; when leaving Ljubiša she hides his photo in a mirror she takes with her; when things with Misa take a bad turn she asks the photographer to 'make' a new photograph of them – instead of the real wedding one – by photo montage. All photos are taken by the Photographer (in the Serbian original he is called The Image-maker) who retouches this record of reality by embellishing and enriching the details. Petrija explains that the embellished photos allow us to remember the past as something that was better and more beautiful, thus imitating the (noble) manipulation of remembrance everyone unconsciously performs. Her simple ways rearticulate André Bazin's 1958 thesis about photography as a means to overcome the ephemerality of life and support a lasting memory that obliterates death. The presence of the photographs – carried in the pocket by the heart or hanged on the wall and thus securing the permanent presence of loved ones – further exemplifies Edgar Morin's claim that photography catches our souls and preserves them.

The Photographer also handles the job with mirrors, linked with a whole range of small rituals and attitudes, which are equally present in the beliefs of the Vlasi and in Morin's film anthropology. When someone dies women cover the mirrors in the house; Misa and Petrija get a mirror as a wedding gift. Because the reflection is understood as a spiritual double of the body through which one could influence the 'original', the Photographer cuts the mirror in half so that Misa would not have to look at the reflection of his crippled leg. Thus the Photographer functions as a male counterpart to Vlajna Ana or as a metaphorical demiurge, his status equated to the position of the film's authors.

The 'frame within the frame' structure creates a web of glances that come together in two of the film's key scenes. The first one is at the market place, where, some time after their separation, Dragiša approaches Petrija and attempts to flatter her. But Dragiša's new wife arrives, baby in arms, and cuts the conversation short. Misa, who wants to pay for the smashing of the *kafana*, comes to Ljubiša, who observes all these developments from a distance. Vlajna Ana silently stops by Petrija and a group of singing partisans with red flags fills the background. The scene brings together all the men that have a defining part in Petrija's life – in the past, the present and the future – and spatially defines her relation to all three of them. Dragiša symbolises bad times; his relationship with Petrija is regularly cut off by the interference of other women (initially his mother, now his new fertile wife). Ljubiša is Petrija's silent protector; Misa appears causally passing by, as somebody who does not play a role yet but who will soon figure powerfully in her life. The scene is further enriched by the double framing, provided by the partisans with the flags (reference to history) and the photographer (reference to record).

The second one is the scene of the demolition of the *kafana*, passively observed by Petrija standing in the back; a crowd of villagers gathering and going away in front of the window and the Photographer taking pictures. Amidst the chaos they leave behind, Ljubiša sits down and invites Petrija to join him for a drink as a companion; his equal.

Both scenes rely on an intricate *mise-en-scéne*, which shows characters standing at the crossroads of life; their circumstances are complex, they both look at others and are simultaneously being looked at. Their ambiguous, almost 'schismatic' position mimics the film's retelling of one's own life from a distance, of looking and participating at the same time. 'My life and me went into different directions; my life went that way and I ended up this way. And somehow it is that this so-called life of mine passes somewhere over there, beside me', says Ljubiša implicitly defining the situation.

*Petrija's Wreath* could be read as a peculiar counterpart to Karanović's earlier *Grlom u jagode* (*Unpicked Strawberries*, 1975), a juxtaposition where *Petrija's Wreath* and this made-for-TV film are put side by side as rural versus urban generational chronicles. The characters in both texts are 'caged in' by Destiny: sometimes visibly (as the metaphorical disguise of Vlajna Ana, for example) and sometimes invisibly yet fatally known and nearly palpable, imposing its constant presence to a degree that is nearly stereotypical. The stories tell of a process of discovering one's true identity and of journeying through life. *Unpicked Strawberries* remains one of the best Yugoslav television series of all time, and is often repeated and still charms new generations of Belgrade teenagers; in 1985 it was followed up by an equally successful feature sequel, *Jagode u grlu* (*A Throatful of Strawberries*). In time, the protagonists of the *Strawberries* films finally grew up and fulfilled the demanding expectation of entering – although quite reluctantly – the world of responsible adults. Their hopes to become like the rest of the normal (slightly grey) world were presented as predictable and moderately optimistic, be it with a touch of resignation.

Karanović's most recent film *Sjaj u očima* (*Loving Glances*, 2003) can be seen as a variation of the *Strawberries* theme, imbued with the same sentimental optimism. The story is a love triangle set among a group of refugees in Belgrade in the late 1990s. A cross between *Strawberries* and *Petrija's Wreath*, the film's protagonists, Labud and Romana, possess the same stoicism and soft humorous resignation as Petrija. They also talk with ghosts from the past who – unlike Petrija's ghosts – keep them apart. This talk evokes an identity conflict between the urban identity of the young refugees and the traditional nationalism of their peasant ancestors, translating into the more general oppositions of rural/urban and old/young, all themes explored throughout Karanović's work.

*Loving Glances* can be seen as a nostalgic look back to the traditional Yugoslav cinema, which restores the continuity of the Prague Group but does not reach the heights of its early achievements. These yearning glances could be seen as a contemporary version of Petrija's almost brutal lust for life in spite of everything, as expressed in the gloomy motto of the film: 'Man is good for nothing. He likes to live like an oblivious, stupid animal.'

**Nevena Daković**

REFERENCES

Deretić, J. *Kratka istorija srpske književnosti*. On-line; http://www.rastko.org.yu/knjizevnost/ jderetic_knjiz/ jderetic-knjiz_12.html (accessed 1 August 2003).

Kalafatović, B. (1985) 'Venac stradnja i patnje', in *Znaci sa ekrana*. Beograd: Institut za film.

– Petković, N. (1997) 'Twentieth century literature' in *The History of Serbian Culture*. On-line; http://www.rastko.org.yu/isk/npetkovic-xx_literature.html (accessed 12 July 2003).

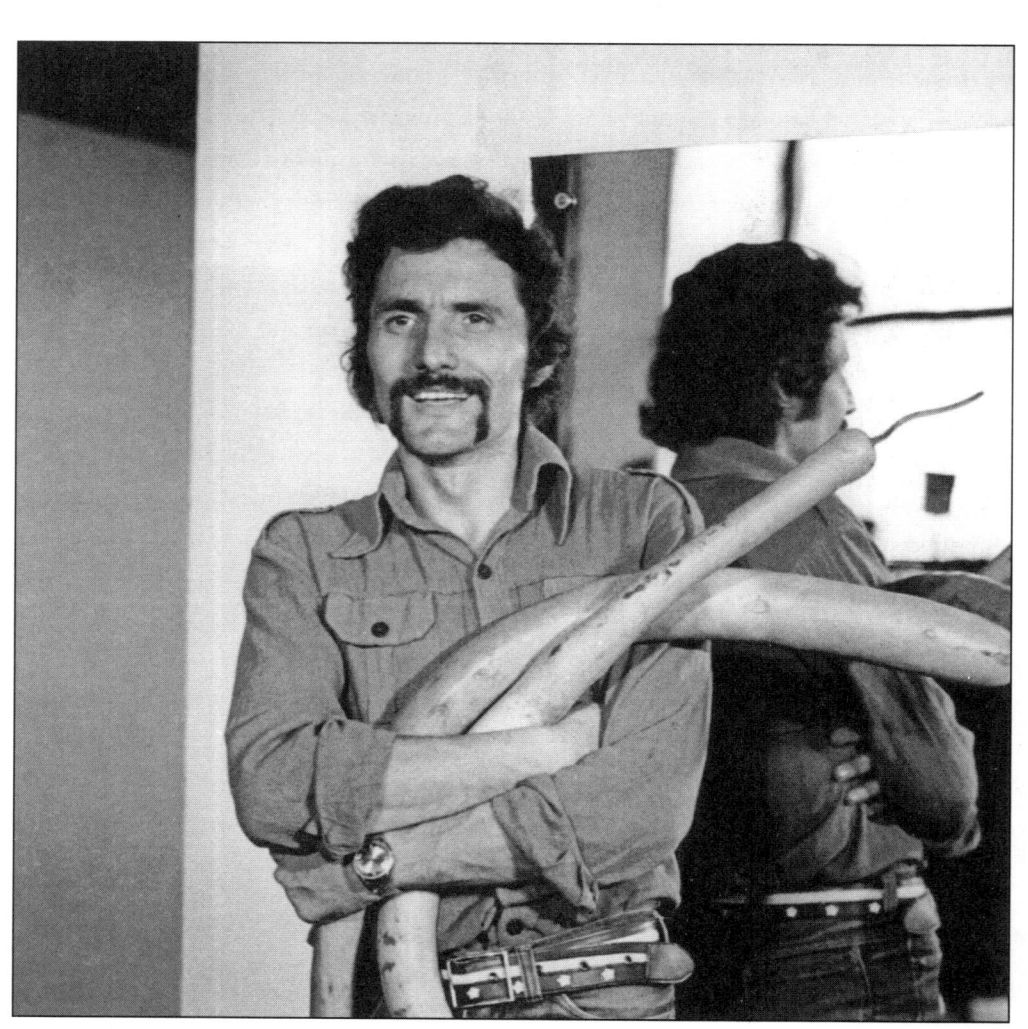

# PROBA DE MICROFON MICROPHONE TEST

## MIRCEA DANELIUC, ROMANIA, 1980

Bucharest Central Station, the late 1970s. Television journalist Luiza and cameraman Nelu (played by director Mircea Daneliuc) are interviewing young people caught traveling by train without proper tickets. Among those interviewed is Ani, a charming factory worker from a small provincial town studying languages at the Popular University in Bucharest. She is returning from a holiday on the seaside and claims that her papers have been stolen together with her train ticket.

Later Nelu receives a phone call from Ani; she invites him for coffee at her temporary home in Bucharest. She confesses that she lied during the interview: she quit factory work some time ago and she is not taking any courses at the University; she just enjoys picking up Italian 'by ear'. Her confession arouses Nelu's suspicion, who knows that contact with foreigners is illegal. Ani suggests that she would rather not have her interview included in the television programme. The next day, part of the Central Station footage is mysteriously missing.

Luiza becomes interested in the case of the young woman whose interview has disappeared and follows Ani to her town to find out more. It turns out that at her former place of work Ani is somewhat of a black sheep. She has given up her job after a dubious episode with a married colleague and has since been involved with a young dolphin tamer working on the Black Sea Coast. The television crew follows Ani throughout the country. A conflict emerges between Nelu and Luiza, as the latter perceives Ani as a threat to her discreet relationship with the cameraman. In reaction to this, Nelu tries to protect Ani from Luiza's 'journalistic' curiosity. The conflict gradually grows into disagreement over ethics: while Luiza is ready to use a hidden-camera to record a discussion between Ani and her boyfriend, Nelu strenuously objects.

Nelu ends his relationship with Luiza, and rushes into a tumultuous affair with Ani. As soon as he does, he sees aspects of her life that the journalistic investigation never touched on: besides being attracted to seaside hotels frequented by foreigners and to smuggle Western goods, Ani is a carer entangled with the rehabilitation of an alcoholic brother whom she follows around the country hoping to find for him an assisted-living home. As Nelu's feelings for Ani grow deeper, he finds out that he will have to join the military reserve in a few months' time.

He tries to postpone it as he has in the past with backing from the television station, but Luiza refuses to help him.

Nelu uses his connections as a television employee to find a job for Ani in Bucharest, as she is under scrutiny by the employment services. But she does not have an ID with a Bucharest address registration, which she needs as a pre-condition for employment in the capital. Nelu suggests that Ani invokes her brother's illness to get work in Bucharest, but she refuses on the grounds that she believes it is unethical.

One of their brief passionate encounters takes them to Central Station. Ani invites Nelu to join her for a train journey without a ticket. But Nelu is unable to jump on to the moving train so she disappears again.

Before embarking on military service, Nelu makes a last attempt to find Ani, who is still seeing the dolphin tamer, hoping he can sort out things between them. During a visit to the town where she used to work, he is once again convinced that she has been lying to him about many aspects of her personal life.

A few months later, Nelu returns from his army reserve service and goes looking for Ani at a factory in another provincial town where she has settled. He meets her in the street on her way from work. Ani is now married and expecting a child. Each of them tries to blame the other for not having been able to express their feelings more clearly at the right time. Their heated discussion causes passers-by to intervene. Ani leaves with her new partner. Alone and confused, Nelu stays behind, lost in the industrial estate's depressing landscape.

'*Microphone Test* is neither the film event nor the masterpiece that it is considered to be. It is rather a *normal* film produced by a film industry which should respect itself.'
— Mircea Alexandrescu

'Nobody can say what would have become of Daneliuc and of others like him under *normal* circumstances.'
— Dan. C. Mihăilescu

The notion that cultural production occurs somehow 'unnaturally' in a repressive political context, that is, mainly as a defensive act or survival strategy, works well in Mircea Daneliuc's case, a graduate in literature and film, who came to prominence in the mid-1970s and who re-emerged as a writer in the mid-1990s.

The specific construction of 'normality' in the context of socialist Romania has a particular resonance for a film director who, around the mid-1980s, had to make a living by knitting cardigans after having given up his Communist Party membership in protest against the shelving of one of his films (*Glissando*, 1984). Rumour has it that, after some practice, Daneliuc even found a way to interweave his signature in the knits, as a necessary transfer of authorship that was not only a source of good money but also a sign of a well-preserved sense of humour in spite of the crippling reality of Ceaușescu's Romania.

The interpretation of Daneliuc's films made during the socialist regime as reactions to the given historical context is logical. His 1997 literary debut, however, written as an expression of dissent with the institutional practices of the post-1989 film establishment comes as a surprise. *Pisica ruptă* (*The Dismembered Cat*, 1997), a bitter and funny autobiographical work, is meant to uncover the metamorphosis within the local film industry during its decades-long relationship with a repressive regime. (The book takes its title from the Romanian colloquial 'a rupe pisica', 'to dismember the cat', which describes a dramatic decision that may have major consequences for both the person who takes that decision and, possibly, for the group. In this case, the 'dismemberment of the cat' refers both to a specific moment from Daneliuc's biography – giving up his Party membership – and to his decision to talk openly about the internal affairs of the local film industry, thus challenging the group's collective identity.) It is a unique 'ethnography' of the Romanian film community living through the change of political regimes, revealing the ambiguous morale of a guild whose past cohesiveness was mainly a result of political numbness. Daneliuc makes unflattering statements and provides not only good contextual background to his isolation but also offers a bitter explanation for the low international profile of Romanian cinema. It is no wonder that his longest period of inactivity as a filmmaker took place not during totalitarian times but only in recent years, around the time of the publication of his critical book: no film by Daneliuc premiered between 1994's *Senatorul melcilor* (*The Snails' Senator*) and 2003's *Ambasadori, căutăm patrie* (*Ambassadors Looking for a Country*).

The harsh truths revealed in *The Dismembered Cat* confirm the anti-establishment aura which has been Daneliuc's main asset since the times of *Proba de Microfon* (*Microphone Test*, 1980). The filmmaker was perceived as the most inconvenient of the so-called Romanian '1970 generation', which also included Dan Pița, Mircea Veroiu, Alexandru Tatos and Radu Gabrea. *Microphone Test* was Daneliuc's third film, and the first real confirmation of his talent after two previous films, *Cursa* (*The Long Drive*, 1975) and *Ediție Specială* (*Special Edition*, 1978) which had established his credibility as a filmmaker.

'When *Microphone Test* was screened for the visa of the Ideological Commission ... I feared what was about to happen and I was ready to "dismember the cat", writes Daneliuc. But contrary to what he expected, the situation did not develop in a way that would make him enter into a radical clash with the system. The film got the commission's stamp of approval rather easily, apparently due to a 'whim' of the secretary. This apparent 'acceptability' provides a good framework for the dialectics of this film's interpretation: the text allowed for an ideologically correct interpretation that simultaneously served as a cover up for its more or less discreet subversive potential. From this perspective, *Microphone Test*, the very title of which suggests tuning in and adjustment to pre-existing codes, is Daneliuc's first chance to play with approved and subversive meanings, a practice in which he would become an expert later on.

*Microphone Test* was produced at the end of a decade marked by the so-called 'July Theses' of 1971 which, after a short-lived liberalisation in the mid-1960s and early-1970s, had ushered in a dramatic process of re-dogmatisation of cultural life. The sudden change in cultural politics left people involved in cultural production in deep shock. Romanian intellectuals took a decade to adjust to the renewed political pressures and to reconsider their position vis-à-vis the system. Released in a world which measured its emancipation in small steps, always compared to previous tighter control rather than to a 'normal' standard of a presumably unrestrained cultural production, *Microphone Test* was enthusiastically received by press and public. Having received several awards at the local festival in Costineşti in 1980 (Special Jury Prize; Best Actress for Tora Vasilescu; Best Supporting Actress for Maria Junghetu) the film was praised as proof of Daneliuc's abilities to strike meaningful balance between scripted and improvised material. The director was also commended for his skills in conveying multiple layers of meanings without losing entertainment value.

A number of other films, including *Filip cel bun* (*Filip the Kind*, Dan Piţa, 1974), *Mere roşii* (*Red Apples*, Alexandru Tatos, 1976) and *Mijlocaş la deschidere* (*Scrum Half*, Dinu Tanase, 1980), have been identified as forerunners of *Microphone Test*, all focusing on the private as mirror of the public, all praised for the freshness of their young protagonists and for their degree of improvisation.

Exiled cultural commentator Monica Lovinescu recalls her first viewing of *Microphone Test* in 1982 in Paris where the film screened as part of a Romanian film week. In a generally disappointing context, *Microphone Test* comes across as a 'double revelation' for Lovinescu: first, there is a Romanian filmmaker who is 'finally contemporary'; secondly, the film displays an 'extraordinary courage'.

The juxtaposition of the relatively good domestic reception on the one hand and of Lovinescu's remark about the dissident nature of Daneliuc's courage on the other, suggests a discreet incongruence between two sets of interpretations. These can be reconciled if one keeps in view the film's assortment of subtexts that allow for two different interpretations (conformist and subversive).

*Microphone Test* combines several narrative layers. First, there is the main narrative provided by the explicitly fictional lives of the protagonists; then come the documentary-style sequences, where the main protagonists mix with non-professional actors in typical socialist contexts and the outcome is introduced as footage resulting from journalistic investigation; third, there are some genuine *cinéma verité* moments with unidentified subjects interspersed throughout the main narrative as short sound (and, sometimes, image) tests.

Seen from today's perspective, *Microphone Test* becomes more than it was accounted for by its initial reviewers, who were interested to ensure public life to the film, so they avoided reference to its more subversive aspects by avoiding discussion of inconvenient meanings and presenting the film as more ideologically compliant than it was. The early reviews concentrated on the main narrative; the documentary-style inserts were treated as stylistic devices rather than as significant in their own right.

The story of a failed attempt to merge two different and inevitably political life philosophies, *Microphone Test* works, at the level of its main narrative, as a commentary on issues of social acceptability. Most frequently the film's plot was summed up as 'a love-hate relationship between a decent man and a less decent woman'. The protagonists are positioned in a classical power imbalance mediated by the camera: Nelu is behind the camera, while Ani is in front of it. As a cameraman, he explores social 'case studies', while she is one of those 'cases', immediately categorised as deviant. Ani is a member of a youth subculture scapegoated by the regime while Nelu is someone who has already internalised the rules of the game. As the plot develops, however, each one of them will be shown as different from the type they are supposed to represent: Ani's compassionate and caring nature will prevail over her eccentric attitudes, her relentless mobility, explosive liveliness and consumerist urges. Nelu's 'decency', on the other hand, will be exposed as pragmatic adaptation to social acceptability criteria: his main preoccupation throughout the film will be to 'fix' things through institutionally-approved arrangements, and his attempts would reveal a rather dubious morality and motivation. Drifters reminiscent of Ani are well represented in the cinema of the Balkans (both *Stella* (Michael Cacoyannis, 1955) and *Evdokia* (Alexis Damianos, 1971) feature such independent and socially marginalised characters; see the chapters on these two films in this volume). Female vagabonds are present, for example, in Goran Paskaljević's *Pas koji je voleo vozove* (*The Dog Who Loved Trains*, 1977), in Rangel Vulchanov's *Valchitsata* (*The She-wolf*, 1965) and in Petar Ppozlatev's *Az, Grafinyata* (*The Countess*, 1989).

The initial reviewers of the film could not equate the male character's ambiguous ethics with the dubious morality of the system. Consequently, what was commented upon was the pair's positioning at opposite poles in terms of social acceptability and their impossibility to 'integrate' each other. But what was seen as 'deviance' in 1980s Romania today would be called simply 'lifestyle'; what was seen as 'decency' today would be called corruption.

A case in point is provided by the only sequence that had to be edited out: during an animated discussion between Luiza and Nelu at the door of her hotel room, an unidentified man in underwear is briefly spotted inside. Nelu freezes and then jokes about Luiza's surprising sexual freedom. The episode was cut in order to avoid any unwanted hints of immorality associated with the journalist. In its original version, the sequence was important in creating the feeling of moral relativism intended by Daneliuc, as Luiza is shown as particularly outspoken in blaming Ani for her promiscuity.

The film's ending allowed for different readings as well. The absence of a happy end was praised by several commentators, who emphasised the uncompromising realism. Yet the decision to deny Nelu and Ani's private reunification was, in a way, providing a different, more politically correct 'happy ending' where a formerly deviant woman, Ani, ends as a properly socially integrated factory worker expecting a baby.

The film's ending was a subversive comment on issues of social acceptability as well: the final freeze frame, showing Nelu alone amidst a depressing industrial landscape, is progressively covered by a series of television control lines scrolling down and gradually covering the screen completely. When the screen is about half covered by straight lines, an irregular line scrolls down but is immediately overridden by several other straight ones that come on top of it, so that the irregular line gets covered and is soon 'straightened' by the others. The frozen final image suggests technical malfunction: the television screen is covered by similar control lines which make Nelu and the landscape almost invisible. The opacity of the screen carried a strong symbolism for the audience of a country entering its worst socialist decade characterised by frustrating media control.

By the end of the film, Nelu has become an object of the camera's gaze; he is no longer the narrator as he was when originally introduced into the narrative. His position has shifted from filming others to being filmed; the shift comes about not as a result of his conscious switching sides in solidarity with his subjects but rather as a consequence of his 'wrong' choice of partner. Unlike Krzysztof Kieślowski's amateur filmmaker from *Amator* (*Camera Buff*, 1979), Nelu is far from critically turning the camera onto himself.

The bureaucratic absurdity of life under communism (compulsory IDs, restrictive freedom of movement, required address registration in cities, arbitrary calls to military reservist service, and so on) that make normal relationships nearly impossible and encourage conformism and opportunism is partially shown in some of the films of Prague Group directors in Yugoslavia (for example Goran Marković's *Tajvanska kanasta* (*Taiwan Canasta*, 1985); Rajko Grlić's *Za srecu je potrebno troje* (*Three for Happiness*, 1985)) and figures prominently in films from Bulgaria (Borislav Sharaliev's *Vsichko e lyubov* (*All is Love*, 1979); Hristo Hristov's *Edna zhena na trideset i tri* (*A Woman at Thirty-three*, 1982); Nikolai Volev's *Margarit i Margarita* (1989)) and Albania (Kujtim Çashku's *Colonel Bunker* (1998); Gjergj Xhuvani's *Slogans* (2001))).

Arguably the film's most innovative, as well as most subversive aspect, is provided by the documentary-style inserts. The late 1970s in Romania were characterised by a certain 'experimental realism', which paralleled the 'official realism' promoted by the state. The erosion of modernist paradigms resulted in a new emphasis on 'the real' which was no longer limited to the legacies of the socialist realist recipe and was developed by artists who used acceptable formats (for example news-reports, journalistic interviews, live broadcasts) in order to make non-conformist statements.

*Microphone Test* was released at the end of a decade marked by the publicly promoted ideology of 'slice of life' as a front for a number of experimental acts such as the quasi-documentary photo-montages of painter Ion Grigorescu or the 'industrial biographism' of writer Alexandru Monciu-Sudinski. Daneliuc's 'sound tests' with average 'socialist citizens' follow a similar approach – from the young man confessing that his greatest dream is 'to be an engineer and be happy' to the middle-aged woman commenting on the relaxed behaviour of the young generation: 'too bad they're allowed to wear long hair' – an apparently conformist *vox populi* which actually engaged ironically with the status quo by exposing the internalisation of ideology by ordinary people.

There was not much stylistic and temperamental congeniality between Daneliuc and other filmmakers of the period, yet *Microphone Test* displayed affinity with the work of a group of Bucharest-based writers who engaged in a similarly 'documentary' subversive re-examination of the status quo (for example Mircea Nedelciu's collection of short stories *Adventures in a Courtyard*, 1979). This 'documentarism' was meant to expose the heavy re-working of reality into the 'factuality' mediated on television: Luiza's tampering with the appearance of the workers she interviews or the punctual, hilarious sequences of reality-staging said much to an audience already familiar with these practices of media manipulation. The film's subversive potential had been properly assessed by Romanian Television still at inception stage: with the exception of several general shots, Daneliuc was not granted permission to shoot on actual television premises.

At least one sequence contains an explicit statement about the relationship between local audiences and national television: the crew's car, bearing the logo of TVR, breaks down; an apparently helpful driver slows down and inquires in an unnaturally friendly manner: 'Are you really from National Television?' And as soon as they confirm this, the driver speeds off, shouting: 'All right then, see you around some other time!'

In the very next sequence Nelu is shown sitting in a room, eating salami on a newspaper and discussing with Luiza the prospect of 'fixing' his army service; on the background a television set is on, playing an edited version of some of the material taken earlier in the film: slow-motion footage of a dog running on the seaside, accompanied by a soundtrack which combines romantic music and sugary poetry recited in voice-over. It is a hilarious example of 'bad TV', explaining why the driver from the previous episode did not care to help. It is also an illustration of the slot filling 'poetical intermissions' which would become a key television attribute during the 1980s as part of the regime's strategy to employ lyricism in order to de-politicise the media.

The 'TV poetry' example also testifies to Daneliuc's strong reliance on the subversive power of language. Similar to most of his other films, *Microphone Test* uses a casual dialogue and thus secures good contact with the audience. Starting from the striking 'sound test' that opens the film (the monologue of a poorly-educated woman talking about her would-be abduction ending at Central Station), the language spoken in *Microphone Test* grasps the dynamics of socialist 'newspeak' revealed in a range of personalised individual vocabularies. It is a mutating language, providing exasperating examples of the impact of the 'mobilisation system' that was in effect in Romania at the time. The news-reporter herself is shown addressing this issue explicitly by asking during an interview: 'Don't you have your own words? Why do you have to speak in clichés? You are still young ... when did you manage to learn this already?'

Romanian critics have frequently noted Daneliuc's extraordinary sensitivity to the nuances of spoken language as the main reason for the rather disappointing international response to his films: his colloquialisms are not easy to interpret. Although regularly selected for major festivals, Daneliuc's films have been bypassed for awards, suggesting that his work does not translate easily, both in linguistic and in cultural terms, and that the full scale of his message can only be grasped by an 'informed audience'.

If approached by focusing more on the documentary excerpts rather than the main narrative, *Microphone Test* can be seen as a commentary on the impossibility to document a given 'reality' through the governing conventions of the time. The falsely investigative yet disinterested attitude of journalist Luiza does not leave space for ordinary human concerns. Therefore Daneliuc needs to rely on a fictional narrative that works as 'ethnography', as an in-depth case study. Luiza's inability to seek deeper truths makes her, according to Monica Lovinescu, resemble Securitate; in a way Luiza is exactly the opposite of Agnieszka, the relentlessly questioning distrustful protagonist of Andrzej Wajda's *Człowiek z marmuru* (*Man of Marble*, 1976) which made Lovinescu call *Microphone Test* 'anti-*Man of Marble*'.

From today's point of view, more than twenty years after the film's premiere, the subversive nature of the inserts dominates the straightforward message of the main narrative. Today, *Microphone Test* works rather as a glossary of 'memory sites'. While strongly reactivating the memory of the informed audience, most sequences of *Microphone Test* require pre-existing familiarity with the context as this is the only way to grasp the ironical references to the Romanian socialist status quo idiosyncrasies: the 'poeticisation' and 'folklorisation' of the media, the 'Bucharest ID', the 'Eugenia' biscuits (the only biscuits widely available during the socialist period).

The approach and structure of *Microphone Test*, its strong local impact and minimal international circulation, are all explained by the film's production context: the film was made at the end of a decade marked by the return to a tighter censorship and a subsequent refining in the textual practices of resistance employed by filmmakers. It was Daneliuc's rehearsal for his next film, *Croaziera* (*The Cruise*, 1981), which was considered by many to be his most accomplished critique of the system and was equally critical of the work of media. Some well-known sequences in *The Cruise* cleverly exposed the deep discrepancies between what was happening on the screen and in front of it and signalled the necessity of more critical reception, a type of audience attitude that the director always counted on.

Today, Daneliuc can be considered as one of those who, in Slavenka Drakulić's words, 'survived Communism and even laughed'. Or, even better, he can be described through the joke of the Eastern European intellectual who, when asked how he survived Communism, replied: 'Did I?'

After 1989 Daneliuc added to his repertoire of subversive acts the engineering of a collective hunger strike for the purposes of gaining autonomy for the local film industry from the Ministry of Culture early in the 1990s, the free public opening of his 1993 *Patul conjugal* (*Conjugal Bed*) where only 61.5 per cent of the film was shown (corresponding to the percentage of votes received by Ion Iliescu, who was elected president of Romania with a landslide in spite of having been exposed as stalwart of Ceaușescu's regime), and the refusal to accept a medal from the same president as part of a pompous ceremony that included a double award for his more accommodating fellow filmmaker Sergiu Nicolaescu. But Daneliuc's post-1989 career also included a gesture which can be seen as giving symbolic consent to his inclusion in the 'film generation' of the 1970s: up to the early 1990s, in spite of his chronological belonging to the '1970 generation', Daneliuc's personal profile was not fully integrated into that of the group, as his passionate preoccupation with the status quo made him stand out for his courage alongside his strictly professional qualities. By taking the managerial position of a film unit (Alpha) where he scripted, directed and produced his own films, he joined the club of those established filmmakers who, after the clash with the socialist regime, were only able to concentrate on running their own publicly-funded filmmaking units and proved more or less unwilling to create a supportive working environment for the younger filmmakers.

The irreverent flamboyance of Daneliuc's 1980s work (*Microphone Test, The Cruise, Glissando*) gradually gave way to a bitter frustration that dominated his post-1989 films such as *Conjugal Bed* or the recent *Ambassadors Looking for a Country*, and not least his professional auto-biography, *The Dismembered Cat*.

Looking in retrospect, Daneliuc appears to be a good example of a freedom-loving artist affected equally by the lost opportunities brought about by a repressive political regime and by the petty rivalries of a narrow-minded film community. The 'normality' invoked by the two reviewers quoted earlier refers to the main limitations of Daneliuc's career: the suppressed freedom of speech, and the inescapable Balkan marginality. Daneliuc desperately needed international legitimisation but, when it came, it was too little too late. A few years after *Microphone Test*, Daneliuc gave up his Party membership to avoid the cutting of *Glissando* in 1984, thus coming close to a professional suicide. But soon thereafter he made cuts to the film himself, responding to a request from the Venice Film Festival, thus asserting the bitterly ironical realisation that 'normality' is always context-specific.

**Adina Bradeanu**

Author's note: My warmest thanks to Mrs Maria Neagu, Mircea Daneliuc's long-standing film editor, for providing me with detailed contextual information hard to grasp from printed sources.

REFERENCES

Alexandrescu, M. (1980) 'Proba de microfon,' *Contemporanul*, April 25, 6.

Daneliuc, M. (1997) *Pisica ruptă*. Bucharest: Univers.

Drakulić, S. (1992) *How We Survived Communism and Even Laughed*. New York: Harper Perennial.

Lovinescu, M. (2002) 'Un cineast scriitor: Mircea Daneliuc,' in *Diagonale*. Bucharest: Humanitas, 101–4.

Mihăilescu, D. C. (2002) *Pisicile lui Daneliuc: definirea prin negație*. Online; http://www.ournet. md/~paulgoma/pg-daneliuc.htm (accessed 15 June 2003).

# PAD ITALIJE THE FALL OF ITALY

## LORDAN ZAFRANOVIĆ, YUGOSLAVIA, 1981

In 1943, a small town on the Adriatic island of Šolta became the focus for communist fighters and a succession of cruel intruders (Italian fascists, Nazi-backed Ustasha, monarchist Chetniks). The story of *Pad Italije* (*The Fall of Italy*, Lordan Zafranović, 1981), referring to actual events, presents a mosaic of different characters and tragic destinies, with the ongoing cruelties leaving the closely-knit community deeply traumatised.

Davorin, a young revolutionary, is the commander of a communist squad from the small town. His family, as well as the population in general, is split between maintaining their traditional lifestyle and the necessity to make harsh choices imposed by the war, the Catholic Church, the fascists and the communists. Davorin's cousin, Niko, has an affair with a young woman who mingles with the Italians and is exposed as an informer. Davorin is ordered to execute the woman (and Niko, if he does not renounce her). Niko refuses to give up his lover and opts to be executed, which Davorin reluctantly carries out after fulfilling the couple's last wish to be pronounced husband and wife. Ironically, Davorin himself will soon fall in love with an equally unsuitable woman – the daughter of a local landowner, called 'the princess'.

June 1943. The Sveti Jovan (St John the Baptist) celebration takes place in the public square. A group of Italian Blackshirts are stationed here. One of them is harassing Božica, a communist who shows sympathies for Davorin; she shoots the troublemaker. Her act leads to an open fight between communists and Blackshirts. The Italians are stronger and punish the community by ruthlessly executing a number of randomly picked townspeople, among them Davorin's younger sister.

September 1943. The capitulation of Italy is announced. A violent revolt breaks out; the town's people take their revenge by savagely killing some of the Italians. The communists return to town to celebrate the fall of Italy. The estate of the wealthy landowner, the princess's father, is pillaged by a hungry crowd; he is brutally beaten in front of his family. When Davorin witnesses the mugging, he stops the mob and insists that the communists do not approve of such anarchy. But being in love with the princess (whom he weds in lavish nuptials), Davorin's allegiance to the cause is tarnished and he comes to be seen as disloyal and prone to compromising his ideals. From now on, he will grow weaker as fighter and revolutionary and will delay important decisions, thus exposing the island's population to danger.

Before long, Germans and their collaborators, the Ustasha, move in and take over. After a bloody fight the communists succeed in pushing them out and defending the island. But soon another group of violent warriors arrives, this time a motley raggedy band of monarchist loyalists – Chetniks, Cherkez and Hungarians – who prove equally violent and destructive and even more bloodthirsty and inhumane.

That all these cruelties are not prevented suggests inadequate defences. The person in charge, Davorin, has grown insensitive to the dangers; his passivity and irresponsible acquiescence has led to loss of life and destruction. Božica accuses him of delaying in securing the island's defence; the revolution should be above anything personal, she insists. By marrying the princess, Davorin has sold out. It is his oblivious behaviour that has made it possible for the Chetniks to set fires and slaughter many of the town's inhabitants, adults as well as children. His younger brother, who has come of age during the revolution, is now associated with a group of committed partisans who confront and condemn Davorin. His execution takes place at the edge of a cliff overlooking the shining blue waters of the Adriatic.

Lordan Zafranović, director of *The Fall of Italy*, graduated from Prague Film School (FAMU) in 1971, and then lived and worked in Zagreb where until 1991 he directed more then fifty documentaries and shorts, and 13 features, almost all of which were very popular. Unlike other members of the so-called Prague Group, he has a pronounced preference for historical themes and takes particular interest in confronting issues of politically-sanctioned violence and historical responsibility, all issues which he approaches in a non-conventional manner. Most of Zafranović's films challenge the deepest foundations of nationalism with daring investigations into the hushed theme of the Nazi-sanctioned cruelty of the Ustasha regime in Croatia during World War Two. Questions of delayed justice and postponed accountability and of the blurred definition of guilt for genocidal crimes are raised not only in his features but also in his impressive documentaries *Krv i pepeo Jasenovca* (*Blood and Ashes of Jasenovac*, 1985) and *Zalazak stoljéca (Testament L.Z.)* (*Decline of the Century: Testament of L.Z.*, 1994).

*The Fall of Italy* is part of a loose trilogy dealing with the historical reality of Croatia during World War Two; the other two are the acclaimed *Okupacija u 26 slika* (*Occupation in 26 Scenes*, 1978) and *Večernja zvona* (*Evening Bells*, 1986). All three films are scripted by Zafranović in collaboration with the well-known writer Mirko Kovać, for which they both gained a reputation of audaciousness: to address the controversial issues of the Civil War during Tito's time was one of the most sensitive undertakings someone could risk. Kovać is responsible for the scripts of many influential Yugoslav films, such as *Occupation in 26 Scenes*, *Mali vojnici* (*Playing Soldiers*, Bahrudin 'Bato' Čengić, 1968), *Lisice* (*Foxes*, Krsto Papić, 1970) and *Tetoviranje* (*Tattoo*, Stole Popov, 1991, co-scripted with director Živojn Pavlović); no matter during which historical period his films are set (World War Two, the aftermath of the war or the present-day) his interest is always on issues of totalitarian oppression and politically sanctioned violence.

In the 1980s, after Tito's death, the re-interpretation of World War Two became a dominant subject in Yugoslav film, but still remained a delicate and uneasy issue. *The Fall of Italy*'s predecessor, *Occupation in 26 Pictures*, is considered one of the most important Yugoslav films. The film is set in the Dalmatian city of Dubrovnik during World War Two and tells the story of three friends – Croat, Italian and Jew – who end up on opposite sides after the fascist regime is established in Croatia (each one of them becoming respectively close to the Ustasha, to the Italians and to the Partisans). The film displays shocking hard-hitting violence and condemns the Ustasha, at the times a muted and contentious topic the very choice of which suggests a certain degree of civil courage. *Occupation in 26 Pictures* won a range of awards, among them a Golden Arena at the Pula festival as well as a Palme d'Or nomination at Cannes. (*The Fall of Italy* also won the Golden Arena and did well in cinemas but never reached *Occupation in 26 Pictures*' popularity)

Ustasha and Chetniks, the conflicting fractions shown in *The Fall of Italy* besides the communist partisans, not only had different political aims but also different historical trajectories. Like in Greece, where multiple occupying and other forces were in place in different parts of the country during World War Two, Yugoslavia's territory also saw the presence of a range of occupiers (German Nazis, Italian, Hungarian and Bulgarian fascists) as well as a range of local warring factions. It is important to keep in mind that the population of these regions was also politically split, and while many supported the partisans, there were also many who actually welcomed the Nazis. In the aftermath of World War Two the uneasy issues of controversial political alignments within Yugoslavia were hushed from the public agenda in favour of building 'brotherhood and unity', and so no real process of the 'truth and reconciliation' type ever took place.

The fascist Ustasha movement had started in Mussolini's Italy some years before the German-led invasion of Yugoslavia in 1941. After this invasion, the country was divided into parts that were respectively controlled by various Nazi allies (Italians in the West, Hungarians in the North of Serbia and Bulgarians in the East). Ustasha leader Ante Pavelić proclaimed the 'Independent State of Croatia' in 1941 with the Germans' blessings and engaged in genocidal policies against Croatia's Jews, Serbs and Gypsies. Yet the Dalmatian coast and most of the Adriatic islands (one of which is the island in the film), were not part of the Ustasha state, but were ceded to Italy and were claimed by Pavelić only after the fall of Italy in 1943. The Chetniks, who had started as a pro-monarchist guerrilla movement led by Draža Mihailović, gradually came to collaborate more and more with the Germans and finally fought against Tito's partisans, hoping to establish a 'Greater Serbia' out of the ruins of Yugoslavia.

The protagonist, Davorin, functions on two levels – on one hand he plays a key role in the life of the town and, on the other, he is part of his own family. In such a small place it is the collective and not the individual that is the more powerful entity, and the film reflects this set-up. Davorin's tragic downfall can, therefore, be seen as an allegory for the crisis of the nation. *The Fall of Italy* is a carefully constructed mosaic representing the island's micro-cosmos and showing the volatility and the violent extremes that rocked the whole region during the war. Davorin's relatives function as a representative cross-section for this micro-cosmos; it encompasses representatives of nearly all warring fractions. The clashes between different ideologies (communists/fascists, poor working-class/rich landowners) and between believers and atheists form the basis of investigation in the film. The tension between loyalty towards the party and loyalty towards the family is a dominant theme in Zafranović's oeuvre. In all three films of the cycle, Zafranović shows situations where family members are divided along political fault lines leading to betrayal of best friends and fratricidal-type executions; these are situations of rupture where the traditional family loyalties and the respect to the elderly, embedded in the patriarchal structures of the region, are profoundly undermined.

Brutality is a wide-spread phenomenon of this historical period, not limited to Italians, Germans or Croats. *The Fall of Italy* enacts a symbolic 'trojka' of yet another villainous gang, comprising of monarchist Chetniks, murderous Cherkez from the Caucasus and degraded Hungarian aristocrats (symbolising a further potential coalition of macabre forces). United by a common interest in fighting Communism they all support the occupying force in the region. They arrive on a boat and reach the town on a horse-drawn carriage, terrorising the local 'enemies'. The assassination of the little Catholic boy who has come to show them the way is one of the most shocking scenes in the film: his little body is soon dumped out of the carriage with a slit throat.

The collaboration between the Ustasha and the Catholic Church is another persistent theme in the film. In one of the scenes the local priest, a Franciscan, is trying to force the people in the church to support the Ustasha; he even keeps a gun on the altar, prepared to face dissent. But Zafranović introduces also a counter-part figure, an open-minded and more humane clergyman who behaves quite differently, thus suggesting that not all who were affiliated with the Church actively collaborated with the Ustasha regime.

On a closer look it also becomes clear that even though Zafranović presents clashes between the Church and the communists, he ultimately sees both sides as stringent doctrines that are equally dedicated to authoritarian and thus fundamentalist moral codes, resulting in occasional yet intense similarities in their practices and approaches. Indicatively, toward the end of the film, just before being sentenced to death, Davorin will be told that a commander of a partisan group has to be like a priest.

The local hunchback, who always happens to be around when crucial events happen, is a symbolic figure for the subservient attitudes to the occupiers. He can be seen as a 'borderline figure': on one side he is shown as a mindless freak that cannot be held responsible for his actions yet on the other he displays the fairly rational behaviour of an evil traitor and conspirator.

Apart from the more general philosophical approach to history, which examines themes of violence and power, Zafranović makes a range of subtle contemporary political statements. The director clearly has problems with those aspects of communist dogma that border on fundamentalism and require the ascetic suppression of human desire. He also exposes the hypocrisy of revolutionary rhetoric: after a temporary victory of the communists, the peasants ransack the rich man's lair and beat up the landlord, an episode clearly suggesting that the line between revolution and pilfering is blurred. Another key moment suggesting Zafranović's critical take on contemporary politics is the sequence featuring the wedding between Davorin, the poor communist, and the rich princess, daughter of the capitalist class enemy, a union that stands in for the symbolic marriage between communists and the affluent classes that came about in Yugoslavia after the communists took power. Both sequences contain implicit critique of the Yugoslav political system, which turned the formerly ascetic communists into members of the well-to-do 'red bourgeoisie', oblivious of their earlier idealistic beliefs and elevated anti-materialist principles.

The story of a communist male of lower-class origins who rises in the world due to a relationship with a woman of higher bourgeois social standing (played out in *The Fall of Italy* in the relationship between Davorin and the Princess), has been interpreted as a generic Yugoslav/

Balkan dramatic plot called 'Reverse Pygmalion' by anthropologist Marko Živković. It can be traced in other popular films such as Rajko Grlić's *Samo jednom se ljubi* (*You Love Only Once*, 1981), Darko Sorak's *Oficir s ružom* (*Officer with a Rose* 1987) and Gorčin Stojanović's *Ubistvo s predumišljajem* (*Premeditated Murder*, 1995).

Zafranović also unmasks the demagogy of situations where declarations of acting morally are clearly refuted by the inhumane acts that accompany this same rhetoric of high moral ground. At the moment of Niko's killing, for example, Davorin insists that it was actually Niko's choice to die, thus snubbing responsibility and passing the blame on to the victim. At the end of the film, Davorin is treated the same way by his own younger brother. In both episodes, those who execute the punishment are shown ridden by an inner conflict; in both cases the victim is held responsible for his own execution.

The director never shuns away from showing shocking levels of visceral cruelty, usually linked to mass violence. When showing individual violent acts he often intertwines them with erotic scenes. It is an approach that foregrounds the specific tension between evil and beauty, death and life. Niko and his lover's serene lovemaking amidst the blue waters of the Adriatic, for example, is interrupted by gunshots that brutally disrupt the drawling Dalmatian folk song of the score. The melancholic tune (*klapa*) speaks of love and introduces the tragic narrative that will follow. The abrupt shooting immediately maps out the potential spectrum of the tensions that will unravel. The same song resounds when Davorin executes Niko and his lover as well as when he makes love to the princess for a first time, a scene that takes place at the same location where the other couple was killed.

Zafranović implements a high dose of symbolic and metaphorical language and colour symbolism. He even uses certain signs to hint at the direction that the future fate of a character may take. At the opening of the film, for example, Davorin is seen in the fields drinking red wine from a bottle; he spills wine on his white shirt. The image is clearly associated with blood, especially as the gunshots of the previous sequence still reverberate in the viewer's mind, positioning Davorin as a tragic character who is likely to die sooner or later. There will be other similar set-ups where red wine stands in as a signifier for blood at moments when other individuals are about to get killed. Another 'red' symbol is the apple, standing in for sin: Niko's lover, who is exposed as a traitor (like Eve in the Bible) will bite into a red apple while Davorin interrogates her.

Black and white are the two other important colours: when Davorin meets his future love for the first time, she wears a pure white dress; the female communist, on the contrary, is in black throughout the film. The usage of black is associated with death, darkness, pollution, guilt and substance; white is predominantly associated with life, brightness, purity, innocence and spirit.

It is the dialectical correlation of black and white, however, that is more important in the film's symbolic palette. The princess, for example, is introduced swimming in the clear waters of the lake and then pausing for a prayer; her appearance is immaculate. Davorin happens to be on the shore; he is fascinated to look at her and stops to wash his face in the water, thus washing away the sin he has just committed (Niko's execution). But even though the princess is positioned as a *white* icon of innocence, her very social standing makes her mingle with the occupiers; it is she who at the Sveti Jovan celebration hands a *black* rosary to the little Catholic boy as a present. This gracious act turns out to be a curse: it is the same boy who, still holding on to the rosary, will be mercilessly slaughtered by the violent band. In another instance black and white are brought together in an even more close and contradictory proximity: in a symbolic scene, clearly hinting at the collaboration between the Catholic Church and Pavelić's regime, one of the Ustasha villains is shown wearing a black shirt with a pair of white angel's wings attached to it. This quasi-surrealistic interplay of black and white subverting any clear-cut colour symbolism suggests that the vicious circle of violence cannot be avoided or suppressed.

Other scenes contain interesting insertions of surrealist elements in the context of a principally realist approach: in the sequence showing villagers plundering their landowner's store their faces get all white from the flour that sifts out of the sacks; those grotesque white-faced figures look like a carnivalesque celebration, reminiscent to the ransacking of the mansion in Luis Buñuel's *Viridiana* (1961). The image of white and black papers thrown out of the manor's balcony and slowly falling down comes across as a reference to Federico Fellini's *Amarcord* (1973), where, during the spectacular fascist celebration a sprinkling of red and white paper is dropped over the main square. On the whole, however, Zafranović is more influenced by the work of Italian directors such as Pier Paolo Pasolini and Bernardo Bertolucci, most notably by their respective 1976 films *Salò o le 120 giornate di Sodoma* (*Salo, or The 120 Days of Sodom*) and *Novecento* (*1900*); one can also discover the influence of Hungarian master Miklós Jancsó, particularly of his *Csillagosok, katonák* (*The Red and the White*, 1967) where different warring factions, whose political doctrines make little difference on the ground and where everybody is equally violent and destructive, consecutively take over a place bringing death and destruction.

Apart from the colour coding, natural elements such as light (bright sunshine) and water (sea, rain) are given prominent symbolic presence. A key scene of the film is set amidst heavy rain: a woman, who will mercilessly kill the Blackshirts' commander shortly thereafter (an unforgettable minor role entrusted to leading Yugoslav actress Mirjana Karanović), is running through town shouting the news about Italy's capitulation. The joy of the liberated town residents almost immediately turns into a savagely cruel attack on the handful of Italians who are cornered into the water and brutally beaten and killed with whatever agricultural tools the townspeople have managed to grab in their rant and rage; the scene of this pitiless showdown is deliberately shot in dimmed light, hazy from the falling rain, suggesting that terror cannot be fully faced. The rain here has a blurring function, provoking the audience toward even more intense participation and response to those scenes.

The triumph of the townspeople who have pushed the occupiers away ferociously is accompanied by a belligerent musical score that greatly enhances the visual power of the scene. The basic instrument is the organ, again an element that is unconsciously associated with the Church. This type of subversive use of religious symbolism is dispersed throughout the film. The heavy rain in this scene can be interpreted as an endorsement of the exoneration of the place after the occupation. At the same time this scene is the stylistic climax of the film. It is elaborately choreographed; the high degree of staged elements is reminiscent of an opera performance, an association that powerfully confirms Zafranović's skill in putting together the vigorous energies of cinematic motifs and in creating an atmosphere that leaves a forceful emotional impact on the viewer. It is a visually sumptuous scene which nonetheless is fully coherent with the other artistic aspects.

In responding to critics who accused the film of 'visual excess, self-indulgent baroque imagery and shallow political perspective', Daniel Goulding remarked that these were 'some of the same criticisms one often hears (especially by leftist critics) concerning Fellini's films and those of Zeffirelli (both directors that Zafranović greatly admires)'. 'Some of these visual "excesses" of the film,' Goulding comments, 'represent genuine instances in which substance is inflected into style ... In *The Fall of Italy*, even more than in *Occupation in 26 Pictures*, Zafranović builds a complex set of stunning antithetical and antipodal visual motifs that transcend mere historicity and "chronicle".'

As in *Occupation in 26 Pictures*, *The Fall of Italy* also makes the most of the relentless sunshine and the intense blue of the Adriatic sea providing a contrasting backdrop for some of the most cruel scenes. It is in accordance with this general set-up that Davorin's execution at the very end of the film takes place on a cliff overlooking the blue waters of the Adriatic bathing in abundant sunshine. The melancholic folksong resounds for one last time, closing a full circle linking the sea with the island and the sunshine, and the prolonged melody with the resounding gunshots.

As Zafranović tends to see violence as an aspect of human behaviour that is enhanced by specific historical circumstances provoking a circle of atrocities, the events in *The Fall of Italy* let him show that taking (or switching) sides is intrinsically linked to cruelty and that violence comes about even when it may not be an inherent part of the ideology of the factions involved in the conflict. In his later film, the deeply personal documentary epic *Decline of the Century,* he stated: 'Isn't history just cycles which open and close? We are helpless to do anything for our salvation and to soften a cruel fate.' The fatalism of these words dominates Zafranović's view of history in general.

About the time of Yugoslavia's break up, Zafranović was working on *Decline of the Century*. The film uses footage from the trial of the notorious Andrija Artuković, former minister of Internal Affairs in the Ustasha government, who at the time was 87 years old and already frail and senile. The film asks uneasy questions of historical responsibility, critically examines the dialectics of individual and nation, and exposes instances of pragmatic forgetfulness and opportunist readjusting of historical record.

The new Croatian government, led by Franjo Tudjman, propagated a new type of nationalism; it was not happy with Zafranović's digging into these embarrassing episodes in Croatia's history and would have much preferred if the director, openly regretting the Yugoslav federation's break-up, had not raised these painful questions of remembrance and responsibility. The defamation soon extended over Zafranović's entire work, a situation that made the director even more determined not to give up his ambitious and highly original documentary project even if this would have meant to be treated as a dissident. In the early 1990s Zafranović left Croatia to finish the film abroad with Czech and Austrian support. It was not until after Tudjman's death in 1999 that the director was rehabilitated and *Decline of the Century* was shown in Croatia as part of a retrospective.

*Decline of the Century* clearly shows Zafranović's preoccupation with the most traumatic periods of Croatia's history; in a very personal manner the director invites the viewers to take part in his own identity quest as part of the nation's past. *The Fall of Italy*, on the contrary, cannot be seen only as a film that focuses solely on the Ustasha version of fascism; while exposing the Ustasha it simultaneously shows that other war factions were similarly fixated on violence:

brutality and cruelty here are postulated as a recurring 'state of mind' that cuts across borders and cultures. It is a film that, at the time of its making, seemed to warn that the future is not immune to the resurgence of brutality.

**Margit Rohringer**

REFERENCE

Goulding, D. (1998) *Occupation in 26 Pictures*. Trowbridge: Flicks Books.

# MERA SPORED MERA MEASURE FOR MEASURE

## GEORGI DYULGEROV, BULGARIA, 1981

The film trilogy *Mera spored mera* (*Measure for Measure*, Georgi Dyulgerov, 1981) takes place at the turn of the twentieth century in Macedonia, at which time it is still part of the Ottoman Empire. It focuses on the revolutionary struggle of the Macedonian population that still remains enslaved by the Ottomans. For hundreds of years, this province has been inhabited by an ethnically mixed population, which has now been split between the territories of the newly emancipated Greece and Bulgaria on the one hand, and the Ottoman Empire on the other. An underground organization, VMRO (Internal Macedonian Revolutionary Organization), is set to free Macedonia from Ottoman rule.

The story is told from the point of view of a minor rank-and-file revolutionary Macedonian, Dilber Tanass, whose memories and thoughts illustrate the dramatic path of his personal maturing. An uneducated and primitive shepherd at the beginning of the film, he gradually turns into an active participant in historical events and surmounts his previously marginal existence. The filmmakers follow his wanderings in 'the nether land' – a world of bondage, fear and resignation, as well as in 'the upper land' – a realm of freedom, and bold ideas of national and spiritual liberation.

The path of Tanass begins with his early naïve observations on life in his enslaved land and with choices he makes more out of intuition than conviction. Soon, however, he accidentally meets the leaders of the 1903 Ilinden uprising, Gotze Delchev and Yane Sandanski, and becomes involved with the revolutionaries. Tanass lives through a painful metamorphosis, which plays out as a personal drama that extricates him from the realm of emotion and elevates him to the realm of reason. He gradually comes to understand complex truths about the struggle for emancipation; his moral dilemmas grow more complex.

*Part I, 1901–02.* Dilber Tanass is a shepherd; his secluded routines revolve around earning the daily bread by taking care of a flock of sheep. He is isolated from politics, and it is only the accidental encounter with Postol, the leader of a rebel group, that will lead to his connecting with the insurgents. Gradually, Tanass begins to feel respect for the rebels, who have put their lives at stake in the name of freedom. The uneducated shepherd grows fascinated with the revolutionary idea and takes on the chance to participate in their perilous activities. This part of the film also features the notorious 1902 kidnapping of American missionary Miss Ellen Stone.

*Part II, 1903.* The Ilinden uprising takes place and is soon crushed. Dilber Tanass is among the revolutionaries. Together with the other rebels he lives through the romantic excitement of the revolt and witnesses the tragic outcome of its brutal containment.

*Part III, 1906–12.* In the aftermath of the uprising the survivors have to face new realities and continue in different directions. Dilber Tanass finally decides to marry; family life is about to change many of his attitudes. A chance encounter with some former rebels, however, will make him once again return to the great ideas of national emancipation and the struggle for freedom.

The title of Georgi Dyulgerov's film, *Measure for Measure*, is taken from a popular poem by renowned poet Peyo K. Yavorov whose series of poems, *Haydushki pensai* (*Rebel Songs*, 1903) is a classical work of Bulgarian national poetry. These outstanding poems were inspired by the poet's immediate involvement with the struggle for the liberation of Macedonia at the turn of the twentieth century; Dyulgerov takes on the intellectual continuity and the patriotic fervour of this emblematic work of poetry. The film interprets complex historical material rich in human drama and examples of heroic sacrifice.

The so-called 'Macedonian question' relates to a thorny issue in the modern history of the Balkan region, born when the clauses of San Stefano's peace treaty of 1878 were revised by the Berlin Congress in 1885 and a new territorial division of the Balkans was established. Macedonian lands were once again relegated to the Ottoman Empire. The population of Macedonia, however, did not accept the secretive manoeuvring of European diplomats and took up arms to fight for emancipation. It was not until 1912–13, however, that Macedonia acquired political emancipation from the Ottoman Empire and only as a territory split between Greece, Serbia and Bulgaria.

A powerful underground revolutionary organization, the VMRO, was established at the turn of the twentieth century, and functioned clandestinely, sometimes resorting to extreme revolutionary methods. The Ilinden uprising of August 1903 was the culmination of this struggle for national liberation against the oppressive Ottoman rule. Doomed to failure from a military standpoint, the uprising won widespread support as it relied on a sole alternative – that of independence and self-determination. The rebellion was drowned in blood, but it nonetheless inflicted a mortal wound on the ailing Ottoman Empire. Its outbreak set off various dramatic changes in the political status quo across the Balkans.

The events that followed – the Balkan Wars of 1912–14 and World War One – had a decisive impact on the resolution of the Macedonian question; with the advent of a new Yugoslav state union in 1918 that included a significant part of Macedonian lands within its borders, 'Macedonia' ended up being situated in a completely new and unexpected geopolitical context. The continuous redrawing of the political map of the region resulted in substantial population movements. One strand of these migrations was the flux of refugees toward Bulgaria in the early 1920s; director Dyulgerov himself came from one such refugee family.

For decades, Macedonia was to remain a contested territory where various irredentist stakes were set out by multiple players and where various factions diverged in their view of further goals and methods. The resulting ideological incoherence lay in the roots of various conflicting interpretations of these events that have been in circulation for many decades; even today, when the countries of the region are trying hard to patch up old controversies, there are moments where these lands are still the object of intricate and extremely contentious nationalist speculation. With the exception of films made in Macedonia (for example, *Solunski atentatori* (*The Salonika Terrorists*, Žika Mitrović, 1961); *Makedonska krvava svadba* (*Bloodshed at the Wedding*, Trajče Popov, 1967) or *Dust*, Milcho Manchevski, 2001), important aspects of the Macedonian struggle for national emancipation remain unexplored in cinema as they are still deemed controversial and are generally avoided.

Dyulgerov's film is an attempt to reconstruct the epic scale of the Ilinden uprising, and to provide an insight into the drama of ordinary people without employing chauvinistically charged clichés. *Measure for Measure* thus casts a fresh look at these issues, one that is not burdened by the cumbersome legacy of decades of 'Macedonian question' disputes. It is a well-researched film: instead of merely reconstructing the epic-scale battles and filming the well-documented bloodshed, the film's authors make the conscious choice to emphasise the human dimension of the conflict. Like Gillo Pontecorvo's classic national liberation story *La battaglia di Algeri* (*The Battle of Algiers*, 1965), *Measure for Measure* offers a unique take on the ideology and motivation of a guerrilla organisation the members of which are prepared to use extreme and often objectionable methods to further their cause (not least because it is only such methods that are available to them).

At the beginning of the 1980s, the historical genre received a powerful impetus for development, which would remove it from the lethargy of the primitive illustrative technique governing the aesthetics of Bulgaria's historical cinema of the 1950s and the 1960s. To commemorate the 1,300th anniversary of the creation of the Bulgarian state, several epic productions were funded, most notably *Khan Asparukh* (1981, aka *Velichieto na hana* (*681 AD: The Glory of Khan* (1984)) and *Vreme na nasilie* (*Time of Violence*, 1988), both directed by Lyudmil Staykov; *Zapiski po bulgarskite vastaniya* (*Notes on the Bulgarian Uprisings*, 1976) and *Boris I* (*Boris the First*, 1985) directed by Borislav Sharaliev; and *Konstantin Filosof* (*Konstantin the Philosopher*, 1983), directed by Georgi Stoyanov. All these films recreated dramatic historical events and played an identity-building function for Bulgarian audiences.

By that time, director Georgi Dyulgerov had already proven his own partiality toward creative challenges – his early films (*I doyde denyat* (*And the Day Came*, 1973), *Avantazh* (*Advantage*, 1977) and *Trampa* (*Swap*, 1978)) demonstrated an acute interest in situations and dramatic collisions where psychologically convincing yet internally confused protagonists are shown navigating in a complicated social milieu. Contrary to the dominant aesthetic norms at the time, these characters are shown as live human beings full of doubts and contradictions, and with a share of mistakes and small victories. The novel point of view that Dyulgerov actively develops disputes the widespread straightforward augmentation of heroic characters and the glorification of events and values.

It is in this context that Dyulgerov's trilogy marked a further development in the director's previous aspirations. The films barely resembled the popular historical super-productions, with their abundance of extras, extravagant battles, costumes and elaborate sets. Unlike those, Dyulgerov's ascetic style is foreign to any kind of showy and self-congratulatory approach. Each specific event in the artistry of his film is only a pretext for the study of the historical processes.

*Measure for Measure* is loosely based on the novel by prominent Bulgarian historical writer Svoboda Bachvarova, *Liturgy for Ilinden* (1973). In addition to this text, however, the film relies on supplementary research materials, memories of participants in the events and academic studies which give the film a further degree of authenticity. Together with the screenplay's co-author, actor Russi Chanev who also plays Tanass, director Dyulgerov breaks away from the rules of traditional storytelling and builds up the film's storyline as an intimate confession told in the first person. On the one hand, this style successfully quells the high passion of the events; on the other, it allows the viewer to focus on the main character, Dilber Tanass. Thus, the filmmaker is able to achieve diverse nuances of his interpretation of specific historical events. It also allows for delicate distancing from the familiar historical episodes that time has already managed to mythologise. Tanass's voice-over imparts interesting nuances laden with self-irony, which softens the otherwise coarse reality of the facts, an approach that allows for a considerably more complex interpretation of the historical events closely linked to suffered human experience.

A good example is the use of the story of the 1902 kidnapping of an American missionary, Miss Ellen Stone, and her fellow missionary Ekaterina Tzilka, by Macedonian rebels, who hoped to raise ransom money for the purchase of ammunition and guns. The event unfolds over the course of the first part of the film as a colourful fragment from the height of revolution. The rebels are depicted as noble and self-respecting. The episode allows the filmmaker to reveal and defend the dignity of the revolutionaries. Their cause attracts the sympathy of the two women, who gradually come to understand the kidnappers and their motives behind the kidnapping.

The director wisely leaves aside all sensational facts around the two missionaries' kidnapping, as well as the concrete details around their stay with the rebels. He does not offer an investigation of the intricate state of mind of the female heroines. This had been the approach of another film, inspired by the same events: *Mis Ston* (*Miss Stone*, 1958), directed by Serbian veteran director Žika Mitrović. It focused more on the details of the event and the psychological motivations behind the kidnapper's actions.

*Measure for Measure* is constructed on the principle of the jigsaw puzzle – fragment after fragment assembled to create the overall picture, and each one of the pieces occupies a strictly defined place in the dramatic structure. Seemingly chaotic at the beginning, the narrative is in fact a cleverly conceived composition whose inner logic follows the whimsical footsteps of Dilber Tanass's personal notes, where the hero re-lives the history of his life. The filmmaker relies on a simple structural principle: he constructs the important from the least important; he weaves in the whole from the separate fragments; he reaches out to the universal from the particular and the personal. As the film progresses, the audience accrues the necessary vital knowledge about the times and the even0ts, about the people and their actions. Thus, the trilogy is charged  with those values of epic storyline, which allow for in-depth coverage of a specific historical event, and for its study against a background of concrete human characters and fates.

The 1903 uprising is shown in the second part of the film without superficial and decorative grandiosity – instead, the director heavily emphasises its raw texture. Dyulgerov shied away from showy effects and epic scale taking precedence over narrative content. The director trusted the impact of authentic documents, and thereby strove to create a feeling of truthfulness. The film was shot entirely in the region where the uprising took place, thus avoiding the construction of lavish sets. The landscape, the props and the characters' costumes were carefully chosen to be as authentic to the spirit of the times as possible, and so is their manner of speaking. The feeling of authenticity is also reinforced by the large number of non-professional actors playing parts of various degrees of significance.

The directorial approach successfully integrates well-known actors within a cast of non-professionals. The actors literally dissolve in this truthful environment, which largely contributes to the overall acceptance of the film as a unique document on the uprising and its historical era. Dyulgerov, who also teaches at the Bulgarian film academy, invited students from his class to take part in the making of the film. They work as his assistants but also take on small parts next to the myriad of professional and non-professional actors.

Nor are the film creators of *Measure for Measure* tempted by the incentive to portray already legendary characters in great detail, by now a part of the mythology of these historical events. Indeed, revolutionaries like Gotze Delchev and Yane Sandanski – ideologists and heads of the revolutionary organisation – are actively present throughout the course of the film. Similar to other real figures, such as Miss Stone and various political leaders, they are an inseparable part of the film's narrative without dominating the plot. In its dramaturgical aspect, the film is constructed like a folk epic where a multitude of characters are given equal weight despite their different importance in the social and political hierarchy. This colourful conglomerate of human fates is firmly consolidated by the main idea of the film, thereby underlining the deeply populist character of the Ilinden uprising fully supported by the people of occupied Macedonia.

Dilber Tanass acts as a unifying figure for the film's plotline. His personal growth is followed throughout the three parts of the film. The character's evolution reveals an unconditional willpower for self-realisation and functions as an idiosyncratic metaphor for the spiritual growth of an entire nation.

The events around the build-up and the breaking-out of the 1903 Ilinden uprising, as well as the subsequent developments of the fight for national determination of Macedonia, utterly alter the spirit of ordinary people. The grey mass of tired peasants and farmers, living at peace with their ability to sacrifice in the name of the common good, now transforms into a united society of people brought together by the national idea. Previously familiar only with the primal emotions of personal vengeance and the daily worries of family upkeep, now these people begin to live with higher thoughts of freedom and emancipation.

Tanass is the artistic emanation of this complex process, quite characteristic of the era of Macedonian national liberation struggles. His experience is enriched by a further dimension of knowledge, unattainable by his contemporaries. The hero enters a previously unknown world where rebellion, guns, freedom and independence are at the centre of all discussions. Learning the ABC of applied politics, Tanass labours hard to figure out the harsh rules of underground conspiracy. Soon enough, he masters the tricks and the tactics of guerrilla conspiracies. Fate confronts him face to face with unforgettable and contrasting examples of human degradation and noble self-sacrifice; Tanass also discovers the feeling of love, and learns to suffer. Unbeknownst to himself, the unknown shepherd grows into a human being with a deeply personal outlook of the world. He walks a path full of controversy and ordeals, from the margins of society to the conscious and prominent embrace of a noble cause. The leaders of the national liberation movement become his tutors in life; it is from them that he receives the ideal of liberated homeland as the highest value deserving utmost sacrifice. A certain sense of the significance of the events that he is involved with is awakened in him, and the previously illiterate shepherd now sets out to describe his thoughts and observations. Thus, Dilber Tanass travels full circle in his intense individual existence, which leads him to uncover the truth about the history and the psychology of his own people.

From a structural point of view, the film follows all the stages of Tanass's personal development. The three parts correspond to the three representative stages in the hero's biography. In the first part (1901–02), the character is revealed as a primitive human being whose interests are limited to his small village, the animals and the house. The restricted horizon, archaic lifestyle and the elemental needs of the protagonist imply the poverty of his existence, both literally and figuratively. He finds himself in the rebels' company out of pure curiosity, but the strange world of these rough men, relentlessly hateful of the Ottomans, attracts him powerfully; yet the philosophy of fighting for a national ideal is still foreign to him. At this point, he squarely and quite naïvely sympathises with the rebels as he sees them as his people's protectors. Later, deep in his soul, he starts forming a new outlook toward the world; the metamorphosis of his consciousness is just beginning.

The second part (1903) portrays Tanass's maturing; he now seems to have cast the dice of his fate. He is now part of the ever-growing net of organised underground-armed groups; he begins to think of himself as a part of a nation fighting for independence. The realisation of the significance of the battle with the oppressors inspires Tanass; he intuitively finds a revered and meaningful social role for himself. In a certain sense, it is the antithesis of the unstressed existence that he was shown leading in the first part of the film. He has to overcome multiple ordeals and obstacles in order to recreate himself as a free-willed person.

The third part of the film (1906–12) is the most important one as it is the artistic synthesis of the entire dramaturgical material. Although the epic outburst of the peoples' impatience and thirst for freedom has already culminated, the fight is not over. The protagonists take different paths. Some find peace in the cosiness of family life, others get well-paid government jobs, but the staunchest supporters of the national idea continue their doomed battle with the oppressors. Fate decides to give Dilber Tanass a taste of everything as it puts his morality and integrity to the test. He starts a family but proves incapable of keeping it. Then he becomes a forest guard but yields to the petty temptations of power and vanity. Despite all this, the flame of idealism is still burning deep inside his rebellious soul. Thus, Tanass takes the critical decision to look for his old brothers in arms. Together with them, he hopes to participate again in the unequal battle for the complete liberation of his homeland.

However, the political reality has already changed. New times have come about, and the crucial national question is seen in a completely different context. In this altered social situation, governed by widely-spread compromise and conformity, Tanass and hundreds of other freedom fighters have suddenly become redundant; their revolutionary idealism is dissolved in the crude pragmatism of daily existence. Here the hero's diary comes to an abrupt end, and so does the chronicle of his nation's struggle for national liberation.

*Measure for Measure*, however, is by no means a biographical film. The portrayal of one person's life, though educational and colourful, is only the cause and instigation of an in-depth study of regional history and national character. Due to an intricate knot of delicate political sensibilities, all issues related to Macedonia were banned from Bulgarian public discourse for decades; cinema was either silently avoiding them or was treating them in cryptic terms. Dyulgerov's trilogy was released at an important moment when society resolutely needed this raw and painful facing of the past and the knowledge of the complexity and significance of the Macedonian question. In this sense, *Measure for Measure* played a particularly positive role as it not only articulated silenced facts into the public sphere but, most importantly, it eased the emancipation of public opinion on the so-called Macedonian question in its historiographic and political aspects. Later on, in 1988, the feature film material was used as the basis for a six-part television miniseries.

*Measure for Measure* is a seminal achievement of Bulgarian cinema with its search for synthesis between the raw primal force and the psychological complexity of fictitious narrative. Naturally, the question is not about establishing a more or less successful balance between the two opposites. The film's polyphonic structure allows the director to fully recreate the epic scale of history without going into the extreme of supplying too much detail, and without being absorbed in an intentional burdening of the theme with ideology. The wide range of meanings is reminiscent of multimodal folk ballads. The storyline steers clear from one-dimensional characters and the events are shown in their multifaceted intricacy; no fervent heroic behaviour or self-aggrandising words are featured here. However paradoxical at first, the dialogue in *Measure for Measure* is not the main means of expression; the film's impact relies on the multilayered build-up of various other cinematic elements, such as the plasticity of the shot and the colour coordination, the level of noise and the delicate musical phrases, the editorial links between the separate episodes, as well as the actors' behaviour and speech.

All elements in the film appear subjugated to the desire for maximisation of authenticity. In *Measure for Measure*, this applies as much to the dialogue as to the performance of the actors. The non-professional actors and the extras bring immediacy and spontaneity that remains unperturbed by the presence of professional performers, as they were all carefully selected on the basis that they should not stand out from the myriad of authentic-looking faces. Dyulgerov's directorial approach bars every use of acting clichés and all attempts to act 'professionally' on the screen, however unintentional they may be. Only a spectator who has previously seen the actors in other films could tell apart their performance from the multitude of non-professionals.

In this regard, Russi Chanev's work in the central role of Dilber Tanass impresses deeply with his creation of an emotionally and psychologically convincing character. The actor, who had become an audience favourite from an earlier collaboration with Dyulgerov (*Advantage*), seems to dissipate in the epic scenes, and the episodes where he performs are dominated by his extraordinary charisma. The astounding change in his physical appearance, his facial expression and the sparkle in his eyes are all manifestations of this character's transformation and his maturation as a person with his own views and opinions. Chanev is quite cautious in using the range of his acting skills: a well-planned gesture, a sudden look, grimace or a smile can be a part of the expressive and purely visual strokes, which represent his inner state of mind and his interaction with the rest of the heroes on the screen.

The well-paced rhythm of the storyline is another noteworthy accomplishment of the film. For a trilogy, the rhythm is of utmost importance as all elements of the story have their own place in the dynamic unity of the whole. The first part is more detailed, as the basic characters and conflicts are being laid out here. The second part is charged with strong drama as it shows the uprising's culmination. The third part is one of retrospective thinking, analysis of and reconciliation with what has been experienced thus far. The director skilfully shifts the film's accents in search of a more active contact with the audience. For most of the film, movements within the frame are preferred to fast-paced editing, as this gives more freedom both to the director of photography, the remarkable Radoslav Spassov, who is thus able to choreograph expressive compositions, and the actors, who achieve a more organic presence on the big screen. The strict form and laconic means of expression in *Measure for Measure* are the product of careful stylisation. Dilber Tanass's voice-over monologue places the viewers in the position of co-participants in the historical events taking place in front of their eyes with all the peculiarities of inconspicuous observation while it simultaneously maintains the feeling of historical distance.

Bulgarian audiences appreciated this film as a real insight, not least because it dared to raise such a fiery issue as the Macedonian question. The widespread positive public reaction was the true testimony of the film's honest and well-documented approach toward this knotty historical theme which had either been silenced or had been adapted to fit the ideological schemes of powers-that-be. The trilogy stands out with an artistic strength that overcomes all prevalent propaganda clichés, and outstandingly reveals the tragic significance of the Ilinden uprising with remarkable maturity. *Measure for Measure* is a call for an unprejudiced reading of the past and its contradictory events. All this places the film among those works of contemporary Bulgarian culture which contribute to establishing a more responsible approach to history.

**Alexander Grozev**

# CRVENIOT KONJ THE RED HORSE

## STOLE POPOV, YUGOSLAVIA, 1981

By 1949, the Democratic Army of Greece (DAG) is losing the civil war. Near the Albanian border, a group of combatants of mixed ethnicity (Greeks and Macedonians) receive orders to surrender weapons and go aboard a ship that sails off to an unidentified destination. The men expect a short passage to Peloponnesus, but soon realise they are crossing the Bosphorus into international waters, and sailing across the Black Sea toward Soviet territory. Once in the USSR, the combatants are put on a train; this leg of the journey will last five full days and every minute of the journey will be taking them farther away from their native land. The destination is again unknown; all they see through the window is endless steppe. Upon arrival they finally learn they are now in Uzbekistan, the Central Asian republic of the Soviet Union. From now on they will live in a specially built camp, where Stalin's portrait hangs alongside the Greek flag; DAG leaders solemnly promise a glorious return one day. The men have no choice but get on with life and adjust to the foreign land, amidst occasional squabbles between ethnic Greeks and Slav Macedonians.

The story of *Crveniot Konj* (*The Red Horse*, Stole Popov, 1981) focuses on Boris Tušev (Bata Živojnović), an ethnic Slav from the village of Kroncelevo in Aegean Macedonia (Greece). He is a widower; his grandfather, three daughters and his brother's family are left behind. In Uzbekistan Boris begins work at a factory. After some time he meets Olga, a Russian widow, and with the approval of his comrades, Greek Nikifor and fellow-villager Vanche, moves in with her. Around 1953, Boris falls ill; after a hospital stay he is seen departing to a sanatorium in the Caucasus, taking a sad farewell from Olga and the young Macedonian Vanche at the station.

Boris spends years away, finally returning in the early 1960s. In the meantime, Vanche succumbs to cancer and dies. On visiting Vanche's grave, Boris feels guilty about abandoning his friend and leaving him to die alone in a foreign land. Although he has risen through the ranks, he still feels an outsider within the Soviet system.

In the 1970s, just after the military junta is removed from power, the Greek government declares a conditional amnesty for exiled DAG combatants. Boris realises he no longer trusts the DAG and its leaders, who endlessly postpone the date of glorious return. He chooses to repatriate. The Greek embassy in Moscow informs him that in order to be allowed back he must renounce his communist affiliation and confirm that he is of Greek ethnicity, which he consents to.

After 25 years of absence, Boris is finally on the way to his beloved native place. It is early spring; on the way he buys a red horse and rides it into the village. He is soon reunited with members of his extended family, yet they do not seem overjoyed at his return. His part of the family house is in disrepair. Boris settles there and begins rebuilding his home and his lost domestic life. Yet he somehow fails to reconnect, perhaps because the place is completely transformed: people of leftist views are under constant surveillance, Slav Macedonians are fully assimilated by the Greeks. Boris is as much a foreigner here as he was in the USSR. Rather than overcome the alienation, the gap with family members and fellow-villagers widens by the day.

It seems unlikely that Boris will ever find peace. One frosty morning he wakes up to find that during the night someone has killed his red horse; the body of the animal hangs from the tree in the yard. Enraged, he dashes to the pub where he violently confronts the young Hellenised Macedonian whom he suspects of killing the horse.

The camera cuts to an interior view of Boris's house as seen through the eyes of someone who climbs the stairs breathing heavily, looks at the ceiling and encounters familiar faces. Upset relatives and distraught women in black all look into the camera, cry and cross themselves. It becomes clear that the camera looks through Boris' eyes. Church bells are heard ringing from afar, announcing his death. The final shot presents a distant view of the village nestled among snowy hills.

*The Red Horse*, director Stole Popov's remarkably mature feature debut, was made around the time of Tito's death in a period that saw the release of some the most important Yugoslav cinematic breakthroughs, such as Slobodan Šijan's *Ko to tamo peva* (*Who's Singing Over There?*, 1980), Rajko Grlić's *Samo jednom se ljubi* (*That Melody Haunts My Reverie*, 1981) and Emir Kusturica's *Sjecas li se, Dolly Bell?* (*Do You Remember Dolly Bell?*, 1981).

Born in 1950, Popov comes from a filmmaking family (his father, Trajče Popov, is one of the doyens of Macedonian cinema) and established a reputation as an outstanding documentary filmmaker from early on. His *Australija, Australija* (*Australia, Australia*, 1976), a feature-length documentary exploration of Slav Macedonian migrants who settled in the remote outback powerfully introduced the subject of anxiety-ridden passage as a central theme of his work. His Academy Award-nominated short *Dae* (1979) featured a Romani celebration of St George's day (and directly influenced the way in which the key scene of the St George's Day celebration is staged in the much wider-seen film by Emir Kusturica *Dom za vešanje* (*Time of the Gypsies*, 1989).

Made long before the themes of exile and dislocation were at the centre of public discourse, *The Red Horse* is a work of great contemporary resonance. It is a film that is far ahead of its time with its focus on migration, displacement and the difficult identity questions that are associated with them. It raises issues of identity and exile as they are played out at the intersection of strained ideological and ethnic loyalties. It shows how dedication can turn into disillusionment and subtly explores the existential failure of commitment to ideas, the tragic detachment from loved ones and the loss of people to believe in and of places to call home.

*The Red Horse* is a Yugoslav film, yet the events depicted in it are more closely linked to the history of neighbouring Greece. International diplomatic agreements made at the end of World War Two left the country within the Western sphere of influence, even though the leftist partisan movement here was reportedly one of the strongest in the region. While the neighbouring states, assigned to the Soviet sphere of influence, soon see communist governments installed in power (even though their partisan resistance has never been as strong as the Greek one), the left-wing forces in Greece (DAG) do not receive any further official support from the Soviets. Nonetheless, they engage in another five years of bitter and futile civil war on their own, a period which Lefteris Xanthopoulos describes as 'the most traumatic experience of Greek society in the twentieth century'. After DAG's defeat in 1949 more than 100,000 combatants are forced into exile, mostly to the Eastern Bloc countries and to the Soviet Union. In order to avoid alleged retributions, thousands of Greek children from leftist families (reportedly up to 28,000; 3,000 of which were of Slav Macedonian ethnicity) were evacuated abroad and raised away from their immediate families, thus setting up one of the most painful examples of forced exile in the history of the region. Due to Cold War divisions many of these exiled children have not been able to visit their native places and relatives in Greece well into their adulthood and have had to hide their true identity for decades. Many Balkan documentaries deal with the harrowing story of these forced political migrations; in Macedonia in particular these issues have been tackled in *Bratska pomoc* (*Brotherly Support*, George Zorz and Trajče Popov, 1950) and *Tuglesh* (Kole Manev, 1971).

The suffering of exiled leftist Greeks, presented through the fate of one such émigré who returns in search of an imaginary nourishing homeland, is the theme of Theo Angelopoulos's

*Taxìdi sta Kìthira* (*Voyage to Cythera*, 1984). Other films also deal with the displaced DAG combatants and with the fate of those Greek children sent into exile, often from different ideological angles. The leftist version is represented in Lefteris Xantopoulos's *Kalì patrìda, sìntrofe* (*Welcome Home, Comrade*, 1986), featuring the life of a village in Hungary where the Greek exiled community still sticks together and dreams of return after 35 years in forced exile. The US production *Eleni* (Peter Yates, 1985), based on Nicholas Gage's autobiographical book, presents an outspoken anti-communist point of view; the forced exile of Greek children here is shown as a cruel totalitarian uprooting. British documentary *Next Year in Lerin* (Jill Daniels, 2001) features testimonies by many of these now grown-up children; many have never been able to return to the native places in Greece and still have to hide their identity.

During the Civil war, ethnic Slav Macedonians and Greeks fought side by side. In the aftermath of the war, however, their unity began to crack. *The Red Horse* clearly shows how the new ethnic division lines emerge and gradually take over, depicting the Macedonians as particularly vulnerable because of their low self-esteem and minority standing. The Macedonians have never been considered as really committed; their loyalty is constantly challenged and tested in rough and violent ways. Even though all combatants are on the same side in terms of political loyalties, in Uzbekistan the ethnic rifts grow deeper; a Macedonian man even murders a Greek who is harassing him. In the eyes of their Soviet hosts, however, they are all democratic Greeks and no differences within the group are acknowledged. At the same time, there are also stories of friendship and support: Boris's closest friend, for example, is Nikifor, a Greek teacher.

It is a strange feeling to end up living in a place one did not even know existed, surrounded by endless vastness, camels and Uzbek men, squatting and gazing in the distance. It is an outlandish sensation to hear drawling Macedonian songs sound over the shallow water of the Uzbek rice fields. Can they be peasants once again somewhere else on Earth? They work the fields, deceiving themselves that they really are settling down. But they cannot help thinking they have no news of their old parents (are they still alive?) nor do they know what became of their fellow-combatants, dispersed all over. They gather frequently in their crammed living rooms to sing nostalgic songs; they are lonely together, they get drunk, embrace, cry and sometimes dance ritualistically. Young Vanche confesses he feels unbearably lonesome; it is the illness of exile that turns this cheerful accordion player into a susceptible tragic hero. He does not want to marry because he hopes to go back home, not knowing he has only a little more time to live and will be consumed by illness in this foreign land.

It is in this context of displacement, of concerns over roots and identity, that the disillusionment with communist ideals will come for Boris. He begins as a committed leftist but by the end of the film he sees his life ruined over his blind allegiance to ideology; he begins as an ethnic Macedonian but by the end of the film it is clear that, if he does not want to perish in a foreign land, he must become Greek.

From beginning to end Boris is, in the words on film historian Miroslav Čepinčić, a 'polyphonic protagonist', whose disillusionment and failure to reconnect upon arrival is reminiscent, as Miron Chernenko has pointed out, of Ulysses' disenchantment and painful homecoming. However, return is not as easy as it seems. He may now be back, yet Boris has difficulty in reconnecting; his uprooting has taken a permanent hold. He has become a stranger and is detached from the place. Dusty family photographs hang on the wall; sweet hubbub coming from the yard brings childhood memories. But the encounter between Boris and his brother, both aging and weary men, is dominated by bitterness: over the house being abandoned, over a life spent in vain. It is difficult to reconcile: both admit they are lonely, yet each one blames the other for not having been there when it could have made a difference. In a key episode Boris and his brother sit together and remember of the time when, during World War Two, they had a draw to see which of them will go to war with the DAG and which will stay at home to take care of household and family. Now they know that it all went wrong: 'Neither you, my brother, were victorious in the struggle, nor I was able to take care of the family, we both failed,' the brother concludes bitterly.

The realisation of impossibility to resist extrication and the horror of distance first comes to Boris with the shock of witnessing the endlessness of the desert on the way to Uzbekistan. The camera shows Boris in a close-up at the train's window; his strained facial expression reveals that he is already grasping that this seemingly innocent protracted journey into the unknown, this moving for days and nights through an infinite steppe, is doing something awful to him. Every hour takes him farther and farther away from where he belongs. Boris has a nightmarish vision: he sees himself walking alongside the train in the desert, struggling against the dust that the wind blows onto his face; he is soon all sunk in sand. 'What will I tell Grandpa?,' he cries out to himself. 'I'll not leave you here, taken over by sands! Grandpa!' But this is crying out into an abyss, surrounded by infinite nothingness, uprooted and displaced. By the time he will manage to return his Grandpa will be dead for a long time.

It does not take long for Boris to become doubtful over the DAG's uncritical loyalty to the Soviets; as early as 1953, the year of Stalin's death, he loses hope that they will ever go back.

It will take another ten years until he fully rejects the DAG and its leaders, who, fixated on the idea of return to power, have denied the right of personal choice to ordinary people like him. He is now prepared to sign that he is not a communist, that he is Greek and has been forced to come to the USSR. His longing for return proves stronger than confessed fidelity to socialist dreams.

But once back, he finds village life dominated by tensions escalating along political and ethnic lines. It is just after the time of the junta dictatorship (1967–74) and all those with left leanings have been under tight surveillance. These people are completely ostracised: all they can do is get drunk, and any mention of Russia or Stalin triggers violent outbursts. The villagers avoid Boris: he is a stranger to them; it is known he is a communist. After so many years of absence his speech is littered with the occasional (incomprehensible) Russian expression; he is a living embodiment of the dreams for democracy that people would rather chase out of their minds. They have no idea what exile means or how difficult it was for Boris to escape the endless sands of Uzbekistan and come back to be with them. Why has he returned? What does he want?

All those of leftist beliefs have been isolated from public life and relegated to the corner spots of smoky pubs. Boris's nephew, a communist (played by leading Macedonian actor Meto Jovanovski), is reduced to alcoholism; he has been handicapped during interrogations and now has to use crutches. He is angry with the DAG combatants who went into exile; they 'run away', he claims, escaping the harassment that those left behind lived through, letting them be 'fucked up'. Both men drive off into the snowy mountains in a taxi. It is only there, among the silent hills, that the nephew can enjoy a moment of freedom, crying out his pain and hearing the echo (an episode that is directly reminiscent of a similar scene featuring Thanassis Vengos in Theo Angelopoulos's film *To Vlemma tou Odyssea* (*Ulysses Gaze*, 1995); it is noteworthy that this episode takes place in approximately the same part of Greece). The nephew feels free only when alone; all he wants is to be with like-minded Boris for a few minutes, to shout out and get the pain off his chest. But Boris does not seem to feel the same way: he has been around and has seen it all, he has witnessed the communist ideas put into practice in the USSR and knows it does not work, he is bitterly returning from the land where the nephew strives to be. The wisdom he has acquired has turned him into a weary cynic; he has nothing left to believe in, he knows that crying out for freedom in the wilderness is delusional.

It does not matter, however, that Boris might be disillusioned with Soviet ideology: in the eyes of everyone around he remains a 'Red' one. 'Even his horse is red', someone remarks. 'Go and report on me, then!' Boris shoots back. No wonder it all ends in a fight. Universally resented, from that moment on Boris will sit alone in the pub, clutching an axe under the table.

And then, there is the ethnic assimilation. Public space is completely taken over by Greek language and culture. The church service is in Greek only, no Macedonian is spoken at the pub where drunk young men dance sirtaki while, in a silent confrontation, old Slav Macedonians look on, seated under the poster of touristy Greece that hangs on the wall. Weary Boris knows that there is no avoiding the assimilation: even in the Soviet Union he was treated as a Greek, and now, to be able to return, he has signed papers renouncing his original ethnicity.

Throughout the film, director Popov uses a range of imaginative stylistic devices. One of these is, for example, the staging of Boris's vision of himself going down in the desert sands while on the train to Uzbekistan: a quasi-surrealist enactment that makes the nightmarish feeling of displacement almost palpable. In another instance Popov relies on intertextuality: the young Macedonian Vanche is shown sitting in a cinema and watching the Soviet war film *Letyat zhuravli* (*The Cranes Are Flying*, Mikhail Kalatozov, 1957); the specific scene is the famous sequence showing the lonely death of the protagonist (who is shot in a swamp and, at the moment of death, has a dream of wedding his beloved). Vanche is lonely and displaced; seeing this episode only enhances his feeling of forlornness and dislocation.

Another sequence that is heavily reliant on allegory is the scene in which Boris meets with his Greek friend Nikifor to discuss his decision to return. The conversation takes place in a zoo, the men are shown standing in front of the tiger's cage with the animal nervously moving in the background, thus setting up direct (yet somewhat contrived) parallels between the trapped animal and the way the protagonist feels. And, last but not least, there is the original point-of-view shot at the very end of the film, where the camera is looking through the eyes of Boris at the moment of his death: he has been mortally injured in the pub fight; the people he sees have actually gathered around his casket for his wake and what the camera shows is the last subjective gaze of a departing soul. This assortment of diverse stylistic strategies is meant to reveal the multidimensionality of the identity conundrums the protagonist has to face in his lifetime. But as each one is used only once, the final impression is that the director's ambitious approach is markedly eclectic.

Besides *The Red Horse*, many more Macedonian films are preoccupied with issues of identity, sovereignty and self-determination. As Miroslav Čepinčić observes, the Macedonian discourse on the past often looks at history as an adverse power and a source of existential anxiety. Classical Macedonian films – like Branko Gapo's *Istrel* (*Shot*, 1972) and *Vreme, vodi*

(*Time, Waters*, 1980) – have functioned as tools for emancipation in telling stories of people that, like the protagonist of *The Red Horse*, are deprived of their own name and identity and who struggle to preserve their distinctiveness in interaction with other, more powerful, ethnic groups (variably with Greeks or Serbs who want to assimilate them, with irredentist Bulgarians who deny the specificity of their culture, or with Albanians who try to redefine the Slavic Macedonian distinctiveness).

It is the complex nature of the region's politics that makes many of the Macedonian films deal with contentious and awkward affairs and episodes. *The Red Horse*'s classical predecessor, Kiril Cenevski's artistic masterpiece *Crno seme* (*Black Seed*, 1971), for example, is another unique film that exposes the mistreatment of Slav Macedonians in the aftermath of the Civil War while making a distinctive contribution to the iconography of violence. Set on a remote island, it shows the systematic mistreatment and torture of Macedonian DAG fighters under a merciless burning sun; all for the sake of renouncing their Slavic identity. Including *Black Seed*, however, would have made it possible to create parallels with other Balkan films that are aesthetically very near as they are also set on isolated islands where rough nature and relentless violence dominate the lives of inmates, like the Bulgarian film *Na malikya ostrov* (*On the Small Island*, Rangel Vulchanov, 1958) or the Greek film *Haroumeni Imera* (*Happy Day*, Pantelis Voulgaris, 1976).

Both *Black Seed* and *The Red Horse* are based on novels by Taško Georgievski, whose work is dedicated to depicting the systematic destruction of Slav ethnic identity in Aegean Macedonia, a province which is administratively part of Greece but had a predominantly Slav population until a few decades ago. Both films are controversial because they depict people that are *de facto* foreign subjects and events that take place on foreign territory. Film historians writing on Macedonia, such as Miron Chernenko, believe that these subject matters are important to address as the fate of people like *The Red Horse*'s protagonist Boris Tušev can be seen as an allegory for the 'tragedy of the divided nation'. Yet it is important to stress that these issues are considered highly controversial and remain routinely hushed and regularly avoided in public discourse.

After *The Red Horse*, Popov directed a film from a script by noted Serbian screenwriter Gordan Mihić, *Srećna nova '49* (*Happy New '49*, 1985). Dealing with the devastating effect that an accusation of collaborating with the Soviets has on a Skopje family at the time of the Tito-Stalin split, the film is a grim political melodrama comparable to Emir Kusturica's Palme d'Or-winner *Otac na službenom putu* (*When Father Was Away on Business*, 1985). This second feature established Popov's reputation as a leading Macedonian cineaste. The director's later work, however, which included well-received films (*Tetoviranje* (*Tatoo*, 1991) and *Gypsy Magic*, 1997), has been of more mainstream character and does not live up to the conceptual and artistic originality of his earlier work.

Velimir 'Bata' Živojnović, who plays the lead in *The Red Horse*, is a titan of Yugoslav cinema; he has been cast in over 250 films by nearly every important Yugoslav director. His name is traditionally associated with partisan roles, yet he has played in films of all genres and across all Yugoslav republics. Živojnović also plays the leads in two more films discussed in this volume, *Tri* (*Three*, Aleksandar Petrović, 1965; see Vlastimir Sudar's chapter) and *Valter Brani Sarajevo* (*Walter Defends Sarajevo*, Hajrudin 'Šiba' Krvavac, 1972; see Rada Sešić's chapter), and has a supporting role in *Pad Italije* (*The Fall of Italy*, Lordan Zafranović, 1981; see Margit Rohringer's chapter). Thus his rich and versatile work is well covered in this volume.

*The Red Horse* is a film on a universal theme. While relying on a concrete historical narrative, its essence is in making explicit the existential distress of emigration, in divulging the constant emptiness and yearning for roots that exile generates. It is a film that shows how forced expulsion and displacement account for the detachment from beliefs and for the failure of ideas. It shows how regaining a lost homeland, even if it is physically achievable can prove emotionally impossible.

**Dina Iordanova**

Author's note: I am grateful to Vesna Maslovarik for introducing me to the work of Stole Popov and other Macedonian directors, and to Petar Volnarovski for supplying the film on video.

REFERENCES

Čepinčić, M. (1999) *Makednoskiot igralen film*, vol. II. Skopje: Kinoteka na Makedonija, 155–69; 400–1.

Chernenko, M. (1997) *Makedonskiot film*. Skopje: Kinoteka na Makedonija, 152–6.

Xanthopoulos, L. (2000) 'La diaspora Greca', in S. G. Germani (ed.) *La meticcia di fuoco: Oltre il continente Balcani*. Venice: La biennale di Venezia, 129–33.

# PETRINA HRONIA STONE YEARS

## PANTELIS VOULGARIS, GREECE, 1985

The plot of *Petrina Hronia* (*Stone Years*, Pantelis Voulgaris, 1985) would be considered hopelessly melodramatic and unrealistic were not it based on actual events. The drama begins in the summer of 1954 in rural Greece. Eleni and Babis, a young couple on the cusp of romance, are preparing to distribute leftist political leaflets of the clandestine Communist Party of Greece. In a swift rush of events, Babis is arrested for engaging in subversive activities and Eleni is forced to flee to Athens. Over the next twenty years, one or the other or both of them will be in jail. Only for a few months in late 1966 are they both simultaneously free. That brief period ends when Eleni is arrested as a long-sought fugitive. During their time together, Eleni has become pregnant. Her son will be born in prison. Following the military *coup d'état* of 21 April 1967, Babis is also arrested. He is able to catch glimpses of his infant son through the bars of his cell, across the courtyard from the cells where Eleni is kept. A number of years pass and the authorities allow the couple to be married in a somewhat bizarre ceremony held in the prison. Not until the junta falls in 1974 will Eleni and Babis be free to live a normal life. In a haunting final sequence set in what will be her new home, Eleni is seized with the realisation of the nearly unbearable costs of two decades of loneliness. She further realises she barely knows the man for whom she has endured so much.

The Greek military dictatorship of 1967–74 was a watershed regime for Greek political life and for Greek cinema. The junta proved to be the final act in a conflict between the Greek right and the left that had raged since the 1930s and had reached a horrific climax in the Civil War of 1946–49. The rule of the colonels proved to be so dreadful that the Greek nation was forced to re-evaluate the historical period that had produced such an unacceptable form of government.

The impact of the junta on Greek cinema was just as decisive, if less direct. The establishment of the dictatorship happened to coincide with the introduction of television. Rather than going to the movies, most of the Greek public preferred to stay home and watch television. Such a phenomenon is not unique to Greece. Even in the United Sates, movie attendance fell by 75 per cent when television was first introduced. Yet such a loss was not sustainable in Greece. The situation was further worsened by an industry that was churning out increasingly mediocre fare. The rigid censorship imposed by the colonels, which even included the banning of bouzouki music, was the final blow; the commercial Greek film industry imploded.

The responsibility for making quality Greek-language films now rested with a small core of predominantly male filmmakers who loathed popular cinema as banal entertainment that should be replaced by an artistic cinema. Greatly influenced by French notions of auteurism, what became known as the New Greek Cinema enthusiastically endorsed the notion that the director's creative vision was paramount in the making of quality films. Even during the junta era, they would be able to produce remarkable films. Much like filmmakers who worked under Soviet censors, the Greeks resorted to artful means of dealing with forbidden topics.

Among the new filmmakers was 25-year-old Pantelis Voulgaris. As he would explain in later years, he had been profoundly influenced by Italian Neorealism. In contrast to the farces and cheap melodramas that characterised Greek popular cinema, the Italians had managed to shape a popular cinema of artistic merit that dealt with everyday life in a serious yet engaging manner. Voulgaris hoped he could do the same with films about Greece. His first three films, shorts of fifteen to thirty minutes in length, which he wrote and directed, show this Italian influence. *O Kleftis* (*The Thief,* 1965) focuses on a poor man who has become a petty thief; *Tzimis O Tigris* (*Jimmy the Tiger*, 1966) deals with a street performer; and *O Horos Ton Tragon* (*The Goat Dance,* 1971) represents the Carnival on the island of Skyros with ancient Dionysian rites.

Voulgaris's first feature, *To Proxenio tis Annas* (*The Engagement of Anna*, 1972) slyly took on the morality of the colonels' 'Greece of Christian Greeks' by offering a poignant view of a young domestic worker trapped in a cruel class society in which even her mother is party to the oppression of women. With the grip of the junta on public life beginning to slip, Voulgaris further tested artistic limits with *O Megalos Erotikos* (*The Great Love Songs*, 1973). He used ten poems by some of Greece's greatest poets (Sappho, Elytis, Cavafy, among others) set to music by Manos Hadjidakis to again challenge the junta's vision of Hellenic culture. The musical format and use of classical poets and Nobel Laureates was sufficient to get past the not very sophisticated eyes of the censors. With the fall of the junta, Voulgaris was able to express his views openly. His *Haroumeni Imera* (*Happy Day*, 1976) used expressionistic humour to mock the brutal culture of the military and the monarchy in a story set in one of the concentration camps established by the Greek government after the end of World War Two and reopened by the junta. Four years later in *Eleftherios Venizelos: 1910–1927* (1980), Voulgaris examined the political career of Greece's most famed republican leader.

*Stone Years* would take the political themes Voulgaris had been developing to a logical conclusion that would trouble many Greeks. In valorising the lives of two communist militants, Voulgaris took on a subject that would have been impossible at any time between the end of the Civil War and the fall of the junta. In a retrospective of his work at New York's Museum of Modern Art in 1995, Voulgaris would comment, in the interview with Cleo Cacoulidis, on film censorship in Greece:

> One has only to consider the fact that after the Civil War of 1949 and the defeat of the leftist movement, censorship of one form or another, at times grim and obvious, at times devious and subtle, has kept the true history of this country far from motion picture screens. And so for many of my generation who view it as an obligation, the allusion to the past is necessary. Events that have lain for years in the shadows, decisive moments for my country that have been concealed, must now be addressed. The adventures of these two people whose story I have told are historically true, but they are not unique … Their personal odyssey represents the great segment of the Greek people. This film is a small tribute to all that these simple people lived through from 1954–74. Those twenty stone years.

*Stone Years* begins in 1954, a time when the radical/liberal alliance of the war years had been destroyed and an ultra-conservative regime with the backing of the United States holds political power. Although the Greek Communist Party has been outlawed and thousands of its cadre are in exile and thousands more are in prison, a skeletal underground continues to exist. Among the communist activists in the Thessalian countryside is 18-year-old Eleni (Themis Bazaka), who lives with her mother. Her two sisters are in exile and all the males in her immediate family have been killed by Greek or German fascists. She is in love with 22-year-old Babis (Dimitris Katalifos), who has a comparable family history. We first encounter the couple in a gorgeous country setting, where they could be any two young people experiencing the magic of a first romance.

Barely together as lovers, Babis is denounced by a local informer and arrested for distributing subversive literature. Eleni has also been named, but she manages to escape to Athens. To illustrate the complex interaction of family and politics in Greece, Voulgaris creates an interesting scene on a train. Two policemen examining identity cards in a search for subversives come upon Eleni. One of them recognises her and understands her documents are bogus; but he does not arrest her. He is a relative and as he whispers to her later, he cannot bring himself to turn her in. For the next dozen years, Eleni will live a clandestine life, aided by various comrades who range from left-wing intellectuals such as the fashionable Cleo (Irini Inglessi) to laborers such as Michael (Ilias Katevas). Her prime political function appears to be simply to not get caught while maintaining a fragile system of leafleting and communication. Years pass before she can see her mother (Maria Martika) again. Even that meeting is arranged as a near-clandestine encounter in a small taverna.

In the summer of 1966, Eleni learns that Babis is going to be transported from a prison in Crete to one on Aegina. Against the advice of her comrades she takes the enormous risk of getting on board the ferry transporting the prisoners. Her only goal is to get a glimpse of him, almost to reassure herself that he still exists; to remind herself of what he actually looks like. The desperate gamble is successful as they are able to exchange furtive glances. Their love is still viable, but any thoughtful viewer must realise that it is a strangely abstract relationship. The lovers are no longer the relatively innocent youths attracted to one another twelve years earlier. Each has surely grown, but as there has been no personal communication between them, they have grown in different ways and separate from one another. Their love seems more like a desperate hope, somehow related to their dreams of a better Greece, than conventional *agape* or *eros*.

Later that year, Babis and other political prisoners are released under an amnesty involving strict supervision. The two lovers are finally able to live together. But it is a period of great political turmoil. The centre-left forces in Greece are on a political upswing. The political scene includes assassinations and mass public demonstrations. Babis and Eleni are engaged in these events to the degree their circumstances allow, but even this relatively positive period is cut short when a now pregnant Eleni is arrested. In a trial that generates enormous publicity, the government paints Eleni as a 'super red' long wanted by the police and a clear and present danger to the state. Eleni's eloquent account of her dreams for a democratic Greece and the travails of her family are discounted; and she is sentenced to a lengthy prison term. A few months later, on 21 April 1967, a group of colonels stage a tank-driven coup. Eleni's prison ward is now filled with many women who had known each other from previous incarcerations. Among them is Cleo and other women who have personally worked with Eleni. The jailers are also veterans who greet the reprisoned women almost as old friends. A benefit in these events for Eleni is that she now has a score of very well organised, 'red grandmothers' to watch over her through the final weeks of her pregnancy and early childrearing, before the child is sent to relatives to be taken care of.

The colonels rescind the amnesty that had been granted to Babis. Before long he is brought to the male quarters across the prison yard from where the women are kept. The new mother and father communicate by sending coded messages through the iron bars that separate them by reflecting sunlight off hand-held mirrors. They demand that the authorities allow them to be married. A number of years pass before the authorities are forced by law to allow a ceremony to take place in the prison. As no adult male is allowed to mingle with the prisoners, the role of best man falls to their infant son! In keeping with Greek Orthodox ritual, 'the best man' will place the wedding wreaths on the head of his mother and father in what may be the most surreal wedding scene in Greek cinema.

Only with the fall of the junta in 1974 are Eleni and Babis finally permanently set free. Rather than a conventional happy ending to such a sad tale, Voulgaris gives his film an additional powerful twist with a final sequence featuring Eleni in her new home. Babis is calling to her from outside and we hear the usual noises of a Greek street. Eleni looks about her new home carefully. In a brilliant piece of acting, without the use of words or voice-over, we understand that Eleni knows little about Babis. What kind of man is he really? What kind of husband and father will he be? Their youth has been consumed in loneliness and despair. Can they recreate anything of the romance of 1954? Can they ever leave behind the burden of those lost years? Eleni does not turn away in despair. She simply communicates the profound price she has paid for her choices and the price that she will continue to pay.

The immediate intentions of Voulgaris in making *Stone Years* was to defend the spirit of the National Liberation Front (EAM-ELAS) of the 1940s. Eleni and Babis are decent working-class Greeks who give their all to create a democratic and just nation. We are impressed by their commitment and their skills. We also see that most of the time they do little more than survive to fight another day. Their major weapons are not arms but ideology. While all this is true enough and even admirable, there is almost no examination of the specific ideology that sustained these brave people or the differences between the personal vision of party militants and some of the party's Stalinist public positions and actions. Surely Eleni and Babis would not have approved of the Soviet gulag, but their party was always silent on that topic. Nor do we get any sense of the issues that drove a wedge between the communists and their erstwhile liberal allies of the war years.

These omissions leave the portraits of Eleni and Babis incomplete and somewhat super-ficial. Their political views are made to appear largely circumstantial, psychological and even simply familial rather than ideological. We can see that Eleni is not the vile subversive the right insists she is, but we have no sense of why the right should feel so threatened by such a person. Nor do we understand why the various rightist regimes commanded substantial public support at various times. The informers are drawn harshly and given vile motivations, but there was no huge pubic outcry to defend the rights of the defeated left. Voulgaris offers a Manichean good versus evil dynamic. As a result, the left-oriented viewer will be moved by his sympathetic portraits, the right will consider the tale a whitewash made by someone with communist sympathies, and the apolitical viewer is likely to see the story as a touching real-life melodrama.

Voulgaris is aware of these shortcomings, but like the majority of Greeks he wanted to bring the old conflicts to some kind of closure. In various talks and interviews, he has noted that the dictatorships that have marked so much of recent Greek history are intolerable. Although given the opportunity to leave Greece by a Ford Foundation grant in 1968, he chose to remain and exercise passive and later active resistance. He only left the country briefly when he was wanted by the police for his involvement in a critical uprising by students at the Polytechnic Institute in November 1973, the revolt that set the stage for the collapse of the colonels the following summer.

The broad revisionist intent of *Stone Years* is not readily apparent in its opening sequences. The significance of the political activism shown depends to a large degree on the viewer's pre-existing knowledge of Greek politics. As the story unfolds, however, it rests more firmly on its own givens and increasingly offers an adroit blending of humour and pathos. The musical score by Stamatis Spanoudakis, which won awards at several international film festivals, is particu-larly effective in setting the tempo for the second half the film. The cinematography by Yiorgos Arvanitis is also most memorable in the second half of the film as his camera captures the ambiance of the prison, particularly the wedding and the mirror communications. Although Katalifos is a credible Babis, his Babis remains a man whom we know only from the outside. In contrast, Bazaka is brilliant in evoking the evolving interior life of Eleni. The shy girl of 1954 progresses subtly to the complex woman of 1974. Bazaka's acting received special mention at the Venice Film Festival.

Greek audiences responded enthusiastically to the message and the art of *Stone Years*. It was awarded Best Film, Best Direction and Best Actress at the Thessaloniki Film Festival and Best Film, Best Actress and Best Music at the State Awards, presented by the Ministry of Culture. In many ways, *Stone Years* marked a closure for the discussion of the Civil War that had been launched with Theo Angelopoulos's *O Thiassos* (*The Traveling Players*, 1975) and elaborated on in a number of films of the New Greek Cinema. The 'official story' of the causes, nature and results of the Civil War had largely been rewritten by the filmmakers of the post-junta era, less with the idea of simply reversing the roles of heroes and villains than replacing such analysis with a sense of the tragic nature and costs of fratricide in all its various forms. By the mid-1980s, Greece was relishing its new image as the leading democracy of the Balkans and was an enthusiastic advocate of the values of the European Union.

Voulgaris has continued to enjoy a substantial following in Greece. After *Stone Years*, he would make *I Fanela Me to Enia* (*The Striker with the No. 9*, 1988), *Isscihes meres tou Avgoustou* (*Quiet Days in August*, 1991), *Akropol* (*Acropole*, 1995) and *Ola ine dromos* (*It's a Long Road*, 1998). Each of these films is set in contemporary Greece, often weighing what elements of tradi-tional culture should be saved and what elements should be discarded. Voulgaris was given a major retrospective at New York's prestigious Musuem of Modern Art in 1995 and another at the Thessaloniki Film Festival in 2002.

Despite a distinguished body of work, Voulgaris remains relatively unknown to interna-tional audiences compared to his contemporary Theo Angelopoulos. He is often referred to as 'that other Greek director'. When asked in 1995 about living in the shadow of Angelopoulos, Voulgaris made a comment that is often heard from artists residing in nations at the periphery of world power. Asked to comment on Angelopoulos in interview with Cleo Cacoulidis, he noted that Angelopoulos being so well known outside of Greece 'creates a climate where critics and audiences expect that all filmmakers from Greece make films like him, or they expect to see something that resembles his style. This can be positive, but it is also negative because Greece is truly a small country. For most of the international film festivals and film critics, it seems, one filmmaker from Greece is enough.'

What is most certain is that the stylistic approach of Voulgaris is quite distinct from that of Angelopoulos. Equally relevant is that Voulgaris has escaped most of the problems that have engulfed other filmmakers associated with the New Greek Cinema. After the first burst of creativity, the auteurism of the New Greek Cinema has often led to a kind of intellec-tual elitism. Eccentricities and mannerisms have often been passed off as style. Long running times frequently are not justified by the content offered and scripts have been notoriously idio-syncratic. In contrast, Voulgaris has been steadfast in trying to fuse the entertainment values of the old Greek cinema with the artistry of the New Greek Cinema as he offers a vision of Greece quite different from the gorgeous seascapes, imposing ruins and mysterious icons of tourist brochures. As *Stone Years* illustrates, while that vision is not always pleasant, it remains hopeful.

**Dan Georgakas**

**Works Cited**

Cacoulidis, C. (1996) 'Chronicles of Modern Greece: An Interview with Pantelis Voulgaris', *Cineaste*, 22, 2, 34–6.

Georgakas, D. (1986) '*Stone Years*', *Cineaste*, 15, 1, 45–6.

Kokolanis, B. (2003) *Pantelis Voulgaris*. Athens: Greek Film Centre/Aigokeros.

# LEPOTA POROKA THE BEAUTY OF SIN

## ŽIVKO NIKOLIĆ, YUGOSLAVIA, 1986

In the rock-strewn mountains of Montenegro, some time in the past, a woman dressed in traditional clothes prepares a flat loaf of bread and removes her wedding ring. Outside, among the rocks, she places the loaf on top of her head as her husband delivers her a deadly blow with a mallet. The traditional ritual of punishing adulterous women by killing them has been practiced for generations.

The same ritual will be played out at the end of the film, but then it will be set in the present day and will involve its main protagonists – Jaglika and Luka. They are a young couple whose everyday life in the remote mountains of Montenegro is hard and far from prosperous; the outlook for the future is similarly bleak. They decide to accept the invitation of cousin and best man, Djordje, who has told them stories about his success in the tourist industry further-away, near the sea, where they could earn well and live at ease.

Earlier, we have seen Djordje with a group of young men he hired to carry his car up the rocky mountain to the village, so that he can impress the peasants with his boisterous arrival on four wheels. Djordje also pays a brief visit to his weak and exhausted wife who has stayed in the village to take care of their many children.

We catch up with Djordje at a coastal railway station on a lookout for women to recruit for work at the nudist resort popular with foreign tourists. He meets an outgoing and sexually emancipated provincial woman, Kosara, and invites her to stay in his charming seafront house. That night, their noisy lovemaking is interrupted by the arrival of Jaglika and Luka. Djordje (or George, as he is known locally), finds a job for Luka at the salt works. There, in the midst of hard labour in difficult conditions, Luka gets into a fight with a colleague to defend George's name.

The manager of the nudist resort is putting pressure on George to find more staff. George's accommodation and lifestyle depend on the resort and he is keen to get Jaglika to work there. Initially, Jaglika and Luka's traditional philosophy is a big obstacle to Jaglika taking the job, but when George secretly arranges for Luka's sacking, the couple are forced to accept the offer.

While Jaglika takes a ferry every morning to work as a maid at the secluded resort crowded with naked foreigners, Luka remains in town, confused and disappointed. At work,

Jaglika becomes fascinated with a beautiful young Western couple. Intrigued by her innocence, they begin teasing her by displaying playful intimacy, like when they ride on horsebacks naked on the beach. Meanwhile, she is under pressure to join a rich client, a Greek shipping tycoon, who has requested her company for a two-week cruise.

George's wife turns up with their children. She is losing her eyesight and needs treatment. George is incensed by her arrival, which also prompts Kosara to leave him, despite his protestations that this woman is his aunt. Kosara, too, has children and a husband, who emerges looking for her. He gets into a fight with Luka, who is quick to protect his best man; both are arrested and spend the night in prison.

After glimpsing the affectionate lovemaking of the tourist couple, Jaglika tries to introduce some gentleness into her own mechanical sex life, but Luka is shocked and responds by telling her that she should leave her job at once. Despite their argument, she goes to work the next day. At the resort, Kosara's husband begs her to come back to their children, but Kosara breaks down in tears, saying that she is ruined and that they would be better off thinking that she is dead.

Jaglika joins the nudist couple on a boat ride; she does not take the ferry but stays at the resort and all three of them dance together at the bar in the evening. At their room, a game of hide-and-seek leads to a kiss and Jaglika runs away. At home, Luka is devastated when he realises Jaglika has not returned. George has an aggressive fit and his wife humbly returns home.

In the morning, Jaglika joins the couple for a passionate, but tender, naked swim. A little later on, back in her maid uniform to clean their room, she is shocked to realise the couple have left without saying goodbye, as the new guests, an older plump naked couple, greet her there. George is made a manager of the nudist complex. On the way to their village, their visit to a shrine is cut short by Jaglika's announcement that she has sinned.

Back home, the ritual from the beginning of the film is re-enacted. But, at the decisive moment, Luka drops the mallet and walks away. From inside the house a gunshot is heard.

The sinister beauty of its landscape, the tradition of proud warriors, the ancient customs of its people, the myth of a genetic tendency relating to their tall stature, the very name – Montenegro (evidently coined by the conquerors), all evoke a theme-park of otherness in the Westerner's imagination.

The inconsistent history of cinema on Montenegrin soil begins with the exploitation of these preconceptions. Foreign cameramen flocked to Montenegro to record the exotic spectacle surrounding the inauguration of King Nikola in 1909. Numerous show reels followed during the Balkan War of 1912–13. After World War One, its rustic environment provided producers (mainly German) with a picturesque and cheap setting for both documentaries and feature films. But it was not until 1948, when the Yugoslav government enterprise Lovćen Film was set up, that the Montenegrin film industry really came to life. This studio financed feature films by local directors, like Velimir Stojanović and Zdravko Velimirović, and developed foreign co-productions. In 1962, the Federal Film Industry Advancement Fund was abolished, and decentralisation of the Yugoslav film industry followed. According to the new model, all the republics were to run their own film funds relying on their own financial resources. Montenegro, the smallest and poorest of them all, could not sustain feature film production in such circumstances. Nevertheless, a lively new generation of filmmakers, including Vlatko Gilić and Živko Nikolić, still managed to establish themselves through the production of outstanding shorts and documentaries.

Živko Nikolić, the director of *Lepota Peroka* (*The Beauty of Sin*, 1986), made his first feature film *Beštije* (*The Beasts*) in 1977 and over the course of the next few decades he became the only consistent face of Montenegrin cinema. He was born in the village of Ozrinići in northern Montenegro. He studied painting in the coastal town of Herceg-Novi before enrolling at the Academy for Theatre, Film, Radio and Television in Belgrade. He was a singularly idiosyncratic figure who wrote most of his films, which were entirely set and shot in Montenegro. Sadly, Nikolić spent the last few years of his life in illness and poverty. He is said to have depended on the good will of a local supermarket manager for food, while endless repeated runs of his comedy series *Djekna* (1988) were still dominating television schedules.

His work can be placed in a diverse and exciting cinematic lineage of male directors who have challenged the existing social, ideological and aesthetic orders through films that centre on female characters: Carl Theodor Dreyer, Kenji Mizoguchi, Douglas Sirk, Luis Buñuel, Rainer Werner Fassbinder, Walerian Borowczyk and, more recently, Lars von Trier. In his interest in female protagonists, however, Nikolić was probably closest to the acclaimed Soviet-Moldovan director Emile Loteanu: both directors had a special talent for discovering extremely good-looking women and casting them in their films by delicately and unobtrusively exploring sexual awakening and sensual eroticism.

A strong woman at odds with her male-dominated community is a central theme of Nikolić's films. *Jovana Lukina* (1979) concerns a young peasant woman who gets corrupted by the pain of the strangers she meets as they pass by her house. This mesmerising and idiosyncratic work is carefully composed to hover all the way through in an ambiguous socio-temporal framework. The film's brutal and violent world likened medieval Montenegro to contemporary reality, and many have found this offensive.

The often angry debates around the question of patriotism continued to follow Nikolić throughout his career. The fact that for so long he had been the prominent Montenegrin voice in the most widely influential art form enforced a special kind of responsibility upon his work. For a great number of those who lived in other parts of former Yugoslavia, his television series *Djekna*, a vicious satire of Montenegrin rural life, is the first thing that springs to mind when Montenegro is mentioned. *The Beauty of Sin*, distributed around the world, was a major box-office hit in Israel, for instance. His other important films, such as *Čudo nevidjeno* (*Unseen Wonder*, 1984), *U ime naroda* (*In the Name of the People*, 1987) and *Iskušavanje djavola* (*Tempting the Devil*, 1989) also depict incredibly conservative and unhealthy societies, populated by selfish, narrow-minded individuals and governed by unfair, irrational traditions. Such representations of his homeland were criticised for being unpatriotic. However, Nikolić's dedicated human and artistic honesty allowed for nothing less than the uncompromising clash with what he perceived as the hypocrisy of his own culture.

*The Beauty of Sin* is probably the most illustrative case in this thorny dispute. It is not difficult to see why Nikolić was accused of exploiting and promoting the prejudice about the exotic/backward Montenegro: the narrative is formally framed by a gruesome 'custom' involving bizarre and cruel executions of young women; another 'tradition' requires a wife to cover her face with a black cloth during marital sex; a shady macho-type, George, is the only one who succeeds in this world, while his wife is treated worse than a slave. But, while many aspects of the characters, habits and circumstances featured in the film are farcical or historically displaced, it is also true that such a ceremonious approach enhances the appreciation and the impact of the intended social and political critique.

Luka embodies an archetypal Montenegrin male, blessed with all the moral qualities that epic history prescribes: he is brave, honourable and loyal. However, he is also more naïve than Don Quixote. When transposed into the real contemporary world, he disintegrates. He is exposed to public humiliation through a series of encounters with individuals from the margins of society: first, with the gay manager of a textile company who is shadowing him; then, with a widow whom he tries to sway into the 'naturist industry'; and, finally, with a prostitute that George sets him up with. His humiliation is repeatedly heightened by the *Commedia dell'arte* device – loud laughter of the strangers who happen to witness it.

As part of the film's depth relies upon the viewer's familiarity with certain key elements of local culture, myth and ethics, it is important to elucidate these elements here. It does not seem possible to write about a Montenegrin film, or book, or sculpture, or indeed any cultural product without placing it within the context independent of a key nineteenth-century literary work – *Gorski vijenac* (*The Mountain Wreath*) by the poet-ruler Petar II Petrović Njegoš. A small-scale violent historical event, the re-conversion of Slav Muslims to Christianity, is a backdrop for this masterpiece fusion of rich oral epic tradition with the sublime poetry of metaphysical romanticism. *Gorski vijenac* outlines the past and present of a people forever involved in brutal struggles arising from their historically tragic predicament. The world as seen through Njegoš's lyrical perspective exists in permanent disharmony, fuelled by the perpetual conflict between mutually opposed forces – between the mind and the body, sea and land, between two animals, two people, two civilisations. These cruel dialectics lie at the core of the Montenegrin national ethos.

It is significant that *The Beauty of Sin* also appears to be structured around a series of philosophical and visual dichotomies: masculine/feminine, peasant/urban, pre-modern/post-modern, wild/civilised, patriarchal/emancipated, light/darkness, custom/commerce, and so on. Harsh rocky mountains of the North are juxtaposed with the softness of the sand and the sea in the South. The nudity of the tourists is comically contrasted with the uniform worn by the staff at the resort, resembling monastic attire. Both appear absurd as a result. The uniform metaphorically relates to the elaborate, abiding system of values, whose end product is the suppression of the most basic emotional and sensual needs. Jaglika's initial encounter with the Western couple is an odd moment: faced with their naked bodies, she breaks down in tears. It is as if she has suddenly been presented with a vision of the world stripped bare of its customary artificial shell. Meanwhile, the foreign couple's nakedness signifies freedom from inhibition, but not only that, this is also a freedom from responsibility, commitment and empathy. The sound design, with their voices dubbed, adds to the air of detachment around them.

Like Kaspar Hauser, Luka and Jaglika are suddenly thrown into the middle of this complicated world. They rely on George on the one hand and the foreign couple on the other to introduce and guide them through it. To betray this child-like dependence would be cruel, but this is precisely what George and the foreigners do, without a hint of guilt or regret.

Aesthetic and symbolic interplay between the indoor and outdoor world is particularly complex. Almost all the shots of domestic interiors are characterised by low, dramatic, chiaroscuro lighting. The nameless couple's living room from the beginning of the film, Jaglika and

Luka's wedding party, as well as all the other scenes inside their house, the sequences within George's village home, the staff dining area in his seaside house and the married couple's bedroom there – all of these are arranged like *tableaux vivants* evoking the atmosphere, the colours, the contrast and composition of classical painting. The tie between tradition and oppression is thus re-emphasised by visual means – the interior is a symbolic setting for their convergence. The interior is, after all, where Luka retreats at the very end, to take his own life.

The exterior shots, on the other hand, bear a stamp of the great Montenegrin twentieth-century painter Petar Lubarda, whose historical Belgrade exhibition in 1951 signalled a radical modernist split with the socialist-realistic style prevalent in Yugoslavia after World War Two. Lubarda's work is strongly rooted in the powerful Montenegrin landscape, which he rendered through the abstraction of mood and ambiance. The human form, reduced to unfixed bestial outlines, dwindles, becoming no more prominent than any other element of the scenery.

Nikolić had always been keen to acknowledge that his cinematic expression owed much to Lubarda and other visual artists. His films do not represent such a radical challenge to the dominant film form like the late 1960s work of better-known Yugoslav directors Dušan Makavejev, Živojin Pavlović, Aleksandar Petrović or Želimir Žilnik. Nevertheless, it is primarily thanks to his painterly approach and references that the visual language of Nikolić's films is specific and unmistakably unique.

Lubarda inhabits *The Beauty of Sin* in more than one aspect. This is Montenegro removed from its postcard beauty, observed with far more nuance and sensitivity for the atmosphere inherent in the changing cast of natural light across mountains and coast. The backdrop for the opening murder scene is like a Lubarda painting come to life, with blue residues of the day in the top left-hand corner and the reddish grey of the rocks hiding the dark crooked figures of gloomy old women clambering for a view of the 'spectacle'.

Humans group into an ominous bunch in another memorable set piece later on. When Kosara's dishevelled husband breaks into the resort looking for her, he is chased by the resort's manager and the security officer, as well as several other figures eager to join them. Their ageing and ungracious appearances add to the simultaneously pathetic and menacing atmosphere punctuated by the sound of weighty footsteps. His run ends when he reaches the beach where unengaged naked tourists are moving around the showers. It is much like an encounter between two different animal species.

Another set of references is evoked here. The manhunt is used as both the narrative and the philosophical framework for two major works of Montenegrin modern literature: *The*

*Chase* by Mihailo Lalić, a psychological novel set in Montenegrin mountains during World War Two, and the existential novella *The Mouth Full of Earth* by Branimir Šćepanović, who was a scriptwriter on another feature film directed by Živko Nikolić, *Smrt Gospodina Goluže* (*The Death of Mister Goluza*, 1982).

But, to return to the long list of conflicted forces shaping the language of *The Beauty of Sin*, a few more words ought to be said about the character of Djordje/George. He has picked up pompous phrases that were created at that time by careerist politicians in an attempt to mask the truth about the disintegration of the country's socialist economy and values. 'Naturism has its developmental perspective', he says, trying to entice vulnerable smalltown and country women into the biggest local business, set up to satisfy particular Western consumerist leisure needs.

His distorted interpretation of female liberation is remarkably displayed when he explains to Luka that 'woman is a social being, and as such she belongs to the society to use her as it sees fit'. He is a monster, created in a freak collision between two systems: predatory patriarchy and collective socialism. Somewhere between the two is also where women's social progress remains suspended.

The picture of women in the film harshly subverts the communist vision of emancipation. The only woman in a position of power, the nudist resort's manager, is an androgynous disciplinarian, whose abilities and desires are entirely subordinated to the demands of her career. The others are either a languid slave to domestic and family duty (George's wife), or a woman who rebelled against slavish submissiveness only to grow into a remorseful emotional wreck (Kosara). And let us not forget the woman (played by the director's wife) who dies at the beginning of the film, after reciting words of comfort to her husband, saying that he is not about to kill *her*, but his disgraced loaf of bread.

These are the models on view for Jaglika, a young woman whose capacity for love is repressed by her community and exploited by her workplace. Her part is played by Mira Furlan, one of the leading Yugoslav actors of the 1980s, who was twice awarded the Golden Arena, the most prestigious film award in former Yugoslavia (including Best Leading Actress for this role). She appeared in such films as Emir Kusturica's *Otac na službenom putu* (*When Father Was Away on Business*, 1985), Rajko Grlić's *Za sreću je potrebno troje* (*Three for Happiness,* 1985) and *Gluvi barut* (*Silent Gunpowder*, 1990) directed by Bahrudin-Bato Čengić. After the break-up of Yugoslavia, she left her native Croatia to continue her career in the US, where she is known for her part in the science fiction television series *Babylon 5*. Considering that Jaglika is the central character of the film, it is striking how little she says. What she sees and what she is able to see are of much more importance. The camera is more concerned with offering us a portrait of Jaglika, rather than her point of view. We are invited to reflect upon her inner world and the world around her, but also to assess the philosophical and political value of seeing.

The film's narrative begins with Jaglika's contemplative gaze. It is an enigmatic and beautifully 'plastic' image. Her face and posture exude beauty and strength, but, like the gusts of wind playing with her hair on the warm bright day, hints of disquiet can be detected. A cut suggests that the gaze is directed towards hazy Montenegrin mountains. While this functions in terms of drawing us into the story – it is her wedding day and she, together with the rest of the party, is expecting the arrival of the best man Djordje – her look does not indicate the petty anxiety of her family and husband-to-be. Instead, it is as if these mountains convey the premonition of the burden and struggle she is about to face.

Seeing, in the female context, is used as a symbolic instrument of liberty. When Jaglika takes the cloth away from her face in the bedroom and tries to kiss Luka, she irrevocably challenges the ridiculous injustice of her position. Her first physical contact with the two foreigners also takes place in the darkness – for the little game they play, she wears a band over her eyes. But she interrupts the play and leaves, joining them the next day in the daylight. At the same time, the misery of George's wife is pointedly highlighted by her illness: she is losing sight.

The male gaze, on the other hand, is no more than a means for the accomplishment of voyeuristic desire, epitomised by the men hiding in the bushes on the outskirts of the naturist camp. And, while the young and attractive Jaglika becomes a fetish for the Western couple, the camera never turns her into one for the audience. That is not to say that Nikolić is not interested in the erotic. On the contrary, he adoringly projects a romantic idea of 'pure' sensuality onto his central female characters. Like those played by Merima Isaković in *Jovana Lukina* and Savina Geršak in *Cudo evidjeno* (*Unseen Wonder*, 1984), Mira Furlan's character responds to this representation. Such an image of sexuality stands out in his films, propped up by the presence of the other two recurrent female types: a casually promiscuous type – the 'whore', and a sexually-deprived woman – the 'slave'. In *The Beauty of Sin*, Kosara and the prostitute involved in the incident with Luka belong to the first category, while George's wife and the manager fit the second.

Jaglika's swim with the pair is a gratification of desire for freedom rather than for sexual fulfilment. The couple awaken love in her, but this love is never defined in clear gendered or sexual terms. She is not drawn to the man, or the woman, but to a promise of the liberation of feelings and needs elaborately repressed until that moment. Their company, together with the setting, have helped to bring these feelings and needs to the surface.

The film's conflicts and contradictions unite finally in the most dramatic conflict of all: the price of Jaglika's self-discovery is Luka's death. Tragic as this ending may be, it is far from didactic. But, more than that, it is imbued with a strange and difficult kind of beauty. His suicide is a painfully poetic sacrifice to the force of womanhood. A force so overwhelming even in a society organised around the superficial norms aimed at its suppression. Essentially, man is as confined by this duplicitous system as is woman.

And to touch upon the most sensitive of Balkan subjects – that of the national identity – Nikolić's critique implies that even though the patriarchal and the parochial may sit at the core of Montenegrin national character, this does not mean that the radical modification of these concepts would result in the loss of that character. However, the film draws attention to the lack of affirmative ideological or ethical perspective necessary for such transformation.

Another aspect of the identity issue is addressed in a very funny moment earlier in the film: after arriving at the coast, Luka sits down to take a moment's rest at a town square and starts playing the Montenegrin national instrument, the *gusle*, which may sound a little strange to an ear accustomed to Western music. While a couple of tourists are keen to photograph this unusual sight, a policeman is quick to interrupt the song. 'Get lost,' he orders, 'you're not amongst sheep! What will these people think of us!?' This attitude is a well-observed summary of the confused cultural politics recurrent among small nations struggling to find their place in a global system, which they have such little power to affect.

**Nikola Mijović**

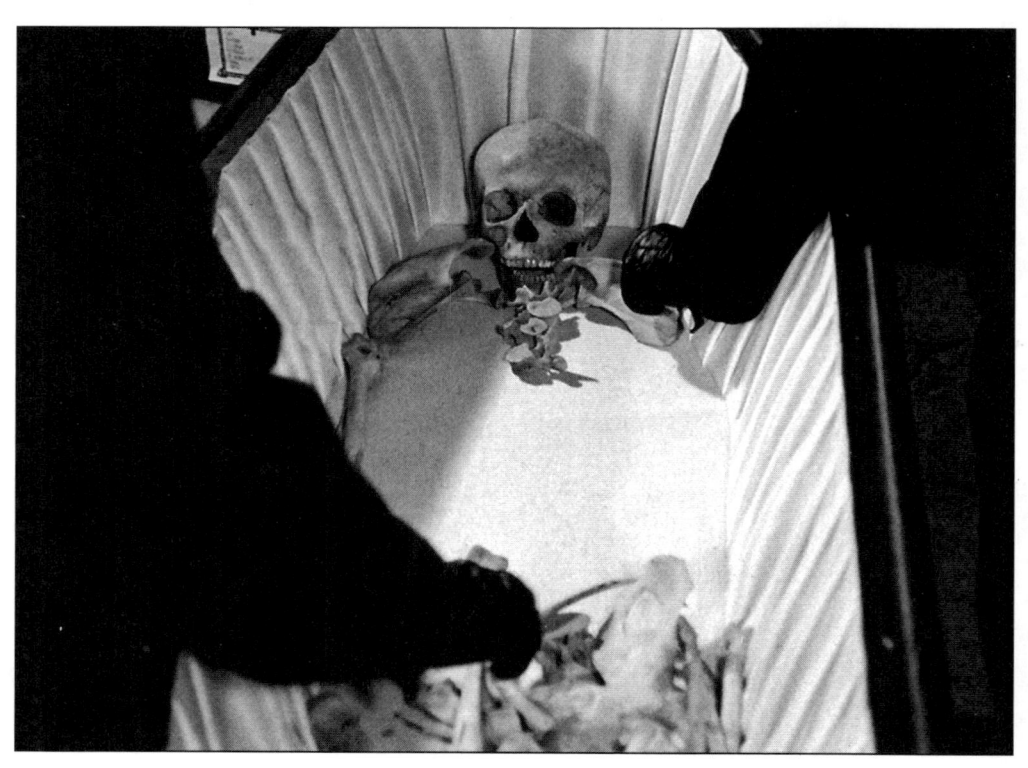

# KTHIMI I USHTRISË SË VDEKUR RETURN OF THE DEAD ARMY

## DHIMITËR ANAGNOSTI, ALBANIA, 1989

It is the early 1960s. Twenty years after Italy's capitulation in 1943, an Italian General and a Catholic Priest embark on a mission to Albania. They are to arrange for the exhumation and repatriation of the remains of some 3,000 Italian soldiers who perished during the occupation of Albania during World War Two. The dead soldiers' relatives expect them to have the remains returned; the Priest and the General compete for the favours of the rich and influential Countess Betty, whose husband, Colonel Di Zetta, also vanished under mysterious circumstances in the war.

The couple arrive in Albania, armed with maps, rosters, measurements and dental records and are received by local officials who are to facilitate the mission. They go on a reconnaissance trip across the barren mountains of Albania's northern countryside where they organise exhumations, assisted by locals who participate in the digs yet display silent hostility to their efforts. In the process of recovering the soldiers' remains, the General discovers that the members of the so-called Blue Battalion have tarnished their reputation with acts of brutality. The story that emerges is far from the myth of heroic death in foreign lands. Tales of brutal rape and murderous revenge haunt the General, who reads excerpts of letters and diaries found in the unmarked graves and experiences nightmarish flashbacks. He cannot endure the silent hostility of the Albanian countryside, the unwelcoming weather, and the suppressed yet overwhelmingly present resentment of the local labourers; there are moments when he feels the mission is doomed. The General feels his grim task is hopeless; it can only lead to unwanted exposure of past crimes and cowardice. He enters into open disagreements with the Priest who is much more pragmatic and optimistic of the mission's outcome.

On one of the trips the Italian General comes across a German General who works on a similar mission of recovering the remains of his Albania-stationed dead German countrymen. They get drunk together and bond, united by shared cynicism and despair, both disillusioned and sceptical, both feeling the curse of silent condemnation.

The searches go on for more than a year; the remains of many are recovered, identified and classified. The Blue Battalion is reconstructed, except for the remains of Colonel Di

Zetta whose disappearance remains as mysterious as it was on the first day of the expedition. One night the General and the Priest attend a village wedding where they enter an unanticipated confrontation with the mother of a girl who committed suicide after she was raped by the Colonel. It now transpires that the Colonel died in a revenge killing committed by the mother, who buried his body under the doorsill of her own house. The bones of the Colonel are exhumed and now the General can bring his mission to conclusion. But, during an agitated dispute with the corrupt Priest, in a bout of rage the General hurls the bag with the Colonel's bones into the nearby gorge.

In the concluding scene the General is seen working on documents in the mortuary while the Priest looks on with silent animosity. The General and the Priest take a set of human bones out of an ordinary wooden coffin and move them to the lacquered casket designed for the remains of Colonel Di Zetta, and begin putting them in order – skull, then the other bones – thus 'reconstructing' his skeleton. Does anybody really care whose skeleton this is? He is as dead as all the others. Set against the sounds of a glorious trumpet tune calling his imaginary 'dead army' to arms, the General can now complete the assignment: he closes the folder containing the notes of his mission, and stores it in a cabinet which he then locks.

*Kthimi I Ushtrisë së Vdekur* (*Return of the Dead Army*, Dhimitër Anagnosti, 1989) is immersed in the labyrinthine universe of writer Ismail Kadaré, who wrote the novel from which the film was adapted. Albania's foremost poet and novelist and one of the most important Balkan authors, Kadaré grew up in the ethnic Tosk city of Gjirokastër, near Albania's southern border with Greece and later graduated from the Maxim Gorky literary institute in Moscow. The 1963 publication of his debut novel *The General of the Dead Army* set off a spectacular literary career that has so far spanned four decades so. Important books by Kadaré include *The Castle* (1970), *Chronicle in Stone* (1971), *The Three Arched Bridge* (1978), *Doruntine* (1980) and *The Palace of Dreams* (1981). After the death of Albania's idiosyncratic communist leader Enver Hoxha in 1985, Kadaré turned to overtly political themes – his novel *The Concert* (1988) focused on Albania's split with China, and the collection of essays *Albanian Spring* (1991) was openly critical of the reformist government. In 1990s the writer, who had been a party member, became an outspoken dissident which led to his emigration to France; his acclaimed novel *The Pyramid* was published in 1992. Kadaré's work is translated worldwide and is regularly referred to as a 'tour de force' and a 'masterpiece'; he has been nominated for the Nobel Prize on several occasions.

The gripping magical style of Kadaré takes the reader into a claustrophobic universe where innocuous protagonists wander in the oneiric labyrinthine spaces of monstrous autocratic regimes. Hidden agendas and conspiracies are perpetrated by faceless shadows hiding in the corners; the annals report endless examples of twisted political mentality and duplicity, and Kadaré's fascinating cosmos brims with ancient rituals and tales of petrified human beings, betrayals and blood feuds. The protagonists of his novels move in a hallucinatory environment of grotesque bureaucracies full of archives and classified stacks where, nonetheless, legends and oral culture cancel the validity of pedantically kept records and subvert attempts to keep a dispassionate historical account. The eerie spaces of these novels are inhabited by ghostly state structures that give rise to despotic regimes governed by subservient cliques and by the confining rule of the unwritten ancient law (*Kanun*). It is a semi-lit world dominated by existential anxieties, a world where truth is ambiguous and elusive and events are anachronistic and timeless, a world where the imaginary and the real are mixed up in an atmospheric and enigmatic universe of surrealist dream works and nightmarish riddles.

Maybe due to his background (Gjirokastër was also Enver Hoxha's native town), Kadaré was tolerated and even praised by Hoxha, even though his work clearly deviated from the socialist realist canon. On the whole, it is believed that during the years of communist rule Kadaré acted as a subversive presence in Albania and that his writings, mixing fairytale elements and political satire, uncovered the failings of Hoxha's totalitarianism. But Kadaré's creativity is much more complex; to see Kadaré's oeuvre as a relentless chronicling of Hoxha's gruesome totalitarian regime would be too simplistic. First, because he was an adversary of the regime but he was also its proponent. Secondly, because his interest in exposing indoctrination and tyranny goes far beyond condemning one concrete form of dictatorship.

The most adapted Kadaré novel is *Broken April* (1978), exposing and essentially denouncing the tradition of family vendettas required by the *Kanun*. Kujtim Çashku's Albanian adaptation, *Te paftuarit* (*Broken April*, 1985), is a beautifully shot story of revengeful mountaineers and treacherous townsmen. Liria Bégéja's French adaptation, *Avril brisé* (1987, co-written by Olivier Assayas), shows a hesitant protagonist who gets entangled in the vicious circle of vendettas while not particularly convinced of the merits of this revenge philosophy. Brazilian director Walter Salles insisted that Kadaré's tragic tale was sufficiently universal to represent the confrontations between landowners' families in the Brazilian hinterlands, so he set his adaptation, *Abril Despedaçado* (*Behind the Sun*, 2001) in 1910 Brazil. (And while Latin American specialists have treated Salles' adaptation of a Balkan novel as fairly contrived, this may be the place to mention that other directors – like Emir Kusturica – have repeatedly insisted there are significant similarities between the equally peripheral and unruly cultures of the Balkans and Latin America.)

*The General of the Dead Army* has also been adapted more than once: its first cinematic version was the ambitious Italian-French co-production *Il Generale dell'armata morte/Le Général de l'armée morte* (1983) scripted by Jean-Claude Carière and directed by acclaimed cinematographer Luciano Tovoli. The film featured a distinguished cast including Marcello Mastroianni (the General), Michel Piccoli (the Cardinal) and Anouk Aimée as Countess Betty; the costume design was by Karl Lagerfeld. It was a cerebral highbrow adaptation that never reached wider audiences and did not manage to win the critics' endorsement.

But it is not only this film: all Kadaré adaptations are unsatisfactory in their own right, maybe because no film can measure up to the fascination that one experiences when reading his novels. In this respect Kadaré compares directly to Kafka and Kundera: masters of absorbing writing which has never matched the potency of the literary original when adapted for the screen. While Kafka and Kundera's fiction can be deemed representative of *Mitteleuropa's* murky and claustrophobic atmosphere, Kadaré's supreme skill is in putting across the Balkan spirit of ineptitude and clumsy officialdom. The symbolism of his novels, often using metaphors of institutional machinery – his favourite image is the one of file storage full of putrid index-cards; his preferred protagonist is the featureless civil servant – does not translate well to the big screen. Kadaré's work is thus not easily adaptable.

Albanians, a nation where Christianity and Islam co-exist, trace their origins from the ancient Illyrians and, like other smaller nations in the Balkan region, have been historically conquered and integrated within the Byzantine and Ottoman empires. A short-lived fifteenth-century rebellion led by national hero Skenderbeg drove out the Turks temporarily. Albanians gained a defiant reputation for resisting the Ottomans, even though their final independence came only in November 1912, followed by tempestuous political twists and turns throughout the following decades. Fascist Italy occupied Albania in 1939 and used it as a base for expansion toward other Balkan countries. Italy's capitulation in 1943 and subsequent withdrawal was followed by a civil war between several groups which ended with the communists seizing control in November 1944 and the declaration of a People's Republic of Albania in 1946 under the leadership of Enver Hoxha. The post-World War Two history of Albania is one of self-imposed isolation. Opposed to de-Stalinisation, Albania broke with the Soviet Union in 1961 (and developed close ties with communist China, a friendship that did not last long either).

The action of *Return of the Dead Army* takes place soon after the break-up with the Soviets when the country had already isolated itself from Europe. It is remarkable that Kadaré had a clear impression of the effects of Albania's isolationism as early as 1963, as in the novel he makes his Western protagonist comment on the people of Albania as 'rough' and 'backward'.

Reportedly, the novel is based on some actual recovery exhumations carried out on agreement between the Italian and Albanian governments. It has proved particularly difficult, however, to establish to what extent the events described in the novel are actually based on real occurrences. According to Albanian specialist Peter Bartl the novel deals with a factual experience; in support of this view Bartl quoted conversations with the late Albanian literary historian Arshi Pipa. But no further details are available. At the same time, in his preface to the English translation of the novel, David Smiley calls it an 'unlikely happening', given the isolationist stance of the Albanian government at the time. In any case, even if based on real events, the focus of the film is on an existential quest impregnated with macabre absurdity, where the exploits of the Italian and German generals are an allegory for the clashing foreign interests everpresent in the Balkans.

As the mission slowly progresses, there is a growing feeling of hostility and unsettling discomfort, coming in equal measure from the people and from the weather. Even though greeted and escorted by civil servants, the General cannot help sensing the resentment of the Albanian peasants who silently observe how, during the exhumations, skeletons are put back together. The General's voice-over commentary to these scenes augments his escalating anxiety. While the camera's impassionate narrative simply registers the exhumations and shows peasants looking on silently, the General's voice-over provides a specific narrative angle which imposes an interpretation, turning the scene from a quiet exhumation site into a battlefield where antagonistic sides clash mutely. At a moment when a local man who must have been in his twenties during the war silently approaches to look into the opened graves, the General comments: 'He hates me – he is only a labourer. He feels superior because he was a partisan.' When another old man wearing medals comes to look on, the General describes him as 'a psychopath'. The silent contempt of the locals is driving him mad, and he hates them. While disagreeing on many other things, both the General and the Priest share the view of Albanians as a tragic but frighteningly primitive nation whose people have a taste for getting themselves killed or for killing others. The Italians see Albania as a backward culture that worships violence. The gun, they observe, occupies a special place in the Albanian psyche: these people carry the umbrella as if it is a rifle; the lyrics of their songs compare bullets to wives. We have killed, the Italian General admits; yet they, obsessed with vengeance and rifles since the cradle, are much worse than us.

'This devilish country, scarcely more than a pinprick on the map, had filled the mouths of our brave, beautiful children with dust', the General comments in the novel; he feels compelled to confront the members of this 'wild barbarian tribe': 'I saw myself walking proudly among them, looking down at them with hatred and contempt as if to say: "Savages, look what you have done!"'

The 'savages' prove stronger, however. The wintry rugged landscape of Albania's northern mountains – patches of snow melting in the rain, endless drizzle, fog and mud – increase the General's sense of fragility and alienation. He looks up to the moon, asking: 'Why are we here, what do we want? Even stones and trees felt more like home.' Alone in his tent, among skulls and skeletons, he feels he is going mad.

There are moments when it seems the mission is cursed. An Albanian consultant gets a mysterious illness and is rushed to the hospital but dies soon in terrible pain. It is because of his involvement with the exhumations, everyone is convinced. The same feeling of being cursed prevails during the wedding celebration at the village pub: in the company of the Priest but amidst glances of suppressed animosity, the General observes a ritualistic male dance; his anxiety grows out of proportion, heightened by too much *raki* and the accelerating beat of the drum. He can never understand these people; they are so remote, different and intimidating.

The only moment of human closeness is the encounter between the Italian and German generals: it is a meeting of soul mates, both tormented by breathing death, both hoping to leave these barbarian lands soon. At an early point in the encounter the German General is shown observing a local girl through binoculars: a scene suggestive of the indirect and mediated manner in which they communicate with the local culture. In a collegial exchange the men admit to each other that they both have nightmares; in fact, nothing but nightmares. They are shown in medium close-up facing each other, yet somehow their eyes never meet. They have plenty of tips to exchange: on disinfection, for example, inevitably concluding that theirs is a 'filthy business'. They get seriously drunk, describing themselves as 'migratory birds'. They bond in delirium, at the height of which each one of them sees the skull transpire behind the live facial features of the other. The Italian accuses the German of stealing eleven of his skeletons yet the fact that they are so immersed in morbidity brings them close together. They disagree over whose national army is superior, the German or the Italian one. But it is a friendly squabble, which will end in complete drunkenness with the two men lying on top of each other in a hotel room, exhausted and intoxicated, but having reached remarkable consensus and serenity.

In the novel the narrative is delivered in the third person, the General is predominantly spoken of as 'he' and his first-person notes are added only at the end of chapters. In the film the storyline is dominated by the General's voice-over commentary, thus his point of view defines most of the narrative. Yet a further narrative thread is interwoven here: the point of view of the Albanian mother who toward the end of the film will admit she killed Colonel Di Zetta to avenge her dishonoured daughter. The mother's point of view is maintained from early on as an alternative yet secondary narrative voice, inserted through associative flashbacks. It is an interesting attempt to assert awareness of the different possible ways to tell the same story and of the different histories that emerge this way: to the Italian General Colonel Di Zetta may be a highly esteemed military hero but to the Albanian mother he is the villain who invaded her home and destroyed her family. The mother's flashbacks, however, are not given a particularly prominent place and are largely absent from a significant part of the film, so the forceful re-emergence of this added point of view toward the end fails to work as convincingly as it could to provide a viable counter-narrative.

Yet a third account is introduced through reconstructing scenes from the diary of a dead Italian soldier who has deserted. The passages from the journal come alive in flashbacks as the General reads them, chronicling lively episodes from the deserter's life with an Albanian family. This added subplot asserts once again the possibility of multiple narratives; evidently some Italians felt at home with the Albanians.

Throughout his mission the General, a handsome bearded man with a penchant for white suits, is not only shadowed but closely controlled by the Catholic Priest; the film thus reveals the suppressed tensions between clerical and secular powers. General and Priest spy on each other; they are often shown sitting in a restaurant and one of them is called to the phone to receive instructions from a superior command centre: the very set up of the scene makes it clear that the Priest is significantly closer to the powers-that-be. Disillusioned with politics back home, the General often plays out his confrontations with the Priest in silent monologues. He may still think of the Albanians as 'savages', yet as he learns of the brutality they suffered, he begins feeling uncomfortable and somewhat guilty with the locals; he even feels the urge to apologise and show that he and his army clearly denounce the Colonel's despicable deeds. The Priest insists that remorse makes no sense. His only interest in Albania is to recover the

Colonel's remains; he may be a spiritual man but seems immune to the moral qualms that torment his allegedly tougher colleague.

The General may be engaged in the 'absurd and gruesome mission' of war archaeology yet never comes to like the white plastic gloves, the disinfection and the formaldehyde. From a single skeleton he reconstructs a whole army and arranges it in squads of coffins. Rather than producing a moving account of heroism, this problematic reconstruction more and more turns the ideas of war bravery into a meaningless, hopeless effort, drowning amidst the resentments of the present.

The excavations continue over a year, seasons change and the General grows more and more anxious in re-examining his own motives for being here. He drinks a lot, hears voices and, every time he talks to living people, he sees their skulls transpire under the skin of their faces. He is no longer a warrior; he inhabits the kingdom of bones, of pure calcium. The mortuary is his commanding centre, where, among index cards, filing cabinets and boxes full of human remains and ID plaques he spends his days piecing skeletons together, cataloguing the dead and compiling the records of the unidentified: head missing, dental records not matching, and so on.

Unlike living people, skeletons are interchangeable and we are all equal in death; one can easily substitute the villain for the victim and vice versa. The missing Colonel, the deserter and many other dead bodies appear to be all the same. Who cares whose remains will be put in Di Zetta's coffin?; it is about skeletons of the same measurement and no longer about people whose convictions or cultural background matter in any way.

*Return of the Dead Army*'s ultimate objective is the denouncement of war. One day the General unearths a trumpet covered in mud; glorious combat tunes resound in his mind and he bitterly realises that a whole army of dead men is under his command. But the dead army cannot possibly line up, obey or fight, nor be mobilised or excited. The General's growing madness produces a cacophony of disoriented voices: disillusioned and cynical, he now knows that no cause can be compelling enough for his dead soldiers to be called to arms.

Director Dhimitër Anagnosti began in filmmaking as a cameraman in the early 1960s, then worked on shorts and documentaries and as screenwriter, coming to directing features only in the 1970s. He worked in various genres (drama, comedy, war, musical), often adapting important works of literature, usually working in to the realist mode. With over twenty films to his name, Anagnosti is a prolific director (especially given that the total Albanian feature film output since 1953 comprises of about three hundred titles). His most important earlier films include the acclaimed anti-fascist resistance drama *Lulekuqet mbi mure* (*Red Poppies on the Wall*, 1976), set in an orphanage during the Italian occupation, and *Përralle Nga e Kaluara* (*A Tale from the Past*, 1987), a comedy of mores denouncing Albania's patriarchy through the farcical litanies in the arranged marriage of a 14-year-old boy to an older female.

Shot in the fading shades of Orwocolor, *Return of the Dead Army* is slow and stylistically uninspired, thus suggesting that it may be better to re-read Kadaré. Like other works from the region, where war archaeology is not about digging in the mud but more about excavations into people's national memory, the film painfully resonates with recent macabre exhumations of mass graves scattered all over former Yugoslavia. As forensic experts pile the remains of the victims from Srebrenica and other massacres in small mucky heaps, one cannot help thinking of Ismail Kadaré as an excruciatingly prophetic Balkan visionary.

**Dina Iordanova**

REFERENCES

Bartl, P. (1995) *Albanien*. Regensburg: Verlag Friedrich Pustet.

Kadaré, I. (1968) *The General of the Dead Army*, trans. W. H. Allen. London, New York and Melbourne: Quartet Books.

# I EARINI SYNAXIS TON AGROFYLAKON THE FOUR SEASONS OF THE LAW

## DIMOS AVDELIODIS, GREECE, 1999

*I Earini Synaxis Ton Agrofylakon* (*The Four Seasons of the Law*, Dimos Avdeliodis, 1999) is an absurdist comedy, the title of which translates literally as 'The Spring Gathering of the Field Guards'. It is divided into four parts, one for each of the four seasons, and chronicles the efforts of four different field guards to police the produce grown around the farming village of Tholopotami (on the island of Chios), which has a reputation for uncanny occurrences.

A field guard is seen collapsing and dying in a tulip field after trying to chase a young girl engaged in stealing potatoes with her grandmother. The incident is shrouded in mystery. Tempted by the bonus payment offered by the Tholopotami village council at the summer gathering of the force, four volunteers declare an interest in taking up the position of their late colleague. The Agronomist, a stern, formal man, chooses the disheveled, tardy Kakavalos.

It is summer and as Kakavalos and his dog approach Tholopotami on a scooter, two men booby trap the road, causing him to crash into a haystack. They are Sideris, a well-heeled farmer and owner of the village tavern-*cum*-coffee shop, and his younger brother Michalis. Believing them to be good Samaritans, Kakavalos agrees to watch over their prized watermelon patch. For the most part, he sleeps his watch away. But one day his dog disappears and he sees the ghost of his predecessor. The memory of the apparition does not leave Kakavalos, even after he is treated to folk music, dancing and alcohol at the local tavern. Kakavalos is too afraid to go back to the patch in the dark and as a result the watermelons are stolen. The Agronomist threatens to report him for corruption unless he helps restore the credibility of the corps. To that end, he must focus his investigation on Kyra Vassiliki and the granddaughter. Kakavalos, however, only pursues the girl. Unperturbed by his following her, she escapes him via a pond only she can jump over. The girl's ability to fly over the 'escape pond' appears superhuman. Kakavalos's tenure finally comes to an inglorious end when he falls victim to a bee attack, as he attempts to catch a glimpse of the girl swimming naked.

By autumn, the only volunteers to show up at the guards' meeting are those who had previously been rejected. Patsaganas, an authoritarian boor who takes his job too seriously, is given the assignment, but ignores the Agronomist's warning not to succumb to anger. He immediately begins abusing his power and terrorising the villagers needlessly. They resist by refusing to cooperate with his investigation of Kyra Vassiliki and their children pelt him with stones. The girl intimidates him. Finally, after forcing a group of schoolboys he caught stealing oranges into a punitive march to headquarters, Patsaganas is fired. The bully returns to the village to drown his misery in cognac and *rembetico* music. Passed out, he dreams about the dead guard and tries to follow his ghost around the village without success. He tries to redeem himself by attempting to catch the girl, only to sink into a pond that lies on her escape route.

By winter, it is Lavidas's turn at the position. A gentle, bookish, older man, he impresses the locals at the pub with his politeness. But he is drawn to the village's hard-core card players who gamble away property and livestock in a seedy tavern. Lavidas soon loses his rifle and a donkey he had been loaned. By Christmas, the girl finds him stealing wood. Out of pity, she allows him to take it. Drifting away, Lavidas dreams of the Agronomist and his fellow guards calling him back into real time but he can only measure his life in card games. Eventually, the police raid the gamblers' hideout. As they march to the station, Lavidas gazes at a blooming almond-tree and recites a few Romantic verses.

By spring, only young Sitaras, who has regularly been seen offending the Agronomist's civilian-bureaucratic sensibilities with mock militaristic mannerisms, is available to take up the assignment. The dead guard appears in Sitaras's dream and tells him that he was bewitched by Kyra Vassiliki and her granddaughter. Sitaras comes across as active and brave. He engages in making fireworks with the village kids and enjoys a growing popularity, even though the Agronomist disapproves of his infantile behavior. He nearly catches the girl stealing potatoes and throws a cherry bomb at her, from which she flees. More chases follow across the same tulip field where the first guard died a year earlier. Although the girl outruns, hits and swears at Sitaras, she is not unperturbed this time but stares back at him across the pond. Sitaras and the children target their Easter bottle-rocket escapades at the girl's house. For this, Sitaras is scolded and suspended by the Agronomist. Sitaras and the girl have a dream encounter. She wakes up crying but tries on a pretty dress. Sitaras is finally fired, but he is more relieved than worried and addresses the Agronomist with a mock military salute. He and the girl are now free to resume their playful chase. No thieves are ever arrested.

*The Four Seasons of the Law* delights in mocking the common understanding of modernisation (that is, Westernisation), on the basis of which Greeks judge themselves and their history. The film draws on stereotypical distinctions between the East (pre-modern or in the early stages of modernisation) and the West (modern), only to subvert them, leaving the viewer in a state of charmed and thought-provoking uncertainty. Through its narrative organisation and visual style, the film is an invitation to indulge in nostalgic flashback of traditional rural life governed by the timeless cycle of the seasons. The farming village of Tholopotami follows a regular pattern dictated by the laws of nature: planting, tending, harvesting and passing time during the winter. This is the idyllic dimension of Greece's uneven and belated development: a time of simplicity and predictability when people identified with the land and aligned their work with nature's rhythms. *The Four Seasons of the Law* could certainly be mistaken for a nostalgic depiction of Greek pre-modernity. Yet Avdeliodis refuses to assign to modernity and pre-modernity their comfortably familiar and expected attributes. He turns the reified watchwords long used to describe Greece's relationship to modernity – religion, the bureaucratic state, authoritarianism, economic modernisation – into the symbolic framework of a magical realist fable where the natural order of things cannot be taken at face value.

The short filmography of Dimos Avdeliodis betrays his predilection for comic fables that mock modernisation, but are also aware that their critique might no longer be relevant. His first film, the short *Athemitos Synaghonismos* (*Unfair Competition*, 1982), and his third, the feature-length *Niki tis Samothrakis* (*Nike of Samothrace*, 1990), both feature various types of scruffy, beaten-down Greek manhood, trying to take advantage of capitalist laws of competition and technological obsolescence, with distinctly surreal results. *Unfair Competition* features Avdeliodis and his young nephew as Greek versions of Chaplin's bum and the 'kid', hijacking a truckload of watermelons and engaging in a furious underselling war with a Romany family of roadside watermelon peddlers. Once the 'competition' takes on a life of its own and the watermelons become missiles in a race for mutually assured destruction that even a goddess *ex machina* – in this case Themis, the ancient Greek goddess of justice who makes a tardy incongruous appearance – is powerless to rectify. *Nike of Samothrace* depicts a comic rivalry between a garage and a blacksmith in the 1950s that finds an outlet in opposing football teams. The football match takes on carnivalesque dimensions when the goddess Nike, the world-famous ancient statue now in the Louvre, suddenly appears in flesh and blood to fulfill the men's elusive dream of happiness and economic success. The message of *Unfair Competition* and *Nike of Samothrace* seems to echo traditional critiques of the mis-adaptation of Western-style market economics and development to Greece. Avdeliodis, however, places the very critique of modernisation under question with his visual gags – the silent-era slapstick and his off-the-wall failed goddesses *ex machina* (the iconic blind justice with the balance and the Louvre exhibit). These visual and stylistic references are now commodities in a transcultural global image exchange, empty icons endlessly reproduced around the world. They are thus a symptom both of the kind of political and economic homogenisation that Avdeliodis seems to decry and of the incompatibility of Greek and Western modernity. As commodified simulacra, moreover, Chaplin's bum, the blind justice and the Nike statue offer only the most cursory affirmation of Greece's cultural connection to the West.

Avdeliodis's ironic attitude towards his own mistrust of modernisation is matched by his wariness of nativist nostalgia. The 'village' has special status in the Balkan imaginary, as a special isolated, wild and simultaneously mystic place inhabited by peasants endowed with a specific brand of stubbornness and of idiosyncratic mentality and mores. The village in Avdeliodis' film is even more isolated because of its island location. In his first feature-length film, *To Dhendro pou pligoname* (*The Tree We Hurt*, 1986), which is based on his childhood memories of growing up in Chios, Avdeliodis overlays a loving reconstruction of island village life in the late 1950s with a jarringly anachronistic electronic music-track. According to the director, this was a deliberate choice intended to warn against the illusion that one can recapture the psychic plenitude of one's childhood connection to landscape and people. In casting *The Tree We Hurt*, Avdeliodis used his extended family along with other native residents of southern Chios – mostly locals with no acting experience. He also filmed in the village where the action is set and its immediate topographical settings without even changing their names. In the 1980s, this would have been a way to reclaim the cinematic representation of the local from the conservative ideologies of modernisation that had hijacked it during the 1960s and 1970s. Commercial films and publicly-funded documentaries promoted the touristic and industrial development of the Greek countryside advocated by the authoritarian regimes of the 1960s and the conservative governments that succeeded them. Until 1981, the representation of the local in mainstream Greek cinema was sacrificed to the common cause of modernisation, escapism and right-wing politics. As critics have pointed out, in constructing a pre-modern past at a local as well as intimate, familial level, *The Tree We Hurt* paid tribute to the independent Greek documentarists of the 1960s (*mikromikadhes*) who looked for the untapped diversity of Greek geography and culture at the regional and local levels. Avdeliodis credits two of these documentarists, Kostas Sfikas and Stavros Tornes, for an early insight into the difficulty of conceptualising an innocent relation to the land before folklore and tourism.

In *The Four Seasons of the Law* Avdeliodis is just as thorough in mapping the narrative onto the existing topographical markers of his native southern Chios and as faithful in casting local amateurs – family members and acquaintances. But the local is no longer familial and intimate as it was in *The Tree We Hurt* and has become instead abstract and allegorical. It has also lost the artless, unprocessed visual impact it had in the earlier film and is now highly stylised – arranged in painterly tableaux and shot in lush, vivid colours manipulated in post-production, with an eye for the picturesque. Avdeliodis uses a different director of photography for each episode of *The Four Seasons of the Law* as a sign that the local is no longer attached to his singular, personal vision but can now circulate in multiple versions and different aesthetic styles. Perhaps the most startling example of the film's synthesised visual style is the choice of Leonardo Da Vinci's painting *The Last Supper* as the central visual motif. The incongruous mixing of emblematic Western high art with a Greek rural, folksy setting is repeated on the soundtrack. Instead of the seamless aural envelope of Dimitri Papadimitriou's original electronic music, which in *The Tree We Hurt* represented the conscious act of remembrance, the soundtrack of *The Four Seasons of the Law* is an acoustic mish-mash of East and West. Vivaldi's *Four Seasons* is the dominant musical accompaniment of the narrative, with sprinklings of Greek folk music, Greek urban blues and an Orthodox hymn. Another important transformation of the local in *The Four Seasons of the Law* is the characters' lack of interiority and tendency to speak an elliptical language coded to reference ethnic, professional and class stereotypes or a single behavioural trait. The schematic nature of the characters seems to reflect Avdeliodis's work in theatre adapting traditional Greek shadow puppet-plays and fairytales. The final crucial transformation of Avdeliodis's cinematic localism, however, is that the narrative world of *The Four Seasons of the Law*, unlike that of *The Tree We Hurt*, is no longer subject to the laws of nature and ordinary causality.

These transformations have much to do with the retreat of the progressive political climate of the 1980s during which the bureaucratic state, the avatar of modernity, was the centre of Greek public discourse. While its interactions with traditional society continued to be criticised as dysfunctional or irrational by liberal and Marxist Greek thinkers alike, the Greek state under the socialists also became an agent of social justice as well as a sponsor of Greece's first public evaluation of its authoritarian past. As a result, the cinematic explorations of authoritarianism and modern alienation that had discreetly begun in the 1970s took on full force. Previously taboo subjects, like the victimisation of the politically 'undesirable' during the Civil War and the Cold War militarisation of civilian structures, became regular film fare in the 1980s. In the 1990s, however, the secular, state-based, civilian-driven understanding of modernity that had dominated Greek anti-authoritarian discourse since the 1970s lost its relevance. As progressive politics became mired in privatisation and scandals, Yugoslavia disintegrated creating a new, 'symbolic' kind of geopolitical insecurity for Greeks and new inroads for religion-based interpretations of Greece's contested modernity. Greek church leaders and neo-orthodox thinkers found new authority in re-evaluating Greece's relationship with the Balkans and the European Union. The de-polarisation of Greek political culture during the 1990s and the cultural fatigue with the 'politically correct' modes of representing the past were reflected in the kinds of films that won critical and popular acclaim at the time: de-politicised, de-historicised nostalgia films and cynical, materialistic comedies. The visual style and narrative construction of *Four Seasons of the Law* capitalise on the trend for nostalgia films as a way to challenge both the progressive certainties of the 1980s and the post-progressive escapism of the 1990s without alienating mainstream audiences.

In each of the four episodes that comprise *The Four Seasons of the Law*, the relationship between the state (the Agronomist and the field guards) and traditional society (the Tholopotamians) breaks down in a way that mocks stereotypes of underdevelopment. The village council repeatedly invites the state to regulate and police the agricultural economy, with no result. According to standard explanations of Greece's problematic relationship to modernisation, the state is supposed to try to impose a Western-style rationalisation of economic and social relations from above but is weakened by the resistance of the traditional society undermining it from below. The tricking of Kakavalos by Sideris and his brother seems to conform to this model. It is a clear example of 'clientelism'; diverting the state from protecting the general interest. Yet the brothers fail to benefit from their 'pre-modern' ways because they undermine their own con game. Out of both self-interest and pity, they try to distract Kakavalos from his shock after the apparition of his dead predecessor and the loss of his dog by getting him drunk and encouraging him to dance. In so doing, however, they also help cause his failure to protect their prime watermelons from thieves and thus their manipulation of the state is in vain.

The Agronomist's ineffectiveness, in turn, has much to do with his efforts to fully realise the promise of modernity, that is, to keep the state untainted by both militarism and religion. Patsaganas is the only guard who tries to enforce economic modernisation by demanding proper book-keeping from a blithely sloppy olive-press operator and verifying olive crop yields. But he is also a pious bully, which makes him distasteful, as an agent of modernisation, to both the Agronomist and the villagers. The Agronomist is a civilian bureaucrat who at every opportunity reminds the guards that 'this is not the army' and is offended by Sitaras's mockery of the distinction. Patsaganas, by contrast, has no understanding of what constitutes appropriate use of force. He shoots a villager's rooster to retaliate against her for refusing to cooperate in his investigation of Kyra Vassiliki. He uses his rifle to terrorise the village boys during their forced march to headquarters and to get the village barber to give him a shave in the middle of the night. He even drinks his cognacs with his rifle in hand. Patsaganas also has a tendency to blur the boundaries between his authority and that of the Church. For instance, he outrages the Agronomist by inappropriately ringing the bell of the little church that neighbours the head-quarters in order to summon him to punish the schoolboys. Furthermore, when he gets drunk after his dismissal, Patsaganas impersonates an archangel to rouse the village barber from his sleep telling him that he has come to take him to heaven.

It is tempting to interpret *The Four Seasons of the Law* as a parable on the origins of Greek authoritarianism. Patsaganas's comic conflation of religious symbolism and military coercion echoes the rhetoric of the Colonels' dictatorship (1967–74). But the Agronomist's punctilious anti-authoritarianism and secularism belongs to the post-dictatorship era and especially the 1990s, when the old left was faced with the popularisation of neo-orthodox critiques of Western modernity that rejected Greece's European pretensions and reclaimed its Balkan/Eastern roots. One could, however, argue that the guards' failure to shed light on the crop thefts represents the socialist state's fear that the legitimate enforcement of the law might at any moment lapse into authoritarianism. With the exception of Patsaganas, who takes his job too seriously, the guards' attitudes towards their official policing functions range from discomfiture and forgetfulness to outright distaste. Kakavalos is naïve. The dreamy Lavidas forgets his function and joins the local illegal gamblers. Sitaras sees no legitimate function in the state at all and abandons his duties on principle. Thus while authoritarianism is symboli-cally neutralised in the film, as it was in 1980s Greece, the promise of creating a just economic order is not fulfilled. The state, in the person of the Agronomist, fails to distinguish between subsistence gleaning and large-scale crop theft for profit. It is content to designate Kyra Vassiliki and the girl as the primary suspects for all the thefts without bothering to confirm innocence or guilt or establish degrees of culpability.

The key to the state's failure to impose economic justice in the film rests in the super-natural realm with the spectre of the guard who died chasing the girl. The ghostly messenger points to the victimisation of women and girls that result from the misrecognition of desire as law-enforcement. Because the guards have trouble keeping their field patrols from turning into libidinal chases, the danger of rape always inheres in their encounters with the girl. Rape is averted every time because the film's internal organisation as a comic fable allows for the suspension of the ordinary course of nature. The girl's effortless escapes mark her as a fairytale heroine endowed with supernatural abilities and thus destined to confound the guards' ordinary plodding maleness. The rapes that never happen, however, expose the diversion of male sexual rapaciousness into the state's mission and the blanket scapegoating of women and girls for society's ills. This is a blind spot at the heart of the law that the Agronomist's scrupulous efforts to distinguish militarism from legitimate policing or the authority of state from that of the Church are doomed to ignore. Even the anarchic, anti-authoritarian Sitaras re-enacts the imaginary entanglement of male desire and state violence. He courts the girl with fireworks in a carnivalesque inversion of the state's authority to use deadly violence.

Avdeliodis has a very pessimistic view of the fate of women and girls in Greek social reality, a view that twenty years of progressive, anti-authoritarian politics only reinforced. While he abhors the sexual cynicism of many mainstream Greek films in the 1990s, he is also mistrustful of feminist militancy in cinema. By exempting the young heroine from ordinary causality and biological limitations, he alludes to the real and continuing untenability of women's and girls' lives without destroying the romantic illusion of smooth and uncontroversial gender relations.

Avdeliodis is more openly sceptical about another romantic illusion that became particularly popular in the 1990s, the neo-orthodox view of modern Greek identity. He opens *The Four Seasons of the Law* with a sequence that underscores this scepticism. After the title and in the place of credits we see a planimetric frontal medium-long shot of the Agronomist and twelve field guards sitting at a long table facing the audience. Their postures mimic Leonardo Da Vinci's *The Last Supper*. The Agronomist occupies the central position of Christ with the guards as the twelve disciples surrounding him reverently. The centre of the company's attention, however, is not the Agronomist but Patsaganas, the Fall guard, seated on his right. He is solemnly singing a traditional religious song from Constantinople customarily performed by Greek Orthodox Church cantors after the regular service. The song celebrates the Creator's benevolence towards nature's creatures. It will not be heard again in the film and it is the only part of the soundtrack not to be identified in the closing credits. During the song, the camera simply pans along the table reinforcing the flat *tableau vivant* effect. The sequence is clearly demarcated from the rest of the film, suggesting its function as a general framing motif. It will re-emerge in the form of a crude folk rendition of the Da Vinci painting hanging in the gamblers' den and again in Lavidas's dream where the apostles are transformed once more into field guards wearing wings made out of giant playing cards.

By transplanting the Greek field guards and their superintendent in their 1950s garb listening to a Byzantine-style melody into an icon of Western art, Avdeliodis questions the possibility of conceptualising an entirely self-referential and self-sufficient Eastern Orthodox culture. The sequence can be seen as a visual gag on the difficulty of disentangling the neo-Orthodox critique of Western modernity from its targets – secularism, Catholicism, cultural imperialism, humanism. Christ's absence from the picture and his substitution by the Agronomist signal the irreversible process of secularisation while the choice of Patsaganas as the hymn's singer seems to question the righteousness of the devout. Although by refusing to acknowledge the hymn's single, touching performance in the credits, Avdeliodis seems to want to preserve it from entering the commodified, over-exposed system of transnational cultural references to which the rest of the film belongs.

Avdeliodis came to filmmaking from a literary and theatrical background without any prior formal training. Not only did he skip the common pathway to 'quality' filmmaking, which usually involves schooling in Europe or the United States, he also bypassed the channels of professional apprenticeship and political networking in the Greek culture industry that most successful practitioners follow. As a result, his films defy the expectations of audiences and critics. *The Four Seasons of the Law* seems to be one of those Greek 'art' films that do well in international festivals and are praised by Greek critics but are met with total apathy or scorn from Greek audiences. It is slow-paced, 178 minutes long, and lacks a conventional plot with a satisfying development and resolution. Its visual composition is highly aestheticised and painterly and the dialogue elliptical and sparse. Yet the film received the audience award at the 1999 Thessaloniki Film Festival, Greece's annual competitive showcase for national and international films. Avdeliodis was also honoured by the Greek Film Critics' Association and by FIPRESCI and received the Caligari Prize at Berlinale in 2000. Finally, the entire Greek popular press –from urban publications catering to a diverse movie-going readership to the small regional and provincial media adopting a less specialised, nativist-populist and entertainment-oriented approach to film – were united in its praise. The reviewers found the film to be a poetic expression of quintessential Greekness and saw no problem in representing Greek culture with Vivaldi and Da Vinci. They showed little inclination, however, to debate the film's cultural criticism.

**Vassiliki Tsitsopoulou**

# TIRANA YEAR ZERO

FATMIR KOÇI, ALBANIA/FRANCE, 2001

Tirana, 1997. Niku is a 23-year-old slacker, who scrapes together a living by taking on freelance jobs with his dilapidated truck. Everyone tells him he should dump the old vehicle, but the truck belonged to his father, Kujtim, with whom he still lives, and his father is keen that Niku earns his living in the way he once did. Although Niku has a girlfriend, Klara, he denies it, indicating he is, initially, not so close to her. The distance is underlined when Klara meets a sculptor, Tare, and forms ambitious plans to go with him to Paris to embark on a modelling career. Niku is less than impressed and tells her that he has been to Italy and knows 'how shitty it is over there'. Their different perspectives on life in the West start to drive Niku and Klara apart.

When the couple go to a run-down cinema in a moment of reconciliation, a power cut leads to a group of disgruntled viewers grabbing a torch, pulling out guns and taking to the stage to present their own raucous entertainment. The incident appals Klara and galvanises her determination to leave the country. For a while, Niku seems more receptive to the idea, but when insulted by Klara's brother-in-law while asking for money for plane tickets, he gives up on the plan and vanishes from Tirana without telling anyone. Travelling along the mountainous southern coast, he meets a variety of strange characters, including a crazed German hippy (played by Austrian art-house regular Lars Rudolph) who buys a concrete bunker and enlists Niku's help in transporting it home, a blind man who is addicted to 'watching' films on television, a couple of old ladies who bemoan rural depopulation, and a French journalist who has been robbed of everything except her camcorder.

Meanwhile, with Niku nowhere to be found, Klara proceeds with her plan to go to Paris, although at Tirana airport she shows signs of growing reservations. When Niku returns to the capital, he not only finds that Klara has gone but also that his father is seriously ill. Kujtim's deteriorating health fails to bring about reconciliation. In a nightmarish dream sequence, Niku sees his father offering his skull to him to eat so that son would become like father, which only serves to antagonise Niku's feelings. This Freudian battle is partially resolved when Niku loses control of his father's beloved truck while making a commercial for an egotistical director, and the vehicle, transporting an oversized statue of Stalin, plunges over a cliff. Niku seems happy to be telling Kujtim the bad news.

Things come to a head in an argument netween two of Niku's neighbours: Xhafa, the arrogant neighbour, arrives to antagonise Besim with the news that he is going to America. Given Xhafa's propensity to tell people that Besim's daughter in Milan is a whore, he is greeted with a Kalashnikov. As the tension escalates, Besim and another neighbour fire their assault rifles out of the window and into the air. Finally, Besim throws his two television sets out of the window at Xhafa, who is down below shouting up. Things only quieten down when it becomes apparent that Niku's father has died. His mother's reaction to this is that she and Niku should 'sell everything and leave'. Meanwhile, their neighbour, Nexhi, has already departed for Italy with her cousin's boss, Paolo, leaving her children in the care of her husband, who drunkenly mourns his loss.

Niku then bumps into Klara, who says she has returned from Paris to see him and reveals that she witnessed the gun-firing and television-throwing incident at Niku's apartment block. The film ends with the couple reunited but reflective, walking along a road while the camera moves ahead to survey the landscape: burnt-out cars and abandoned bunkers form a boundary between the dirt track and a wasteland beyond, with uninviting tower blocks in the distance.

*Tirana Year Zero* (2001), the second feature film by Fatmir Koçi, was made in reaction to Albania's current situation, as 'a call to the Albanian people not to abandon their native land'. Emigration has played an important role in the country's post-communist history. During the totalitarian years between the end of World War Two and 1991, leaving Albania illegally would result in the imprisonment of any family remaining, which severely limited the numbers of those willing to try. However, with the easing of political conditions in the years since the early 1990s, Albanians responded with a mass wave of emigration, either legally by queuing up at an embassy for the necessary paperwork or, more likely, illegally via a perilous journey across the Adriatic Sea to Italy (a popular destination for Albanians, many of whom understand or speak some Italian from watching Italian television).

In 1992, the post-communist government of Aleksander Meksi began to introduce 'shock therapy' – the sudden and complete removal of state support for industry and the application of free-market conditions regardless of the short-term social cost – in order to kick-start the flagging economy. This lead to higher prices, more unemployment and a general degradation in the already low living conditions of the populace.

Things only got worse. In 1997, Albanians saw the collapse of a series of 'pyramid' schemes that had been supported beyond their natural life by the Albanian government. Around two-thirds of the country's population had collectively invested an estimated two billion dollars in the scams. In the ensuing crisis, angry anti-government protests around the country degenerated into anarchy. More than 1,500 people died in the unrest and some 600,000 weapons from state armouries went missing as ordinary people helped themselves in order to protect their families. Despite a government programme to encourage people to hand back the looted arms, only a fraction of the missing weapons was recovered, and gun-related deaths, frequently arising out of minor arguments, were common in the years following 1997. Again, many in the population reacted to the traumatic circumstances by either leaving or at least contemplating it. From a country of four million people at the end of the communist era, nearly a quarter of the population left Albania in 1990s (although in the early 2000s some started to return as conditions in the country improved).

*Tirana Year Zero* takes place in 1997, after the worst of the anarchy had died down, and uses a style that balances elements of neo-realism with comedy to document the interest in emigration, gun culture and the general state of corruption and lawlessness, while touching on many other issues that define Albanian mentality, such as the country's long-standing fascination with television. Koçi developed the script working from events he witnessed, newspaper stories and friends' anecdotes. Anecdote-telling is an important part of the film itself. Just as significant as the overarching story of Niku and Klara, yet acting out the film's discourse are also many conversations between minor characters, almost all of whom seem to have a tale of someone they know abroad or of their own experiences there. (Perhaps it is this focus on a large number of episodic encounters that has lead to the film being described as a 'road movie'.)

*Tirana Year Zero* is representative for a wide range of films made in the region (for example *Patul conjugal* (*The Conjugal Bed*, Mircea Daneliuk, 1993); *Rane* (*Wounds*, Srdjan Dragojević, 1998); *Dunav most* (*Danube Bridge*, Ivan Andonov, 1999)) all featuring the post-communist impoverishment and economic crisis causing feelings of social frenzy, disorientation and chaos. It is a rough and drab reality amplified by mafia hostilities, street crime and domestic violence, a context in which many see emigration as the only viable solution.

Although billed as a call for Albanians to stay in their homeland, Koçi is unsparing in his portrayal of the reasons for wanting to leave. Again, this is played out in small incidents: power cuts at Klara's flat and the cinema, a train grinding to a halt for lack of fuel, the petty-mindedness of a government official and the black market, shown through Albanian antiquities being sold at historic sites (although these are more than likely to be fakes). More than anything else, though, *Tirana Year Zero* shows the harshness of life, not in the physical condition of the infrastructure but in the behavioural psychology of a nation that has been brutalised by persistent poverty, and economic and social change. Indeed, it is probably as much this focus on psychological trauma as on physical ruination that Koçi saw parallels between his film and Roberto Rossellini's *Germania anno zero* (*Germany Year Zero*, 1947), and which is clearly alluded to in the film's title. Gun-related incidents and anecdotes, and even a background news story concerning the collection programme for weapons, are particularly important among these, but there are also many other scenes in which characters respond to their surroundings in a tense and confrontational manner. This aggressiveness is presented as female-degrading machismo, painfully felt by Klara who is sexually harassed by her boss at the bar she works in and whose sister is married to an aggressive bully who freely admits to being an 'asshole'.

When the cinema is taken over during the power cut, it is as much the overt sexism of the revellers, who make remarks about Klara's looks and lust over a picture of a topless woman, which disturbs Klara, as their waving weapons in a public place. In this climate, women can only find a high self-opinion by flaunting their sexuality, illustrated by a secretary who hates men because they do not find her sexy, the French journalist who insists on sunbathing naked on a beach and Nexhi, who abandons her family and cashes in her good looks to get a free ride to Italy with Paolo. Klara, too, tries to use her body, but the result is failure. As well as her unrealised plan to become a model, she also poses for Tare in a swimming costume, looking somewhat frail and vulnerable against the large, ungainly space of the artist's studio. When Niku shows up, she is instantly embarrassed about what she has done and hurriedly dresses to run after him, offering apologies.

Niku, by contrast, exhibits few tendencies of excessive masculinity. Although strong and somewhat muscular, he has a gentle soul. His soul-searching and desire to 'stick' with his homeland can be associated with a mature 'feminisation' of his personality, especially in contrast to the histrionic machismo of other male characters, such as his father and Xhafa, and the aspirations of hyper-sexuality in some of the female characters. The times when Niku does lose his temper are when his masculinity is questioned: first, when he catches his girlfriend posing in a swimsuit for Tare; and secondly, when he battles with his father to assert his independence. Perhaps in this, Koçi is suggesting that it is desirable for Albanian males to find a softer side, while at the same time being sympathetic to those that react violently to challenges to their masculinity, personal space and identity. This sympathy does not extend too far and the film's titular allusion to a work that is primarily about children underlines the immaturity of the posturing characters. This juvenile side to Albanians is further emphasised by the recurring theme of the father/son struggle. Alongside Niku's personal conflict, the country as a whole appears to undergo its own battle to shake off the yoke of the ultimate all-seeing and strict father figures: Josef Stalin and Enver Hoxha, Albania's own communist dictator. The former is present in statue form, while the latter's legacy of paranoia is still evident throughout the Albanian landscape (and the film) in the shape of the ugly concrete bunkers that were manufactured by the hundreds of thousands in the 1970s, to defend the country in the event of an attack. (The story behind this massive exercise in totalitarian hubris was recorded in Kujtim Çashku's 1996 film, *Kolonel Bunker*.) Framed in these terms, emigration becomes not just a quest for material betterment but a mental journey to overcome societal psycho-sexual tension and an attempt to escape the metaphorical patriarchy of the past and the literal patriarchy of the present.

If conditions in the homeland are portrayed with stark honesty, there is little evidence presented that emigration is ever a positive experience. We are told nothing about Niku's own experiences in Italy, but it is clear they were negative and various reports from minor characters who have relatives overseas do nothing to contradict this view. The negativity of emigrating is also underlined in that those wanting to leave are rarely able to express why they want to do so or what they want to achieve there. This is most explicitly stated in the exchange between Niku and a young Romany (probably a prostitute) who plans to go to Italy. When Niku asks what she will do there, she replies 'I don't know. I'll just go and see.' Similarly, when Nexhi promises her children to take them to Italy, they tearfully reply that they do not want to, to which a Nexhi can only snap, rather illogically, that 'Everyone wants to.' Klara, on the other hand, does have a specific reason for wanting to travel: modelling. But it is a false one and she clearly has no contacts in Paris that would keep her involved in the legitimate side of the business of showing off her body.

The portrayal of foreigners also points to a negative view towards emigration. Particularly strong in this regard is the depiction of Paolo, Nexhi's cousin's boss, who has the briefest appearance of any of the foreign characters, but the most damning. It is never explained exactly what Nexhi's cousin does (something in itself which might raise suspicions), and Paolo is shown to have enormous interest in Nexhi while expressing an unctuous fatherly understanding when her children say they do not want to travel with her to Italy. When Nexhi does leave the country with Paolo, she leaves behind her children in the care of her husband, the irresponsibility of both partners underlined by the husband's inability to cope and consequent reliance on alcohol. This effectively paints Paolo as a parasitic sexual opportunist. Günther, the German tourist whose mind seems affected through excessive drug use, on the other hand, is a largely likeable character, but not one who really seems to understand Albania or its people, despite travelling with an Albanian fiancée (who has very little to say). Virginie, the French journalist, has a far sharper mind, but she too is out of place. There is a documentary element in this depiction of Westerners coming to revel in the chaos of the Balkans, but Koçi in these scenes also plays against stereotypical presentations of Western travellers in the Balkans (as visible in films such as Michael Cacoyannis's *Zorba the Greek*, 1964), in which a rigid, identity-confused Westerner meets chaotic Balkan emotionality and finds his 'true' personality in the resulting clash of cultures. In *Tirana Year Zero*, the roles are reversed and Niku is the young man in search of who he is, and Günther and Virginie are the wild and free spirits that he comes up against. Except that they can provide him with no answers, and their eccentricities provide no formula by which to understand life. The portrayal of this pair of out-of-place foreigners is immediately followed by a scene in which Niku picks up two old women carrying bundles of wood, and it is clear that Niku has far more to learn from this serene, sensible, hard-working elderly pair than he possibly could from the care-free tourists.

There are plenty of stark portrayals of life in urban Albania, but the cinematography (by Austrian Heinzi Brandner) oscillates between creating visual harmony and capturing the mundanity of life. The ruins are only foregrounded in the bleak closing shot, and there is certainly no aesthetic of decay, as there is in the cinema of Hungarian director Béla Tarr. Expansive establishing shots that take in the surroundings are only common when Niku leaves Tirana, and most of these images are positive if rather dry and dusty: vertiginous mountain views, sparkling seas and a village picturesquely perched on a hillside. The overall affect is to create a rather nostalgic visual style that yearns for rusticism.

The closing shot remains a notable exception. The last words we hear in the film are those of Klara asking Niku what he is thinking. He gives no verbal response, but the camera hints at a possible answer. If Klara and Niku do decide to stay in Albania, it is certainly not a triumphal turning point where the young couple discover their national consciousness, thus making the film a rather ridiculous melodrama, in the style of Socialist Realism (in which the great hero discovers his political consciousness, and a genre that is also alluded to in the film in its dialogue and in the ironic use of Stalin's statue). It is a decision laced with regret and perhaps, in the case of Klara, overshadowed by feelings of unrealised yearning for something better abroad.

The only positive element suggested in what may happen after the final credits roll occurs earlier in the film's action when one of the two old ladies Niku picks up in his truck gives him her ring. It is a gift that hints at a figurative marriage to his homeland and its traditions but also possibly a literal one to Klara.

Undoubtedly, it is this ambiguous ending that gives *Tirana Year Zero* much of its power, and the film certainly has more narrative strength and originality when compared with other works from former communist countries that have sought to change how a country perceives itself. The Albanian response to Koçi's 'call' to them was mixed, however. The film opened for theatrical release on 26 October 2001 and was programmed for two weeks in cinemas. Whilst in any other country this would be no remarkable feat, in Albania it was something of an achievement given the fact that the cinema distribution and exhibition system in Albania had almost totally collapsed and films were shown in impromptu venues such as community centres and theatres. By 1996 all the major cinemas had been converted to more profitable bingo halls. Cinema had been all but surpassed by the power of television and proliferation of pirated videos. Gjergj Xhuvani's *Slogans* (2001), which had opened earlier that same October, was the first Albanian film to get a release in a proper cinema. That *Slogans* and *Tirana Year Zero* were able to be released theatrically in Tirana illustrates an enormous advance in the cinema climate.

In contrast to the international acclaim, critical response to the film in Albania was largely negative and Koçi was accused by the media of blackening the country's name. The theatrical run even had to be suspended after one week, when cinema-owners refused to continue screening the film because of the negative picture it portrayed (the second week of the run resumed in April 2002). However, according to Koçi, box-office receipts for the two-week total were positive – six thousand admissions for Tirana and four thousand for other towns – and screenings were mostly full, with a strong attendance by younger people, among whom the film was better received. Émigré Albanians were the harshest critics of all, as Koçi discovered in March 2002 when he gave a two Q&A sessions after screenings at the Museum of Modern Art in New York. The 'discussion' of his film, the director claimed, degenerated into a shouting match in Albanian, with audience members accusing the film of being 'a lie' and Koçi of being an enemy of Albania. Others complained he had not concentrated on the more positive aspects of Albania, or more honourable moments of the country's recent history (as other Albanian directors such as Kujtim Çashku did), such as when Albania absorbed half a million ethnic Albanian refugees escaping the ethnic cleansing in neighbouring Kosovo, in 1999. Koçi, in response to this, has expressed his surprise that people who had left Albania should be among those most willing to brand him an enemy.

Koçi also found that ethnic Albanians also responded negatively when the film screened in Pristina (Kosovo) and Skopje (Macedonia). However, at other Balkan screenings the film was received positively, including Belgrade (Serbia), Motovun (Croatia), Sofia (Bulgaria) and the Thessaloniki International Film Festival (Greece) in November 2001, where the film played in competition and won the highest prize, the Golden Alexander. Whilst Albania's mass exodus may be extreme, the Balkan-wide identification with emigration in reaction to poverty, lack of opportunities and lawlessness may explain the success of the film in the region. (Perhaps it is no coincidence that the poorest and most isolated of these countries in the late 1990s, Serbia, also gave *Tirana Year Zero*, according to Koçi, its warmest reception, despite historical bad relations between the two countries.)

As a region-wide phenomenon, emigration has appeared as a topic in many Balkan films, and some of the area's finest directors have viewed it from a number of perspectives: Goran Paskaljević's *Andejo čuvar* (*Guardian Angel*, 1986) and Emir Kusturica's *Dom za vešanje* (*Time of the Gypsies*, 1989) both deal with the exploitation of Yugoslav Roma children in Italy; Milcho Manchevski's *Pred doždot* (*Before the Rain*, 1994) has an émigré Macedonian decide to return home, despite the risk that war is about to break out; Iglika Trifonova's *Pismo do Amerika* (*Letter to America*, 2000) is a personal search for the main character's Bulgarian roots sparked off by an inability to visit a dying friend in the USA; Cristian Mungiu's *Occident* (2002), like *Tirana Year Zero*, plays off the lack of opportunities at home against uninviting prospects abroad; and Serbian veteran Želimir Žilnik's re-enacted documentary *Tvrdjava Evropa* (*Fortress Europe*, 2000) and Damjan Kožole's fiction feature *Reservni deli* (*Spare Parts*, 2003) both look at the desperate measures people use to cross into the prosperous European Union, while Faruk Sokolović's comedy *Mliječni put* (*Milky Way*, 2000) does the same thing with New Zealand's border. The fascination is not one-sided, and Western European directors have also made films about Balkan emigration, including Michael Haneke's *Code inconnu: Récit incomplet de divers voyages* (*Code Unknown*, 2000) and Gianni Amelio's *Lamerica* (1994), which takes place in Albania against the backdrop of the 1991 wave of emigration.

On a larger scale, the interest in *Tirana Year Zero* can be seen as part of a global trend in the early years of the twenty-first century towards films about the movement of people, a trend that includes films such as Michael Winterbottom's *In This World* (2002), a tale of two Afghan refugees trying to get to England. This widespread interest has been aided by migration being a hot topic in both political circles and the press. Social issues such as the lack of assimilation among immigrants vs. preserving cultural identity, allegiance of the immigrant to the host country, concentration of refugees in one place vs. splitting up ethnic groups, uncoordinated policies on the international level, preserving human rights vs. maintaining national security and the surge of interest in anti-immigration political groups have fired media pundits and politicians around the globe. Whereas politicians and media outlets tend to look at the macroscopic consequences of migration, filmmakers have usually focused attention on the causes and on telling the stories of individuals caught behind the wider statistics and the headlines. Therefore, as much as *Tirana Year Zero* is a response to a specific set of circumstances in one country and addressed to a certain ethnic group, it can be aligned with a regional and global trend in humanistic filmmaking about a worldwide crisis issue.

**Andrew James Horton**

# FILMOGRAPHY

To find video copies of most of the films covered in this book was next to impossible just a few years ago. The only title that was commercially available was the Greek *Stella*. Over the four years I worked on this project, however, the situation changed a lot. Various internet-based media shops that mostly cater to the respective diasporas have appeared and it is now possible to find more of these films, some even in subtitled copies. Here I would like to list some of the outlets that I know of:

An ever growing range of Bulgarian films on VHS or DVD (some with English subtitles) are available from Salt Lake City-based *GoBgMedia*, http://www.gobgmedia.com. In early 2005 the site listed all four Bulgarian titles included in this collection.

Toronto-based *DS Sound*, http://www.dssound.com, carries a wide selection of films on video from former Yugoslavia, yet most have no subtitles. In 2005 they had listed films like *Petrija's Wreath* and *The Beauty of Sin*. Having visited the store in person, I can confirm that they have a wider selection available than listed on the website.

A large number of films from former Yugoslavia are listed on the website *Gerila*, http://www.gerila.com/video/index.htm. These include *Three*, *The Fall of Italy*, *When I am Dead and Pale* and *Walter Defends Sarajevo*, even though some titles are marked as 'temporarily unavailable'.

Another Toronto-based store, *Greek City Music and Video* on Danforth, http://www.greekcity.com, carries a wide selection of Greek-language films; in the store they have more films than are actually listed on the website.

An Albanian site, http://www.albanianshopping.net/shop, has a listing for *Return of the Dead Army* and many more Albanian films. Various Chinese web-shopping sites list more Albanian films on DVD with subtitles in Mandarin.

Films that I have come to believe are not available through any commercial channels include all the Romanian titles, *Early Works*, *The Red Horse* and *The Raft of Medusa*. For Romanian films, however, it may be worthwhile to try the Romanian Cultural Centres in London and New York; both have websites and contact information.

It is particularly disconcerting to realise that the two most recent films included here, *Four Seasons of the Law* and *Tirana Year Zero*, both widely acclaimed winners of various festival awards, do not appear to have been released on video or DVD neither in their respective countries nor internationally.

Still, if one spends time looking around in the dusty video/grocery stores in the respective ethnic neighbourhoods in New York, Chicago, Toronto and London, one can make surprise discoveries of cinematic gems. Even though it may sound like an unlikely development, more and more local films are becoming available commercially in the large media stores run by international chains.

**STELLA** 1955
Country of Origin: Greece
Director: Michael Cacoyannis
Production: Milas Films (Greece)
Screenplay: Iakovos Kamabanellis (based on his play *Stella with the Red Gloves*)
Photography: Kostas Theodoridis (b&w)
Editing: Michael Cacoyannis
Music: Manos Hadjidakis
Costume Design: Denni Vachilioti
Cast: Melina Mercouri (Stella), Alekos Alexandrakis (Alekos), Yiorgos Foundas (Miltos), Voula Zoumboulaki (Annetta), Sophia Vembo (Maria), Kostas Kakavas (Andonis), Christina Koloyerikou (mother of Miltos).
Running time: 97'

**KRADETSAT NA PRASKOVI** THE PEACH THIEF 1964
Country of origin: Bulgaria
Director: Vulo Radev
Production: Boyana Film Studio
Screenplay: Vulo Radev (based on the novella *The Peach Thief* by Emilian Stanev)
Photography: Todor Stoyanov (b&w)
Editing: Lyuben Stanev, Yanko Yankov
Music: Simeon Pironkov
Cast: Rade Marković (Ivo), Nevena Kokanova (Liza), Mikhail Mikhailov (The Colonel), Naum Shopov (de Greville), Vassil Vachev (Colonel's orderly), Georgi Georgiev (Varenov), Ivan Bratanov (Gandev), Ivan Manov (Lefterov), Nikola Dadov (the old soldier)
Running time: 80'

**PĂ DUREA SPÎNZURAȚILOR** FOREST OF THE HANGED 1964
Country of Origin: Romania
Director: Liviu Ciulei
Production: Bucharest Film Studio
Screenplay: Titus Popovici (based on the novel *Forest of the Hanged* by Liviu Rebreanu)
Photography: Ovidiu Gologan (b&w)
Editing: Yolanda Măntulescu, Dan Naum
Music: Theodor Grigoriu
Costume Design: Ovidiu Bubulac, Ileana Oroveanu
Cast: Victor Rebengiuc (Lieutenant Apostol Bologa), Liviu Ciulei (Captain Ottokar Klapka), Ștefan Ciobotarășu (Orderly Petre), Ana Széles (Ilona), Mariana Mihuț (Marta), György Kovács (General von Karg), Gina Patrichi (Roza Janosi), Andrei Csiki (Lieutenant Varga), Emmerich Schäffer (Private Johann-Maria Müller), Lászlo Kiss, M. Mereuța, V. Arnăutu, M. Crizan.
Running time: 158'

**TRI** THREE 1965
Country of origin: Yugoslavia (Serbia)
Director: Aleksandar Petrović
Production: Avala Film Belgrade
Screenplay: Aleksandar Petrović, Antonije Isaković (based on the collection of stories *Paprat i vatra* by Antonije Isaković)
Photography: Tomislav Pinter (b&w)
Editing: Mirjana Mitić
Cast: Velimir 'Bata' Živojinović (Miloš Bojanić), Senka Veletanlić-Petrović, Voja Mirić, Ali Raner, Slobodan Perović, Mića Tomić
Running time: 75'

**KAD BUDEM MRTAV I BEO** WHEN I AM DEAD AND PALE 1968
Country of origin: Yugoslavia (Serbia)
Director: Živojin Pavlović
Production: FRZ Srbije (Centre of Film Workers' Cooperatives, Serbia)
Screenplay: Gordan Mihić, Ljubiša Kozomara
Photography: Milorad Jakšic-Fandjo (b&w)
Editing: Olga Skrigin
Music: archival and Crni Biseri (Black Pearls)

Cast: Dragan Nikolić (Jimmy Barka), Ruzica Sokić (Duška), Neda Spasojević (Lilica), Dara Čalenić (Mica), Severin Bijelić (army officer), Slobodan Aligrudić (Milutin), Zorica Šumadinac (dentist's assistant), Snezana Lukić (dentist's assistant II), Ljiljana Jovanović (mother), Milivoje Tomić, Nikola Milić, Petar Lupa, Aleksandar Gavrić, Janez Vrhovec, Milan Jelić, Miodrag Andrić, Milorad Spasojević.
Running time: 74'

**RANI RADOVI** EARLY WORKS 1969
Country of origin: Yugoslavia (Serbia)
Director: Želimir Žilnik
Production: Avala Film (Belgrade), Neoplanta film (Novi Sad)
Screenplay: Želimir Žilnik, Branko Vučičević; additional text dialogue by Karl Marx and Friedrich Engels
Photography: Karpo Aćimović–Godina (b&w)
Editing: Karpo Aćimović-Godina
Music: music from the archives
Cast: Milja Vujanović (Yugoslava), Bogdan Tirnanić, Čedomir Radović, Marko Nikolić, Slobodan Aligrudić
Running time: 78'

**MIHAI VITEAZUL** MICHAEL THE BRAVE 1970–71
Country of origin: Romania
Director: Sergiu Nicolaescu
Production: Romania Film
Screenplay: Titus Popovici
Photography: Mircea George Cornea (c)
Editing: Yolanda Mintulescu
Music: Tiberiu Olah
Cast: Amza Pellea (Mihai), Sergiu Nicolaescu (Selim), Mircea Albulescu, Ion Besoiu (Szigmond Báthory), Constantin Codrescu (Prince Alexandru), Ilarion Ciobanu, Ioana Bulca (Stanca), Irina Gardescu (Countess Ventini), Fory Etterle, György Kovács, Mihai Mereuta, Florin Piersic, Colea Rautu (Murad), Aurel Rogalschi, Emmerich Schäffer, Klára Sebök, Nicolae Secareanu, Olga Tudorache
Running time: 200'

**TI EKANES STON POLEMO, THANASSI?** WHAT DID YOU DO IN THE WAR, THANASSIS? 1971
Country of Origin: Greece
Director: Dinos Katsuridis
Production: Dinos Katsuridis
Screenplay: Dinos Katsuridis and Asimakis Yialamas
Photography: Yiorgos Arvanitis (b&w)
Editing: Dinos Katsuridis
Music: Mimis Plessas
Cast: Thanassis Vengos (Thanassis), Efi Roditi (Froso), Katerina Yoyu, Andonis Papadopulos, Manolis Destounis, Hristos Kalavruzos, Keti Lambropoulu, Nikitas Platis, Grigoris Evangelatos, Mihalis Gianatos, Dimitris Veakis, Stelios Lionakis, Yiannis Firios, Giorgis Hristofilakis, Yorgos Hristopulos, Tasos Papadakis, Irini Emirza, Keti Prekete, Tzeni Stefanaku, Patritsia Adamu, Evi Kasimati, Efi Arvaniti, Dinos Dulyerakis, Yiorgos Morogianis, Yiorgos Mihalakis, Spiros Pantzas, Yianis Sidiropulos, Mihalis Costopulos, Spiros Papafratzis, Tasos Polihronopulos, Yiorgos Kaitsis, Yiannis Emanuil, Yiorgos Faturos, Thanassis Sirmakesis, Vasilis Katsulis, Costas Stavrinudakis, Dimitra Katerinaki, Filipos Dres, Nikos Karatasos, Fotis Litharis, Takis Tatsiopulos, Manolis Papadakis, Hristos Maroyianis, Manolis Dimitrianakis, Mihalis Mihail, Paraskevi Karteru.
Running time: 85'

**EVDOKIA** 1971
Country of Origin: Greece
Director: Alexis Damianos
Production: Artemis Kapasakali
Screenplay: Alexis Damianos
Photography: Christos Mangos (c)
Editing: Matt McCarthy
Music: Manos Loizos
Cast: Maria Vassiliou (Evdokia), Yiorgos Koutouzis (Yiorgos), Koula Agagiotou (Maria), Christos Zorbas (Yiorgos), Vassilis Panayiotopoulos, Pavlos Roussos
Running time: 97'

**VALTER BRANI SARAJEVO** WALTER DEFENDS SARAJEVO 1972
Country of origin: Yugoslavia (Bosnia and Herzegovina)
Director: Hajrudin 'Šiba' Krvavac
Production: Bosna Film Sarajevo
Screenplay: Djordje Lebović, co-writers: Hajrudin 'Šiba' Krvavac, Savo Predja, Momo Kapor
Photography: Miroljub Dikosavljević (c)
Editing: Jelena and Vanja Bjenjaš
Music: Bojan Adamič
Cast: Velimir 'Bata' Živojinović (Walter), Ljubiša Samardžić (Zis), Slobodan Dimitrijević (Suri), Dragomir Bojanić Gidra (Condor and fake Walter), Rade Marković (Sead Kapetanović), Etela Pardo (Azra Kapetanović), Neda Spasojević (Mirna), Faruk Begolli (Branko), Pavle Vujisić (Train Dispatching Clerk ), Jovan Janićijević Burduš (Uncle), Stevo Žigon (Dr. Sreten Mišković)
Running time: 133'

**KOZIYAT ROG** GOAT'S HORN 1972
Country of origin: Bulgaria
Director: Methodi Andonov
Production: Boyana Film Studio
Screenplay: Nikolay Haytov from his *Wild Stories*
Photography: Dimo Kolarov (b&w)
Editing: Svoboda Buchvarova
Music: Maria Neykova
Cast: Katya Paskaleva (Maria, Maria's mother), Anton Gorchev (Karaivan), Milen Penev (Shepherd), Nevena Andonova (little Maria), Todor Kolev (Deli), Kliment Denchev (Turkish rapist 1), Marin Yanev (Turkish rapist 2), Stefan Mavrodiev (Turkish rapist 3), Krasimira Petrova, Ivan Obretenov, Andrey Mihaylov, Prodan Nonchev, Iliya Georgiev, Tzanko Petrov, Petar Bozhilov
Running Time: 96'

**NUNTA DE PIATR** STONE WEDDING 1972
Country of origin: Romania
Director: Mircea Veroiu & Dan Pița
Production: Romaniafilm
Screenplay: Mircea Veroiu, Dan Pița based on two short stories by Ion Agârbiceanu
Photography: Iosif Demian (b&w)
Editing: Dan Naum
Music: Doru Liviu Zaharia

Cast: Leopoldina Balanuța (Fefeleaga), Petrica Gheorghiu, Ursula Nussbacher, Radu Boruzescu, Mircea Diaconu, George Calboreanu
Running time: 90'

**LACHENITE OBUVKI NA NEZNAINIYA VOIN** THE PATENT LEATHER SHOES OF THE UNKNOWN SOLDIER 1979
Country of Origin: Bulgaria
Director: Rangel Vulchanov
Production: Boyana Film Studio
Screenplay: Rangel Vulchanov
Photography: Radoslav Spassov (b&w)
Editing: Svoboda Bachvarova, Mikhail Kirkov
Music: Kiril Donchev
Cast: Borislav Tzankov (Mone), Ivan Stoichkov (Grandfather Dobrin), Slavka Ankova (Grandmother Slava), Emilia Marinska (White Aunt), Nicolay Velichkov (Black Uncle), Rangel Vulchanov (Simeon)
Running time: 85'

**SPLAV MEDUZE** THE RAFT OF MEDUSA 1980
Country of origin: Yugoslavia (Slovenia)
Director: Karpo Aćimović-Godina
Production: Viba film
Screenplay: Branko Vučičević
Photography: Karpo Aćimović-Godina
Editing: Karpo Aćimović-Godina
Music: Predrag and Mladen Vranešević
Costume design: Jasmina Ješić and Gordana Rothstein
Cast: Olga Kacjan-Srdić (Kristina Polič), Vladislava Milosavljević (Ljiljana), Boris Komnenić (Mišić), Erol Kadić (Ljiljana's brother), Frano Lasić (Aleksa Ristić), Radmila Živković (Nadežda), Miloš Battelino ('Giant' Žnidaršič), Predrag Panić (Borivoje Lazarević), Gisela Siebauer, Petar Kralj, Miodrag Radovanović, Mitja Šipek, Grozdana Stefanović.
Running time: 97'

**PETRIJIN VENAC** PETRIJA'S WREATH 1980
Country of origin: Yugoslavia (Serbia)
Director: Srdjan Karanović
Production: Centar Film
Screenplay: Srdjan Karanović and Rajko Grlić based on the novel by Dragoslav Mihajlović
Photography: Tomislav Pinter (c)
Editing: Branka Čeperac
Music: Zoran Simjanović
Art direction: Miodrag Mirić, Miljen 'Kreka' Kljaković.
Cast: Mirjana Karanović (Petrija), Marko Nikolić (Dobrivoje), Ljiljana Krstić (Vela Bugarka), Olgica Petrović (Milana), Pavle Vujisić (Ljubiša), Dragan Maksimović (Misa), The Photographer (Mića Tomić)
Running time: 99'

**PAD ITALIJE** THE FALL OF ITALY 1981
Country of origin: Yugoslavia (Croatia)
Director: Lordan Zafranović
Production: Jadran Film, Centar Film (Belgrade), RTV Zagreb

Screenplay: Mirko Kovač, Lordan Zafranović
Photography: Božidar Nikolić (c)
Editing: Josip Remenar
Music: Alfi Kabiljo
Art Direction: Drago Turina
Cast: Daniel Olbrychski (Davorin), Dragan Maksimovic (Rafo), Dusan Janicevic (Ljubo), Ena Begovic (Veronika), Frano Lasic (Niko), Gorica Popovic (Božica)
Running time: 113'

**PROBA DE MICROFON** MICROPHONE TEST 1980
Country of origin: Romania
Language: Romanian
Director: Mircea Daneliuc
Production: Casa de filme 3
Screenplay: Mircea Daneliuc
Photography: Ion Marinescu, Constantin Chelba (for 16 mm documentary sequences)
Editing: Maria Neagu
Cast: Tora Vasilescu (Ani), Gina Patrichi (Luiza), Mircea Daneliuc (Nelu), Maria Junghetu (Gabi), Vasile Ichim (Ani's brother), Adrian Mazarache (Sile)
Running time: 108'

**MERA SPORED MERA** MEASURE FOR MEASURE 1981
Country of origin: Bulgaria
Language: Macedonian, Bulgarian, Turkish, English
Director: Georgi Dyulgerov
Production: Boyana Film Studio
Screenplay: Georgi Dyulgerov, Russi Chanev (based on the novel *Liturgy For Ilinden* by Svoboda Buchvarova)
Photography: Radoslav Spassov (c)
Editing: Tzvetana Kolarova
Music: Bozhidar Petkov
Cast: Russi Chanev (Dilber Tanass), Grigor Vatchkov (Postol), Stefan Mavrodiev (Hristo Tchernopeev), Katya Ivanova (Slava), Dimitar Buynozov (Gotze Delchev), Bogdan Glishev (Yane Sandanski), Tzvetana Maneva (Tasha), Christine Bartlet (Helen Stone), Rumena Trifonova (Ekaterina Tzilka), Martina Vachkova (Limbiyka), Vulcho Kamarashev (Dickinson), Margarita Karamiteva (Anika), Vladimir Yotchev (Krastyo Assenov).
Running time: 288' in three parts: part I, 100'; part II, 84'; part III, 104'

**CRVENIOT KONJ** THE RED HORSE 1981
Country of origin: Yugoslavia (Macedonia)
Director: Stole Popov
Production: Vardar Film (Macedonia), Macedonia Film (Skopje)
Screenplay: Taško Georgievski (based on his own novel)
Photography: Branko Mihajlovski (c)
Editing: Dimitar Grbevski
Music: Ljupčo Konstantinov
Art direction: Vlastimir Gavrik
Sound: Yordan Yanevski
Cast: Velimir 'Bata' Živojnović (Boris), Ilija Džuvalekovski (Nikifor), Dančo Čevrevski (Vani Josmov), Kole Angelovski (Sujde), Radmila Živković (Olga), Meto Jovanovski (Vani Urumov), Lile Georgieva (Drita), Stole

Arandjelović (Nikola), Dušan Janićijević (Commander), Ilija Milčin (Defter), Aco Jovanovski (Sabrija), Risto Šiškov (Stavropoulos), Vladimir Svetiev (Veljo's Son)
Running time: 126'

**PETRINA HRONIA** STONE YEARS 1985
Country of origin: Greece
Director: Pantelis Voulgaris
Production: EKK/Greek Film Centre, EPT A.E./ ERT S.A.
Screenplay: Pantelis Voulgaris
Photography: Yiorgos Arvanitis (c)
Editing: Andreas Andreadakis
Music: Stamatis Spanoudakis
Cast: Themis Bazaka (Eleni), Dimitris Katalifos (Babis), Maria Martika (Eleni's mother), Irini Inglessi (Cleo), Nikos Birbilis (Policeman), Ilias Katevas (Michael)
Running time: 142'

**LEPOTA POROKA** THE BEAUTY OF SIN 1986
Country of origin: Yugoslavia (Montenegro)
Director: Živko Nikolić
Production: Centar Film, Belgrade
Screenplay: Živko Nikolić
Photography: Radoslav Vladić (c)
Editing: Zoltan Wagner
Music: Zoran Simjanović
Art Direction: Miodrag Mirić
Cast: Mira Furlan (Jaglika), Milutin-Mima Karadzić (Luka), Petar Bozović (Djordje/George), Alain Noury (foreign male nudist), Ines Kotman (foreign female nudist), Dobrila Cirković (Kosara), Eva Ras (George's wife), Mira Banjac (Manager of the resort), Boro Stjepanović (Manager of the textile company), Boro Begović, Drago Malović, Gojko Kovacević, Milo Miranović, Miodrag-Miki Krstović, Mladen Nelević, Svetolik Nikacević, Veljko Mandić, Vesna Pecanac, Žarko Lausević
Running time: 111'

**KTHIMI I USHTRISE SE VDEKUR** RETURN OF THE DEAD ARMY 1989
Country of origin: Albania
Director: Dhimitër Anagnosti
Production: Albfilm, Tirana
Screenplay: Dhimitër Anagnosti (based on the novel of Ismaïl Kadaré *Gienerali ushtrisë së vdekur* (*The General of the Dead Army*))
Photography: Bardhyl Martiniani (c)
Editing: Mimoza Nano
Music: Gjon Simoni
Cast: Bujar Lako (Italian General), Guljelm Radoja (The Priest), Rajmonda Bullku (Countess Betty), Liza Vorfi (Contessa Dizeta), Ndriçim Xhepa (German General), Roza Anagnosti (old Nicë), Kastriot Ahmetaj, Vasillaq Godo.
Running time: 107'

**I EARINI SYNAXIS TON AGROFYLAKON** FOUR SEASONS OF THE LAW 1999
Country of origin: Greece
Director: Dimos Avdeliodis

Production: Greek Film Centre, Dimos Avdeliodis, E.T.1
Screenplay: Dimos Avdeliodis
Photography: Odysseas Pavlopoulos (Summer), Alekos Giannaras (Fall), Linos Meitanis (Winter), Sotiris Pereas (Spring) (colour/ b&w)
Editing: Kostas Iordhanidis
Music: Antonio Vivaldi, Vassilis Tsitsanis, Stelios Kazantzidhis
Art direction: Charlotte Van Gelder, Nikos Khatzis
Cast: Angeliki Malanti (Elisso), Angelos Pantelaras (Spring Field Guard), Takis Aghoris (Summer Field Guard), Yannis Tsoumbariotis (Patsaganas: Fall Field Guard), Stelios Makrias (Lavidas: Winter Field Guard), Ilias Petropouleas (Agronomist)
Running time: 178'

**TIRANA YEAR ZERO** 2001
Country of origin: Albania/France
Director: Fatmir Koçi
Production: KKoçi Production, Ciné-Sud Promotion, Alexis Films
Screenplay: Fatmir Koçi and Heinzi Brandner
Photography: Heinzi Brandner (colour)
Editing: Thomas Kühne-Tomk and Michel Klochendler
Music: Artëm Denissov
Art direction: Andon Koja
Cast: Nevin Meçaj (Niku), Ermela Teli (Klara), Rajmonda Bulku (Marta, Niku's mother), Robert Ndrenika (Kujtim, Niku's father), Bahar Mera (Xhafa), Birçe Hasco (Besim), Lars Rudolph (Günter), Juli Hajdini (Linda), Laura Pélerins (Virginie), Nigda Dako (Dessi), Vladimir Metani (Vladimir), Artur Gorishti (Tare), Monika Lubonja (Nexhi), Gesim Rudi (Titi), Fatos Sela (City Hall official), Jorida Meta (Romany girl), Blegina Hasko (Klara's sister), Alfred Muçi (Klara's brother-in-law), Eridan Kellici (secretary), Ledio Topalli (policeman), Muharrem Hoxha (barber)
Running time: 89'

# BIBLIOGRAPHY

## GENERAL WORKS

Bakić-Hayden, M. (1995) 'Nesting Orientalisms: The Case of Former Yugoslavia', *Slavic Review*, 54, 4, 917–32.

Bjelić, D. and O. Savić (eds) (2002) *Balkan as Metaphor: Between Globalisation and Fragmentation*. Cambridge, MA: MIT Press.

Elsaesser, T. (2005) 'Our Balkanist Gaze: About Memory's No Man's Land', in *European Cinema: Face to Face with Hollywood*. Amsterdam: Amsterdam University Press, 356–73.

Germani, S. G. (ed.) (2000) *La meticcia di fuoco: Oltre il continente Balcani*. Venice: La biennale di Venezia; Torino: Lindau s.r.l.

Goldsworthy, V. (1989) *Inventing Ruritania: The Imperialism of the Imagination*. New Haven, CT and London: Yale University Press.

Goulding, D. J. (ed.) (1989) *Post New-Wave Cinema in the Soviet Union and Eastern Europe*. Bloomington, IN: Indiana University Press.

Grbić, B., G. Loidot and R. Milev (eds) (1995) *Die Siebte Kunst auf dem Pulverfass: Balkan Film*. Graz: Blimp.

Horton, A. J. (ed.) (2000) *The Celluloid Tinderbox: Yugoslav Screen Reflections of a Turbulent Decade*. London: Central Europe Review, 62–89. On-line; http://www.mirhouse.com/ce-review/Yugofilm.pdf.

Iordanova, D. (1996) 'Conceptualising the Balkans in Film', *Slavic Review*, 55, 1, 882–91.

_____ (1996–97) 'Women in New Balkan Cinema: Surviving on the Margins', *Film Criticism*, 21, 2, 24–40.

_____ (1998) 'Balkan Film Representations since 1989: The Quest for Admissibility', *Historical Journal of Film and Television*, 18, 2, 263–80.

_____ (1999) 'College Course File: Eastern European Cinema', *Journal of Film and Video*, 51, 1, 56–77.

_____ (2000) 'Are the Balkans Admissible? The Discourse on Europe', *Balkanistica*, 13, 1–35.

_____ (2001a) *Cinema of Flames: Balkan Film, Culture and the Media*. London: British Film Institute.

_____ (2001b) 'Balkan Cinema: An Overview', *Afterimage: The Journal of Media Arts and Cul-

*tural Criticism*, 28, 4. Online; http://www.findarticles.com/cf_dls/m2479/4_28/76560786/p2/article.jhtml?term.

Jameson, F. (2004) 'Thoughts on Balkan Cinema', in Atom Egoyan and Ian Balfour (eds) *Subtitles: On the Foreignness of Film*. Cambridge, MA; MIT Press/Alphabet City Media, 231–59.

Kolar-Panov, D. (1997) *Video, War and the Diasporic Imagination*. London and New York: Routledge.

Liehm, M. and A. J. Liehm (1977) *The Most Important Art: Soviet and East European Film After 1945*. Berkeley and Los Angeles: University of California Press.

Milev. R. (ed.) (1996) *TV auf dem Balkan: Zur Entwicklung des Fernsehens in Südosteuropa*. Hamburg: Hans-Bredow-Institut, 17.

Nonevski, B. (2003) (ed.) *Razvojot i proniknuvaneto na balkanskite natsionalni kinematografii vo periodot od 1895 do 1945 godina*. Skopje: Kinoteka na Makedonija.

Slater, T. J. (ed.) (1992) *Handbook of Soviet and East European Films and Filmmakers*. New York: Greenwood Press.

Stoil, M. J. (1974) *Cinema Beyond the Danube: The Camera and the Politics*. Metuchen, NJ: Scarecrow Press.

_____ (1982) *Balkan Cinema: Evolution after the Revolution*. Ann Arbor: University of Michigan.

Taylor, R., J. Graffy, N. Wood and D. Iordanova (eds) (2000) *The BFI's Companion to Eastern European and Russian Cinema*. London: British Film Institute.

Todorova, M. (1997) *Imagining the Balkans*. New York: Oxford University Press.

_____ (ed.) (2004) *Balkan Identities: Nation and Memory*. London: C. Hurst.

Ţuţui, M. (2004) *Manakia Bros or the Moving Balkans*. Bucharest: Romanian Film Archive.

Tozi, N. (2000) *The Creation of the Brothers Manaki*. Skopje: AM.

Vincendeau, G. (ed.) (1995) *Encyclopedia of European Cinema*. London: British Film Institute.

Virag, K. (2002) 'Boundaries and Revolving Doors: Some Thoughts on Europe, Balkan Cinema and Identity', *Spaces of Identity*, 2, 1. On-line; http://www.spaceofidentity.net.

## ALBANIA

Hoxha, A. and F. Papleka (eds) (1987) *Filmi artistik shqiptar 1957–1984*. Tirana: Shtepia.

_____ (1994) *Arti i shtate ne shqiperi 1900–1944*. Tirana: Albin.

_____ (1999) *Enciklopedi e kinematografise shqiptare*. Tirana: Lira & Albanian-American Academy of Arts-European section.

_____ (2002) *Enciklopedi e kinematografise shqiptare*. Tirana: Teona.

_____ (2002) *Vjet Kinema 1897–1997*. Tirana: Marin Barleti.

Lako, N. (2000) 'Cinema albanese', in G. P. Brunetta (ed.) *Storia del cinema mondiale*, vol. III. Turin: Einaudi, 1173–91.

_____ (2004) 'The Birth of Balkan Cinematographic Art in an Albanian Colonial Period', *MovEast 9*, Hungarian National Film Archive: Budapest. Online; http://www.filmintezet. hu/uj/kiadvanyok/moveast/moveast_9/lako_albanian.htm.


## BULGARIA

Brossard, J.-P. (1986) *Aspects nouveaux du cinéma bulgare*. La Chaunx-de-Fonds, Cinédiff.

Cervoni, A. (1976) *Les écrans de Sofia: Voyage français dans le cinéma bulgare*. Paris: Pierre L'Herminier.

Dimitrova, G. (1999) *Kino v kraya na veka*. Pleven: EA-AD.

Gencheva, G. (1988) *Bulgarski igralni filmi, Vol. 2. 1948–1970*. Sofia: BNF.

Grozev, A. (1985) *Nachaloto: Iz istoriyata na bulgarskoto kino, 1895–1956*. Sofia: BAN.

Holloway, R. (1986) *The Bulgarian Cinema*. Rutherford, NJ: Fairleigh Dickinson University Press/London: Associated Presses.

Ignatovski, V. (1982) *Filmovo desetiletie: Shtrihi ot portreta na 70-te godini v bulgarskia igralen film*. Sofia: Nauka i izkustvo.

Iordanova, D. (1998) 'Canaries and Birds of Prey: The New Season of Bulgarian Cinema', in J. D. Bell (ed.) *Bulgaria in Transition*. Boulder, CO: Westview Press, 255-77.

Kurdzhilov, P. (1987) *Bulgraski igralni filmi, Vol. I, 1915–1948*. Sofia: BNF.

Marinchevska, N. (2001) *Bulgarsko animatsionno kino, 1915–1995*. Sofia: Colibri.

Micheli, S. (1971) *Il Cinema bulgaro*. Padua: Marsilio Editori.

_____ (1981) *The Bulgarian cinema today*. Sofia: Bulgariafilm.

Mikhailovska, E. (1985) *Natsionalnata kulturno-xudozhestvena traditsiya i bulgarskoto kino*. Sofia: Nauka i izkustvo.

Milev, N. (1982) *Bulgarskiyat istoricheski film*. Sofia: Nauka i izkustvo.

*MovEast 6* (2001) *Bulgarian Cinema of the 1990s*. Hungarian National Film Archive: Budapest.

Petrova, V. (2003) *V syankata na Lai: Metafori na vlastta v kinoto*. Sofia: Titra.

Radev, V. (2002) *Izgubeni prostranstva*. Sofia: Literaturen Forum.

Ratscheva, M. and K. Eder (1977) *Der bulgarische Film: Geschichte und Gegenwart einer Kinematografie*. Frankfurt: Kommunales Kino.

Stanimirova, N. (1984) *Bulgarski kinorezhisyori*. Sofia: Nauka i izkustvo.

Terziev, J. (2000) 'Cinema bulgaro', in G. P. Brunetta (ed.) *Storia del cinema mondiale*, vol. III Turin: Einaudi, 1225–51.

Yanakiev, A. (ed.) (2000) *Ot A do Ya: Encyclopedia na Bulgarskoto kino*. Sofia: Trtra.

_____ (2003) *Cinema.bg: 100 godini filmov process; lichnosti/filmi/kritika*. Sofia: Titra.


## GREECE

*25 Years of Greek Movies* (1985) Athens: Ministry of Culture, Film Department.

*1981–1986 New Greek Cinema/Nouveau Cinéma Grec* (1987) Athens: Greek Film Centre.

*1987–1990 New Greek Cinema/Nouveau Cinéma Grec* (1990) Athens: Greek Film Centre.

Arecco, S. (1978) *Thodoros Angelopoulos*. Firenze: La Nuova Italia.

Athanasatou, G. (2001) *Ellinikos kinimatografos, 1950–1967: Laiki mnimi kai ideologia*. Athens: Finatec.

Bacayannopoulos, Y. ans A. Tyros (eds) (1993) *Cine-Mythology: A Retrospective of Greek Film*. Athens: Greek Film Centre.

Constantinidis, S. (2000) 'Greek Film and the National Interest: A Brief Preface', *Journal of Modern Greek Studies*, 18, 1, 1–12.

_____ (2002) 'The Greek Studio System, 1950–1970', *Film Criticism*, 27, 2, 9–30.

Demopoulos, M. (1995) *Le Cinéma grec*. Paris: Centre Georges Pompidou.

Demopoulos, M., B. Aktsoglou, P. Mavromoustacos and C. Gapanopoulou (2003) *Cinemythology: Greek Myths in World Cinema*. Thessaloniki: Thessaloniki International Film Festival.

Dimitriou, A. (1993) *Lexiko ellinikon tenion mikrou mikous* (1939–1992). Athens: Kastaniotis.

Eleftheriotis, D. (1995) 'Questioning Totalities: Constructions of Masculinity in the Popular Greek Cinema of the 1960s', *Screen*, 36, 3: 233–42.

Georgakas, D. (2002) 'Greek Cinema for Beginners: A Thumbnail History', *Film Criticism*, 27, 2, 2–8.

_____ (2005) 'From *Stella* to *Iphigenia*: The Woman-Centred Films of Michael Cacoyannis', *Cineaste*, 30, 2, 24–30.

Georgakas, D. and A. Horton (2002) 'Editors' Introduction', *Film Criticism, 27*, 2, 1.

Goutos, C. and C. Noulas (eds) (1996) *Leksiko skinotheton tou ellinikou kinimatografou*. Athens: Aigokeros.

Herzfeld, M. (1987) *Anthropology Through the Looking-Glass: Critical Ethnography in the Margins of Europe*. Cambridge: Cambridge University Press.

Hess, F. L. (2000) 'Sound, Film, and the Nation: Rethinking the History of Early Greek Cinema',

*Journal of Modern Greek Studies*, 18, 1, 13–36.

_____ (2003) 'Close Encounters of the Common Kind: The Theoretical and Practical Implications of Popular Culture for Modern Greek Studies', *Journal of Modern Greek Studies*, 21, 1, 37–66.

Horton, A. (1997a) *The Films of Theo Angelopoulos: A Cinema of Contemplation*. Princeton, NJ: Princeton University Press.

_____ (ed.) (1997b) *The Last Modernist: The Films of Theo Angelopoulos*. Westport, CT: Praeger.

*Incontro con il cinema greco* (1975) Venice: La Biennale di Venezia.

Koliodimos, D. (ed.) (1999) *The Greek Filmography, 1914 through 1996*. New York: McFarland.

Kolonias, B. (ed.) (1995) *Mihalis Cacoyiannis*. Athens: Kastanioti.

Koussumidis, M. (1981) *Istoria tou ellinikou kinimatografou*. Athens: Kastaniotis.

Kymionis, S. (2000) 'The Genre of Mountain Film: The Ideological Parameters of its Subgenres', *Journal of Modern Greek Studies*, 18, 1, 53–66.

Kyriakidis, A. (ed.) (1993) *Jules Dassin*. Athens: 34th Thessaloniki Film Festival.

Mercouri, M. (1973) *I Was Born Greek*. New York: Dell.

Mikelides, N. F. (2000) 'Cinema greco', G. P. Brunetta (ed.) *Storia del cinema mondiale*, vol. III Turin: Einaudi, 1285–305.

Mitropoulou, A. (1980) *Ellinikos kinimatografos*. Athens: Themelio.

Papadimitriou, L. (2000a) 'Travelling on Screen: Tourism and the Greek Film Musical', *Journal of Modern Greek Studies*, 18, 1, 95–104.

_____ (2000b) 'More than a Pale Imitation: Narrative, Music, and Dance in Two Greek Film Musicals of the 1960s', in B. Marshall and R. Stilwell (eds) *Musicals: Hollywood and Beyond*. Bristol: Intellect, 117–24.

_____ (2006) *The Greek Film Musical: A Critical and Cultural History*. Jefferson, NC and London: McFarland.

Pappas, P. (1976) 'The Engagement of Anna: Toward the Definition of a New Greek Cinema', *Jump Cut*, 9, 4–6. Online; http://www.ejumpcut.org/archive/onlinessays/JC09folder/EngagementofAnna.html.

Rutherford, A. (2004) 'Precarious Boundaries: Affect, *Mise-en-scéne* and the Senses in Angelopoulos' Balkan Epic', *Senses of Cinema*, 31. Online; http://www.sensesofcinema.com/contents/04/31/angelopoulos_balkan_epic.html.

Schuster, M. (1979) *The Contemporary Greek Cinema*. Metuchen, NJ: Scarecrow Press.

Soldatos, Y. (1979–91) *Istoria tou Ellinikou kinimatografou*. 6 vols. Athens: Nefeli and Aigokeros.

Sotiropoulou, C. (1995) *I diaspora ston Elliniko kinimatografo*. Athens: Themelio.

Stassinopoulou, M. A. (1995) 'Geschichten aus Griechenland: Zur Konstituierung eines Spielfilmkorpus für die Sozial- und Kulturgeschichte', *Filmkunst*, 148, 4–14.

_____ (2000) 'Creating Distraction after Destruction: Representations of the Military in Greek Film', *Journal of Modern Greek Studies*, 18, 1, 37–52.

_____ (2002a) '"It Happened in Athens": The Relaunch of Greek Film Production during World War II', *Kampos: Cambridge Papers in Modern Greek*, 10, 111–28.

_____ (2002b) 'Gefährliche Erbschaften – Griechische Antike im griechischen Kino', in M. Korenjak and K. Töchterle (eds) *Pontes II: Antike im Film [Comparanda 5]*, 35–43.

_____ (2006) *Greek National Cinema*. New York and London: Routledge.

Theodosiou, N. (2000) *Ston palio sinema: I ilikia tou kinimatografou stin Ellada*. Athens: Finatec.

Triantafyllides, I. (1996) *Sto telos milaei to pani*. Athens: Ammos.

_____ (2000) *Tainies gia filima: Afieroma ston Filopimena Fino kai tis tainies tou*. Athens: Exantas.

Tsitsopoulou, V. (2000) 'Greekness, Gender Stereotypes, and the Hollywood Musical in Jules Dassin's *Never on Sunday*', *Journal of Modern Greek Studies*, 18, 79–93.

Valoukos, S. (1998) *Filmografia tou ellinikou kinimatografou, 1914–1998*. Athens: Aigokeros.

## ROMANIA

Blaga, I. (2003) *Fantasme și adevăruri: O carte cu Mircea Săucan*, Bucharest: Editura Hasefer.

Căliman, C. (2000) *Istoria filmului românesc, 1897–2000*. Bucharest: Editura Fundației Culturale Române.

Cantacusino, I. and B. T. Rîpeanu (1970) *Productia cinematografică din România 1987–1970: filmografie adnotata*. Bucharest: Archiva Nationala de Filme.

Cantacusino, I. (ed.) (1971) *Contribuții la istoria cinematografiei în România 1896–1948*. Bucharest: Editura Academiei RSR.

Caranfil, T. (2003) *Dictionar de filme românesti*. Bucharest/Chisinau: Litera International.

Cernat, M. (1982) *A Concise History of the Romanian Film*, trans. Andrei Bantas. Bucharest: Editura Științifică și enciclopedică.

Corciovescu, C. and B. T. Râpeanu (1996) *1234 cineaști români*. Bucharest: Editura Științifică.

De Hadeln, M. (ed.) (1990) *Romania: The Documentary Films 1898–1990*. Nyon: Festival International du film documentaire.

Jäckel, A. (1999) 'The Grand Theatre of the World: The Films of Lucian Pintilie', *Cineaste*, 25, 1, 27–9.

\_\_\_\_ (2000a) 'Franco-Romanian Reconstruction is also an Ethical Issue', *Forum for Modern Language Studies*, 36, 2, 165–78.

\_\_\_\_ (2000b) 'France and Romanian Cinema 1896–1999', *French Cultural Studies*, special issue on French Culture and Eastern Europe, 11, 3, 409–24.

\_\_\_\_ (2000c) 'Film Policy and Cooperation between East and West: The Case of France and Romania in the Nineties', *International Journal of Cultural Policy*, 7, 1, 131–50.

\_\_\_\_ (2001) 'Too Late? Recent Developments in Romanian Cinema', in W. Everett (ed.) *The Seeing Century: Film, Vision and Identity*. Amsterdam/Atlanta: Rodopi, 98–110.

*MovEast* 8 (2002) *Contemporary Romanian Cinema*. Budapest: Hungarian National Film Archive.

Nasta. D. (2000) 'Cinema rumeno', in G. P. Brunetta (ed.) *Storia del cinema mondiale*, vol. III Turin: Einaudi, 1459–95.

Pintilie, L. (2003) *Bricabrac*. Bucharest: Humanitas.

Potra, F. (1979) *Profesiune: Filmul*. Bucharest: Meridiane.

Potra, F. (1987) *Aurul filmului*. Bucharest: Meridiane.

Rîpeanu, B. T. (ed.) (2004) *Filmat în România 1911–2004* (Vol. I, 1911–1969). Burharest: Editura Fundației PRO.

Sava, V. (1999) *Istoria critică a filmului românesc contemporan 1*. Bucharest: Meridiane.

Țuțui, M. (2004) *A History of Romanian Cinema*. Bucharest: National Center of Cinema.

## YUGOSLAVIA

Alagjozovski, R. (2004) 'The Postmodernism in the Macedonian Film', *MovEast 9*, Hungarian National Film Archive: Budapest. Online; http://www.filmintezet.hu/uj/kiadvanyok/moveast/moveast_9/alagjozovski.htm.

Blaževski, V. (ed.) (1988) *Dušan Makavejev: 300 Čuda*. Belgrade: Studenski kulturni centar.

Boglić, M. (ed.) (1988) *Film kao sudbina*. Zagreb: Nakladni zavod Matice hrvatske.

Bouineau, J. M. (1993) *Le petit livre de Emir Kusturica*. Garches: Spartorange.

Boni, S. (ed.) (1999) *Emir Kusturica*. Torino: Paravia Garage.

Čepinčić, M. (1992–99) *Makednoskiot igralen film* (Vol. I, 1992; Vol. II, 1999). Skopje: Kinoteka na Makedonija.

Chernenko, M. (1997) *Makedonskiot film*. Skopje: Kinoteka na Makedonija.

Cohen, R. (1995) 'A Balkan Gyre of War, Spinning Onto Film', *The New York Times*, Section 2, 12 March, 1.

Čolić, M. (1984) *Jugoslovenski ratni film*. 2 vols. Belgrade: Institut za film.

Daković, N. (1996–97) 'Mother, Myth, and Cinema: Recent Yugoslav Cinema', *Film Criticism*, 21, 2, 40–50.

_____ (2001a) 'The Threshold of Europe: Imagining Yugoslavia in Film', Online; http://www. spaceofidentity.net.

_____ (2001b) 'Documentaries from Post-Yugoslavia: Serbian War Discourse', *Afterimage*, 28, 4, 16–18.

_____ (2003a) '*Skupljaci perja/I Even Met Happy Gypsies*', *Framework: Cinematic Images of Romanies*, 44, 2, 103–8.

_____ (2003b) 'The Unfilmable Scenario and Neglected Theory: Yugoslav Film Avant-garde: 1920–1990,' in D. Djuric and M. Suvakovic (eds) *Impossible Histories: Historical Avant-Gardes, Neo-Avant-Gardes and Post-Avant-Gardes in Yugoslavia, 1918–1991*. Cambridge, MA: MIT Press, 466–90.

_____ (2003c) '*Pretty Village, Pretty Flame:* Conflicting Identities', in K. Ross and D. Derman (eds) *Identity Politics and Mapping the Margins*. Cresskill, NJ: Hampton Press, 147–63.

_____ (2004) "War in the Hall of Mirrors: NATO bombing and Serbian Cinema', in A. Hammond (ed.) *The Balkans and the West: Constructing the European Other, 1945–2003*. Aldershot: Ashgate, 199–213.

Durgnat, R. (1999) *WR: Mysteries of Organism*. London: British Film Istitute.

Germani, S. G. (2000) 'Cinema jugoslavo', in G. P. Brunetta (ed.) *Storia del cinema mondiale*, vol. III. Turin: Einaudi, 1327–61.

Gocić, G. (2001) *The Cinema of Emir Kusturica: Notes from the Underground*. London: Wallflower Press.

*Goran Marković* (2001) Belgrade: Centar film/Prizma Kragujevac/Slovenska kinoteka/Ljubljana/Zepter International/International Thessaloniki Film Festival.

Goulding, D. J. (1988) *Liberated Cinema: The Yugoslav Experience*. Bloomington, IN: Indiana University Press.

_____ (1998) *Occupation in 26 Pictures*. Trowbridge: Flicks Books.

Holloway, R. (1972) *Z is for Zagreb*. Cranbury, NJ: A. S. Barnes.

_____ (1985) *Slovenian Film: Slovenian Post-War Cinema, 1945–1985*. Berlin: Kino.

_____ (1996a) *Macedonian Film: A History of Macedonian Cinema, 1905–1996*. Berlin: Kino.

_____ (1996b) *Goran Paskaljevic: La tragicomedia humana*. Valladolid: Semana International de cine.

Horton, A. (1988) 'Oedipus Unresolved: Covert and Overt Narrative Discourse in Emir Kusturica's *When Father Was Away on Business*', *Cinema Journal*, 17, 4, 64–81.

_____ (1995) '"Only Crooks Can Get Ahead": Post-Yugoslav Cinema/TV/Video in the 1990s', in S. P. Ramet and L. S. Adamovic (eds) *Beyond Yugoslavia: Politics, Economics and Culture in a Shattered Community*. Boulder, CO: Westview Press, 413–31.

_____ (1998) 'Cinematic Makeovers and Cultural Border Crossings: Kusturica's *Time of the Gypsies* and Coppola's *Godfather* and *Godfather II*', in A. Horton and S. V. McDougal (eds) *Play it Again, Sam: Retakes on Remakes*. Berkeley: University of California Press, 172–91.

*Hrvatski filmski letopis: Godišnjak hrvatskog filma i videa* (1996) Zagreb: Hrvatski državni arhiv/Hrvatska kinoteka.

Huffman, K. R. (1998) 'Video from Bosnia: A Meeting Point of Memory and Reality', *Convergence*, 4, 2, 102–10.

Ilić, M. (ed.) (1970) *Filmografija jugoslovenskog filma, 1945–1965*. Belgrade: Institut za film.

_____ (1971) *Godišnjak 1969: Kinematografija u Srbiji*. Belgrade: Institut za film.

_____ (1974) *Filmografija jugoslovenskog filma, 1966–1970*. Belgrade: Institut za film.

*Filmografija srpskog dugometražnog igranog filma 1945–1995* (1996). Belgrade: Institut za film.

Iordanova, D. (1999) 'Kusturica's *Underground*: Historical Allegory or Propaganda', *Historical Journal of Film, Radio and Television*, 19, l, 69–86.

_____ (2000) 'The Cinema of the Dispersed Yugoslavs: Diasporas in the Making', *CineAction*, 52, 69–72.

_____ (2002) *Emir Kusturica*. London: British Film Institute.

Jončić, P. (2002) *Filmski jezik Želimira Žilnika*. Belgrade: Studentski Kulturni Centar.

Kastratović, G. (1999) *Crnogorska kinematografija i filmovi o Crnoj Gori*. Podgorica: Društvo za očuvanje baštine.

*10 najboljih igranih filmova. 50 godina filma BH: Anketa filmskih kritičara* (1997). Sarajevo: Kinoteka Bosne i Hercegovine.

Kosanović, D. (1966) *Dvadeset godina jugoslovenskog filma, 1945–1965*. Belgrade: Savez filmskih radnika Jugoslavije I Festival jugoslovenskog filma.

_____ (1976) *Uvod u proučavanje istorije Jugoslovenskog filma*. Belgrade: Univerzitet Umetnosti.

_____ (1986) *Počeci kinematografija na tlu jugoslavije 1896–1918*. Belgrade: Institut za film.

_____ (ed.) (1995) *Vek filma*. Belgrade: Galerja Srpske akademije nauka i umetnost; Jugoslovenska kinoteka.

Krstić, I. (1999) 'Representing Yugoslavia? Emir Kusturica's *Underground* and the Politcis of Postmodern Cinematic Historiography', *Tijdschrift voor Mediageschiedenis. Media & Orlog* (Amsterdam), 138–59. Online; http://www.othervoices.org/2.2/krstic/index.html.

Kusturica, E. and S. Grünberg (eds) (1995) *Il était une fois … Underground*. Paris: Cahiers du cinéma/CiBY 2000.

Levi, P. (2001) '*Underground*: jedna estetika nacionalističkog uživanja,' *Republika*, 270–1, 48–54.

_____ (2002) 'O filmskoj formi i medjuetničkim odnosima u post-jugoslovenskom filmu', *Prelom*, 4, 135–47.

Makavejev, D. (1960) *Poljubac za drugarica parolu*. Belgrade: Nolit.

Munitić, R. (1977) *Te slatke filmske laže*. Belgrade: Vuk Karadžić.

Novaković, S. (1965) *Dvadeset godina jugoslovenskog filma*. Belgrade: Festival jugoslovenskog filma.

_____ (1970) *Vreme otvaranja: Ogledi i zapisi o novom filmu*. Novi Sad: Kulturni centar.

_____ (1971) *Dve decenije-dve generacije*. Belgrade: FEST 71.

O'Grady, G. (ed.) (1995). *Makavejev Fictionary: The Films of Dušan Makavejev*. Boston: Harvard Film Archive and the American Museum of the Moving Image.

Obradović, B. (ed.) (1981) *Filmografija jugoslovenskog igranog filma, 1945–1980*. Belgrade: Institut za film.

_____ (1987) *Filmografija jugoslovenskog igranog filma, 1981–1985*. Belgrade: Institut za film.

Passek, J. L. and Z. Tasić (1986) *Le Cinéma Yougoslave*. Paris: Centre Georges Pompidou.

Pavlović, Ž. (1969) *Djavolji film*. Belgrade: Institut za film.

Peterlić, A. (ed.) (1986) *Filmska enciklopedija I–II*. Zagreb: Jugoslavenski Leskikografski Zavod 'Miroslav Krleža.'

Petrović, A. (1971) *Novi film*. Belgrade: Institut za film.

Ramet, S. (2002) *Balkan Babel* (fourth edition). Boulder, Co: Westview Press.

Rosenstone, R. (2000) (ed.) Special issue on Milcho Manchevski's *Before the Rain, Rethinking History*, 4, 2.

*25 Godina Bosansko Hercegovačke Kinematografije* (1974) Sarajevo: Sineast.

Skrabalo, I. (1984) *Između publike i države. Povijest hrvatske kinematografije 1896–1980*. Zagreb: Znanje.

Slapšak. S. (2000) 'Žensko telo u jugoslovenskem filmu: status žene, paradigma feminizma', in *Žene, slike, izmišljaji*. Belgrade: Centar za ženske študije, 121–37.

Slijepčević, B. (1982) *Kinematografija u Srbiji, Crnoj Gori, Bosni i Hercegovini 1896–1918*. Belgrade: Univerzitet umetnosti/Institut za film.

Stojadinović, M. J. (1994) 'Alexander Petrović (1929–1994),' *Balkanmedia*, 3, 3, 11.

Stojanović, D. (1974) *Sistematizacija teorija filma u svetu i u naš*. Belgrade: Institut za film/Zagreb: Zagreb Filmoteka 16.

_____ (1984) *Film kao prevazilaženje jezika*. Belgrade: Institut za Film/Universitet Umetnosti.

Stojanović, M. (ed.) (2003) *Želimir Žilnik: Above the Red Dust/Iznad crvene prašine*. Belgrade: Institut za Film.

Tasić, Z. and J. Passek (eds) (1986) *Le cinema Yougoslave*. Paris: Centre Georges Pompidou.

Turković, H. (1985) *Filmska opredjeljenja*. Zagreb: Cekade.

Vecchi, P. (1999) *Emir Kusturica*. Rome: Gremese Editore.

Volk, P. (1983) *Savremeni jugoslovenski film*. Belgrade: Institut za Film/Universitet Umetnosti.

_____ (1986) *Istorija jugoslovenskog filma*. Belgrade: Institut za film/Partizanska knjiga.

*Živojin Pavlović* (1998) Belgrade: Centar film/Prizma/Kragujevac/Radio-Television Serbia/International Thessaloniki Film Festival.

## RECOMMENDED WEBSITES

*Belgrade Fest* – http://www.fest.org

*BG Media* – http://www.gobgmedia.com/home_page.html

*Centrul National al Cinematografiei – Romania* – http://www.cncinema.abt.ro

*Cinema.bg* – http://www.cinema.bg

*Cinematheque of Macedonia* – http://makedonija.at/kinoteka

*DS Sound – Toronto* – http://www.dssound.com

*Film Festival of East European Film, Cottbus* – http://www.filmfestivalcottbus.de

*goEast - Festival of Central and Eastern European Film Wiesbaden* – http://www.filmfestivalgoeast.de/engl/01.htm

*Goran Paskaljevic* – http://www.paskaljevic.com/main/index.html

*Greek City Video – Toronto* – http://www.greekcity.com

*Greek Film Centre* – http://www.gfc.gr

*Istanbul International Film Festival* – http://www.iksv.org/film/english

*Kinoeye* – http://www.kinoeye.org

*Macedonian Cinema Information Centre* – http://www.maccinema.com/e_kinoteka.asp

*Matthieu Dhennin's Emir Kusturica* – http://www.dhennin.com/kusturica

*Milcho Manchevski* – http://www.manchevski.com.mk

*Motovun Film Festival* – http://www.motovunfilmfestival.com

*MovEast* – http://www.filmintezet.hu/uj/kiadvanyok

*Pula Film Festival* – http://www.pulafilmfestival.hr

*Sarajevo International Film Festival* – http://www.sff.ba

*Sofia International Film Festival* – http://www.cinema.bg/sff

*Thessaloniki Documentary Festival* – http://www.docfestival.gr/docfestival/uk/index.htm

*Thessaloniki International Film Festival* – http://www.filmfestival.gr/index_uk.htm

*Transylvania International Film Festival* – http://www.tiff.ro

*Želimir Žilnik* – http://www.zelimirzilnik.net

# INDEX

emigration   69, 102, 215, 238, 258–64

village-city migration   61, 69, 102, 164, 197, 209, 264

Mihajlović, Dragoslav   59, 163

Mihić, Gordan   55, 152, 214

Milošević, Slobodan   67, 154

Mitrović, Žika   197, 199

modernisation   127, 133, 139, 143–4, 248–52

Moldavia (Moldova)   76

Montenegro   5, 49, 66, 227–30, 232

Morgenstern, Maia   10, 20, 166

Moscow   79, 208, 238

Munk, Andrzej   47

Mureşan, Mircea   34, 41

Muşatescu, Tudor   35

Muslim   83, 107–9, 124–5, 231

Năstase, Doru   79

Negulesco, Jean   20

Neorealism   100–1, 218

Neretva   8, 47, 50, 81, 110

Nero, Franco   81, 90, 101, 118, 154

New Greek Cinema   5, 99–100, 104, 223–4

New Yugoslav Film   54, 58–9

Nicolaescu, Sergiu   7, 35, 75–8, 80–5, 111, 180

Nikolić, Dragan   55, 81

Nikolić, Živko   8, 55, 118, 227, 229–30, 232–5

nouvelle vague   46, 99, 157

Novi Sad   62, 67, 69

Ottoman Empire   26, 75, 79, 83, 195–7, 240

Ottomans   75, 78, 83, 195, 201, 240

Papas, Irene   10, 20, 111

Papić, Krsto   59, 185

Partisan   6, 10, 43–51, 81, 107–14, 166, 168, 184–7, 209, 215, 241

Paskaleva, Katya   122

Paskaljević, Goran   8, 161–3, 176, 264

Pasolini, Pier Paolo   101, 189

patriarchy   1, 7, 18, 70, 124, 233, 245, 261

Pavelić, Ante   186

Pavlović, Živojin   4, 8, 46, 53–62, 70, 153, 166, 232

Pellea, Amza   75, 82–3

Petrescu, Camil   134

Petrović, Aleksandar   8, 25, 43–50, 59, 70, 111, 124, 154, 231

Pinter, Tomislav   49

Pintilie, Lucian   7, 10, 20, 34, 40, 59

Piţa, Dan   34, 40, 127–35, 174

Pontecorvo, Gillo   197

Popovici, Titus   35–6, 81–2

Popov, Stole   185, 207–8, 215

Popov, Trajče   197, 209

Prague Film School (FAMU)   161, 163, 184

Prague Group   153, 161–9, 184

Prague Spring   145

Praxis   59–60

Radev, Vulo   23–30, 37, 48

Rebengiuc, Victor   33, 40

Rebreanu, Liviu   34–6, 128

Renoir, Jean   28, 58